After the Rubicon

**CHICAGO SERIES
ON INTERNATIONAL &
DOMESTIC INSTITUTIONS**

Edited by William Howell and Jon Pevehouse

After the Rubicon

Congress, Presidents, and the Politics of Waging War

DOUGLAS L. KRINER

THE UNIVERSITY OF CHICAGO PRESS   CHICAGO AND LONDON

DOUGLAS L. KRINER is assistant professor of political science at Boston University and coauthor of *The Casualty Gap: The Causes and Consequences of American Wartime Inequalities.*

The University of Chicago Press, Chicago 60637
The University of Chicago Press, Ltd., London
© 2010 by The University of Chicago
All rights reserved. Published 2010
Printed in the United States of America
19 18 17 16 15 14 13 12 11 10   1 2 3 4 5

ISBN-13: 978-0-226-45355-2 (cloth)
ISBN-13: 978-0-226-45356-9 (paper)
ISBN-10: 0-226-45355-3 (cloth)
ISBN-10: 0-226-45356-1 (paper)

Library of Congress Cataloging-in-Publication Data

Kriner, Douglas L.
    After the Rubicon: Congress, presidents, and the politics of waging war / Douglas L. Kriner.
       p.   cm.
    Includes bibliographical references and index.
    ISBN-13: 978-0-226-45355-2 (cloth : alk. paper)
    ISBN-13: 978-0-226-45356-9 (pbk. : alk. paper)
    ISBN-10: 0-226-45355-3 (cloth : alk. paper)
    ISBN-10: 0-226-45356-1 (pbk. : alk. paper)   1. Executive-legislative relations—United States.   2. Politics and war—United States.   3. Executive power—United States.
4. United States. Congress—Powers and duties.   5. United States—Military policy.
6. United States—History, Military.   I. Title.
    JK585.K75   2010
    355.020973—dc22
                                                                        2010018918

♾ The paper used in this publication meets the minimum requirements of the American National Standard for Information Sciences—Permanence of Paper for Printed Library Materials, ANSI Z39.48-1992.

Contents

Figures

Tables

Acknowledgments

I am very grateful to many individuals who helped me through every stage of this project. William Howell, Lisa Martin, Eric Schickler, and Charles Stewart offered guidance from the start, read every chapter, and always steered me in the right direction. For their rich insights and thoughtful suggestions I would also like to thank Barry Burden, Neta Crawford, Linda Fowler, John Gerring, Cathie Martin, Paul Peterson, Christine Rossell, Liam Schwartz, Francis Shen, Theda Skcopol, and my anonymous reviewers. Seminar participants at Harvard University, the American Political Science Association, and the Midwest Political Science Association offered still more valuable feedback and ideas.

For generous financial support, I thank the Dirksen Congressional Center, the Weatherhead Center for International Affairs at Harvard University, the National Science Foundation Graduate Research Fellowship Program, and Boston University.

I would also like to thank everyone at the University of Chicago Press for all of their efforts to bring this project to fruition. I am especially indebted to my editor, David Pervin, for his guidance throughout the project. Renaldo Migaldi, Shenyun Wu, and Robert Hunt also played key roles in shepherding the manuscript through production.

Finally, I thank my family for their love and encouragement. My parents, Gary and Deborah Kriner, sacrificed much to give me every opportunity, and for this I am eternally grateful. I dedicate this book to my wife, Jillian, who continually supports me in every endeavor and vastly enriches my life.

CHAPTER ONE

Introduction:
Domestic Politics and Waging War

In 49 BC Julius Caesar and his legions crossed the Rubicon, a small river marking the border between the province of Cisalpine Gaul and Italy itself. The move triggered a bloody civil war between Caesar's forces and those of the Senate under the command of Pompey the Great. For two millennia scholars have analyzed every facet of Caesar's fateful choice, and with good reason: the decision irrevocably altered the course of Western history itself. As a testament to its importance, the phrase "crossing the Rubicon" remains in our vernacular to indicate a transformative decision. As serious students of both classical and European history, the Framers of our Constitution recognized the paramount importance of the power of war and peace.[1] Notes from the 1787 Constitutional Convention capture the fervent debate in Philadelphia over who in the new government should hold the power to initiate war, and the question remained heatedly contested in the early republic. For example, lambasting President James K. Polk's aggressive assertions of military power in taking the nation to war with Mexico, a young Congressman named Abraham Lincoln warned: "This our convention understood to be the most oppressive of all kingly oppressions, and they resolved to so frame the Constitution that no one man should hold the power of bringing this oppression upon us."[2] Today, decisions to dispatch American military might abroad remain the most consequential and scrutinized

---

1. For the influence of classical civilizations on the Framers' thinking, see Richard 1995.
2. Lincoln 1953 [1848], 451–52.

actions of our body politic. Reflecting this, the vast majority of scholarship in political science focuses almost exclusively on these decisions to initiate military ventures and on the relative influence that the president and Congress have in making them. Because of this exclusive emphasis, however, prior scholarship tells us surprisingly little about how interactions between the executive and legislative branches continue to shape the conduct of these military ventures once they are launched. Moreover, by overlooking these later dynamics, existing scholarship yields an incomplete picture of the calculations made by forward-looking strategic actors when deciding whether or not to use force.

After the recourse to arms, policymakers are confronted with a myriad of decisions about a martial venture's scale and conduct. Ultimately, they must also decide when and how to bring American troops home. These decisions plainly are of considerable political, strategic, and historical import; yet it is not clear how, within our system of separated institutions sharing power, the two branches interact to chart the course of military affairs. The ambiguous constitutional distribution of war powers—what the great legal scholar Edward Corwin called the "invitation to struggle"—entrusted to both branches enumerated powers and bases of authority from which to shape these decisions.[3] As a result, over the course of American history starkly different views, both constitutional and normative, have emerged concerning who should play the lead role in shaping the conduct of American military ventures. In the early days of the republic one of the chief architects of the Constitution, James Madison, wrote, "Those who are to *conduct a war* [i.e., presidents, by virtue of the commander-in-chief clause] cannot in the nature of things, be proper or safe judges, whether *a war ought* to be *commenced, continued* or *concluded*. They are barred from the latter functions by a great principle in free government, analogous to that which separates the sword from the purse, or the power of executing from the power of enacting laws."[4] Congress and not the president, in Madison's view, should stand at the helm of the ship of state in wartime, particularly in deciding when and how an armed conflict will end.

Such sentiment may sound foreign to contemporary ears, given that many of our beliefs and opinions have been forged in an era of aug-

3. Corwin 1940, 200.
4. James Madison writing as Helvidius, reproduced in Corwin 1970 [1917]. Emphasis in original.

mented presidential war powers. President George W. Bush's assertions of plenary commander-in-chief powers to direct an ongoing military operation as he alone saw fit may better accord with our understanding. During a 2007 Iraq War appropriations battle with Congress, for example, Bush made clear his belief that the legislature should play virtually no role in shaping the conduct of military operations. "I don't think Congress ought to be running the war," he curtly remarked to the media. "I think they ought to be funding our troops. I'm certainly interested in their opinion, but trying to run a war through resolution is a prescription for failure, as far as I'm concerned, and we can't afford to fail." When pushed further by a reporter, Bush rejoined, "Let me make sure you understand what I'm saying. Congress has all the right in the world to fund. That's their main involvement in this war, which is to provide funds for our troops. What you're asking is whether or not Congress ought to be basically determining how troops are positioned or troop strength. And I just—I don't think that would be good for the country."[5]

No observer of contemporary American politics could mistake Madison's vision with the current state of affairs. Modern presidents are undoubtedly the preeminent actors directing the conduct of the nation's major military engagements. Yet Bush's protestations remind us that sometimes the legislature does rise up, engage the military policy-making process, and attempt to reassert its constitutional prerogatives in deciding whether a military venture is "continued" or "concluded." Whether such actions have any tangible policy consequences, and ultimately how these competing conceptions of the roles of the executive and legislative branches in shaping the conduct of major military operations are resolved, remain among the most important political and constitutional questions in contemporary politics. Ironically, however, these are questions that existing political science scholarship in American politics is woefully unprepared to answer.

The Politics of Initiating War versus Waging War

Virtually every prior study of the dynamics governing American uses of force abroad has focused exclusively on the politics driving the *initia-*

5. George W. Bush, "The President's News Conference." *Public Papers of the President*, July 12, 2007.

tion of a military action. As a result, the existing literature has paid scant attention to the impact of various factors—from reactions in Congress to swings in public opinion to changing conditions on the ground—on a joined action's subsequent conduct and eventual termination.

When constitutional scholars discuss war powers, they begin and all too often end with the power to initiate military actions abroad. Perhaps no single semantic change at the Philadelphia Convention has received more intense scrutiny than James Madison and Elbridge Gerry's motion that "moved to insert 'declare,' striking out 'make' war; leaving to the Executive the power to repel sudden attacks."[6] Most legal scribes contend that the constitutional power to initiate military actions resides exclusively with the legislature; even the power to authorize limited military actions is granted to Congress through Article I, Section 8's provisions on letters of marque and reprisal.[7] Revisionists counter that through Gerry's switch and the vesting clause of Article II, the Founders gave both branches the authority to launch military ventures short of total war.[8] In stark contrast to this voluminous literature on the distribution of the power to initiate war, legal scholars have paid much less attention to the balance of constitutional powers to shape the scale and duration of a military venture once begun.

Although more concerned with the political forces shaping policy decisions than with constitutional provisions and powers, use-of-force scholarship in political science has also focused almost exclusively on the political dynamics governing the initiation of major military actions. Citing a string of precedents since the Korean War in which presidents have refused even to consult Congress, much less seek its blessing, before launching major uses of force abroad, most scholars have decried an unambiguous devolution of the power to initiate military actions from Congress to the president, culminated in the "imperial presidencies" of Lyndon Johnson and Richard Nixon.[9] While a number of analyses in the immediate aftermath of the Vietnam War proclaimed a "resur-

6. James Madison, reproduced in Farrand 1966 [1787], 318. Though see Lofgren (1972) for ambiguity in the precise meaning of this phrase.

7. See Lofgren 1986, Koh 1990, Ely 1993, Silverstein 1994, Adler and George 1996, Glennon 1990.

8. Inter alia, see Yoo 2005.

9. See Wildavsky 1966; Schlesinger 1973; Fisher 1995, 2000; Rudalevige 2005; Hinckley 1994; Meernik 1994; Meernik and Waterman 1996; Peterson 1994; Gowa 1998, 1999; Moore and Lanoue 2003.

gent Congress" in foreign affairs, assessments of congressional influence in military policymaking again quickly soured.[10] This dour historical appraisal of congressional weakness has only been buoyed in recent years by the aggressive military policies of Presidents Ronald Reagan, George H. W. Bush, and Bill Clinton, all of whom deployed American troops abroad, even into open hostilities, absent any prior congressional authorization.

Finally, even the more empirically focused literature at the nexus of American politics and international relations has shared both this conventional view of congressional weakness and, more importantly, the exclusive analytic focus on the initiation of military actions. At the core of this literature is a host of quantitative studies examining the factors driving the frequency with which the United States uses force abroad. Some scholars, such as James Meernik, explicitly searched for empirical evidence of congressional influence and found little; this led Meernik to assert that the president alone "exercises supreme control over the nation's military actions."[11] This statement is unique in the literature if only for the bluntness, not the tenor, of its assessment of the balance of power between the branches. Many other studies are loath even to afford any attention to Congress, their silence speaking as loudly as any words proclaiming congressional irrelevance.[12]

Recently a growing number of scholars have challenged this received wisdom of congressional impotence in military affairs and have demonstrated that the partisan composition of Congress strongly influences both the frequency with which presidents use force abroad and the probability with which they respond militarily to international crises.[13] These advances by William Howell, Jon Pevehouse, David Clark, and others provide an important corrective to our understanding of military policymaking in the United States, and they assert the continued importance of interbranch politics, even in the martial arena. However, while this new research yields considerable insights into the rich interplay of politi-

10. For studies proclaiming a "resurgent Congress," see Franck 1981, Rourke 1983, Ripley and Lindsey 1993.

11. Meernik 1994, 123.

12. See Ostrom and Job 1986, DeRouen 1995, James and Oneal 1991, Fordham 2002.

13. For empirical analyses, see Howell and Pevehouse 2005, 2007; Clark 2000; Wang 1996. For qualitative work asserting congressional influence in the military arena, see Johnson 2006, Carter and Scott 2009, Hersman 2000, Trubowitz 1998, Lindsay 1992, Brands 1987.

cal forces shaping the initial decision to use force abroad, it tells us little about whether Congress continues to influence the scope and duration of major military operations once launched.

The role that Congress plays in deciding whether a war is continued or concluded is of intrinsic interest to academics, policymakers, and casual observers of contemporary American politics alike. Yet the belief that Congress retains some capacity to shape the conduct of military affairs after a venture is launched is also a critically important and untested proposition underlying most theories asserting congressional influence over the initiation of military action. Why, according to this emerging literature, do presidents facing a strong opposition party in Congress use force less frequently than do their peers with strong partisan majorities in Congress? The most commonly offered answer is that presidents anticipate Congress's likely reaction to a prospective use of force and respond accordingly.[14] Presidents who confront an opposition-led Congress anticipate that it is more willing and able to challenge the administration's conduct of military action than a Congress controlled by their partisan allies. Therefore, the frequency with which presidents use force abroad covaries with the strength of their party in Congress. However, this anticipatory logic requires that Congress has the ability to raise the costs of military action for the president, once that action has begun. If Congress lacks this capacity, presidents have little reason to adjust their willingness to initiate the use of force in anticipation of an adverse congressional response.[15] As a result, determining whether and how Congress can influence the scope and duration of ongoing military operations is critically important even to evaluating prior research that asserts congressional influence over the initiation of military actions. Without it, such analyses rest on shaky ground.

Unfortunately, because the dynamics change dramatically once American troops are deployed abroad, simply drawing lessons from existing studies of interbranch dynamics in military policymaking at the

14. For seminal works on the "second face of power," see Bachrach and Baratz 1962, Nagel 1975.

15. Of course, all that is required for anticipatory mechanisms to work is that the president *believes* that Congress has the capacity to impose costs on him if he pursues military policies that do not possess legislative sanction. However, it is highly unlikely that presidents will believe this if Congress does not, in fact, have mechanisms at its disposal to inflict such costs on the administration.

conflict initiation phase and applying them to the conflict conduct phase is unlikely to offer much insight.[16] The decision-making environment at the conflict conduct phase differs from that at the conflict initiation phase along at least three key dimensions: the incentives and constraints governing congressional willingness to challenge presidential discretion; the relative institutional capacities of the executive and legislative branches to affect military policymaking; and finally, the ability of unfolding conflict events to change further the political and strategic environment in which the two branches vie for power.

With regard to the political constraints that limit would-be adversaries in Congress, the president may be in an even stronger position after American troops are deployed in the field. Ordering troops abroad is akin to other unilateral presidential actions; by seizing his office's capacity for independent action, a president can dramatically change the status quo and fundamentally alter the political playing field on which Congress and other actors must act to challenge his policies.[17] Once the troops are overseas, the political stakes for any congressional challenge to the president's policies are inexorably raised; any such effort is subject to potentially ruinous charges of failing to support the troops. Georgia Senator Richard Russell's conversion from opposition to U.S. intervention in Vietnam in the early 1960s to stalwart support for staying the course after Lyndon Johnson's escalation of the American commitment there illustrates this change: "We are there now, and the time for debate has passed. Our flag is committed, and—more importantly—American boys are under fire."[18] Russell's sentiment was loudly echoed forty years later in the allegations by the Bush administration and its partisan allies in Congress that any legislative efforts to curtail the war in Iraq undermined the troops. As a result of these potentially intense political costs, there are reasons to question whether Congress can mount an effective challenge to the policies of the commander in chief. If it cannot, this would compel a reassessment of prior theories asserting congressio-

16. Indeed, past scholars have explicitly acknowledged that the politics governing military action change dramatically after troops are deployed. See, for example, Russett 1990, 130; Howell and Pevehouse 2007, 14. See also Bueno de Mesquita, Morrow, and Zorick 1997; Bueno de Mesquita, Morrow, Siverson, and Smith 1999.

17. See Howell 2003; Moe and Howell 1999a, 1999b; Cooper 2002; Mayer 1999, 2001.

18. Quoted in Herring 1987.

nal influence over the initiation of military actions through the logic of anticipated response. Certainly, more empirical analysis is needed to answer this question.

Congress may, however, have considerably greater capacity to check presidential discretion after a military action has begun than when it is merely anticipated. Particularly since the enactment of the War Powers Resolution in 1973, which critics then and now have charged tacitly recognized the president's extra-constitutional authority to order American forces abroad absent any prior congressional authorization for up to ninety days, Congress is in a weakened position in the lead-up to most military endeavors. Because of the informational advantages enjoyed by the president and his access to unparalleled intelligence resources, Congress frequently finds itself in the dark as initial military decisions are made. Indeed, legislative leaders first learned of impending actions as varied as the 1962 quarantine of Cuba during the missile crisis, the 1983 invasion of Grenada, and the 1986 bombing of Tripoli only hours before, or even after, they began. Recognizing this state of affairs, which perhaps was made necessary by the exigencies of the Cold War and America's role as a global superpower, Congress with the War Powers Resolution effectively delegated the power to initiate the use of force to the president and attempted to reserve ex post facto authority to terminate an action of which it disapproved. In light of this explicit delegation, we must be wary of assessing the extent of congressional power in military policymaking solely in terms of Congress's capacity to prevent military ventures which it does not support, without also examining Congress's ability to retain a check on war powers delegated to the president through its ability to shape the scope and duration of a military action once begun.

Despite the complex incentive structure and real constraints governing congressional attempts to influence the president's handling of military affairs, Congress's capacity to challenge the president may actually increase in two important respects after a military action begins. First, the influx of information from the field begins to attenuate the informational asymmetries that presidents exploit to demand deference when making the initial case for a military response. When force is merely contemplated, members of Congress have little access to critical information on the nature of the threat or the conditions on the ground that might justify a military intervention. Instead, they have little choice but to defer to the executive. However, the presence of American troops on the ground opens new conduits of information to legislators. They can hold hearings, demand reports, and vigorously question administration officials and commanders in the field. The twenty-four-hour news cycle provides legislators with up-to-the-minute independent accounts of the situation on the ground. And, ultimately, members of Congress can count the number of Americans who have given what Lincoln termed "the last full measure of devotion" in service to their country. Equally important, members of Congress also have a range of legislative tools at their disposal to seek influence over the conduct of a military intervention. Article I grants to Congress alone the power of the purse; this, coupled with the War Powers Resolution's ninety-day withdrawal clock, gives Congress formal legal authority to terminate wayward presidential military ventures. Moreover, as recent experience in Iraq has demonstrated, opponents of the president's policies can also employ more creative legislative maneuvers to try to hamstring the flexibility of the commander in chief.

Finally, in addition to the different capacities of the two branches and the altered incentive structures governing their behavior in the pre- and post-conflict initiation phases, developments on the ground hold the potential to transform even further the political and strategic environment in which the two branches vie for influence over the conduct of military affairs. The unfolding of events on foreign battlefields can greatly influence public opinion and dramatically reshape the political capital and position held by both the president and opponents of his policies in Congress.[19] Such swings may insulate the president from congressional attack, or weaken his political clout and make him particularly vulnerable to congressional challenges. Moreover, conflict developments can also directly alter the partisan balance of power across the branches by affecting both presidential and congressional electoral outcomes.[20]

Because the politics governing military action fundamentally shift after American troops are deployed abroad, we cannot simply assume that

19. See Mueller 1970, 1973; Brace and Hinckley 1992; Eichenberg, Stoll, and Lebo 2006; Gelpi, Feaver, and Reifler 2005/06, 2007; Voeten and Brewer 2006; Berinsky 2007.

20. For the influence of military actions, particularly combat casualties, on congressional elections, see Kriner and Shen 2007, 2010; Grose and Oppenheimer 2007; Cotton 1986; Carson, Jenkins, Rohde, and Souva 2001; Gartner, Segura, and Barratt 2004. For the influence of major military actions on presidential contests, see Karol and Miguel 2007; Gelpi, Reifler, and Feaver 2005; and more generally Aldrich, Sullivan, and Borgida 1989; Nincic 1990; Nincic and Hinckley 1991.

the balance of power between the president and Congress described by previous scholars at the conflict initiation phase describes the politics governing a military venture's conduct. Moreover, because decisions at the conflict initiation and conduct phases are inextricably linked, examining the first in isolation, with little attention to decision-making after force is used, yields only an incomplete picture of the policy process.

The decision to use force is not a simple, static decision; rather, presidents are forward-looking strategic actors who make this fateful choice based in large part on their anticipations of how events and politics will play out and evolve should they deploy American troops abroad. Because decisions at the conflict initiation and conduct phases are interlinked, we cannot completely understand even the initial decision of whether or not to intervene militarily unless we expand the scope of analysis to include interbranch politics after American troops are deployed. Moreover, once the die is cast, events may not unfold according to plan. At the conflict conduct stage, decision-making is dynamic as actors respond continuously to changes in the strategic and political environment. Thus, new theorizing, data, and analysis are needed to gain a full picture of the dynamics governing American military policymaking and the indirect yet still significant role that Congress continues to play in shaping military policy outcomes.

Congressional Influence through Indirect Means

When looking for signs of congressional influence over the conduct of American military policymaking, the most obvious place to begin is to search for concrete legislative assertions of Congress's constitutional powers. Even most revisionist scholars acknowledge that the Framers equipped Congress with significant constitutional powers to make the legislature *a* principal, if not necessarily *the* principal, actor in our polity directing the nation's course in the international arena.[21] Yet on this metric Congress is historically weak. Time and again throughout two cen-

21. For example, in their afterword to Robert Kennedy's (1999 [1971]) memoir of the Cuban Missile Crisis, Richard Neustadt and Graham Allison assert a strong constitutional role for the president in military affairs, but acknowledge that "in warmaking, the Constitution contemplated enforced collaboration between the President and his fellow

turies of American history, presidents, not members of Congress, have emerged as the motive force charting the nation's military policy course. Presidents have launched a myriad of military ventures across the globe, most without any legislative sanction. And even when criticism of presidential policies has emerged on Capitol Hill, Congress has failed in all but the rarest of cases to employ any of the panoply of constitutional powers granted it to bring a wayward commander in chief to heel. It is this historical record that first gave birth to, and today sustains, the conventional academic and popular wisdom of an "imperial presidency."

Congress clearly is not the principal actor guiding the nation's military policy that at least some of the Framers intended it to be. Indeed, this book contends that in most instances it is not a principal decision-maker at all in the military policymaking realm. However, this does not mean, as so many prior studies have supposed, that Congress exerts *no* significant influence over the conduct of American military policy. Rather, by serving as a constraint—and sometimes a very powerful one—on the strategic calculus of both the president and the foreign leader of the target state, Congress can influence the initiation, scope, and duration of the nation's military endeavors even when it cannot legislatively mandate its preferred policy course.

The theoretical puzzle then is how Congress can serve as a strong constraint, given the rarity with which members have succeeded in using their legislative powers to write their foreign policy preferences into law. Anticipatory mechanisms suggest one possible answer: if presidents anticipate perfectly when Congress will act legislatively to block a new use of force or end an ongoing military deployment, then they will adjust their policies ex ante to avoid being overruled by Congress. According to this logic, we should only rarely, if ever, see Congress striking down presidential military policies. This is not because Congress is weak, but because the president anticipates when Congress will act and adjusts his conduct of military affairs accordingly. The problem with this hypothesis is that presidents surely recognize that Congress faces tremendous institutional and political barriers that all but preclude it from legislatively overriding their military policies except in extraordinary cases. Given this reality, this simple anticipatory logic begins to break down.

---

politicians on Capitol Hill." They note, however, that the ideals of this dual principal model are frequently not met in practice.

Without a credible threat of congressional action, why would presidents incorporate congressional preferences, either expressed or anticipated, into their strategic calculations? They will do so only if Congress is able to affect the costs and benefits more broadly that presidents stand to reap first for launching and then for continuing a military action. This book argues that through a variety of formal and informal actions taken on the chamber floors, in the committee rooms, and on the airwaves, members of Congress can affect both the political and the strategic costs of military action for the president, even when they cannot legally compel him to alter his preferred policy course.[22] For example, by introducing legislation authorizing or seeking to curtail a use of force, holding oversight hearings, and engaging the debate over military policymaking in the public sphere, members of Congress can play a critically important role in shaping the public's reaction to a military mission. Congressional support can provide the president with invaluable political cover either to launch a new or to continue a current use of force. Conversely, vocal opposition to the president's policies from Capitol Hill can both forestall a rally in popular support behind a proposed military venture and erode public support for an ongoing overseas deployment. In these and other ways, Congress may play a critical role in either raising or lowering the domestic political costs the president stands to reap from his preferred military policy course.

In a similar vein, highly visible congressional actions send important signals of domestic resolve or unease to the target of a threatened or ongoing military action. The leaders of the target state can then incorporate this information about the state of the political climate in Washington into their strategic calculations when deciding whether to capitulate to or resist the president's demands. In this way, even informal actions taken in Congress may unintentionally shape the strategic costs of different military policy options for the president through their influence

22. In his foreword to *The Imperial Presidency*, Schlesinger (1973, ix) also discusses such informal constraints and calls them "unwritten checks" once exercised by Congress, public opinion, and other forces that the president "had to take into practical account before he made decisions of war and peace." However, whereas Schlesinger argued that these unwritten checks had all but disappeared in the twentieth century, this book argues that through a variety of maneuvers Congress can still serve as a significant constraint on presidential discretion in war-making in certain political and strategic environments through informal means.

on the calculus of target state leaders. Finally, because presidents recognize the political and strategic costs that congressional opposition may generate, even when it cannot legislatively compel the administration to alter its preferred policy course, they face strong incentives to anticipate Congress's likely reaction to different policy options and to adjust their conduct of military policymaking accordingly. When making these calculations, Congress's partisan composition provides perhaps the best insight into its likely response.

Through each of these mechanisms, Congress and its members can serve as an important constraint on presidential policymaking and can retain a significant measure of influence over both the initiation and subsequent conduct of major military ventures. The empirical analyses in the chapters that follow marshal extensive empirical, historical, and archival data to examine these indirect pathways of congressional influence and the conditions in which Congress has proved most effective at exercising them to shape the course of American military policymaking from the end of Reconstruction to the ongoing war in Iraq.

Interinstitutional Dynamics and Military Policymaking

In making its theoretical and empirical claims, this book contributes to multiple literatures across subfields of political science. Most directly, it addresses the live debate at the nexus of American politics and international relations on the factors driving the presidential use of force. A host of studies asserts that Congress possesses little to no influence over presidential decisions of whether and when to dispatch American troops abroad, while a handful of recent analyses challenge this dominant view. This book brings a wealth of new empirical evidence to bear on this question and also expands the theoretical and empirical scope of analysis to examine whether Congress continues to influence military policymaking in the dramatically transformed post-deployment environment.

In so doing, the book also speaks to larger literatures within both American politics and international relations. Beginning with the latter, the posited theoretical mechanisms of congressional influence draw heavily on recent advances within the international relations subfield that emphasize the importance of domestic politics in shaping state conflict actions and outcomes.[23] This emerging literature examines the influence of public opinion, ballot box pressures, and even the signals sent by institutionalized opposition parties on executives' military decision-making. Yet many existing studies pay scant explicit attention to the role of legislatures in shaping each of these domestic pressures. By illuminating pathways through which the U.S. Congress can influence the popular and electoral pressures the president faces when charting the nation's military policy course, as well as the credibility of the signals he is able to send to foreign actors, this research may encourage further cross-national analysis into the roles that legislatures play in shaping state conflict behaviors and how this influence varies across states and contexts.

This analysis of interbranch dynamics in the military arena also has important synergies with wider literatures within American politics. In recent years scholars have made great strides in moving beyond old schemas that analyzed governing institutions in isolation, and instead have emphasized the importance of examining how multiple institutions interact simultaneously and strategically within a separation of powers framework. Recent works in this separation of powers literature have demonstrated how interinstitutional concerns shape politics and a myriad of policy outcomes including, but certainly not limited to, how Congress reforms its internal institutional structures to increase the legislature's capacity vis-à-vis the executive; how the president weighs the congruence between congressional policy preferences and his own when deciding where to draft his legislative initiatives; and how bureaucrats navigate a course of competing incentives from the executive who nominally heads them and the congressional committees responsible for appropriating their funds.[24] The vast majority of this scholarship, however, has focused solely on the domestic arena. Applying a similar interinstitutional lens to questions of foreign policymaking holds considerable

23. See, inter alia, Bueno de Mesquita, Morrow, Siverson, and Smith 2003; Fearon 1994; Schultz 2001; Auerswald 2000.

24. Inter alia, on the role of institutional incentives in spurring legislative institutional reform, see Schickler 2001; on where presidential policy decisions are drafted, see Rudalevige 2002; and on the implications of separation of powers dynamics for bureaucratic politics, see Carpenter 2001. For other important recent works in this separation-of-powers tradition, see Cameron's (2000) formal analysis of interbranch veto bargaining; Canes-Wrone's (2005) analysis of presidential public leadership strategies; Howell's (2003) analysis of the logic of unilateral action; Krehbiel's (1998) pivotal model of lawmaking; and Lewis' (2003) analysis of the interbranch tensions driving federal agency creation.

promise for broadening our understanding of how actors in our separation of powers system interact to shape politics and policy. This and future research into interinstitutional dynamics in foreign policy may, in turn, yield fresh perspectives from which to reexamine interbranch tensions and contests in the domestic arena.

Finally, this research agenda has broader implications for assessments of the relative balance of power between the executive and legislative branches. For much of the post–World War II era, students of American politics have decried the increasing institutional weakness of Congress. A robust literature documents the institutional flaws, such as collective-action dilemmas and a cumbersome legislative process riddled with transaction costs and supermajoritarian requirements, that severely circumscribe Congress's capacity to wield the strong legislative check on presidential usurpations of power that the Founders intended.[25] Indeed, the data in this book confirm that such barriers do limit Congress's ability to check the president legislatively in military affairs. However, if Congress continues to exert influence over policymaking through more indirect means—even in foreign affairs, an arena long held to be dominated by the executive—then Congress may not be as institutionally weak as is often proposed. The three historical case studies that follow endeavor to show how these indirect pathways operate and afford Congress some influence over one of the most important aspects of a use of force: its duration.

Interbranch Politics and War-Making: Three Cases

From the earliest days of the republic, the executive and legislative branches have vied for influence over the nation's military affairs. For example, only five years after the ratification of the Constitution, George Washington's Proclamation of Neutrality prompted outcry from pro-French factions in Congress that the president was reserving for himself alone the right to interpret the nation's treaty obligations with its Revolu-

---

25. For collective-action dilemmas, see Olson 1965, Mayhew 1974, Wawro 2000. For transaction costs in Congress, see Weingast and Marshall 1988, Epstein and O'Halloran 1999, Moe and Wilson 1994, Moe and Howell 1999a, Howell 2003. On the pivotal importance of supermajoritarian requirements to understanding U.S. lawmaking, see Krehbiel 1996, 1998; Brady and Volden 1998; Cameron 2000.

tionary War ally. This episode prompted the famous Pacificus-Helvidius debate between Alexander Hamilton and James Madison on the proper balance of foreign policy powers between the branches. Less than twenty years later when Madison himself inhabited the White House, the tables were turned as pro-British Federalist leaders in Congress attempted to block funding for the War of 1812, which they sardonically dubbed "Mr. Madison's War."[26]

Throughout American history, these interbranch struggles have taken many forms. In few instances do we observe Congress unambiguously bringing to heel an overzealous commander in chief.[27] However, time and again there are signs that Congress has exerted some measure of influence over the course of military affairs, albeit through indirect means. These brief case studies only begin to probe the various ways in which Congress has historically entered into the president's decision calculus. In none of the cases does Congress legally compel the president to abandon his preferred policy course without his consent. Yet in each, the varied actions taken in Congress influenced the president's strategic calculations and helped shape observable policy outcomes.

Grenada: Operation Urgent Fury, 1983

One of the defining foreign policy priorities of Ronald Reagan's administration was to combat perceived communist expansion in Latin America. As early as the spring of 1983, the administration began to turn its attention to the small Caribbean island nation of Grenada. In a televised address on March 23, the president alleged that the island's communist government under Maurice Bishop was aligning the country ever closer militarily to Cuba and the Soviet Union. To substantiate his claims, Reagan displayed aerial photos of the new airport being built on the island with the considerable help of Cuban military advisors; this airport, he argued, was primarily designed to facilitate a communist military buildup in Grenada.[28]

---

26. See Hickey 2004.

27. It is even rarer that we observe congressional hawks actively pushing a reluctant president to begin a new or continue an existing military conflict against his better judgment.

28. Ronald Reagan, "Address to the Nation on Defense and National Security." *Public Papers of the President*, March 23, 1983.

Despite these concerns, Reagan took no action against Grenada until events in October of 1983 provided the administration with an opportunity to act. A military coup led by even more fervent communist factions within the government deposed Bishop on October 12. While Bishop was freed by supporters on October 19, he was quickly recaptured and killed by military forces loyal to the coup. The new military government instituted a twenty-four-hour curfew with orders to shoot on sight. In response to the assassination and deteriorating situation on the island, planning for a possible military intervention accelerated in Washington. On October 20, Vice President George H. W. Bush convened a high-level meeting to assess the situation; later that day, Reagan ordered a Marine task force in transit to Lebanon diverted toward Grenada in case he decided upon a military response.[29] Various official and secondary sources offer somewhat conflicting chronologies as to the precise sequence of decisions that ultimately led to the American invasion. However, what is clear is that on the evening of October 24, 1983—one day after the terrorist bombing of the Marine barracks in Lebanon that left 241 Americans dead—Reagan signed the order for American forces to invade the island. Two to three hours later, he summoned top congressional leaders to the White House to inform them of his decision.[30] The next day Reagan announced the invasion to the American people and emphasized the necessity for swift action to protect American lives, including those of 600 American medical students on the island.[31]

The immediate reaction on Capitol Hill was mixed. Some Democrats expressed outrage at the administration's move, which they denounced as a violation of both American and international law. Others, including House Speaker Tip O'Neill (D-Massachusetts), defended Reagan and emphasized the need to stand behind the president in a time of international crisis. By contrast, many Republicans openly lauded the invasion, but some expressed concerns about the tenuous military situations in both Grenada and Lebanon. Despite these varying reactions to the

29. For an overview, see Richard Whittle, "Questions, Praise Follow Grenada Invasion." *CQ Weekly,* October 29, 1983, 2221–24.

30. Rubner 1985/86.

31. Ronald Reagan, "Remarks of the President and Prime Minister Eugenia Charles of Dominica Announcing the Deployment of United States Forces in Grenada." *Public Papers of the President,* October 25, 1983.

administration's decision to invade and the justifications for it, the debate in Congress revealed two overriding concerns. First, many members publicly and privately chafed at the administration's failure to consult with Congress before making the decision to invade, as was required by the War Powers Resolution of 1973. As Senator Claiborne Pell (D-Rhode Island) remarked in a Foreign Relations Committee hearing on the invasion, "there is a world of difference between being consulted and . . . being informed . . . we are doing this at 5am tomorrow."[32] Second, regardless of their position on the wisdom of the initial decision, many announced that they were willing to back the president provided that the mission would be short in duration. Senator Joseph Biden (D-Delaware) spoke for many when he told reporters that he was "ready to sign on" in support of the invasion, "conditioned only on the assertion that he doesn't plan on staying there beyond the restoration of peace."[33]

This congressional unease quickly manifested itself in legislative vehicles seeking to limit the duration of the military action in Grenada. Two days after the invasion began, the House Foreign Affairs Committee approved HJ Res 402 triggering the War Powers Resolution's withdrawal clock and requiring that all American forces be removed from Grenada within ninety days unless their continued presence was authorized by congressional statute. The full Senate adopted similar language the following day as an amendment to a bill raising the federal debt ceiling (HJ Res 308).[34] In tandem with these legislative challenges to unilateral assertions of presidential military power, skeptics of the president's poli-

32. Rubner 1985/86.

33. Richard Whittle, "Questions, Praise Follow Grenada Invasion." *CQ Weekly,* October 29, 1983, 2221–24.

34. While both chambers did pass versions of legislation that would invoke the War Powers Resolution's withdrawal clock, members did so knowing that there was very little chance that the language would ever become law. Senate Majority Leader Howard Baker refused to allow the House resolution to come to a vote in the Senate, instead burying it in committee. Republicans also refused to pass the debt ceiling bill (HJ Res 308) as long as it contained the provision invoking the War Powers Resolution. Moreover, as joint resolutions, both the House and the Senate measures would require veto-proof two-thirds majorities to become law. Accordingly, Illinois Republican Henry Hyde labeled these "institutional votes" in which even Republicans could send a signal of standing up for the legislature's war prerogatives with little risk of genuine policy consequences—a classic example of Mayhew's (1974) position-taking. See: Richard Whittle, "Questions, Praise Follow Grenada Invasion." *CQ Weekly,* October 29, 1983, 2221–24; Richard Whittle, "Objec-

cies also launched independent investigations into the administration's pretext for war and the costs of the military campaign. While Senate Majority Leader Howard Baker (R-Tennessee) killed Democratic proposals to send a fact-finding mission to Grenada, Speaker O'Neill quickly dispatched a bipartisan group to the island to investigate publicly the causes and consequences of the American invasion, and the House Foreign Affairs Committee commenced its own inquiry into the administration's policy in Grenada.

Despite this unease on Capitol Hill—and thanks in part to a carefully crafted media strategy that included extensive coverage of returning medical students kissing the ground and exclaiming "God bless America, God bless Reagan, God bless our military"—the public rallied behind the president and the invasion.[35] This helped the administration weather the initial congressional storm and cooled efforts to mandate legislatively the troops' expeditious withdrawal. Some in the Pentagon interpreted the eased political climate as license for an extended American commitment in Grenada. However, the president's special assistant for legislative affairs bluntly warned Chief of Staff James A. Baker III that Reagan must not mistake this temporary lull in congressional opposition for a permanent one:

I'm told [Undersecretary of State] Ken Dam said in testimony this week before the Senate Foreign Relations Committee that it is extremely unlikely that the War Powers Act will become an issue because we don't envision staying in Grenada 60–90 days. Defense, on the other hand, is now saying we have to stay there indefinitely (or at least for an extended period) to keep the Cuban forces from reoccupying the island. The longer we stay the more opposition will grow in the Congress to our decision to send in the troops. *Right now we're in relatively good shape on the Hill on Grenada, but that doesn't mean there's a hell of a lot of support or patience for U.S. troops remaining in Grenada for a lengthy stay.*[36]

tives Achieved, Reagan Says: Congress Examines Causes, Costs of Grenada Operation." *CQ Weekly,* November 5, 1983, 2292–93.

35. Ibid.

36. Memorandum, Duberstein to Baker, October 29, 1983, folder "W.H. Staff Memoranda—Legislative Affairs 7/83-12/83 [1 of 3]," box 5, James Baker III files, Ronald Reagan Library. Emphasis added.

Many in the administration embraced Duberstein's views. Still reeling from the devastating attack on American Marines in Beirut, top administration officials saw more benefit in ending the military mission in Grenada expeditiously than in maintaining a commitment there. Many in the Defense Department argued that an extended military presence would have best served the administration's goals of countering the expansion of communist influence in the region. However, these considerations were outweighed by the political benefits of a quick withdrawal coupled with the potential costs of heightened congressional criticism and resistance should it reemerge in the near future.

Days after Duberstein's memorandum, Secretary of Defense Caspar Weinberger announced the first major withdrawal of American forces from Grenada. On November 3, President Reagan declared, "Our objectives have been achieved, and as soon as logistics permit, American personnel will be leaving."[37] The final American combat troops left the island in December of 1983, well before the War Powers Resolution's ninety-day time horizon.

Somalia: Operation Restore Hope, 1992–94

In January 1991, a coalition of revolutionary clans in Somalia forced the government's totalitarian leader, Mohammad Siad Barre, from power. The coup thrust the country into a bloody civil war pitting various clans against one another. A combination of battle-ravaged crops and severe drought quickly produced starvation on a massive scale. The plight of the Somali people attracted significant attention in Congress even before the crisis featured prominently on the mainstream American media.[38] Senator Nancy Kassebaum (R-Kansas) initiated the congressional

37. Ronald Reagan, "Remarks Announcing the Appointment of Donald Rumsfeld as the President's Personal Representative in the Middle East." *Public Papers of the President*, November 3, 1983.

38. The case of Operation Restore Hope is frequently cited as a prime example of the "CNN effect" by academics and politicians alike. For the former, see, for example, McNulty 1993; Shaw 1993; Robinson 1999, 2002. For the latter, see, for example, Murtha 2003. However, careful research by Jonathan Mermin (1999) notes that sustained media coverage of famine in Somalia, which ultimately prompted the Bush administration to launch Operation Restore Hope, emerged only *after* other political elites, particularly members of Congress, had moved the issue onto the agenda (see also Livingston and Eachus 1995).

response by introducing a resolution calling on President George H. W. Bush to lead a United Nations humanitarian effort to end the suffering in Somalia. In subsequent months congressional committees held multiple hearings on the crisis. Members of Congress sent over a dozen letters to various executive officials pressing for action, and multiple congressional delegations witnessed firsthand the devastation on the Horn of Africa.[39] At least in part because of this pressure for action from Congress, the media, and the public, in the final days of his administration Bush committed U.S. forces to provide food assistance and peacekeeping in Operation Restore Hope.

Just over two weeks after Bill Clinton took office in 1993, the Senate took steps to authorize legislatively the military deployment (SJ Res 45). However, the new president faced considerably greater opposition to the authorization in the House. Some prominent Democrats, including Pennsylvania's John Murtha, expressed considerable unease about the deployment. Most Democrats, however, unwilling to criticize openly their party's first president in more than a decade, relegated their concerns to discussions behind closed doors.[40] House Republicans, by contrast, were more vocal in their objections. New York's Benjamin Gilman, for example, offered an amendment that would have limited the authorization to six months. While the resolution ultimately passed in May of 1993, the final, largely party-line vote testified to the latent opposition to the mission in Congress.

The situation on the ground in Somalia deteriorated considerably soon after the House vote. On June 5, 1993, rebels led by warlord Mohammed Farah Aidid ambushed Pakistani troops dispatched as part of the multinational mission; the raid left twenty-four peacekeepers dead and nearly sixty wounded. American and United Nations forces responded with a combination of air strikes and ground assaults. After the battle, Clinton declared: "This operation is over and it was a success. . . . our nation must continue to exert global leadership as we have done this week in Somalia."[41] Despite Clinton's optimism, peacekeeping forces

39. For an overview of the congressional reaction, see Johnston and Dagne 1997.

40. Carroll J. Doherty, "Anxiety Grows on Capitol Hill over Clinton's Approach." *CQ Weekly*, March 20, 1993, 683.

41. "Presidential News Conference: Clinton Touts Economic Growth, Defends Tax Increases as Fair." *CQ Weekly*, June 19, 1993, 1604.

remained in the war-torn country and the American role continued to shift from one of providing humanitarian relief to a more active posture that included the goals of capturing Aidid and building a more stable Somali state.

While Democratic leaders had largely succeeded in stifling criticism of the new president's policies for much of the summer, in early September a boisterous Democratic critic broke the virtual four-month silence in the Senate. Juxtaposing the Senate's failure to act, West Virginia's Robert Byrd, the rare inveterate defender of the legislature's constitutional prerogatives, reminded the chamber that after the Battle of Actium in 31 BC "the Roman Senate had lost its will to make hard decisions. It had lost its will to lead. It had lost its nerve. It had lost its way." Byrd warned, "All we have to do is to look at a bit of Roman history and see exactly where we are going."[42] Although he had periodically raised concerns over the costs of the mission, Byrd sought to move the issue more firmly onto the congressional agenda by introducing an amendment to the defense authorization bill (S 1298) that would cut off funding for the mission. The strategic changes in the operation, Byrd argued, were neither debated nor approved in the Senate. Moreover, he contended, such actions were not worth "any price in American blood."[43] Many Republicans, sensing Clinton's political vulnerability, also sharply criticized his policies.

Working in tandem with the White House, Democratic and Republican leaders forged a compromise alternative to Byrd's hard-line approach. In the end, the Senate voted 90–7 in favor of a nonbinding resolution attached to the authorization bill that called on Clinton to make a full report of his policy goals to Congress and to seek bicameral authorization for the expanded mission by November 15. The House ultimately passed similar language, but only after the Democratic leadership, in the words of Nebraska Republican Doug Bereuter, "manipulate[ed] the will of Congress to avoid a straightforward vote" on pulling U.S. troops out of Somalia.[44]

Yet the political reprieve for Clinton was short-lived. Less than a week after the administration survived its first showdown in Congress, a

42. Robert Byrd, *Congressional Record*, September 9, 1993, S11264.
43. Robert Byrd, *Congressional Record*, September 8, 1993, S11126.
44. Doug Bereuter, *Congressional Record*, September 28, 1993, H7101.

special operations mission went awry and Somali fighters shot down two American Black Hawk helicopters. In the Battle of Mogadishu, eighteen Army Rangers were killed and scores more wounded. Gruesome images from the battle saturated the airwaves in the United States and around the world. Certainly, the stark loss of life and extensive media coverage of it turned many Americans against continuing the Somali mission. However, as research by James Burk, Christopher Gelpi, Peter Feaver, and Jason Reifler has demonstrated, the most prominent initial response of the American public was not to advocate immediate withdrawal, but to support an expanded American military operation to retaliate against those responsible for the attacks.[45] The political pressure to withdraw expeditiously came first from opponents in Congress, who immediately *prior* to the Black Hawk Down incident had waged an intense campaign to terminate the military mission.

The negative reaction in Congress, from erstwhile opponents and supporters alike, was overwhelming. Senator Byrd inveighed on the floor: "Americans by the dozens are paying with their lives and limbs for a misplaced policy on the altar of some fuzzy multilateralism. . . . why in the world should we drag these fatal cops-and-robber operations on any longer? Let us vote and let us get out."[46] Haunted by U.S. blunders in Southeast Asia, South Carolina Democrat Fritz Hollings admonished, "It's Vietnam all over again," and Illinois Republican Henry Hyde called the debacle a "Johnsonian error."[47] A number of House Republicans signed on to a letter chastising Clinton's foreign policy as "indecisive and naïve."[48] Summing up the sentiments of many on the Hill, Senator John McCain (R-Arizona) plainly stated: "Clinton's got to bring them home."[49]

In his memoirs, Clinton plainly acknowledged the critical importance of congressional pressures in effecting his reversal.

45. Burk 1999; Gelpi, Feaver and Reifler 2009. See also Kull and Destler 1999, Feaver and Gelpi 2004. For a different interpretation of the survey evidence, see Larson 1996.

46. Robert Byrd, *Congressional Record*, October 4, 1993, S12876.

47. Clifford Krauss, "White House Tries to Calm Congress." *New York Times*, October 6, 1993.

48. Carroll J. Doherty, "Clinton Calms Rebellion on Hill by Retooling Somalia Mission." *CQ Weekly*, October 9, 1993, 2750.

49. R. W. Apple Jr., "Clinton Sending Reinforcements after Heavy Losses in Somalia." *New York Times*, October 5, 1993, A1.

I was sick about the loss of our troops and I wanted Aidid to pay. If getting him was worth eighteen dead and eighty-four wounded Americans, wasn't it worth finishing the job? . . . [T]here was no support in Congress for a larger military role in Somalia, as I learned in a White House meeting with several members; most of them demanded an immediate withdrawal of our forces. I strongly disagreed, and in the end we compromised on a six-month transition period. I didn't mind taking Congress on, but I had to consider the consequences of any action that could make it even harder to get congressional support for sending American troops to Bosnia or Haiti, where we had far greater interests at stake.[50]

In the hope of preempting more aggressive congressional restrictions, Clinton responded to the disaster by announcing that, in addition to sending reinforcements to protect American forces in the region, he would set a six-month deadline and end American participation in the mission by March 31, 1994. The president also personally called Byrd and pledged full cooperation in an attempt to prevent a more radical rebellion on Capitol Hill.[51] Ultimately, Byrd, the majority leadership, and Senate Minority Leader Robert Dole (R-Kansas), endorsed the president's plan. After five hours of floor debate, at 1:15 in the morning of October 15, the Senate voted 61–38 against immediate redeployment and 76–23 in support of Clinton's plan, with a provision cutting off funding for operations in Somalia after March 31, 1994. The House continued the debate for several days and voted on alternative Republican-sponsored resolutions moving the funding cutoff date forward, but it ultimately backed the compromise.

To critics, the legislative measures that ultimately passed were not bold enough and still reflected undue congressional deference to the executive.[52] To others, Congress's reaction was a clear and decisive check on presidential war powers.[53] While both perspectives have merit, by President Clinton's own admission, Congress played a critically important

50. Bill Clinton, 2004. *My Life*. New York: Knopf, 552.

51. Thomas L. Friedman, "A Firm Deadline for a Pullout Will Be Set." *New York Times*, October 7, 1993, A1.

52. See, for example, Weissman 1995; Pat Towell, "Cover Story: Clinton's Policy Is Battered, but His Powers Are Intact." *CQ Weekly*, October 23, 1993, 2896.

53. In Byrd's assessment, for example, the legislature's actions in October of 1993 "put Congress in the front seat and on the front row [in military affairs] as it should be under

role in circumscribing both the scope and the duration of the American military commitment in Somalia. Moreover, the institutional scars inflicted by Congress had serious ramifications for the Clinton White House's subsequent decisions in Bosnia, Kosovo, Afghanistan, and Haiti. Perhaps nowhere is the legacy of congressional actions in Somalia clearer than in the administration's feeble response to the Rwandan genocide, a decision that Clinton later called perhaps the most regrettable failure of his presidency.[54]

Afghanistan: Operation Enduring Freedom, 2001–present

The ongoing war in Afghanistan is a qualitatively different conflict from most prior uses of force in American history. It is now an inherited war, waged by a new president from the party previously in opposition. As a result, many of the political dynamics of this case are exceptional. For example, in most cases throughout American history, congressional challenges to presidential military policies have arisen primarily among the ranks of the opposition party. However, in the Afghan war, the strongest opposition to President Barack Obama's policies has paradoxically come from his fellow Democrats, and particularly from his liberal base. The reasons for this anomaly are clear; much of this Democratic opposition built during the Bush years as congressional liberals grew increasingly dissatisfied with the war's spiraling human and financial costs and its extended duration with no end in sight.

As of this writing, it is exceedingly difficult to assess the degree of influence, if any at all, that Congress has had over the Obama administration's conduct of the Afghan war and its likely duration. Nevertheless, the eruption of legislative criticism of Obama's plans to dispatch additional troops to the region in fall 2009 affords some insight into (and raises additional important questions about) how interbranch struggles can shape the conduct of major American military deployments, even years after their initiation.

On the evening of September 11, 2001, as smoke continued to rise from the Pentagon and the World Trade Center, President George W.

---

the Constitution." Carroll J. Doherty, "Byrd's Caution a Vietnam Legacy." *CQ Weekly*, October 16, 1993, 2824.

54. Clinton 2004, 593.

Bush spoke to the nation from the Oval Office and proclaimed the beginning of a "war against terrorism" in which the United States would "make no distinction between the terrorists who committed these acts and those who harbor them."[55] A week later, Congress enacted SJ Res 23, which authorized the president to "to use all necessary and appropriate force against those nations, organizations, or persons he determines planned, authorized, committed, or aided the terrorist attacks that occurred on September 11, 2001, or harbored such organizations or persons, in order to prevent any future acts of international terrorism against the United States by such nations, organizations, or persons."

On September 20, 2001, Bush identified the terrorist network Al Qaeda as being responsible for the attacks on the American homeland, and he described its strong ties to the Taliban leadership of Afghanistan, where most of the group was based. The president issued a series of demands to the Taliban leadership, including the arrest and transfer of Al Qaeda leaders to the United States and the dismantling of terrorist camps and infrastructure. If the regime did not comply, the United States would overthrow it militarily. Yet even as Bush strove to convey America's resolve, he also sought to prepare the American people for the realities of this new type of war. The campaign against terror would be multifaceted and constantly evolving; but perhaps most importantly, Bush warned: "Americans should not expect one battle but a lengthy campaign, unlike any other we have ever seen."[56]

The Taliban leadership rejected Bush's ultimatum the following day, and on October 7, 2001, American and British aircraft and guided missiles began an intensive aerial assault against Al Qaeda and Taliban targets. Operation Enduring Freedom had begun. By the end of December 2001 the Taliban government had fled first the capital, Kabul, and then its stronghold in southern Afghanistan, Kandahar. Yet despite these early victories, Taliban elements survived the initial assault, regrouped, and launched new attacks against both coalition forces and those of the fledgling Afghan government established in 2004 and 2005.

Despite the failure to eliminate the Taliban threat, public support

55. George W. Bush, "Address to the Nation on the Terrorist Attacks." *Public Papers of the President*, September 11, 2001.

56. George W. Bush, "Address before a Joint Session of the Congress on the United States Response to the Terrorist Attacks of September 11." *Public Papers of the President*, September 20, 2001.

for the war in Afghanistan remained strikingly high throughout Bush's presidency. This resilience in public support stands in stark contrast to the dramatic erosion of support for the war in Iraq, which the administration also sought to justify as an integral part of the campaign against global terrorism. For example, in July of 2008, twice as many Americans responded that the war in Iraq was a mistake as believed the same concerning the war in Afghanistan (56% vs. 28%).[57] Indeed, the percentage of Americans judging the war in Afghanistan a mistake at the conclusion of Bush's term in office was only marginally higher than the comparable figure at the midpoint of his presidency.[58]

In the midterm elections of 2006, Democrats exploited this sharp gap in public support for the two conflicts by charging that the Bush administration's misguided invasion of Iraq had diverted scarce military resources from the genuine fight against terror in Afghanistan. This line of attack allowed Democrats to claim credibly that they were "tough" on terrorism, even as it enabled them to score political points by criticizing the administration's bungling of the war in the Middle East. Two years later the Democratic presidential nominee, Illinois Senator Barack Obama, consciously adopted a similar strategy. He repeatedly made a distinction between the "war of choice" in Iraq and the "war of necessity" in Afghanistan. Winding down the American commitment in Iraq, he argued, would free up needed resources to strengthen our military presence in Afghanistan.

Yet, even as the Obama campaign sought to contrast the "good war" in Afghanistan with the distraction in Iraq, the situation on the ground in central Asia was deteriorating. Renewed Taliban offensives made 2008 the deadliest year of the seven-year war for American forces, and intensified fighting spilled over into an increasingly unstable Pakistan. As a result, the situation in Afghanistan that President-elect Obama inherited in early 2009 was significantly worse than what it had been when he began campaigning in 2007.

Nevertheless, having promised during the campaign to bolster the American presence in Afghanistan, Obama quickly ordered twenty-one

57. *USA Today*/Gallup poll [USAIPOUSA2008-27], July 25–28, 2008. http://www.pollingreport.com/afghan.htm. http://www.pollingreport.com/iraq.htm.

58. Gallup/CNN/*USA Today* poll [USAIPOCNUS2004-24], July 25–27, 2004. In July of 2004, twenty-five percent of Americans judged the war in Afghanistan a mistake. http://www.pollingreport.com/afghan.htm.

thousand additional soldiers to Afghanistan. But the additional influx of troops did little to turn the tide on the ground. The much anticipated but ultimately tainted Afghan presidential election shattered hopes that a more stable, competent indigenous government—a central element of the American counter-insurgency strategy—would emerge to serve as a strategic partner in combating the Taliban insurgency and bringing security and stability to troubled regions. Meanwhile, the military situation worsened further still and American casualty tallies in 2009 quickly surpassed even those of 2008.

Against this backdrop, the commanding general in Afghanistan, Stanley A. McChrystal, submitted a report to Secretary of Defense Robert Gates on August 30, 2009, that requested an additional forty thousand troops be sent to the region. Absent reinforcements and a shift in strategy, McChrystal warned, failure was a genuine possibility.[59] The leaking of the report in the *Washington Post* before the administration had completed its review of the document placed considerable pressure on the Obama administration to respond.[60] It also provided the impetus for members of Congress, many of whom had expressed their concerns on Afghanistan primarily in private to that point, to publicly enter the policy debate.

Many on Capitol Hill, particularly within the president's own party, were quick to question the proposed troop increase. The chairman of the Senate Armed Services Committee, Carl Levin, argued that expanding the size of the Afghan army, not sending additional U.S. combat troops to the region, should be the focal point of American strategy in Afghanistan. Senator John Kerry, the chairman of the Foreign Relations Committee and the Democratic Party's nominee in the 2004 presidential election, went even further and evoked the specter of Vietnam in condemning the rush to send more troops. "In Vietnam, we heard the commanding general on the ground saying we need more troops. We heard the president of the United States say if we just put in more troops, we're

59. The *Commander's Initial Assessment* warns (pp. 1–2): "Failure to gain the initiative and reverse insurgent momentum in the near term (next twelve months)—while Afghan security capacity matures—risks an outcome where defeating the insurgency is no longer possible." http://media.washingtonpost.com/wp-srv/politics/documents/Assessment_Redacted_092109.pdf?hpid=topnews

60. Eric Schmitt and Thom Shanker, "General Calls for More U.S. Troops to Avoid Afghan Failure." *Washington Post*, September 20, 2009, A1.

going to see the light at the end of the tunnel." Such logic, Kerry maintained, was fatally flawed "because [it] never examined the underlying
assumptions on which our involvement was based."[61] House liberals also
raised strong objections to any troop increase. In a letter sent to Obama,
members of the Congressional Progressive Caucus expressed their considerable unease "about committing additional US troops and taxpayer
dollars in Afghanistan, especially when the US mission is unclear and
when methods for measuring mission effectiveness are underdeveloped
or nonexistent."[62] Most Republicans, by contrast, supported the call for
increased troop levels; however, a handful, including California's Dana
Rohrabacher, publicly joined forces with the liberals, at least temporarily, in opposing any troop surge.[63]

Faced with a tenuous political climate on Capitol Hill and declining
public support for the Afghan war, the Obama administration engaged
in lengthy deliberations about the nature of its response to McChrystal's
request. On December 1, more than two months after the commander's
assessment arrived in Washington, the president finally announced his
decision to send 30,000 more troops to Afghanistan, a move that effectively tripled the number of American soldiers in Afghanistan since he
took office.

Superficially at least, the strong opposition of many in Congress seems
to have had little detectable influence on Obama's decision-making;
he did, after all, dispatch an additional 30,000 troops to Afghanistan
against the express wishes of many in his own party. Nevertheless, his
announcement and the decision process leading up to it do suggest at
least two areas in which congressional concerns may have entered into
the administration's strategic calculations. The first element of Obama's
policy response that is consistent with assertions of congressional influence is the delicate balance he endeavored to strike between firmly de-
claring to the Taliban and the world his "intention to finish the job" in

61. Scott Wilson. "On War, Obama Could Turn to GOP; Democrats Oppose Larger
War Effort." *Washington Post*, October 1, 2009, A1.

62. "Lawmakers Caution Obama against Afghan Troops." Agence France-Presse, November 17, 2009. http://www.breitbart.com/article.php?id=CNG.9900453d71362e75f82c0e
358cd4ed7e.6c1&show_article=1.

63. Richard Simon, "Opposite Minds Think Alike: A Republican and a Democrat,
Both Against Sending More U.S. Troops, Become Surprising Allies." *Los Angeles Times*,
October 19, 2009, A8.

Afghanistan, and simultaneously reassuring congressional critics that the newly augmented American military commitment in central Asia would not be open-ended.[64] As early as May 2009, Massachusetts Democrat Jim McGovern introduced a bill (HR 2404) demanding that the administration present Congress with a detailed exit strategy for American forces in Afghanistan. On June 25, a majority of House Democrats voted in support of the McGovern measure; only Republican support won the day for the administration.[65] The movement gained renewed impetus during the White House's deliberations over the response to McChrystal's request.[66]

Obama's address to the nation on December 1, 2009, clearly reflected his awareness of these concerns. After summarizing the events that led the nation to this pivotal moment, he declared: "As Commander in Chief, I have determined that it is in our vital national interest to send an additional 30,000 U.S. troops to Afghanistan." And yet, in his very next sentence, he placed restrictions on the duration of the troop surge: "After 18 months, our troops will begin to come home. These are the resources that we need to seize the initiative, while building the Afghan capacity that can allow for a responsible transition of our forces out of Afghanistan."[67] For many, the immediate juxtaposition between the president's desire to convey American resolve and his explicit discussion of the military exit strategy was striking. Indeed, Secretary Gates had ex-

64. For Obama's usage of the phrase "finish the job," see Barack Obama, "The President's News Conference with Prime Minister Manmohan Singh of India." *Public Papers of the President*, November 24, 2009.

65. McGovern's language was offered as an amendment to a defense appropriations bill (HR 2647). The final vote tally on the amendment was 138–278, with Democrats voting 131–114 in favor of the amendment, and Republicans voting 164–7 against it.

66. In the weeks before the administration announced its decision, Raul Grijalva of Arizona vented the frustrations of many on Capitol Hill with the administration's intended decision: "I hope she [Speaker Pelosi] tells him our caucus is not going to be happy about this. . . . An exit strategy to be developed later is not an exit strategy." Mike Soraghan and Jared Allen, "Pelosi, Obama Meet amid Afghan Debate." *The Hill*, November 24, 2009. http://thehill.com/homenews/house/69355-pelosi-obama-meet-amid-afghan-debate. See also Mike Soraghan and Jared Allen, "Afghanistan Troop Surge Could Test Alliance between Obama, Pelosi." *The Hill*, November 28, 2009. http://thehill.com/homenews/house/69631-afghanistan-action-could-test-alliance-between-obama-pelosi.

67. Barack Obama, "Remarks by the President in Address to the Nation on the Way Forward in Afghanistan and Pakistan." *Public Papers of the President*, December 1, 2009.

plicitly rejected the suggestion of setting a timeline only two months before.[68] Moreover, as the administration surely anticipated, Republicans
criticized Obama heavily for the mixed messages these contrasting statements sent to the Taliban and Al Qaeda.[69] Nevertheless, the move makes
sense if the administration calculated that the political costs of Republican criticism and potential strategic costs of the mixed signals were
outweighed by the political need to address deep concerns among congressional Democrats and a majority of the American public over any
escalation of the war.[70]

The second area of paramount concern to many in Congress that
appears to have influenced administration thinking is the financial
cost of the escalation. On this issue, again, the loudest critics on Capitol Hill paradoxically have been members of the president's own party.
As Obama deliberated, House Appropriations Committee Chairman
David Obey lamented that supporters of the surge advocated a double
standard for war spending: "For the last year, as we've struggled to pass
healthcare reform, we've been told that we have to pay for the bill—and
the cost over the next decade will be about $1 trillion. Now the presi-
dent is being asked to consider an enlarged counterinsurgency effort in
Afghanistan. . . . But unlike the healthcare bill, that would not be paid

68. Sean Lengell, "Gates: Afghan Exit Timeline 'a Mistake.'" *Washington Times*,
September 28, 2009. http://www.washingtontimes.com/news/2009/sep/28/gates-afghan-
exit-timeline-a-mistake/?page=2. For Gates's response to allegations of inconsistencies,
see transcript, *This Week with George Stephanopoulos.* December 6, 2009. http://www
.abcnews.go.com/ThisWeek/week-full-transcript-dec-2009/story?id=9262010.

69. Republicans also roundly criticized Obama for his delay in responding to McChrystal's request. Former Massachusetts Governor Mitt Romney, for example, ridiculed what
he termed Obama's "Hamlet performance" on Afghanistan. "The president has known
about this issue for a long time," Romney noted. "He received the report from General
[Stanley] McChrystal four months ago and has not been able to make a decision." This delay may have been due, at least in part, to the discussions over the exit strategy that the administration would make public at the time of the troop surge announcement to allay the
fears of congressional Democrats. For the Romney quote, see Ewen MacAskill, "Obama
Accused of Dithering over Troops." *The Guardian*, November 3, 2009, 17.

70. While Republicans almost uniformly attacked Obama's strategy as sending mixed
signals to the enemy, the president claimed that it sent an important signal to the Karzai
government: that the United States' willingness to prop up the regime militarily was not
open-ended. Barack Obama, "Remarks by the President in Address to the Nation on the
Way Forward in Afghanistan and Pakistan." *Public Papers of the President*, December 1,
2009.

for. We believe that's wrong."[71] To pay for the war, Obey proposed a war income tax surcharge. House Democratic Caucus Chairman John Larson and Defense Appropriations Subcommittee Chairman John Murtha also publicly backed the surcharge idea as the administration deliberated its response.[72]

In the face of such criticism from prominent Democrats, the president brought Office of Management and Budget Director Peter Orszag into his inner circle on war planning, and administration spokesman Robert Gibbs publicly promised that the administration would put forward a plan to pay for whatever option it ultimately endorsed.[73] Even a spokesman for Secretary Gates acknowledged that the costs of the various options played a role in the decision-making process.[74] And in his address to the nation announcing the dispatch of additional troops, Obama specifically referenced the question of costs while rejecting calls for a larger, open-ended surge: "I reject this course because it sets goals that are beyond what can be achieved at a reasonable cost." Obama then alluded to President Dwight Eisenhower's warning of the need to strike a balance between competing national interests when deciding how to spend

71. Janet Hook and Christi Parsons, "Talk of War Surcharge for Afghanistan Expenses Heats Up." *Los Angeles Times*, November 25, 2009. http://www.latimes.com/news/nation-and-world/la-na-war-taxes25-2009nov25,0,2635358.story.

72. Janet Hook and Christi Parsons, "Talk of War Surcharge for Afghanistan Expenses Heats Up." *Los Angeles Times*, November 25, 2009. http://www.latimes.com/news/nation-and-world/la-na-war-taxes25-2009nov25,0,2635358.story. Having been warned by Speaker Pelosi that it might be impossible to secure the needed funding for any surge with Democratic votes alone, the White House and Chief of Staff Rahm Emanuel also began private discussions with Republican leaders. South Carolina Senator Lindsay Graham told the White House that if the troop surge was large enough (at least a number "that began with 3") and the generals supported the move, he would have substantial Republican support. Peter Baker, "How Obama Came to Plan for 'Surge' in Afghanistan." *New York Times*, December 6, 2009, A1.

73. An OMB memo to the president asserted that the cost of fully meeting McChrystal's request for 40,000 troops would be an additional $1 trillion over the next decade. A recent assessment of Obama's decision process by the *New York Times* captures his reaction this way: "The president seemed in sticker shock, watching his domestic agenda vanishing in front of him. 'This is a 10-year, trillion-dollar effort and does not match up with our interests,' he said." Peter Baker, "How Obama Came to Plan for 'Surge' in Afghanistan." *New York Times*, December 6, 2009, A1.

74. Janet Hook and Christi Parsons, "Talk of War Surcharge for Afghanistan Expenses Heats Up." *Los Angeles Times*. November 25, 2009. http://www.latimes.com/news/nation-and-world/la-na-war-taxes25-2009nov25,0,2635358.story.

our limited resources. "Over the past several years, we have lost that balance. We've failed to appreciate the connection between our national security and our economy. In the wake of an economic crisis, too many of our neighbors and friends are out of work and struggle to pay the bills. Too many Americans are worried about the future facing our children. Meanwhile, competition within the global economy has grown more fierce. So we can't simply afford to ignore the price of these wars."[75] Of course, cost concerns factor into any major policy decision. However, it is important to note that such language was absent from Obama's public announcement of his first major reinforcement of American troops in Afghanistan before the intensification of opposition to the war in Congress.[76]

It remains to be seen precisely what influence, if any, these congressional concerns have had and will have on the duration of the war in Afghanistan. It is impossible to discern whether Obama scaled back his ambitions in Afghanistan in an effort to mollify congressional opponents, or whether his rhetorical emphasis on an exit strategy and cost containment simply represents the administration's efforts to package its policy preferences in a way that makes them appear responsive to congressional preferences.[77] Similarly, we do not know what the congressional response to the administration's surge will be when the debate over supplemental funding for the additional troops begins, and how this battle, if one materializes, will affect the political and strategic costs Obama risks incurring by continuing an aggressive military course in Afghanistan.

It is possible that congressional opposition to Obama's plan may dissipate by that time. For example, in sharp contrast to the sometimes viru-

75. Barack Obama, "Address to the Nation at the United States Military Academy at West Point, New York." *Public Papers of the President*, December 1, 2009.

76. No reference was made to the need for a timeline to begin withdrawing U.S. forces from Afghanistan or to cost constraints when the president announced his first dispatch of reinforcements in February 2009. Indeed, the presidential statement stressed that the drawdown of American forces in Iraq "allows us the flexibility to increase our presence in Afghanistan." Barack Obama, "Statement on United States Troop Levels in Afghanistan." *Public Papers of the President*, February 17, 2009.

77. Indeed, in public statements since the president's address, Gates and other officials have emphasized repeatedly that July 2011 is only a start date for the American withdrawal. The speed and scope of this drawdown, they maintain, will be dictated by conditions on the ground. Paul Richter, "Robert Gates Says Afghanistan Withdrawal Will Be Gradual." *Los Angeles Times*, December 7, 2009. http://www.latimes.com/news/nation-and-world/la-fg-gates-afghanistan7-2009dec07,0,5275244.story.

lent Democratic criticism of Obama's escalation plans in the fall, immediately after the president's speech in December 2009 many Democrats,
including some erstwhile skeptics such as John Kerry, publicly fell in line
behind their party leader and his new strategy. Instead, the harshest criticism of the president's plan has come from Republicans, who denounced
both the delays in the decision-making process and the announcement
of a timeline for withdrawal, which, many Republicans charged, undercut the mission even before it began.[78] At first blush the Republican criticism is ironic, given that Obama's announcement fit their policy preferences better than those of many Democrats. However, the reactions
of both parties show that even in this atypical case, interbranch politics
over war powers has a strong partisan dimension.

Alternatively, even if significant opposition to the Afghan surge remains, the Democratic leadership could block any serious challenges
from ever reaching the floor. Indeed, House Speaker Nancy Pelosi, despite her publicly-professed skepticism on Afghanistan, has already announced that she will not allow proposals such as Obey's war tax to move
forward.[79] In a similar vein, while Congress has held a number of hearings on the administration's escalation, those hearings have differed substantially in tenor and scale from the heated and politically damaging inquests into President Bush's Iraq surge in 2007. Undoubtedly, the response
of Democratic investigators to Obama's surge has almost certainly paled
in comparison to what would have emerged if John McCain were president and had announced a tripling of the American force size in central
Asia. Partisan incentives may diminish Congress's potential influence.

As a result, the administration may have calculated that the modest
concessions already offered to the left, coupled with Democratic leaders'
awareness that their own and their fellow members' electoral fates are
tied intimately to the success of the president, will be sufficient to afford
Obama the necessary leeway on the Afghan war. Nevertheless, the growing assertiveness of congressional critics of the administration's war policies attests to the importance of understanding the ways in which such actions might influence the conduct of military operations, even if they fail
to legally compel the president to abandon his preferred policy course.

78. See, for example, Susan Milligan and Lisa Wangsness, "Democrats Wary of the
Commitment." *Boston Globe*, December 2, 2009, 10.

79. CQpolitics.com, December 3, 2009. http://www.cqpolitics.com/wmspage.cfm?
parm1=5&docID=cqmidday-000003258240.

Plan of the Book

The foregoing brief case studies raise as many questions as they answer. Do the Grenada and Somalia cases, in particular, represent the rare exceptions that prove the rule? Does Congress, when it engages the military policymaking process, regularly influence presidential conduct of major military affairs, or does it do so only in isolated instances? How do congressional actions affect the calculations of foreign actors? What are the implications for congressional influence when opposition to a military action arises primarily from the president's own party while many in the opposition party support the president in the middle of an inherited war? However, by hinting at indirect pathways through which Congress can shape the calculations of the commander in chief even when it cannot legally compel him to abandon his preferred policy course, the three cases help set the stage for the more formal theorizing and empirical analysis that follow.

Drawing on a wealth of empirical, archival, and historical data covering American military actions from the mid-nineteenth century to the present, this book investigates how Congress influences both the initiation of major military actions and the presidential conduct of these ventures after troops are deployed abroad. Chapter 2 begins by confronting the most explicit challenge to any assertion of congressional influence over the conduct of military actions—the repeated failure of Congress, in all but the rarest of cases, to use the legislative tools at its disposal either to terminate an ongoing war or to block the use of force altogether. Rather than concluding from this failure that Congress is irrelevant in the martial arena, the chapter proposes alternative mechanisms through which actions taken in Congress may influence the president's strategic calculus, even when it cannot legislatively mandate a change in policy.

Despite its record of failed legislation, Congress has historically been actively engaged in debates over the proper conduct of many major military initiatives. It has proposed, publicly debated, and voted on varied legislative initiatives to authorize or curtail the use of force. Its committees have held thousands of hours of highly public investigative hearings, probing and criticizing the administration's conduct of military operations. And individual members have engaged the public debate over military policy options through their maneuverings in the public sphere. Most prior scholarship has discounted the influence of such actions. In the words of Stephen Weissman, a former staff director on the House

Armed Services Committee, such maneuvers ring hollow and "amount to no more than putting up a fuss, unless they actually culminate in significant legal constraints on presidential power."[80]

By contrast, chapter 2 argues that all of these actions, both formal and informal, hold the potential to influence military policy by shaping the cost-benefit calculations of both the president and the leader of the target state. Vocal congressional support for or opposition to the president's military policies may significantly raise or lower the political costs that the president stands to incur by pursuing his preferred policy course. Even if such initiatives hold little promise of ever becoming law, they can have significant political consequences by shaping real or anticipated public opinion and by determining how much political capital the president must spend to pursue his desired policies in the international arena. Moreover, through these same actions Congress can also affect the military costs the president must pay to pursue his chosen course of action through the signals it sends to foreign actors, who may incorporate information about unity or discontent in Washington into their own strategic calculations. Finally, because both the president and the target state's leader anticipate Congress's reaction to various options when crafting their policy choices (anticipations that are based in large part on Congress's partisan composition), the legislature may exert considerable influence over policy outcomes even when it does not actively engage in the process at all. Thus, by affecting the cost-benefit calculations of both the president and the leader of the target state at both the conflict initiation and conduct phases, Congress may exert considerable influence through indirect means.

By analyzing the impact of the partisan composition of Congress on the initiation, scale, and duration of all major uses of force from 1945 to 2004, chapter 3 affords the first empirical tests of whether and in what political conditions Congress influences military policymaking. The evidence is compelling. The statistical models show that presidents who enjoy strong partisan support on Capitol Hill are significantly more likely to respond to an opportunity to use force abroad than are their peers who are confronted by a strong partisan opposition in Congress. Moreover, the models show that Congress's influence over military policy-

80. Stephen Weissman, letter to the editor, *Foreign Affairs*, May/June 2008. Available online at http://www.foreignaffairs.org/20080501faletter87371/louis-fisher-ryan-hendrickson-stephen-r-weissman/congress-at-war.html. Accessed May 22, 2008.

making does not end once troops are in the field. Rather, presidents facing stiff partisan opposition in Congress employ shorter and more limited military actions to achieve their foreign policy goals than do their peers whose co-partisans hold sway on Capitol Hill. Far from stopping at the water's edge, the statistical models demonstrate that partisan interinstitutional politics have greatly shaped the initiation, intensity, and duration of American military operations in the post–World War II era. Finally, parallel analysis of data concerning the use of force from the end of Reconstruction in 1877 through World War II shows that even in that earlier period, the partisan composition of Congress remains one of the strongest predictors of the duration of a major military action.

Chapter 4 focuses on the subset of major uses of force since 1945 involving the dispatch of ground troops or the sustained use of American firepower to explore the specific actions by which Congress and its members raise or lower the political and strategic costs of an extended military engagement for the president. Duration models with time-varying covariates show that both through formal legislative actions, such as initiatives to authorize or curtail a use of force and oversight hearings, and through members' informal policy recommendations reported in the mass media, Congress is able to influence the presidential conduct of major military actions. The statistical evidence for congressional influence remains robust even after controlling for shifts in public opinion, American casualties, and changes in the situation on the ground.

Supplementing the statistical evidence with extensive archival data from the Reagan Presidential Library, chapter 5 presents an intensive case study of the precise mechanisms through which congressional opposition to the Reagan administration's policies influenced its conduct of the 1982–84 Marine mission in Lebanon. Strongly consistent with the theory developed in chapter 2, internal White House records reveal that top administration officials were carefully attuned to happenings in Congress and openly worried about the varied political costs the president risked by continuing the mission in Lebanon. Other communiqués from administration envoys on the ground warned that the signals sent by public congressional opposition to Reagan's policies were also stiffening resistance in Lebanon and Syria and increasing the military costs that the administration stood to incur if it continued the mission. Ultimately, these dual pressures played a critically important role in precipitating the administration's reversal and decision to withdraw the Marines in February of 1984, even though congressional opponents lacked the votes to legally compel Reagan to abandon his preferred policy course.

Having established the influence Congress exerts over presidential decision-making through its actions on the floor and in the hearing room, chapter 6 explores the dynamics driving whether and when in the course of a conflict Congress chooses to exercise its legislative and oversight powers. Consistent with theoretical expectations that partisan incentives are the dominant motive force behind interinstitutional struggle over the conduct of military ventures, the models show that the partisan balance of power in Congress is the single best predictor of the likelihood of a legislative challenge and of congressional investigatory activity. However, even opposition partisans do not act in a political vacuum. Sensitive to the potentially ruinous charge of failing to support American troops in the field, the president's would-be opponents wait for openings to press the offensive against the administration's martial policies. Political factors, such as popular support for the president and the war, as well as strategic opportunities created by changes in the situation on the ground, also influence the likelihood and timing of such challenges. The chapter then turns to the factors underlying individual members' votes on these initiatives. Partisanship, again, is by far the strongest predictor of congressional behavior. Each member's unique electoral circumstances, veteran status, committee assignments, constituency pressures, and prior voting record also affect vote choice, though at the margins.

Finally, chapter 7 pushes the temporal scope of the analysis beyond 2004, when the statistical models end, to examine the latter years of the Iraq War and how this contemporary case both corresponds to and deviates from expectations derived from the analysis of prior major military conflicts. Consistent with theory, congressional challenges to presidential discretion in the direction of American military policy rose exponentially after the Democratic takeover in 2007. Yet this opposition failed to produce a major change in policy; indeed, President Bush launched his troop "surge" in the face of the Democratic revolt. The chapter explores what Iraq tells us about both the prospects for congressional influence and its limits in the military arena.

CHAPTER TWO

Mechanisms of Congressional Influence

M ost analyses of congressional influence in military policy begin—and end—by examining Congress's capacity to enact its military preferences into law. The reasons for this are clear. Congress's authority to set the nation's military policy course is enshrined in the Constitution itself. Congress has the sole power to declare war. It alone is entrusted with raising, equipping and regulating the American armed forces. Moreover, the power of the purse, in theory, grants Congress almost complete control over the nation's actions in the military arena including the authority to block potential military actions from ever beginning and to terminate ongoing ones of which it no longer approves. Finally, as part of the congressional "resurgence" in the 1970s that sought to reclaim power seized by an "imperial presidency," Congress enacted over President Nixon's veto the War Powers Resolution of 1973, which carved out for the legislature an additional statutory mechanism to shape the nation's military affairs that does not require it to cut off funding for the troops in the field.[1] On parchment at least, Congress has more than enough tools at its disposal to serve as a strong check on presidential power in the military arena.

In rare circumstances, Congress has exercised these instruments to shape the course of the nation's military policy, in some cases by curtailing or even terminating an existing war, in others by blocking the use of

---

1. On the "resurgent" Congress, see Sundquist 1981. For the origins of the term "imperial presidency," see Schlesinger 1973.

force altogether. For example, through a series of Neutrality Acts in the 1930s, Congress greatly circumscribed the Roosevelt administration's efforts to aid the allies against German aggression; in so doing, isolationists in Congress kept the United States out of World War II until the Japanese attack on Pearl Harbor, more than two years after the fighting began in Europe. Three decades later, after extended negotiations with the Nixon administration, Congress enacted HR 19911, cutting off funding for the president's clandestine expansion of the ground war in Indochina into Cambodia.[2] Similarly, after the Paris Peace Accords went into effect in 1973, Congress cut off funds for any future combat operations in Vietnam and placed a strict ceiling on the number of American troops that could be maintained there. These enactments not only helped bring the war in Vietnam to an end, but they also barred the Ford administration from responding militarily, even with air strikes, in 1975 to enforce the terms of the Paris Peace Accords and prevent the fall of Saigon to communist forces. Indeed, Henry Kissinger and others have excoriated these congressional actions and blamed them for ensuring that the United States "lost" Vietnam.[3]

On a much smaller scale, in the post-Vietnam era Congress has used the power of the purse to prohibit certain military activities, particularly military support and training missions abroad. The 1975–76 Tunney and Clark amendments barred covert U.S. assistance to paramilitary forces in Angola, and the Boland amendments of the 1980s banned aid to the Nicaraguan Contras (though the latter case, in particular, may reveal more about the barriers to effective congressional action of this sort than it does about legislative power in military affairs). Similarly, in the 1990s with the memory of Somalia firmly entrenched in the congressional consciousness, the legislature acted to insure that the Clinton administration's very limited aid mission to Rwanda, Operation Support Hope, did not expand by precluding the use of funds to support any mil-

2. Congress succeeded at passing this legislation in 1970 only after extensive negotiations with the Nixon administration, and after the troops in Cambodia had already been withdrawn. However, it is not clear whether Nixon ever would have withdrawn the troops of his own accord absent the outcry and action in Congress.

3. See Kimball 2004, Kissinger 1979. For recent recapitulations of Kissinger's argument, see Henry Kissinger, "Lessons for an Exit Strategy." *Washington Post*, August 12, 2005, A19; Henry Kissinger, "The Lessons of Vietnam." *Los Angeles Times*, May 31, 2007.

itary presence within the genocide-ravaged country, except to protect American nationals (PL 103–335).[4]

However, if Congress can exert influence over military policymaking only by taking a leading role and exercising these formal legislative mechanisms to mandate its preferred policy course, then there are reasons to be skeptical of its ultimate influence. Throughout American history, presidents have deployed American military forces across the globe to pursue a variety of policy objectives. Yet, in all but the rarest of cases, Congress has failed to avail itself of any of these tools to limit the president's authority as commander in chief. When presidents request a congressional authorization to use force, it is almost always forthcoming. When they act unilaterally without prior congressional assent, they almost always evade legislative sanction. Congress has invoked the War Powers Resolution's withdrawal clock only once, and even then it simultaneously authorized an eighteen-month deployment for the Marine mission in Lebanon. And, as recent debates concerning the war in Iraq have demonstrated, in almost every case of interbranch conflict over military policy, the power of the purse has proven to be a blunt instrument whose costs, both strategic and political, have virtually precluded its successful use.[5] Given this record of congressional acquiescence to presidential initiatives and the reality that when members of Congress do rise up against the president's policies they consistently fail to write their preferences into law, why would presidents ever adjust their military policies in response to or anticipation of congressional opposition? What costs can the legislature impose on the president to dissuade him from pursuing his chosen policy course, regardless of legislative unease?

If the only way in which Congress can affect the president's strategic calculus in the military arena is by legally compelling him to abandon his preferred policies, then Congress is indeed all but impotent in military affairs. A host of factors combine to hinder Congress from acting legislatively to constrain the commander in chief. Collective-action problems necessarily plague any effort by 535 atomized, individual ac-

4. For an example of Congress exercising the power of the purse in the pre–World War II era, see Robert David Johnson's (1995) discussion of the peace progressives and the passage of the Dill amendment cutting off funding for U.S. military intervention in Nicaragua in the 1920s.

5. See, for example, Lindsay 1994.

tors to protect their institutional prerogatives as legislators in military affairs.[6] More importantly, the partisan incentives of many members of Congress to support a president of their own party often overwhelm their interest in maintaining the power stakes of their institution. This reality, coupled with a legislative process riddled with transaction costs and supermajoritarian requirements, virtually precludes Congress from building the requisite majorities, or in some cases supermajorities, needed to chart a military course independent of the president.[7] Finally, the courts have long been reticent to intervene and protect legislative prerogatives in war powers that Congress itself is loath to assert.[8] For all of these reasons, presidents act in the military arena secure in the knowledge that they can operate as they please with little risk of Congress exercising its constitutional and statutory prerogatives to compel them to do otherwise. If Congress does retain any influence in the military arena, it must be able to affect presidents' decision calculus through other, more indirect means.

Yet, Congress's failure to play a leading role—the president undeniably is the preeminent actor plotting the nation's course in the international arena—does not mean that it has no place in the equation. Rather, this chapter argues that by influencing the calculations of the president and the leader of the target state at both the conflict initiation and conduct phases of the decision-making process, Congress exerts considerable indirect influence over the course of American military policymaking. Through a variety of actions—from introducing and voting on legislative initiatives to holding oversight hearings to debating the merits of presidential policies in the public sphere—Congress and its members affect the incentives and judgments of the president and foreign leaders alike.

The argument proceeds in four parts. The following section presents a theoretical framework for thinking about the military policymaking process as a series of cost-benefit calculations made by both the president and the leader of the target state. While Congress does not craft

---

6. Inter alia, Mayhew 1974, Olson 1965, Wawro 2000.

7. For transaction costs in Congress, see Weingast and Marshall 1988, Epstein and O'Halloran 1999, Moe and Wilson 1994, Moe and Howell 1999a, Howell 2003. On the pivotal importance of supermajoritarian requirements to understanding U.S. lawmaking, see Krehbiel 1996, 1998; Brady and Volden 1998; Cameron 2000.

8. Silverstein 1997, Fisher 2005.

policy directly in this framework, it nevertheless significantly influences both the initiation and conduct of American military actions by shaping the cost-benefit calculations of both major actors at every step of the policymaking process.

The chapter next revisits the stark differences in the political and strategic environments governing actors' calculus before and after troops are deployed. Once policymaking moves from the conflict initiation phase to the conflict conduct phase, informational asymmetries begin to attenuate, the political and strategic consequences of various courses of action are heightened, and all actors begin to respond to developments on the ground. The issue of how members of Congress navigate this perilous political environment when deciding whether openly to challenge or support the president's military policies is temporarily set aside; it will be examined in detail in chapter 6. However, these differences strongly suggest that the ways in which Congress influences policymaking at the conflict conduct phase may be quite different from the anticipatory mechanisms described by previous studies of decisions made at the conflict initiation phase.

The third section proposes three mechanisms by which Congress can influence the cost-benefit calculations of both the president and the target state. At the conflict initiation phase, Congress can shape the decision calculus of both the president and the target state leader, even without actively engaging the issue, through the logic of anticipated response. However, this mechanism, emphasized in prior studies, presupposes that Congress can subsequently act to impose costs on the president for launching a military action of which it disapproves. Accordingly, the chapter next posits two mechanisms by which Congress, through a variety of formal and informal maneuvers, can affect the president's and target state leader's cost-benefit calculations during the course of an ongoing military venture. First, by shaping real or anticipated public opinion and the amount of political capital the president must expend in the foreign policy arena, congressional engagement of military affairs can significantly raise or lower the political costs that the president stands to pay by staying the course militarily. Second, by sending signals of American disunity or resolve to the target state's leader, these same congressional actions may influence the military costs that the president must pay to achieve his foreign policy goals.

The chapter concludes by developing a set of hypotheses about how real or anticipated congressional support for opposition to a presidential use of force affects three observable policy outcomes: the probability

with which the president uses force in response to an opportunity arising in the international environment; the scale of the American military
response—specifically, whether it involves ground troops or sustained
firepower—and the duration of the military venture. These hypotheses
are tested using a range of empirical, historical, and archival data in the
following three chapters.

Conceptualizing the Military Policymaking Process

Few decisions are as complex as those that take a nation first into and
ultimately out of a war. A host of institutional actors—including the
United Nations, NATO allies, foreign and domestic interest groups, and
other domestic politicians—all influence the conduct of American military policymaking. However, attempting to incorporate the roles, incentives, and interactions of all of these players into a single theoretical framework would obscure more than it would illuminate. Therefore,
this chapter focuses on the decision calculus of two primary actors, the
president and the leader of the target state. For example, how do presidents decide first whether to use force in response to an opportunity
arising abroad, and then whether to continue or terminate a military
venture once launched? A large literature in international relations has
successfully modeled these and similar decisions as cost-benefit calculations. Adopting this framework clarifies the structure of the military
policymaking process and aids in the development of testable hypotheses about the forces making various military outcomes more or less
likely. Moreover, it suggests an alternative pathway through which other
political actors—particularly Congress—can affect the policymaking
process.

Most existing studies of the American use of force have focused solely
on the strategic choices culminating in the final presidential decision of
whether to use force in response to an opportunity abroad. Prior analyses have modeled this pre-conflict decision-making in a variety of ways.[9]
Some model it as a single decision: an opportunity arises in the inter-

9. Some of the works cited below refer specifically to the American case; others model
use-of-force decision-making more generally. For clarity, I describe each perspective on
this decision-making dynamic with respect to the American case, even if the original work
was not tailored specifically to the United States.

national environment and the president decides either to use force or not.[10] Other more game-theoretic approaches conceptualize the process as a number of sequential decisions along a decision tree. For example, one schema common in the literature conceptualizes the use of force as the product of three decisions. Once an opportunity arises, the president must decide whether or not to threaten the target state with the use of force. If he makes a threat, the target state's leader then must decide whether to capitulate or resist. If the target state resists, the president ultimately decides whether to follow through on his threat to use force or to back down.[11] Despite differences across studies, each decision posited as leading to the ultimate observable policy response—the use of force or its absence—can be conceptualized as a cost-benefit calculation. Once the president perceives an opportunity to use force, he calculates the expected benefits of acting militarily, weighs them against the costs, and opts first to threaten and then, if the target state resists, to use force only if the benefits outweigh the costs. In a similar vein, the leader of the target state weighs the benefits of resisting American demands against the anticipated costs of provoking an American military response, and chooses accordingly.

Most analyses of American military policymaking end here. However, the decision to use force is really only the beginning of the military decision-making process. Once he has embarked upon a military response to a foreign crisis, the president must decide the initial scope and scale of that response. These are determined in large part by the specific policy goals the president adopts. For example, after deciding to use force against Iraq in the wake of Saddam Hussein's invasion of Kuwait in August of 1990, President George H.W. Bush had to determine

10. See, for example, Meernik 1994. This is also implicitly the way in which any analysis using event count models of the use of force models the conflict initiation process (e.g., Stoll 1984, Ostrom and Job 1986; James and Oneal 1991; Fordham 1998a, 1998b, 2002; Gowa 1998; Clark 2000; Howell and Pevehouse 2005).

11. See, for example, the crisis signaling analyses of Morrow 1986; Fearon 1994, 1997; Smith 1998; Schultz 1998, 1999, 2001; Tomz 2007. Still others go further and treat the emergence of the opportunity to use force itself as endogenous; see, for example, Howell and Pevehouse 2007. Theories of strategic avoidance behavior suggest that a foreign leader may be wary of engaging in an action that might provoke an American military response if he or she anticipates that such a response is likely. In each case, however, the various choices posited as leading to the ultimate observable policy response—the use of force or its absence—can be conceptualized as the products of cost-benefit calculations.

the ultimate objective of American military aims. Would he seek only to drive Iraqi forces out of Kuwait? Or would he go further and make the overthrow of Hussein's government the nation's ultimate objective? The scale, scope and likely duration of the American military action are in large part a product of the selected mission objectives. This decision can also be modeled as a cost-benefit calculation. The president weighs the benefits of various mission goals and types against the costs each is likely to entail, and crafts the scope and scale of the military operation accordingly.

Finally, once American troops are deployed in a foreign theater, military decision-making enters the conflict conduct phase. In response to each new development on the ground or in the domestic political environment, the president and the target state leader make important decisions that determine the duration of a use of force. The target state leader continuously weighs whether his or her interests are best served by resisting or capitulating to American demands; the president conducts similar cost-benefit calculations that determine whether he continues an overseas military deployment or terminates it. The use of force continues until one of the two actors judges that the benefits of continuing it no longer outweigh the costs.[12] Of course, the decision of whether to continue a use of force is only one such decision that both the American president and the target state leader make in the conflict conduct phase. For example, the president could also choose to escalate or de-escalate the scale of the military commitment or to alter the nature of the military's objectives. However, both because of data limitations and because of the paramount political importance of conflict duration, this analysis focuses squarely on the decision of whether the military mission continues or ends.

The costs and benefits that each actor stands to incur or gain from various courses of action are certainly multifaceted. For example, both the president and the target state's leader may perceive a mix of political, ideological, and strategic costs and benefits associated with different military policy options. Moreover, the relative weighting that each actor places on these components may vary significantly across individuals and over time. Extensive literatures in international relations have explored these important dynamics in great detail. However, rather than seeking to uncover all of the nuances in such calculations, the theoreti-

---

12. This decision to end a military action does not necessarily connote defeat.

cal focus here emphasizes how adopting even an undifferentiated cost-benefit framework suggests pathways for other actors to influence military policymaking without legally compelling either the president or the target state's leader to abandon his or her preferred policy course.

Although Congress only rarely takes center stage to become a lead actor charting the course of military policy, this does not mean that it fails to play an important role in shaping military policy outcomes. Rather, the cost-benefit framework suggests an alternative, more indirect way for the legislature to play a vitally important role in affecting the conduct of American military policy: by shaping both the domestic political and the strategic costs of military action for the president. However, the ways in which Congress influences these cost-benefit calculations can differ significantly in the very different political and strategic environments that govern decision-making at the conflict initiation and conduct phases.

Anticipated Reactions versus Active Congressional Engagement

Previous research asserting congressional influence over military policymaking has focused almost exclusively on conflict initiation. Specifically, several studies have presented empirical evidence that presidents confronted by a strong partisan opposition in Congress both use force less frequently and are less likely to respond militarily to opportunities arising in the international environment than presidents who enjoy greater co-partisan support on Capitol Hill.[13] However, these studies do not argue that this relationship is the result of presidents being systematically handcuffed by ex ante legislative constraints imposed by an activist Congress, or even of presidents repeatedly bowing to sustained, vociferous, public opposition to the use of force on Capitol Hill. Indeed, as William Howell and Jon Pevehouse note, historically "during the lead-up to a military venture, Congress has been notably silent."[14] As discussed in chapter 1, this congressional reticence to challenge presidential military policies may be due in large part to the informational asymmetries that the executive enjoys over legislators at the conflict initiation phase. It also reflects the limited tools at Congress's disposal to check the commander

13. Clark 2000; Howell and Pevehouse 2005, 2007.
14. Howell and Pevehouse 2007, 21.

in chief, and the lack of strong incentives to engage military affairs when the use of force is merely anticipated.[15] The theoretical mechanism most frequently posited to drive congressional influence over policymaking at the conflict initiation phase is anticipatory. When facing a strong opposition party in Congress, presidents anticipate more trouble from the legislature than they do when their partisan allies hold the reins of power. As a result, presidents confronted with an opposition-led Congress are less likely to use force than their peers who are buoyed by strong partisan support on Capitol Hill.

However, such arguments logically presume that Congress can act during the course of a military venture to raise the costs of military action for the president. If Congress cannot do so, then the president has little reason to anticipate its potential reactions during the conflict conduct phase or to update accordingly his strategic calculations at the conflict initiation phase. Thus, that Congress has the capacity to influence presidential decision-making at the conflict conduct phase through alternative, non-anticipatory means is a largely untested, critical assumption underlying almost all prior studies asserting congressional influence over conflict initiation through the logic of anticipated reactions. Once policymaking enters the conflict conduct phase, anticipatory calculations remain important. For example, when crafting the intended scope and duration of a military venture, the president may still anticipate Congress's reaction to military operations of different lengths and adjust his policy goals accordingly. However, for such anticipatory mechanisms to work, Congress must also be able to take affirmative actions that affect the costs and benefits that the president perceives from continuing, curtailing, or even terminating a use of force.

As discussed in chapter 1, when Congress engages the policymaking process and endeavors to shape the conduct of an ongoing military venture, it does so in a dramatically transformed political and strategic environment. The informational asymmetries that the president enjoys at the conflict initiation phase begin to attenuate once American troops

15. Many members of Congress do not have incentives to engage military policymaking until force is used and the abstract possibility of a use of force acquires a tangible electoral connection. For the importance of major military actions on congressional election outcomes, see Kriner and Shen 2007, 2010; Grose and Oppenheimer 2007; Gartner, Segura, and Barratt 2004; Carson et al. 2001. A third reason for the lack of congressional action in the lead-up to war is the frequent celerity of presidential responses to foreign crises. In many cases, presidents simply act before Congress has a chance to do so.

are deployed to a foreign theater. Moreover, the range of legislative and investigative options available to would-be opponents of the administration's policies increases. Yet even as Congress's capacity to challenge the president grows, so, too, do the political risks of such opposition. Once American forces are in the field, any congressional opposition to a military venture is subject to the politically devastating countercharge of failing to support the troops. In such a politically charged environment, would-be congressional opponents must tread carefully. Nevertheless, whereas members of Congress may prefer to remain silent—and they frequently do so when the use of force is merely anticipated—developments on the ground may all but compel them to take a stand and enter the policy debate once a military action has begun.[16]

Chapter 6 returns to the question of how Congress and its members navigate these politically perilous conditions when deciding whether openly to support or oppose the president's military policies. However, the historical data presented in chapter 4 make clear that, throughout the post–World War II era, Congress has repeatedly engaged military policy issues on the floor, in the committee hearing room, and through the mass media during the course of an ongoing martial venture. Through such active engagement of the military policymaking process, Congress has the potential to influence the cost-benefit calculations of both the president and the target state leader and, in turn, to shape policy outcomes. Yet existing scholarship provides little insight into the mechanisms through which such actions taken in Congress can influence presidential cost-benefit calculations once a conflict has begun. This lacuna is particularly serious given Congress's historical inability to enact legislation compelling the executive to change course. New theorizing is thus

16. Focusing more specifically on the presidential cost-benefit calculation, a further difference is that the costs the president stands to face from terminating an ongoing military action before fully achieving his goals are likely to be significantly greater than those he would have risked if he had chosen simply to forego a military response. In addition to whatever policy costs attend from failing to respond to a foreign crisis, once American troops are deployed abroad American credibility is similarly committed to the mission's success. Thus, the president must weigh whatever heightened costs Congress can impose should he continue a military action against the strategic and political costs he stands to incur from appearing to have withdrawn American forces prematurely for political reasons at the expense of the national interest. As a result, the costs that Congress must generate to influence the conduct of a military action once launched may have to be considerable indeed. Previous research focusing only on the initiation of military actions has failed to demonstrate that Congress can impose such costs on the president.

needed to lay bare the mechanisms through which congressional actions influence, albeit indirectly, the calculations of the commander in chief during the course of a military mission.

Accordingly, the next section reviews three mechanisms through which Congress influences both the initiation and conduct of major military ventures. The first mechanism, centered on the logic of anticipated response, draws heavily on previous research and explains how Congress may influence policymaking at the conflict initiation phase, even when it does not engage the policy process directly in the lead-up to a use of force. The chapter then proposes two mechanisms through which congressional actions during the course of a conflict can influence its conduct.

While anticipatory mechanisms remain important even after a use of force begins, when Congress actively engages the policymaking process at the conflict conduct phase, it can raise or lower the costs a president stands to incur by continuing his preferred military policy course. These costs are twofold. The first comprises the military costs that must be paid to defeat the target state and achieve the stated military and policy objectives. These are the costs most emphasized in realpolitik analyses within the realist tradition.[17] If a military action stands to incur minimal tangible costs in men, money, and materiel, then the president will be more likely to continue an ongoing operation to pursue his policy goals. As these costs rise, however, so, too, does the probability that the president will judge that the benefits of military action no longer outweigh its costs. However, the president is also undoubtedly sensitive to the domestic political costs he may incur from his military policy choices. This emphasis on domestic political costs parallels both a long-established literature in American politics on the domestic costs of war and a growing literature within international relations emphasizing the importance of domestic considerations within a cost-benefit framework.[18] Through a

17. Inter alia: Meernik 1994, Gowa 1998, Moore and Lanoue 2003.

18. On the domestic political ramifications of major American military actions, see: Mueller 1970, 1973; Cotton 1986; Gartner and Segura 1998; Mayhew 2005; Karol and Miguel 2007; Kriner and Shen 2010. Within the international relations tradition, much research, for example, analyzes the effect on state conflict behavior of fears concerning the ultimate domestic political cost: removal from office. Research by Bruce Bueno de Mesquita and colleagues has shown, both theoretically and empirically, that executives' responses to this threat produce very different patterns of conflict behavior across different types of political regimes. Bueno de Mesquita and Lalman 1992; Bueno de Mesquita and Siverson 1995; Bueno de Mesquita, Morrow, Siverson, and Smith 1999, 2003. On the impor-

variety of formal and informal actions, which previous scholarship has largely overlooked, Congress has the potential to influence both of these costs and, in so doing, to shape the conduct of major military ventures.

The Mechanisms of Congressional Influence: The Conflict Initiation Phase

The Anticipation of Congressional Reactions

As the empirical analysis in chapter 4 will show, once American troops are deployed overseas, Congress and its members have frequently engaged in a wide range of activities to make their voices heard in the policy process. Yet at the conflict initiation phase, Congress is usually much less actively engaged in the military arena. There are, of course, important exceptions. Before many of our nation's major wars, Congress has publicly debated and even voted on whether or not the country should go to war. In a handful of instances, such as the prelude to the Spanish-American War, congressional war hawks brought pressure to bear on a reluctant president to embrace a military response to a foreign crisis. In other cases, such as the contemporary wars in Afghanistan and Iraq, Congress has authorized military action requested by the president. And in still other cases, including most prominently the Neutrality Acts passed to prevent American involvement in World War II, Congress and its members have considered legislation or spoken out publicly in an attempt to dissuade the president from acting militarily when an opportunity to use force arises. When Congress does act at the conflict initiation phase, presidents and target state leaders alike undoubtedly take notice and incorporate its positions and likely future reactions into their cost-benefit calculations.[19]

---

tance of institutional constraints more generally, see Lake 1992, Prins and Sprecher 1999, Siverson 1995. For studies exploring the importance of legislative constraints, see Morgan and Campbell 1991, Auerswald 2000, Reiter and Tillman 2002. The latter are a part of a growing literature in international relations emphasizing the importance of domestic institutions, particularly legislatures, and the subtle yet tangible influence they wield on a diverse set of foreign policies from treaty arrangements to economic aid to the use of force (Martin 2000, Millner 1997, Schultz and Weingast 2003).

19. In the rare cases in which Congress does act at the conflict initiation phase, such actions should affect the cost-benefit calculations of both the president and the target state's leader in ways similar to those posited for anticipated congressional support or opposi-

However, since World War II presidents have grappled with thousands of opportunities to use force; and in the vast majority of cases, they have done so with little explicit prior input from Congress. Yet this frequent lack of active congressional engagement in military policymaking at the conflict initiation phase does not mean that Congress has no influence over the early stages of the military decision-making process in such cases. Rather, if—and only if—Congress has the potential to shape the costs that the president stands to incur should he pursue a military course of action, then both actors have strong incentives *to anticipate* Congress's likely reaction when forming their cost-benefit calculations at the conflict initiation phase.

But if Congress is often silent in the lead-up to war, how can presidents and other actors judge when the administration is likely to encounter problems from Congress if it deploys American forces abroad? To be sure, Congress has failed to provide the consistent check on the aggrandizement of presidential war powers, particularly war powers, that the architects of the Constitution envisioned. Rather than uniformly rising up to defend their institutional prerogatives as the Framers intended, repeatedly throughout history—from President Harry Truman's undeclared war in Korea to the first four years of American involvement in Vietnam and Iraq—members of Congress have mustered scant opposition to brazen assertions of plenary presidential power in the military arena. Yet in other instances, such as Lebanon in 1983–84, Somalia in 1993–94, and the 2007 legislative battles to alter President Bush's policies in Iraq, Congress has spurred to life and challenged presidential primacy in military policymaking. Thus, Congress does not always timidly defer to the president in the military arena, but its assertiveness does vary dramatically across time and space.

Ironically, the root of the problem and an explanation for this variance in congressional assertiveness is captured in James Madison's own defense of the constitutional separation of powers system. The essential feature of checks and balances, Madison wrote in the fifty-first *Federalist*, "consists in giving to those who administer each department the

---

tion as described in this chapter's penultimate section. Specifically, congressional support should lower the political and military (through signals sent to the target state) costs of using force for the president, thus making the use of force more likely. By contrast, congressional opposition should raise both the political and military costs of the use of force for the president, thus making the use of force less likely.

necessary constitutional means and *personal motives* to resist encroach-
ments of the others. . . . Ambition must be made to counteract ambition. The *interest of the man* must be connected with the constitutional
rights of the place." Madison hoped that, in the pursuit of their personal
power stakes in a system of separated powers, members of Congress
would assiduously protect their institution's war powers every bit as zeal-
ously as presidents would defend the authority of the executive branch.
However, the emergence of partisan politics quickly upset the Framers'
carefully crafted Newtonian system of institutional checks and balances.
As the political "interests" of legislators began to be defined as much
by their partisan relationship to the president as by their institutional
loyalty and affiliation, the incentives to check presidential aggrandize-
ments of power, in war-making as in other realms, became considerably
more complex. As a result, Congress's propensity to challenge the president's military policies—and, in so doing, to raise the political and military costs of the use of force—increases in conjunction with the strength
of the partisan opposition.[20]

Existing literatures within American politics suggest at least three
reasons for this strong partisan dynamic driving congressional assertiveness in military affairs. First, presidents and their co-partisans in Congress may simply share similar preferences about the conditions under
which using military force abroad is appropriate and in the national
interest. For much of American history, many of the most important
cleavages in foreign policy preferences have fallen largely, although not
exactly, along party lines.[21] To be sure, the level of intra-partisan ide-

20. The analysis in chapter 6 will investigate the importance of other factors, in addition to partisanship, on Congress's willingness to use these tools at its disposal during the
course of an ongoing military action.

21. Throughout the twentieth century, the main ideological cleavages first pitted in-
ternationalists against isolationists, then hawks against doves, and more recently those
who adopt a more narrowly realpolitik view of the use of force against those who embrace
a wider conception of the national interest when deciding the proper range of objectives
and uses of American military power abroad. (On this latter cleavage, see Mandelbaum
and Schneider 1978, Reichley 2000, Johnson 2006, Gibbons 1986. Even anticommunism,
a common tenet of both parties' platforms, manifested itself in different ideological approaches across the two parties in the 1940s and 1950s; see Gerring 1998, 154.) Within each
period there are certainly prominent counterexamples on both sides of the aisle. However,
the ideological fault lines have largely fallen along the partisan divide. Partisanship and
ideology are likely even more closely aligned today with the gradual realignment of the
South toward the Republican Party throughout the 1970s and 1980s (Rohde 1991, Car-

ological homogeneity has waxed and waned over the course of American history, particularly within the Democratic caucus. For most of the period analyzed in the empirical models to follow, however, presidents and their co-partisans in Congress were significantly more likely to share preferences on major questions of foreign policy than presidents and members of the opposition party.[22] As a result, when the opposition party is weak, the general congruence of preferences between the White House and Capitol Hill should yield little overt interinstitutional conflict over the conduct of major military actions. However, when the president's partisan opponents hold sway on the other end of Pennsylvania Avenue, the conflict between the dominant ideological beliefs motivating the two branches sets the stage for open confrontation over the course of military policymaking.[23]

Shared electoral incentives between the president and his co-partisans in Congress provide a second reason why both the president and leader

mines and Stimson 1989) and the increasing ideological polarization of the parties in general in recent decades (McCarty, Poole, and Rosenthal 2006; Stonecash, Brewer and Mariani 2003).

22. Exceptions to the rule are certainly possible. One possible counterexample involves Eisenhower's first term: the president and his administration may indeed have been closer ideologically to congressional Democrats in foreign policy matters in 1955–56 than they had been with the Republican majority that held power in 1953–54.

23. If ideology drives interbranch conflict, then some measure of both the *size* and the *ideological cohesiveness* of the opposition party may be a better indicator of the likely level of interbranch conflict over military affairs. Accordingly, all of the models in chapter 3 examining the correlation between the partisan composition of Congress and the duration of all 122 major uses of force were also reestimated using Legislative Potential for Policy Change (LPPC) scores, which account for both the size and the cohesiveness of the majority party caucus, with virtually identical results. For the importance of ideology in driving members' positions on defense votes, see Bernstein and Anthony 1974; Fleisher 1985; McCormick 1985; McCormick and Black 1983; Russett 1970; Wayman 1985; Lindsay 1991; Wittkopf 1990; Wittkopf and McCormick 1992, 1998. In addition to following their personal ideological orientations and policy preferences, members of Congress are also attentive to the preferences of their constituents, even in foreign policy (Erikson 1978, Monroe 1998, Lindsay 1990, Bartels 1991, Hartley and Russett 1992; though see Miller and Stokes 1963). Because the preference divisions seen between Republican and Democratic elites are also largely present at the mass level, and because redistricting and other forces have dramatically increased the number of ideologically cohesive districts over time (Grofman and Brunell 2005, Cox and Katz 2002, Hirsch 2003, Koetzle 1998), constituency preferences should reinforce the expectation that members of the president's party are likely to defer to his military policies while members of the opposition possess the strongest incentives to oppose them.

of the target state look to the partisan balance of power in Congress when anticipating the legislature's likely response to a use of force. A growing number of studies have questioned the old conventional wisdom that voters are relatively unconcerned with foreign affairs, and have demonstrated that major questions of foreign policy significantly influence both presidential and congressional elections.[24] Accordingly, legislative challenges to the president's military policies hold the potential to damage the president's political standing and create a drag on his co-partisans' electoral fortunes, even in midterm contests.[25] Thus, the president's co-partisans in Congress have strong electoral incentives to support the actions of their party's leader in the Oval Office, even though this weakens their own scope of authority and power in military affairs as legislators. Even if conditions on the ground sour, the president's partisan allies have strong incentives not to jump ship prematurely, as doing so would only weaken their party's titular leader and cast a pallor on public perceptions of their party's capacity to govern—an unpalatable prospect for any candidate. Conversely, as congressional Democrats learned in the 2002 midterms, members of the partisan opposition stand to gain little at the ballot box by supporting the president and his military policies. Instead, when given a window of opportunity, opposition members' best hope to turn military policymaking to their electoral advantage is to attack.[26]

24. For the importance of foreign policy concerns more generally, see Kessel 1988; Aldrich, Sullivan, and Borgida 1989; Nincic 1990; Nincic and Hinckley 1991. These studies challenged the old consensus that the general public lacked informed, stable opinions on questions of foreign affairs, and that foreign affairs consequently had little if any impact on national elections. Among others, see Stokes 1966; Miller and Miller 1976; Kagay and Caldeira 1975; Light and Lake 1985; Hess and Nelson 1985; Miller, Wattenberg, and Malenchuk 1986.

25. Jacobson 2004; Bean 1948; Campbell 1991; Waterman, Oppenheimer, and Stimson 1991; Flemming 1995; Mondak and McCurley 1994; Campbell and Sumners 1990; Campbell 1986; Kriner and Shen 2007. For a general discussion of the importance of party labels and how the advantages they afford encourage members to protect and strengthen them, see Cox and McCubbins 1993, Kiewiet and McCubbins 1991, Aldrich 1995. For the critical importance of electoral incentives, see Mayhew 1974, Fenno 1973, Arnold 1990, Smith and Deering 1990, Jackson and Kingdon 1992.

26. To be sure, opposition partisans in Congress do not attack the president's policies blindly. Rather, as chapter 6 will explore in considerable detail, they carefully await openings in the political and international environment to press the offensive. Nevertheless, vocal opposition has the potential to insulate the party's ranks from political fallout should

A final reason to expect that the level of interbranch conflict in the military arena will greatly depend on the partisan composition of the two branches is the considerable power exercised by the majority party leadership to control the business of the legislature.[27] To the extent that the president's opponents in Congress rely on their capacity to introduce, debate, and vote on formal legislative proposals to curtail a use of force, as well as on their ability to hold hearings investigating the administration's conduct of an action and to exploit the public forum they provide, the party leaders of each chamber can short-circuit even a strong minority-led opposition through their power of negative agenda control. While the scholarly evidence of the majority party leadership's capacity to force through legislation opposed by its members is mixed, the leadership can be quite successful at keeping potentially embarrassing legislation from ever escaping committee.[28] In a similar vein, majority party

---

the operation result in casualties or fail to meet public expectations; to forestall a rally in public support for the president in the wake of a military action, often largest among opposition party identifiers (Baum 2002, Brody 1991, Zaller 1992, Lian and Oneal 1993, Berinsky 2007); and to bring public pressure to bear on the president to change course, thus weakening his and his party's electoral clout.

27. Kiewiet and McCubbins 1991, Sinclair 1995. Because the Senate leadership has never developed institutional resources and procedural powers on a par with those of their counterparts in the House (Ripley 1969, Binder 1997, Smith 2007, Sinclair 2000), most analyses of negative agenda control in Congress have focused on the House, with some scholars openly speculating that the phenomenon should be considerably weaker in the Senate (e.g., Smith, Roberts, and Vander Wielen 2006). However, a number of recent studies have found considerable evidence that the Senate majority leadership wields considerable power to keep items it opposes off the agenda, despite the limited tools available to it (Gailmard and Jenkins 2007; Campbell, Cox, and McCubbins 2002; Lee 2008; Den Hartog and Monroe 2008).

28. For the leadership's limited capacity to change votes, see Krehbiel 1993, 1998; Rohde 1991; Sinclair 1983; Brady and Volden 1998. On negative agenda control, see Cox and McCubbins 2005; Gailmard and Jenkins 2007; Smith and Deering 1990; Campbell, Cox, and McCubbins 2002. And even if a majority leadership of the president's party does allow legislative challenges to the president's military policies to come to the floor, they can control how the options are framed and presented. For example, in the wake of Democratic Congressman Jack Murtha's move to push for a phased withdrawal of American forces from Iraq in November of 2005, the Republican leadership was able to keep from the floor more modest resolutions and force Democrats to vote on an unpalatable resolution carefully crafted by California Republican Duncan Hunter to put Democrats in a political bind. Through their skillful control of the agenda, Republicans embarrassed many Democratic advocates of a change in course in Iraq and forced all but three, including Murtha, to vote against the resolution calling for immediate withdrawal (H Res 571).

committee chairmen are able to limit in scope or keep off the agenda altogether potentially embarrassing investigations of the executive branch.[29] This power of negative agenda control thus enables the president's partisan allies in the leadership, even when they are reluctant to support vocally a failing administration policy, to mute pressure for a change in course by keeping the most damaging challenges off the agenda.[30]

As a result, when the president faces a legislature dominated by members of the partisan opposition, both he and the target state leader logically anticipate, ceteris paribus, greater congressional opposition to a potential use of force than if the president's co-partisans held sway on Capitol Hill. In this way Congress can influence decision-making at the conflict initiation phase, even without actively engaging in the national policy debate.

The Mechanisms of Congressional Influence: The Conflict Conduct Phase

The logic behind anticipatory mechanisms only holds if Congress does indeed possess the capacity to impose costs on the president if he launches a military venture of which it disapproves.[31] However, given a myriad of

29. For negative agenda powers, see Kriner and Schwartz 2008. On investigations more generally, see Mayhew 1991; Ginsberg and Shefter 1995, 2003; Aberbach 1990, 2002; Parker and Dull 2009. This dynamic is succinctly captured in congressional Democrats' lament that the Republican-controlled Armed Services Committee held only five hours of testimony on Abu Ghraib, compared to 140 hours of House testimony on whether Bill Clinton had improperly used the White House Christmas card list. Henry Waxman, *Congressional Record*, June 21, 2005, H4829, Vol. 151, No. 83. Moreover, as the party leadership's control over semi-autonomous committee chairs increased with the reforms of the 1970s, so, too, should have their capacity to check committee-led investigations with the potential to damage the party label. See Zelizer 2004, Rohde 1991, Sinclair 1989, Schickler 2001.

30. As with intra-party ideological homogeneity, the degree to which the majority party can use negative agenda control to squash potentially embarrassing legislative or investigative challenges to presidential military policies has also likely varied over time. For example, even during periods of unified government, Franklin Roosevelt and Harry Truman faced a litany of legislative and investigative challenges from 1938 to 1952. On average, however, presidents for most of this period were better protected from serious institutional challenges from the legislature during unified government than they were during divided government.

31. Similarly, in the rare instances in which Congress does weigh in before the decision to use force and openly supports or opposes a military course of action, this congressional

failed past precedents and the multiple institutional barriers to successful congressional efforts to check the commander in chief, presidents
surely realize that the probability of Congress legislatively compelling
them to abandon their preferred military course is virtually zero. From
this perspective, Congress looks irrevocably weak in military affairs.

While most scholarship has emphasized only Congress's failure to enact its military policy preferences into law, when taking a broader view
of congressional action in the military arena we see that, far from being
disengaged on major questions of military policy, Congress historically
has been an active player on the political stage. In the formal legislative realm, even though it has demonstrated little capacity to enact legislation constraining the president, Congress has frequently introduced,
publicly debated, and brought to the floor legislative initiatives to authorize or curtail the president's conduct of ongoing military operations.
These initiatives range from spending measures to cut off funds for policies of which it disapproves, to resolutions invoking the War Powers Resolution and its ninety-day withdrawal clock, to more creative measures,
such as the Webb amendment in the 110th Congress, that endeavor to
hamstring the president's flexibility to conduct military policymaking
solely according to his preferences.

Alternatively, Congress and its foreign policy entrepreneurs have
also sought to engage in and shape the military policy debate in front
of the television cameras through high-profile investigative oversight
hearings. A quick perusal of David Mayhew's list of congressional pub-
licity probes reveals many investigating and criticizing administration
conduct of foreign policy.[32] Repeatedly in the post–World War II era,
major military actions—including the Truman administration's conduct
of the Korean War, the Johnson administration's policies in the Dominican Republic and Vietnam, and President Reagan's military dealings in
Latin America—have attracted significant scrutiny from congressional
committees.

Finally, individual members of Congress are also at times extraor-
dinarily active in shaping the national debate over foreign policy issues
through their informal maneuverings in the "public sphere." Through
speeches on the floor, press conferences, media events, and swings

---

response should only be influential if Congress can later back it up with actions to impose
costs on the president for pursuing a military course of action that it has opposed.

    32. Mayhew 1991.

through their states and districts, members can engage in and shape the national debate over major issues on the political agenda. Indeed, in Mayhew's extensive survey of more than two hundred years of American history, almost a quarter of all informal congressional "actions" in the public sphere involved major issues of foreign policy.[33]

Through all three of these types of action, Congress can retain a measure of influence on presidential conduct of military affairs by significantly shaping both the political and the military costs that the president stands to incur from pursuing a given military policy course. The following sections explore each in turn.

Congress and the Political Costs of Military Action

Presidents and politicos alike have long recognized Congress's ability to reduce the political costs that the White House risks incurring by pursuing a major military initiative. While declarations of war are all but extinct in the contemporary period, Congress has repeatedly moved to authorize presidential military deployments and consequently to tie its own institutional prestige to the conduct and ultimate success of a military campaign. Such authorizing legislation, even if it fails to pass both chambers, creates a sense of shared legislative-executive responsibility for a military action's success and provides the president with considerable political support for his chosen policy course.[34] Indeed, the desire for this political cover—and not for the constitutional sanction a congressional authorization affords—has historically motivated presidents to seek Congress's blessing for military endeavors. For example, both the elder and younger Bush requested legislative approval for their wars against Iraq, while assiduously maintaining that they possessed sufficient independent authority as commander in chief to order the invasions unilaterally.[35] This fundamental tension is readily apparent in the

33. Mayhew 2000.

34. Prior congressional authorization may also dissuade members of Congress from later challenging the president's conduct of military affairs during the course of an engagement. Changing conditions on the ground may eventually provoke legislative opposition; however, by raising the costs of a public reversal, an authorization affords the president a measure of protection from subsequent political challenges by Congress. The analysis in chapter 6 will test this additional observable implication of theory.

35. While presidency scholars may point to Truman's classification of the Korean conflict as a UN "police action" in order to circumvent having to seek congressional authoriza-

elder Bush's signing statement to HJ Res 77, which authorized military action against Saddam Hussein in January of 1991. While the president expressed his gratitude for the statement of congressional support, he insisted that the resolution was not needed to authorize military action in Iraq. "As I made clear to congressional leaders at the outset, my request for congressional support did not, and my signing this resolution does not, constitute any change in the long-standing positions of the executive branch on either the President's constitutional authority to use the Armed Forces to defend vital U.S. interests or the constitutionality of the War Powers Resolution."[36]

Less frequently discussed, however, is Congress's capacity, through its varied formal and informal maneuverings, to influence the president's decision calculus by raising the political costs of clinging to a chosen military course of action.[37] When Congress publicly debates a bill to curtail a use of force or investigates allegations of executive mismanagement of a military operation, or when its members criticize the president's conduct of a war in the mass media, the legislature can isolate the president politically and raise the costs he stands to incur domestically should his military policies fail to match popular expectations.

Archival evidence from the Reagan administration clearly demonstrates the tangible consequences of increased domestic political costs for military policymaking and the importance accorded them by executive branch officials. In the midst of an acrimonious debate with Congress over the War Powers Resolution and the reasons for continuing the American Marine peacekeeping mission in Lebanon in October 1983, Secretary of State George Shultz, an ardent advocate of a strong American presence in Lebanon, acknowledged the very real costs congressional opposition entailed. In a memorandum to the president, Shultz concluded:

---

tion as an example of presidential unilateral power (Howell 2003), other scholars note the political costs Truman paid by failing to seek Congress's blessing (Tanabaum 1987, Fisher 1995).

36. George H. W. Bush, "Statement on Signing the Resolution Authorizing the Use of Military Force against Iraq." *Public Papers of the Presidents*, January 14, 1991.

37. It is theoretically possible that the president's preferred course of action is to end a military engagement, while Congress prefers to continue it. In such a scenario, Congress might act to raise the costs of terminating a war for the president. However, because such cases are exceedingly rare, the theory focuses on the political dynamics that occur when Congress opposes a president's desire to continue a military conflict.

In the end, we need to face up to the real situation that confronts us, and decide whether we are prepared to take the kinds of steps necessary to shape the Lebanese outcome in the desired direction. In effect, the choice is one of accepting the *strategic costs of getting out soon* or the possible *political costs of staying in*.[38]

As the historical case study in chapter 5 will show, the Reagan administration decided in October 1983 to risk the possible political costs of continuing U.S. participation in the multinational force so as not to pay the strategic costs of an embarrassing American defeat in the region. Within the cost-benefit framework, the policy benefits of continuing the mission in Lebanon outweighed the political and military costs of doing so. By February 1984, however, in the face of a full-blown congressional revolt against the administration's policies joined by many even within the president's own party, the administration reevaluated its position, judged that the political costs of staying the course now outweighed the potential benefits of staying, and withdrew the Marines.[39]

But how, precisely, can these formal and informal maneuverings of Congress influence the political costs of a chosen military policy course for the president? While there are many potential pathways, three seem particularly powerful.

Raising or Lowering Political Costs by Influencing Public Opinion

One of the most important ways in which congressional actions can shape domestic political costs is by mobilizing and swaying public opinion for or against the president and his policies. As early as 1917, Edward Corwin wrote in *The President's Control of Foreign Relations*: "For the

38. Memorandum, Schultz to Reagan, October 5, 1983, folder NSPG 0072 13 Oct 1983, box 91306, Executive Secretariat, NSC: Records NSPG, Ronald Reagan Library. Emphasis added.

39. Moreover, such dynamics are not limited to the post–World War II era. A significant pre-1945 example involves the open conflict between Congress and the Wilson administration over the president's unauthorized dispatch of American troops to Russia in the midst of the Bolshevik Revolution during World War I. After a resolution introduced by Senator Hiram Johnson to withdraw funding for the mission failed by a narrow margin, the administration reconsidered its actions and, in light of the political uproar provoked by the Russian venture, promptly withdrew the troops, even though Congress failed to legally compel the White House to do so. See Johnson 1995, Foglesong 1995.

president, even in the exercise of his most unquestioned powers, cannot act in a vacuum. He must ultimately have the support of public sentiment."[40] More recently, Louis Klarevas, echoing Leslie Gelb's 1972 article in *Foreign Affairs*, argued that public support is the "essential domino" of military policymaking. Public support, he contended, is "vital to the successful conduct of military operations" in contemporary American politics.[41]

This view also features prominently in the public assessments of military policymakers themselves. For example, one of the key tenets of the Weinberger Doctrine, articulated by Secretary of Defense Caspar Weinberger in a 1984 speech, was that "before the U.S. commits combat forces abroad, there must be some reasonable assurance we will have the support of the American people." However, Weinberger went further and explicitly recognized the critical role that Congress plays in shaping this support by adding to the above sentence: ". . . and their elected representatives in Congress." Because the two were closely interrelated, Weinberger argued that the support of both the people and their representatives was a critical precondition for the use of force. This belief is clearly captured in his frank recognition of congressional power in military affairs: "We cannot fight a battle with the Congress at home while asking our troops to win a war overseas."[42] By bolstering or diminishing popular support for the president and his policies, Congress can significantly affect the presidential cost-benefit calculation, even after American troops are deployed in a foreign theater.

Scholars have long documented the president's ability to use the office's "bully pulpit" to court popular support for his policy proposals.

40. Corwin 1970 [1917], 45–46.

41. See Klarevas 2002, 417. For other studies asserting the critical importance of public opinion in driving military policymaking, see Gelb 1972; Hurwitz and Peffley 1987; Sobel 1993, 2001; Foyle 1999; Holsti 2004; Baum 2004; Larson and Savych 2005. For the importance of public opinion as a constraint on military policymaking cross-nationally, see Reiter and Tillman 2002.

42. Caspar W. Weinberger, "The Uses of Military Power: Remarks prepared for delivery by the Hon. Caspar W. Weinberger, Secretary of Defense, to the National Press Club, Washington, D.C. November 28, 1984." http://www.pbs.org/wgbh/pages/frontline/shows/military/force/weinberger.html

A Weinberger protégé, General Colin Powell, would espouse similar sentiments when articulating what came to be known as the Powell Doctrine in the aftermath of the 1991 Gulf War.

Recent scholarship demonstrates, however, that presidents are far from the only actors on the political scene who strive to influence public opinion.[43] By introducing, publicly debating, and voting on legislative initiatives either to ratify or alter the military status quo, Congress can recast the dominant lens through which the public views a use of force. High-profile oversight hearings afford another powerful tool by which Congress, particularly members who oppose the president's policies, can seek to dominate the airwaves and mold public opinion against the president's handling of military affairs.[44] Finally and more generally, through a variety of actions from filing suit against the president in federal court to chastising the administration's conduct of military actions to reporters, members of Congress can influence elite public opinion attuned to national policy debates. These findings complement a growing body of research suggesting that members routinely seek to manipulate public opinion to pursue their policy and partisan electoral goals, even in foreign affairs.[45]

In their quest to mold public opinion, members of Congress receive considerable support from the mass media. Scholars have long noted that the news media depend on government officials for information, but W. Lance Bennett goes further and argues that the media also look to Washington when crafting the scale and tone of their coverage. Specifically, the media tend "to 'index' the range of voices and viewpoints in both news and editorials according to the range of views expressed in mainstream government debate about a given topic."[46] Although the indexing hypothesis does not explicitly limit governmental debate to dissension in Congress, every empirical study focuses on vocal congressional opposition as the single most important source of intragovernmental

43. For traditional studies of presidents' command of the bully pulpit, see Tulis 1987, Peterson 1990, Mouw and MacKuen 1992, Kernell 1997, Canes-Wrone 2001, Barrett 2004, Edwards 2006. For analyses of attempts by Congress and other domestic actors to influence public opinion, see Alexseev and Bennett 1995, Edwards and Wood 1999, Walker 1977, Jacobs and Shapiro 2000, Jacobs 2003, Jacobs 2007.

44. For the influence of congressional hearings on popular support for war, see Howell and Kriner 2009, Kriner 2009.

45. Jacobs, Lawrence, Shapiro, and Smith 1998; Jacobs and Shapiro 2000; Caldwell 1991; Carter and Scott 2009.

46. Bennett 1990, 106. See also Bennett 1996. For the media's general dependence on official sources, see Sigal 1973, Tuchman 1978.

debate. In the words of Scott Althaus and colleagues, Congress is "the chief institutional locus of elite opposition."[47] Interbranch consensus in Washington breeds consensual news stories.[48] Only when intragovernmental opposition arises, particularly within the halls of Congress, does the media openly and prominently question the administration's policies and discuss available alternatives. An extensive literature has accumulated supporting the indexing hypothesis, particularly in the reporting of foreign affairs.[49]

Coverage in the mass media does not necessarily connote influence over public opinion. However, a smaller yet growing literature supports the contention that the public claims asserted by Congress and reported in the mass media do have significant influence over popular attitudes toward military affairs.[50] With respect to uses of force in particular, numerous studies have shown that the presence or absence of congressional opposition to the president in the media's reporting on a military venture substantially influences popular reactions to the administration's handling of the crisis.[51] More recently, exploiting variations in news coverage across media markets, William Howell and Jon Pevehouse find that citizens' reactions to the Iraq War were heavily influenced by the balance of elite discourse they observed on local television news. Respondents living in media markets that cited more congressional oppo-

47. Althaus et al. 1996.

48. Jonathan Mermin (1999) even argues that in the absence of official Washington policy debate, the media systematically marginalize external policy concerns such as public opinion polls, protests, and warnings by nongovernmental experts.

49. For example, content analyses of news coverage of a range of foreign policy crises from Vietnam (Hallin 1986) to the Persian Gulf War (Entman and Page 1994) to minor conflicts in Panama, Grenada, and Somalia (Mermin 1999) have shown that news coverage critical of administration policies has risen and fallen with the level of vocal congressional criticism. Additionally, in a quantitative analysis of thirty-five crises from 1945 to 1991, Zaller and Chiu (1996) show that the media also index how "hawkish" or "dovish" its coverage is to the prominence of each position in Congress. Moreover, their regressions even suggest that Congress has a substantially greater capacity to influence the tone of media than the president. However, for a contrasting perspective see Althaus 2003, Entman 2004.

50. Inter alia: Brody 1991, Zaller 1992, Zaller and Chiu 1996, Berinsky 2007, Kriner 2009. For the media's ability to influence public reaction through its framing of a given policy issue in general, see Iyengar and Kinder 1987, Kinder and Sanders 1996, Nicholson and Howard 2003; but also see Druckman 2001.

51. Brody and Shapiro 1989, Brody 1991, Brody 1994, Zaller and Feldman 1992, Zaller 1994, Berinsky 2007.

sition to the Bush administration's war plans were less likely to approve of invading Iraq than individuals from regions with more pro-war coverage, even after controlling for respondents' partisanship, demographics, and other individual characteristics.[52] In a similar vein, research by Matthew Baum and Tim Groeling demonstrates strong correlations between media-reported congressional rhetoric surrounding multiple major military missions in the last quarter century and popular support for those endeavors.[53]

While the relationships between congressional actions and public opinion are undoubtedly complicated and partially reciprocal, many scholars using observational data contend that, particularly in foreign affairs, the causal arrow runs primarily from elites to the public.[54] Furthermore, a number of recent experimental studies have demonstrated the ability of even subtle congressional cues to substantially influence levels of popular support for military action.[55] For example, in a series of survey experiments querying public support for withdrawing American troops from Iraq and for a number of proposed hypothetical military engagements, Howell and Kriner found that even very modest congressional cues have a considerable influence on popular support for maintaining an existing military commitment or launching a new one. Across scenarios, respondents who had been told that many in Congress opposed the president's policies were less supportive of military action than those in the control group who had been told nothing about congressional preferences. Similarly, respondents who had been informed that Congress backed the president's policies were more supportive of military action than those in the control baseline.

52. Howell and Pevehouse 2007.

53. Groeling and Baum 2008.

54. See Zaller 1992, Zaller and Chiu 1996, Jordan and Page 1992, Berinsky 2007.

55. E.g., Howell and Pevehouse 2007, Howell and Kriner 2007, Kriner and Shen n.d., Baum and Groeling 2009. Although their focus is on the ability of international organizations to shape American public support for war, Gelpi, Feaver, and Reifler 2009 and Grieco, Gelpi, Reifler, and Feaver n.d. also find experimental evidence that congressional cues significantly shape popular support for proposed military ventures. Although it lacks the real-world grounding of observational studies, experimental analysis has distinct advantages in alleviating concerns about endogeneity and identification issues. In the laboratory we can be sure that manipulations in the congressional signal are producing the observed changes in public opinion and not the reverse. Moreover, the experimental treatments insure that all subjects receive the congressional signal of interest, a tricky proposition when using only observational data.

In sum, a growing body of research employing both observational and experimental data makes plain that presidents are not the only actors with the capacity to mold public opinion on issues of national import, including major military endeavors. These studies also complement a growing literature which argues that even the effects of seemingly objective conflict events, such as combat casualties, on public opinion are conditional on how these events are framed by political elites. For example, the sensitivity of the American public to casualties may vary considerably according to whether trusted political elites rally behind a military venture or criticize it, and whether the response of these elites bolsters public confidence in the mission's ultimate success or spurs public doubt about the prospects for military victory.[56] While they may not possess the bully pulpit of the Oval Office, members of Congress nonetheless have a number of means at their disposal through which to engage the president in the public sphere, raise or lower the political costs of military action by molding public opinion, and make their own imprint on the conduct of military policymaking.

Raising or Lowering Political Costs by Affecting Anticipated Public Opinion

However, congressional actions need not effect an immediate change in public opinion for the White House to perceive genuine political costs from congressional opposition. Presidents and their advisors are acutely responsive to *anticipated* public opinion. Vocal support for administration policies decreases fears of sudden swings in public opinion. By contrast, open expressions of congressional dissatisfaction with presidential military policies raise the very real specter of future erosion in popular support, leaving the president, shorn of congressional backing, standing alone to incur the public's wrath.

As an example, consider again the calculations of the Reagan administration during the 1982–84 U.S. Marine mission in Lebanon, which chapter 5 will explore in greater detail. In the wake of the October terrorist bombing at the Marine barracks in Beirut that killed 241 American servicemen, the public largely rallied behind the commander in chief. In multiple polls, support for Reagan's handling of the mission actually

56. Inter alia, Berinsky 2007, 2009; Feaver and Gelpi 2004; Gelpi, Feaver, and Reifler 2005/06, 2009; Boettcher and Cobb 2006.

rose, as did his overall job approval rating. Yet the bombing reenergized congressional critics, who only a month earlier had battled the administration over invoking the War Powers Resolution, and it raised the specter of a growing interinstitutional battle when Congress reconvened in January. Despite the current strong public support for the mission, Reagan's chief political advisors were concerned, particularly given the potential for an explosion of opposition in Congress. Writing to White House Deputy Chief of Staff Michael Deaver, political advisor David Gergen presciently warned against complacency. "Most of us agree with Teddy White's observation this week: 'If Reagan has the troops out of there in six weeks, he'll be a hero. If not, you will see the support fade.'" Long before other major players at the State Department and National Security Council agreed to reverse course, the politically astute Gergen surmised, "Clearly we need a set of phased withdrawals, well publicized, the bigger the groups the better."[57] While it would be months before the administration reversed course and embraced proposals for a phased withdrawal, an anticipated decline in public support for the mission, spurred by highly salient opposition to the administration's policies in Congress, was a critically important factor driving many members of the Reagan team to reevaluate the costs and benefits of staying in Lebanon.

Raising or Lowering Political Costs by Affecting Presidential Political Capital

Shaping both real and anticipated public opinion are two important ways in which Congress can raise or lower the political costs of a military action for the president. However, focusing exclusively on opinion dynamics threatens to obscure the much broader political consequences of domestic reaction—particularly congressional opposition—to presidential foreign policies. At least since Richard Neustadt's seminal work *Presidential Power*, presidency scholars have warned that costly political battles in one policy arena frequently have significant ramifications for presidential power in other realms. Indeed, two of Neustadt's three "cases of command"—Truman's seizure of the steel mills and firing of General Douglas MacArthur—explicitly discussed the broader political consequences of stiff domestic resistance to presidential assertions

57. Memorandum, Gergen to Deaver, November 1, 1983, folder ND016 184505, WHORM, Ronald Reagan Library.

of commander-in-chief powers. In both cases, Truman emerged victorious in the case at hand—yet, Neustadt argues, each victory cost Truman dearly in terms of his future power prospects and leeway in other policy areas, many of which were more important to the president than achieving unconditional victory over North Korea.[58]

While congressional support leaves the president's reserve of political capital intact, congressional criticism saps energy from other initiatives on the home front by forcing the president to expend energy and effort defending his international agenda. Political capital spent shoring up support for a president's foreign policies is capital that is unavailable for his future policy initiatives. Moreover, any weakening in the president's political clout may have immediate ramifications for his reelection prospects, as well as indirect consequences for congressional races.[59] Indeed, Democratic efforts to tie congressional Republican incumbents to President George W. Bush and his war policies paid immediate political dividends in the 2006 midterms, particularly in states, districts, and counties that had suffered the highest casualty rates in the Iraq War.[60]

In addition to boding ill for the president's perceived political capital and reputation, such partisan losses in Congress only further imperil his programmatic agenda, both international and domestic. Scholars have long noted that President Lyndon Johnson's dream of a Great Society also perished in the rice paddies of Vietnam. Lacking both the requisite funds in a war-depleted treasury and the political capital needed to sustain his legislative vision, Johnson gradually let his domestic goals slip away as he hunkered down in an effort first to win and then to end the Vietnam War. In the same way, many of President Bush's highest second-term domestic priorities, such as Social Security and immigration reform, failed perhaps in large part because the administration had to expend so much energy and effort waging a rear-guard action against congressional critics of the war in Iraq.[61]

58. See Neustadt 1990, particularly the extended discussion in chapter 6.

59. For the extensive literature on presidential coattails in presidential and midterm elections, see Jacobson 2004; Waterman, Oppenheimer, and Stimson 1991; Campbell and Sumners 1990; Campbell 1986.

60. See Kriner and Shen 2007, Grose and Oppenheimer 2007, Gartner and Segura 2008.

61. By contrast, wartime successes may bolster a president's political capital and success in other policy arenas. For example, the Bush tax cuts of 2002–3 may well have benefited from the strong support he enjoyed for his handling of foreign policy.

When making their cost-benefit calculations, presidents surely consider these wider political costs of congressional opposition to their military policies. If congressional opposition in the military arena stands to derail other elements of his agenda, all else being equal, the president will be more likely to judge the benefits of military action insufficient to its costs than if Congress stood behind him in the international arena.

Congress and the Military Costs of the Use of Force

A growing game-theoretic literature within international relations suggests that these very same congressional actions can, however unintentionally, also raise or lower the military costs for the president of pursuing his preferred policy course. High-profile congressional support for or opposition to the president's military policies does more than shape real and anticipated public opinion and affect the president's levels of political capital in Washington. It also sends important signals of American resolve or disunity to foreign actors. Target state leaders conduct their own cost-benefit analyses when plotting their military policy courses, and they may incorporate congressional signals into these calculations.

An extensive literature in international relations examines the importance of signal credibility for interstate crisis bargaining and the initiation of military action.[62] In the international system, states are constantly sending signals about their expectations of and intentions toward other state actors. When challenged by another country, a state's leaders not only must weigh the costs and benefits of complying with their adversary's demand; but, perhaps even more critically, they must also evaluate the opposing state's willingness to follow through on its threat to use force if necessary to achieve its objective. The decision of Congress to back or oppose the president's threat thus conveys important information about American resolve to the target state. Moreover, when the president decides whether or not to threaten a target state with military action, he may anticipate the effect of likely congressional reactions to

62. For the importance of opposition parties, particularly in legislatures, to determining signal credibility, see Schultz 1998, 1999, 2001. For the effect of domestic institutional structure on signal credibility in foreign affairs more generally, see Cowhey 1993 and Martin 1993. However, Fearon (1994) would argue that all threats to use force from a democratic state are credible, at least to some degree, because democratic leaders face significant and very public "audience costs" should they back down.

his decision on the credibility of the signal he will send to the target. Thus, because they can affect signal credibility, even anticipated congressional support or opposition can affect the cost-benefit calculations of both the president and the leader of the target state at the conflict initiation phase.[63]

Signals of American resolve or disunity may also affect the target state's calculations and, in turn, the military costs to the president of staying the course throughout the conflict conduct phase.[64] Public displays of legislative support for the president's conduct of military operations enhance the credibility of executive commitments to stay the course, and may deter the target state from escalating its resistance in the hope of outlasting American political will.[65] Conversely, as presidents throughout American history have admonished would-be opponents in Congress, open legislative opposition to the president's military course sends visible signals of American ambivalence, which may steel the target state's resolve to continue to resist once a conflict has begun. For example, Vice President Dick Cheney was particularly aggressive in leveling this charge against Democratic opponents of the war in Iraq. In response to congressional efforts to set a timetable for phased withdrawal from Iraq in early 2007, Cheney minced few words: "When members of Congress pursue an antiwar strategy that's been called 'slow

63. President George H. W. Bush explicitly emphasized the importance of the congressional authorization to use force against Iraq as a signal of American resolve that could prompt Saddam Hussein to comply with UN mandates and withdraw from Kuwait. "I asked the Congress to support implementation of UN Security Council Resolution 678 because such action would send the clearest possible message to Saddam Hussein that he must withdraw from Kuwait without condition or delay. . . . To all, I emphasize again my conviction that this resolution provides the best hope for peace." George H. W. Bush, "Statement on Signing the Resolution Authorizing the Use of Military Force Against Iraq." *Public Papers of the Presidents*, January 14, 1991.

64. See also Auerswald 2000.

65. Prefiguring President George H. W. Bush's praise of the positive signals of American resolve sent by congressional authorization of military action against Saddam Hussein in January of 1991, President Reagan also extolled the value of vocal congressional support in helping him achieve administration objectives in Lebanon. Internal White House memoranda make clear that Reagan believed congressional authorization of the continued Marine presence in Beirut "was influential in [obtaining] the present ceasefire," and he warned Congress that any move to retrench that authorization "could be highly detrimental to effective U.S. policy in the area." Memorandum, Duberstein to Baker III, September 28, 1983, folder "W.H. Staff Memoranda—Legislative Affairs 7/83–12/83 [2 of 3]," box 5, James Baker III files, Ronald Reagan Library.

bleeding,' they are not supporting the troops, they are undermining them." Vocal opposition in Congress, he charged, was a prescription for certain defeat as it was tantamount to "telling the enemy simply to watch the clock and wait us out."[66] A number of congressional Republicans echoed Cheney's rhetoric; for example, South Carolina Senator Jim De-Mint asserted in 2007 that responsibility for American deaths in Iraq belonged not to President Bush, but to Democratic opponents of the war in Congress. "Al-Qaida knows that we've got a lot of wimps in Congress," DeMint said. "I believe a lot of the casualties can be laid at the feet of all the talk in Congress about how we've got to get out, we've got to cut and run."[67]

While such scathing rhetoric is obviously calculated to score political points, internal administration memoranda from the Reagan era show that, even far from the public eye, many in the executive branch fervently believe that the signals Congress sends through its actions can have real consequences on the ground. CIA and National Security Council evaluations of the situation in Lebanon in 1983 held that it deteriorated in large part because Syria believed that congressional opposition to the Marine mission was evidence that the United States had "short breath" and was unwilling to pay the costs of staying the course in Beirut.[68] The signals sent by congressional opposition increased the perceived

66. Sheryl Stolberg, "Opposition Undercuts Troops, Cheney Says of Spending Bill." *New York Times*, March 13, 2007. Even the Pentagon publicly embraced similar reasoning in June of 2007. In a formal written reply to questions about American withdrawal by Senator Hillary Clinton (D-New York), Under Secretary of Defense Eric Edelman admonished that "public discussion of the withdrawal of U.S. forces from Iraq reinforces enemy propaganda," and that "such talk understandably unnerves the very same Iraqi allies we are asking to assume enormous personal risks." Associated Press, "Pentagon Rebukes Clinton on Iraq." July 19, 2007.

67. James Rosen, "DeMint Rips War 'Wimps.'" *The State*, May 30, 2007.

68. Foreign Intelligence and National Security Policy Developments, October–December 1983, folder "Foreign Intelligence and National Security Policy Developments, October–December 1983, (1)," box 91129, Crisis Management Center, NSC Records. Directorate of Intelligence, "The Terrorist Threat to US Personnel in Beirut," January 12, 1984, folder "Lebanon, (11/30/1983)," box 43, Executive Secretariat, NSC, country file, Ronald Reagan Library. More broadly, Secretary of State George Shultz in a memo to other top administration officials worried about the lasting strategic implications of these signals of domestic opposition in the Lebanon case for the larger prosecution of the Cold War. Shultz warned that the "world public relations battle is clearly being won by the Soviets" and feared that signals of American disunity in Lebanon hurt the nation's capacity to project resolve in other areas of the globe. Cable, Shultz to McFarlane, Weinberger,

military costs of continuing the Marine mission in Lebanon. Ultimately, this helped tilt the administration's cost-benefit calculation toward ending the venture.

Theoretical Expectations

Through these three mechanisms, the theory argues that real or anticipated congressional support or opposition can affect the cost-benefit calculations of the president and the target state's leader as well as, ultimately, both the initiation and conduct of major military ventures. Empirical testing of the theory proceeds in two stages. First, because assessing Congress's influence on actual policy outcomes is most amenable to large-n, empirical analysis, the models in the following two chapters test a series of hypotheses that are derived from the theory and developed below. However, the posited theoretical mechanisms that link congressional actions with changes in policy outcomes are difficult to test statistically. For example, large-n analyses of hundreds of uses of force may show the predicted correlations between public congressional opposition to the president's policies and decreased conflict duration; however, such models offer little insight into the mechanisms linking cause and effect. Accordingly, to test the proposed theoretical mechanisms described previously more directly, the analysis continues in chapter 5 with a historical case study that draws on extensive archival evidence to trace the causal processes by which actions in Congress produced tangible changes in the conduct of American military policy. For the remainder of this chapter, however, the emphasis is on the ultimate consequences of congressional actions for policy outcomes.

To help generate precise theoretical expectations for the effects of real or anticipated congressional support or opposition on the course of military affairs, figure 2.1 presents a basic sequence of decisions that leads to the three observable policy outcomes explored in the next two chapters: the president's decision about whether to use force in response to an opportunity, the scope and scale of that use of force, and its ultimate duration. While this simple sequence of decisions and presidential-target

Vessey, and Casey, February 2, 1984, folder "Lebanon I (2 of 5)," box 90753, Donald Fortier files, Ronald Reagan Library.

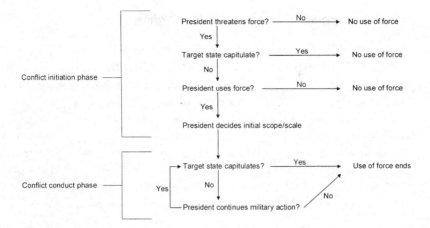

FIGURE 2.1. Military policymaking at the conflict initiation and conduct phases

TABLE 2.1. **Summary of hypotheses**

Hypothesis 1	The stronger the president's party in Congress, the more likely he is to respond militarily to an opportunity to use force arising in the international arena.
Hypothesis 2	The stronger the president's party in Congress, the more likely he is to use large-scale military actions to pursue his foreign policy objectives.
Hypothesis 3	The stronger the president's party in Congress, the longer the duration of the military action he will employ in pursuit of his military policy goals.
Hypothesis 4a	Public congressional support for the president's military policies will, on average, increase a conflict's duration.
Hypothesis 4b	Public congressional opposition to the president's military policies will, on average, decrease a conflict's duration.

state interactions does not account for the full range of possibilities or contingencies that may arise in a given context, it does capture the basic cost-benefit calculations of both the president and the target state leader at the conflict initiation and conduct phases. Table 2.1 summarizes the full set of hypotheses developed below, which relate real or anticipated congressional support for opposition to each of the three observable military policy outcomes.

Congressional Partisanship and the Initiation of a Military Action

We begin by examining the influence of anticipated congressional reactions on the president's cost-benefit calculation of whether or not to use force in response to an opportunity in the international arena.[69] Because Congress is usually silent in the lead-up to a use of force, the logic of congressional influence at the conflict initiation phase is primarily anticipatory. When the president's party is strongly entrenched on Capitol Hill, the chief executive anticipates greater congressional support for a military course of action. This anticipated congressional support decreases the president's fears that the legislature will act to raise the political costs of a military action if chosen. Conversely, when confronted with a strong opposition party in Congress, the president anticipates greater legislative opposition. If the president uses force and Congress does vigorously oppose his policies during the course of a military venture, its actions could both raise the domestic political costs of the action and, by sending signals of American disunity to the target state, increase the military costs that must be paid to achieve the administration's objectives. These dynamics lead to the following hypothesis (hypothesis 1 in table 2.1): The stronger the president's party in Congress, the more likely he is to respond militarily to an opportunity to use force. Conversely, the stronger the opposition party in Congress, the less likely the president is to embrace a military response, ceteris paribus.

Some scholarship in international relations suggests an alternate possibility. In many cases, even before the president makes the final cost-

---

69. The theoretical mechanisms and the discussion in this section focus on the ability of Congress to affect the costs of military action for the president. However, it is also possible that Congress can affect the benefits the president stands to gain from acting militarily. The president may perceive a range of policy benefits from responding militarily to a foreign crisis. Depending on the nature of the crisis, a use of force might protect vital American interests in the region, prevent the destabilization of a region and forestall future problems, or bolster international confidence in American leadership. These benefits are largely unaffected by Congress's anticipated response. However, the president may also perceive political benefits to a use of force, such as a popular rally in approval of his administration. A great deal of scholarship suggests that this rally is contingent upon reaction in Congress. If other political elites line up behind the president, then the public rallies. If other elites, particularly those in Congress, criticize the president's actions, the rally fails to materialize or quickly dissipates. Thus, presidents may logically expect to derive more political benefits from acting militarily when they anticipate greater support, or at least quiescence, on Capitol Hill. This reinforces hypothesis 1 from table 2.1. However, prior research has yielded only very modest evidence that presidents consciously use force in pursuit of personal political reward (e.g., Meernik and Waterman 1996). As such, the primary means through which Congress can affect these calculations is by shaping the costs of military action for the president.

benefit calculation of whether or not to use force, the leader of the target state has the ability to forestall an American military intervention by capitulating to presidential demands.[70] Research on conflict signaling by Kenneth Schultz and others suggests the importance of this target state response to the threat of American military action.[71] If, rather than immediately using force in response to an opportunity, the president first threatens the target state with force if it does not comply with American demands, the leader of the target state must decide whether to capitulate or resist. If the president is backed by strong partisan support in Congress, the target state's leader may deem the presidential threat to use force particularly credible. This could make the target state's leader more likely to capitulate to American demands than he or she would be if the president confronted a strong partisan opposition in Congress. If the target state capitulates, no use of force is observed. By contrast, if the target state's leader anticipates that Congress is likely to oppose the president should he adopt a military course of action, he or she may judge that the president will back down from his threat because he is unwilling to pay the costs of a lengthy military campaign. This signaling logic suggests an alternate possible relationship between congressional partisanship and the initiation of military actions: the stronger the president's party in Congress, the less likely he is to respond militarily to an opportunity to use force, because the target state is more likely to capitulate to American demands to avoid provoking a military response.

While this alternative formulation is plausible, research by James Fearon strongly suggests that, because opposing states know that the

70. In other cases, by contrast, there is no implicit or explicit threat of American military action. For example, after the Reagan administration determined that the Libyan government was behind the attack on a Berlin disco that killed American Marines, the president did not threaten the Libyan leader, Moammar Qadaffi, with force unless he met a set of specified demands. Rather, Reagan ordered an expeditious, secret air strike against the Libyan capital. Thus, some situations follow the outline in figure 2.1 (which draws on the models of Fearon, Schultz, and others) in which the president first decides to threaten force, then the target state's leader decides whether to capitulate, and finally, if the target state resists, the president decides whether to use force. However, other cases involve a simpler process in which an opportunity arises and the president decides whether to use force (this, for example, is similar to the theoretical logic in Meernik 1994 and Howell and Pevehouse 2007).

71. Schultz 1998, 1999, 2001; Auerswald and Cowhey 1997; Auerswald 2000. It should be noted that Schultz does not apply his signaling logic specifically to the American context.

American president stands to pay considerable domestic audience costs if he fails to follow through on a threat to use force, all presidential threats should be deemed highly credible by the leader of the target state.[72] As a result, the anticipation of Congress's likely reaction to a use of force conveys little information about presidential intentions. Once the president has threatened military action, he is likely to follow through on that threat whether or not Congress is expected to support him. Accordingly, the partisan composition of Congress should have only modest influence on the calculations of the target state leader at the conflict initiation phase. As a result, there are strong reasons to believe that hypothesis 1 in table 2.1 captures the net effect of anticipated congressional reactions on the initiation of American military actions.

Of course, both hypothesis 1 and the alternative suggested by the signaling literature presume that Congress can raise the political and military costs of a use of force for the president should he launch one. If it cannot, then the president has little to fear from the legislature, regardless of whether it is controlled by the opposition party or by his co-partisans, and the leader of the target state has little incentive to update his or her strategic calculations based on Congress's anticipated reaction. This leads to the null hypothesis that there is no relationship between the partisan composition of Congress and the presidential initiation of military actions. The empirical analyses in chapter 3 will test between these competing possibilities.

Congressional Partisanship and the Scale and Duration of a Military Action

Up to this point, the discussion has treated the decision to use force as a simple binary choice: either the president deploys American military might abroad in pursuit of his policy objectives, or he does not. Yet, clearly not all uses of force are the same. Once the president decides upon a military response, he must determine the scale, scope, and intended duration of the military action. Anticipations about Congress's likely reaction affect these decisions, too, by altering the president's cost-benefit calculations.

This chapter has argued that when open opposition to the use of force arises within Congress, it can significantly raise the political costs that

---

72. Fearon 1994.

the president risks incurring if he continues an ongoing overseas deployment. Moreover, highly visible opposition to the president's policies in Congress sends signals of American disunity to the target state, which could stiffen its resolve and raise the military costs that must be paid to achieve the administration's policy goals. In many cases the anticipation of these dual pressures encourages the president to forego the use of force altogether. In other cases, he may feel that imperatives on the ground demand a military response. However, anticipating opposition from his partisan adversaries on Capitol Hill, the president possesses strong incentives to moderate his policy goals and, in so doing, to limit the scale, scope, and length of the use of force that is necessary to achieve them. By crafting a military mission designed to be limited in scope and duration, the president may hope to minimize costly congressional objections to his policies. By contrast, a president who enjoys strong co-partisan support in Congress has considerably greater freedom to embrace more ambitious policy goals that require military actions of larger scale and longer duration. This leads to the following hypotheses (hypotheses 2 and 3 in table 2.1) about the relationships between congressional partisanship and a use of force's scale and duration. First, the stronger the president's party in Congress, the more likely he is to use large-scale military actions—specifically, those involving new deployments of American ground troops or the sustained use of firepower—to pursue his foreign policy objectives. Second, the stronger the president's party in Congress, the longer the military actions he pursues, ceteris paribus. The null hypothesis against which the empirical analyses in chapter 3 will evaluate these theoretical expectations is that there is no relationship between the partisan composition of Congress and the scale or duration of American military actions.[73]

73. A possible objection to hypothesis 2 is that presidents who anticipate trouble from a strong partisan opposition in Congress could also conceivably respond by deploying a massive American military intervention (i.e., one whose scale is disproportionate to the mission's objectives) in the hopes of winning a quick victory before significant opposition in Congress can materialize. This is plausible, but the main intended result and observable implication of such a strategy is shortened conflict duration, a policy response captured in hypothesis 3. The historical record since World War II does contain examples of presidents consciously trying to limit the duration of conflicts to avoid congressional interference. For example, as discussed in chapter 1, officials in the Reagan administration urged the president to withdraw American forces from Grenada before the ninety-day War Powers Resolution withdrawal clock expired to avoid a confrontation with Congress, despite the pref-

Congressional Actions and the Duration of an Ongoing Military Action

Heretofore, we have examined only the effects of anticipated congressional support or opposition on the cost-benefit calculations of the president and the target state leader at the conflict initiation phase. However, anticipatory mechanisms alone tell but part of the story. Presidents cannot anticipate Congress's reaction with anything approaching absolute certainty. The partisan composition of Congress affords only a rough baseline estimate of how the legislature and its members will respond to presidential military policies. Moreover, wars, as Sir Winston Churchill presciently warned, are inherently unpredictable. When presidents make early decisions about whether to use force and, if so, what type of military operation to employ, they rely on the best available estimates of how events will unfold once the die is cast. However, the nature of historical contingency virtually insures that, more often than not, all will not go according to plans. When decision-making enters the conflict conduct phase, calculations about what is likely to happen are replaced by actual events unfolding on the ground. The political and strategic environment in which both the president and the target state leader act changes dramatically.

Members of Congress also react to ongoing developments on the ground and to whether or not the operation's progress meets, exceeds, or fails to meet expectations. In some cases, even an opposition-led Congress will respond with greater than expected support. Momentum may build behind resolutions authorizing the president's foreign deployment, or members of Congress may take to the airwaves to express publicly their support for the president and his policies. In other cases, Congress may respond with greater opposition than anticipated. Its members may speak out against the president's policies, its committees may launch investigations into the administration's conduct of military operations, and its two chambers may even introduce, debate, and vote on legislation curtailing the scope and duration of the military action.

Theory suggests that these actions taken by Congress during the course of a military venture shape the calculations of both the president

---

erence of some in the Pentagon to keep American forces on the island for an extended period. Yet there are few obvious examples of presidents employing overwhelming force to achieve their objectives at lightning speed. A seemingly disproportionate American military response could potentially raise more objections than it would silence by shortening the military operation's duration.

and the leader of the target state in the iterative decision-making environment of the conflict conduct phase. Indeed, the aforementioned hypotheses (hypotheses 1–3 in table 2.1) and every prior study asserting congressional influence through the logic of anticipated response explicitly or implicitly rely on this claim. However, the precise consequences of tangible expressions of congressional support for opposition to an ongoing use of force on duration are somewhat complicated because these actions may have different effects on the calculations of the president and the leader of the target state.

When deciding whether to capitulate to American demands or to continue to resist militarily (the first of the iterative decisions at the conflict conduct phase shown in figure 2.1), the leader of the target state may factor congressional actions into his or her calculations. Legislative authorizations and public congressional support for the president's policies signal American resolve to stay the course militarily. Such signals, prior studies suggest, may encourage the target state to capitulate to American demands. By contrast, public opposition to the president's policies in Congress alerts the target state to domestic political pressures on the president to change course. Signaling literatures within international relations suggest that such information could bolster the target state's hopes that it can outlast the political will in Washington to continue a military action. In this way, congressional opposition to the president's policies could conceivably prolong the duration of an American military venture, while congressional support, which may encourage the target state leader to capitulate, could shorten a conflict's duration.

By contrast, the effects of congressional support for opposition to a use of force on the president's cost-benefit calculations of whether or not to stay the course or end a military venture (the second of the iterative decisions at the conflict conduct phase shown in figure 2.1) are essentially reversed.[74] Congressional support decreases the political costs of military

74. Here, too, the discussion focuses on the capacity of congressional actions during the course of a military venture to shape the political and military costs that the president stands to incur by continuing the action. However, congressional actions could also conceivably shape the benefits presidents stand to reap by continuing ongoing military actions. The policy benefits are mostly unaffected by congressional actions, but the political benefits may vary according to Congress's response. Congressional support for the use of force may increase these political benefits, while congressional opposition may diminish them. In this way, on the benefits side of the cost-benefit framework hypotheses 4a and 4b find additional support.

action for the president. It provides him with substantial political cover for his actions, and it marginalizes would-be critics. Moreover, through the signals of American resolve that it sends to the target state, congressional action supporting the use of force may also decrease the military costs of staying the course. By lowering both costs in the president's cost-benefit calculation, congressional support significantly decreases the probability that the president will terminate an ongoing military venture before the target state capitulates and his goals are achieved. Congressional opposition, conversely, raises the costs of staying the course for the president. By effecting real or anticipated decreases in public support for a military action and by forcing the president to expend political capital in keeping his opponents on Capitol Hill at bay, congressional opposition raises the domestic political stakes for the president of staying the course militarily in a foreign theater. Congressional opposition may also inadvertently embolden the target state to stiffen its resistance, and thereby increase the military costs the president must pay to obtain his policy objectives. By raising both the political and military costs of staying the course, congressional opposition generally increases the probability that the president will judge that these heightened costs now exceed the benefits of continuing a military venture, and that he will therefore terminate the American military deployment.[75]

Thus, the theoretical framework developed above, which draws on existing literatures in both the American politics and international relations subfields, suggests competing hypotheses regarding the effects of congressional support or opposition on conflict duration. Ultimately, the question of whether the net effect of congressional opposition is to decrease or increase a conflict's duration—and vice versa for congressio-

75. Furthermore, as discussed previously in this chapter, one of the dimensions on which the politics of conflict conduct differ from those of conflict initiation is that once American troops are deployed abroad, the strategic and political costs of withdrawing the troops prematurely are likely to be considerably greater than those the president risks if he merely chooses to forego using force at the outset. If there is strong support for continuing a military action, the political costs of withdrawing prematurely are very high indeed, as legislative supporters of staying the course will be primed to attack the policy reversal. By contrast, if many in Congress vociferously oppose the military mission, the political costs of terminating it prematurely may be lower. The strategic costs of doing so would still remain; however, fewer in Congress would have grounds for charging the president with endangering the national interest by withdrawing prematurely. This dynamic also supports hypotheses 4a and 4b.

nal support—is an empirical one that the analyses in chapters 4 and 5 address directly. Nevertheless, there are strong ex ante theoretical reasons to believe that the effect of congressional opposition, on average, is to decrease conflict duration, while the effect of congressional support, on average, is to increase it.

First, in many cases congressional signals will likely have only a modest influence on the calculations of the target state at the conflict conduct phase. Uses of force involving the United States are different from most other uses of force occurring in the international system because of the tremendous asymmetric advantages in military capabilities that the United States enjoys over almost every adversary. By the time that the military policymaking process enters the conflict conduct phase, the target state's leader has already decided that his or her interests are best served by refusing to capitulate to American demands, even at the risk of almost certain tactical defeat at the hands of a superior military force. Having made this cost-benefit calculation, congressional signals during the course of a conflict should have only a modest impact on the target state leader's subsequent behavior at the conflict conduct phase.[76] Moreover, the types of states whose leaders are most likely to make this calculation—weak states (including those harboring non-state actors who are the true target of a proposed use of force), failed states, and vulnerable dictatorships—are in many cases very different from most other members of the international community. For these actors, the costs of capitulating to American demands are so high that their cost-benefit calculations should be more impervious to congressional signals.

If the signals sent by Congress have only a modest influence on the calculations of the target state's leader, their effect on the military costs the president stands to pay may also be limited. Yet such signals may still affect the military side of the presidential cost-benefit calculation if the president *perceives* that congressional actions shape the calculations of the target state. For example, the previously cited archival evidence from the Reagan presidential library in the Lebanon case revealed that, in at

76. I thank an anonymous reviewer for encouraging my thinking along these lines. To illustrate this dynamic further, consider, for example, Saddam Hussein's calculations during the American invasion in 2003. Having decided that the costs of capitulating to American demands outweighed even the high probability of military defeat, he was unlikely to be influenced by congressional support for the Bush administration's war policies during the course of the conflict.

least some instances, presidents do believe that congressional signals have a real effect on the behavior of a target state. This in turn shapes their assessments of the military costs that must be paid to continue a use of force and fully achieve their objectives.[77]

Finally, the most direct effect of congressional support of or opposition to administration war policies is to shape the domestic political costs of staying the course for the president. A growing literature has amassed considerable observational, experimental, and archival evidence showing the severity of these costs and the seriousness with which presidents and their advisors attend to them. As a result, there are strong theoretical reasons to expect the effects of congressional support or opposition on the president's cost-benefit calculations at the conflict conduct stage to outweigh those that it has on the cost-benefit calculations of the target state leader.

This leads to the final set of hypotheses (hypotheses 4a and 4b in table 2.1) describing the expected net effect of active congressional support or opposition on the duration of an American military venture: public congressional support for the president's military policies will increase, on average, a conflict's expected duration; by contrast, public congressional opposition to the president's military policies will decrease, on average, a conflict's expected duration. Again, because some ambiguity remains, the direction of the net effects of congressional actions on conflict duration remains an empirical question. Accordingly, the statistical analyses in chapter 4, which employ time-varying covariates to examine the effects of congressional actions taken during the course of a major military venture on conflict duration, will test these hypotheses against the alternatives suggested by the signaling literature as well as against the null hypothesis, dominant in prior scholarship, that congressional actions have no influence on the duration of American military ventures.

A final caveat is in order: it is important to note that the theory developed here does *not* lead to the prediction that congressional opposition *always* leads the president to terminate a use of force more quickly than

---

77. It is likely that congressional signals have a significant effect on the behavior of target states in some cases but not in others. Because it is difficult to measure the precise effect of congressional signals on a target state's behavior in a given instance, a president confronted with highly public congressional opposition may anticipate a possible increase in the military costs of staying the course and factor it into his calculations. Such a dynamic would also support hypotheses 4a and 4b.

he would in its absence. In some cases the president may judge that the benefits of staying the course militarily are so great—or, alternatively, that the costs of backing down are so high—that he will continue a military venture regardless of the domestic political and military costs of doing so. The theory does suggest, however, that congressional opposition makes the president more likely, *on average*, to judge that the costs of continuing a military venture outweigh the benefits of doing so than he would if Congress had remained silent.

Conclusion

Although Congress has repeatedly failed to enact legislation that would legally compel the president to alter or abandon his chosen military policy course, it would be wrong to infer that the president enjoys a free hand in directing the scope and duration of American military commitments abroad. Instead, through a variety of actions, Congress can affect the cost-benefit calculations of the president and the leader of the target state at both the conflict initiation and conduct phases of the military decision-making process. Because Congress can raise or lower the political and military costs presidents risk incurring if they employ a lengthy military engagement to pursue their foreign policy goals, the theory predicts that Congress can influence the probability with which presidents use force in response to opportunities in the international arena, the size and scope of those military actions, and ultimately even their duration.

Much of Congress's influence is exerted through anticipatory mechanisms. Both the president and the leader of the target state anticipate greater congressional challenges to presidential military policies from a legislature controlled by the opposition party than from one dominated by the president's partisan allies. As a result, theory suggests that the stronger the opposition party in Congress, the less likely the president is to use force in response to an opportunity. Moreover, even when the president does embrace a military option, the presence of a strong congressional opposition party encourages him to moderate the mission's scale and even to limit its duration. By contrast, presidents buoyed by strong co-partisan majorities operate under considerably fewer constraints on their freedom of action in the military realm.

However, presidents cannot anticipate congressional reactions to their military policies perfectly. Once a military venture commences and events on the ground begin to unfold, members of Congress have myriad opportunities to respond to the president's policies and either support or oppose them. Concrete, public expressions of congressional support are hypothesized to lower the political and military costs of staying the course for the president and therefore to increase a conflict's expected duration, all else being equal. High-profile expressions of congressional disapproval, by contrast, can raise both the domestic political costs and the strategic costs of continuing to pursue an extended duration military mission. These actions are hypothesized to decrease a conflict's expected duration.

The next two chapters empirically test these hypotheses, summarized in table 2.1, against plausible alternatives and null hypotheses of no congressional influence. Chapter 3 examines the influence of the partisan dynamic on the initiation, scope, and duration of all 122 major uses of force since the conclusion of World War II. Statistical models reveal that presidents confronting strong opposition party ranks in Congress are less likely to launch major military ventures than their peers. Moreover, when they do act, such presidents employ military actions considerably smaller in scope and shorter in duration than do presidents enjoying strong majorities of their co-partisans in Congress.

Chapter 4 then focuses more intently on the specific actions Congress takes during the course of an ongoing conflict to raise or lower the domestic political costs of staying the course for the president, or to send signals of American resolve or disunity to foreign actors. Hazard analyses that allow congressional, political, and conflict-specific factors to vary over time strongly suggest that legislative initiatives to authorize or curtail the use of force, critical oversight hearings, and individual members' rhetorical appeals in the public sphere all strongly affect the expected duration of major military actions in the post-1945 era.

Finally, this chapter has said little about how members of Congress decide whether and when to publicly support or oppose a military venture in the dangerous new political and strategic environment that emerges once American troops are deployed abroad. Both the president and the leader of the target state look to Congress's partisan composition when anticipating its likely response. However, partisanship only goes so far. In many cases a challenge to a president's military policies, particularly once troops are deployed abroad, can be risky even for the president's harshest partisan critics. Any such opposition is subject to the potentially damning charge of undermining the troops in the field. In other conditions, however, even the president's strongest supporters may feel pressure to distance themselves from their party leader. The forces that govern these congressional calculations are critically important to understanding the limits of congressional influence on military affairs. Chapter 6 returns to these questions with additional theorizing and empirical analysis.

CHAPTER THREE

Partisan Politics and the Initiation, Scale, and Duration of War

Throughout American history, the conduct of major military operations has proved a fertile battleground for political conflict between the executive and legislative branches. In most cases, these interinstitutional wars of will have pitted a president of one party against rivals from the opposition party in Congress. For example, only thirty years after the birth of the nation, the War of 1812 threatened to rip it in two as the opposition Federalists in Congress openly defied the administration's call to arms and even sought to block funding for the conflict.[1] Indeed, New England Federalists even discussed secession from the Union in protest of "Mr. Madison's War." In a similar vein, President James K. Polk's expansionist war against Mexico in 1846–48 prompted a vociferous reaction and repeated attacks from opposition Whigs, one of whom was a young Illinois congressman named Abraham Lincoln, whose "spot resolution" openly challenged the Polk administration's casus belli. And despite the conventional wisdom proclaiming a bipartisan Cold War consensus in foreign affairs, many post-1945 military engagements from Korea and Vietnam to Somalia and Iraq have featured a similar dynamic of partisan interinstitutional conflict over the scope and duration of a major military venture.

However, existing scholarship offers little insight into whether this pattern of partisan conflict has any tangible impact on the conduct of major military actions. Does partisan interbranch friction—or the anticipation of it—impose costs on the president and dissuade him from

---

1. For an account of Federalist opposition to the War of 1812, see Hickey 2004.

pursuing lengthy, large-scale military operations to achieve his foreign policy goals? Or does the president—secure in the knowledge that Congress, even when a strong opposition party vehemently opposes his policies, is virtually powerless to *force* him to abandon them—execute his preferred military policies with little regard for real or anticipated congressional opposition?

Several recent studies in political science have examined whether presidents consider Congress's likely reaction when deciding whether or not to deploy the armed forces abroad. Yet the existing literature says virtually nothing about whether partisan politics continue to influence military policymaking in the dramatically different political and international environment that emerges once American forces are deployed in foreign theaters.[2] Simply foregoing a military response altogether is only one policy response that presidents might adopt when confronted with a strong opposition party in Congress. The theory presented in the previous chapter reminds us that presidents who use force despite an entrenched partisan opposition in Congress have strong incentives to moderate the scope and duration of their military actions. Thus, to understand the full nature of congressional influence in military policymaking we must examine legislative influence over both the *initiation* and the *subsequent conduct* of major military ventures.

The chapter proceeds in four parts. First, because of this lacuna in existing scholarship, the chapter begins by assessing hypothesis 3 (see table 2.1): that anticipations of Congress's likely reaction to a use of force based on its partisan composition inform the president's strategic calculus and significantly influence the duration of major military actions. Toward this end, a series of statistical models demonstrates strong linkages between the partisan composition of Congress and the duration of all 122 major uses of force since the conclusion of World War II. Second, because the decision to use force and, once a military venture is launched, calculations about its conduct and duration are inextricably linked, the analysis next endeavors to model these two decision processes simultaneously. The resulting selection models offer strong support for hypothesis 1: that the partisan composition of Congress significantly affects the president's willingness to use force in response to an opportunity arising in the international environment. Moreover, this

---

2. David Clark's 2000 article is an important exception. Clark's model is discussed in more detail below.

expanded analysis again generates strong empirical evidence that Congress continues to influence presidential decisions regarding the conduct and duration of major military ventures.

Most analyses in the quantitative use-of-force literature, including those in the first two sections described above, are limited strictly to data from the post–World War II era; however, the theory articulated in chapter 2 is not time bound to this period.[3] Accordingly, as a further empirical test of its propositions, the chapter's third section presents an additional analysis of the duration of major American military ventures from 1877 to 1945. The statistical evidence strongly suggests that even in this earlier epoch of our nation's history, the partisan composition of Congress was one of the strongest predictors of the duration of a major military action. The analysis concludes with a test of hypothesis 2: that the partisan composition of Congress also affects the scale and scope of major military deployments.

Through these four rounds of analysis, this chapter provides a series of important tests of whether Congress continues to influence presidential military policymaking even after the initial decision to deploy the armed forces abroad. The following chapter focuses even more intently on the politics that emerge once American troops are deployed. It investigates the effects of specific actions taken in Congress during the course of military operations on the duration of the twenty principal postwar uses of force involving the sustained use of firepower, significant deployments of ground troops, or commitments of capital aircraft or naval assets to hostile zones.

The Duration of Major Military Actions, 1945–2004

Data and Methodology

The first set of analyses that follows tests hypothesis 3 from chapter 2, which posits that the partisan composition of Congress significantly influences the duration of major military actions. Blechman and Kaplan and their successors have identified more than four hundred uses of mil-

3. Notable exceptions include Joanne Gowa's (1998, 1999) analysis finding no correlation between unified government and the frequency of American involvement in militarized interstate disputes, and Peter Feaver and Christopher Gelpi's (2004) work on the civil military gap and its influence on United States conflict responses.

itary force abroad since World War II.[4] However, the majority of these
actions are exceedingly minor, and consequently there is little reason
to expect Congress to influence their direction. For example, it is hard
to believe that Congress would have incentives to act to influence President Truman's dispatch of five naval vessels to monitor the inauguration of the Chilean president in 1947. Many similar ventures are unlikely
to attract much congressional attention, let alone action, and as a result
the anticipation of a congressional response should have little effect on
the president's cost-benefit calculation. To capture some of the variation between uses of force, Blechman and Kaplan coded each action on
a five-point scale that accounts for differences in the size and scope of
forces initially deployed in each instance. Because the political dynamics surrounding larger, more intensive uses of force are fundamentally
different from those surrounding smaller-scale operations, this chapter
follows the mold of other scholars and examines the duration of only
those uses of force receiving a 1, 2, or 3 on the Blechman and Kaplan
scale.[5]

The subsequent analysis includes all major uses of force updated
through 2004, with but a few exceptions. First, following Howell and
Pevehouse, the analysis excludes prescheduled military exercises, such
as the Operation Team Spirit maneuvers in South Korea, and operations
carried out by forces already deployed in a crisis area, namely enforce-
ments of the Iraqi no-fly zone.[6] Second, several actions coded as separate uses of force by Blechman and Kaplan that were part of the same
operation were combined into single observations. For example, instead
of coding the dispatch of American troops to the Dominican Republic
as two separate events (the initial deployment constituting the first event
and the decision to keep them in that country after the restoration of civilian government in September of 1965 comprising the second event),
this analysis treats the deployment as a single use of force more con-

---

4. See Blechman and Kaplan 1978, Zelikow 1987, Fordham 1998a, Grimmett 2001,
Howell and Pevehouse 2005.
5. See Fordham 1998a, 1998b; Howell and Pevehouse 2005. Actions of this type involved the initial mobilization of nuclear weapons or multiple naval task forces, air combat
wings, or ground battalions.
6. The exclusion of no-fly zone violations reflects the qualitatively different nature of
this use of force, which is an extension of the informal peace agreement reached between
General Norman Schwarzkopf and Saddam Hussein's commanders after the Persian Gulf
War.

sistent with the reality that American troops first entered the county in April 1965 and did not leave until September of 1966.[7] In the same manner, the current dataset combines the multiple observations for the occupation and garrisoning of Trieste (1945–47), the Berlin airlift, the Persian Gulf War, and peacekeeping missions in Lebanon (1982–84) and Bosnia into single observations beginning with the first use of American troops in military operations and ending with their withdrawal.[8]

Finally and most importantly, because Blechman and Kaplan were interested solely in discrete uses of force crafted to achieve a specific political objective, they consciously excluded the conflicts in Korea and Vietnam from their analysis. They considered these two major conflicts to be full-scale wars, in which military force was used primarily as a "martial instrument," rather than targeted military actions aimed at realizing explicit, limited political objectives.[9] Most scholars of the postwar use of force have followed their lead.[10] However, the goal here is not to investigate Congress's impact on the conduct of political uses of force per se, but to determine its influence over military actions writ large. Any proclamation of congressional war power based solely on the demonstration of congressional influence in more limited military actions may ring hollow. Thus, both this analysis and the more detailed time-varying covariate duration models of the next chapter include the Korean and Vietnam wars.[11]

7. In a similar manner, Zelikow coded the early 1980s U.S. peacekeeping mission in Lebanon as two independent events: the Marine presence itself and the decision to support them with naval and aerial firepower in the fall of 1983. Fordham also identifies five separate uses of force in Bosnia, even though American troops were constantly on patrol either on the seas or on the ground from spring 1994 to December 2004.

8. The data set does code for two uses of force in Lebanon in 1982: the first peacekeeping mission that ended in early September 1982, and the second one that began in late September 1982. This reflects the Marines' withdrawal after the first date, and their return later in the month. The combined uses of force were the multiple actions identified by Zelikow involving the Marine presence and the later use of naval and aircraft bombardment to support their positions.

9. Blechman and Kaplan 1978, 14.

10. Replicating the models in table 3.1 excluding the Korean and Vietnam wars produces very similar results across specifications.

11. While Blechman and Kaplan excluded the greater Vietnam and Korean conflicts from their list of major uses of force, they did include a number of events related to the conflicts, such as incident 38, the end of the Korean War, or incident 278, the withdrawal of troops from Europe because of the Vietnam War in 1965. Because the Korean and Viet-

For the twenty principal uses of force involving ground troops, the sustained use of firepower, or an extended operation of air or naval vessels in hostile zones, which are examined in the second section of this chapter and in the next chapter, the start date is coded as the day on which U.S. ground troops were first deployed to a region where they were not previously stationed, firepower was first used, or an air or naval patrol was begun.[12] The end date for each action is the day on which the last U.S. ground troops were withdrawn from the region except for those intended to form a permanent presence—or, for the Berlin airlift and 1987–88 Persian Gulf reflagging operation, the date on which the U.S. naval or air operations were suspended. Start and end dates for the remaining 102 major uses of force are taken from those provided by Blechman and Kaplan and in updates by Fordham and by Howell and Pevehouse.[13]

Figure 3.1 illustrates the frequency with which the United States engaged in military actions meeting the major use-of-force and principal use-of-force criteria from 1945 to 2004. Most years witnessed between one and three major uses of force, though in ten years no major uses of force took place. The graph also shows two clear peaks in major force activity. The first emerged as the Cold War heated up at the end of the Eisenhower and Kennedy administrations. The second spike occurred in the Reagan era as a result of the administration's active posture in Latin America and the Middle East.

Figure 3.2 summarizes the dependent variables for the statistical analyses of this chapter and the next, the durations of both sets of military actions. The median duration of a Blechman and Kaplan major military action was relatively short, just over a month at 43 days. There is considerable variance around that median, however, as a quarter of the actions continued for more than four months and more than 15 percent of the

---

nam wars themselves are included in my analysis, I exclude all such incidents as repeat uses of force.

12. For example, because American ground forces were already stationed in Kuwait and Saudi Arabia, the beginning of the aerial bombardment of Iraq on March 19, 2003—not the Bush administration's reinforcing of these contingents in 2002—is coded as the start date for the Iraq War.

13. The only major changes in duration for the twenty principal uses of force are due to combining events coded by Blechman and Kaplan as separate uses of force; any other modifications of start or end dates were only by a few days here or there, and the changes were based on government and military chronologies.

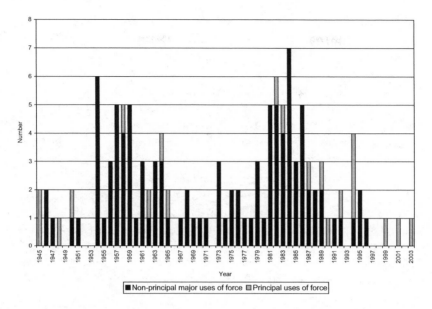

FIGURE 3.1. Frequency of U.S. major and principal uses of force, 1945–2004

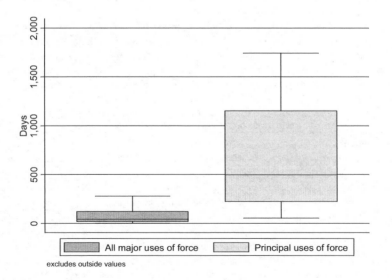

FIGURE 3.2. Durations of U.S. major and principal uses of force, 1945–2004

actions involved the deployment of American forces for more than one year. These are not visible on the box plots because outside values are left undisplayed to preserve some semblance of scale.[14] The median duration of the subset of principal uses of force was considerably longer—almost 500 days. A handful of even these most intense military actions were short in duration, with two (10 percent) lasting less than two months, but the vast majority of the principal military actions were of extended duration, with an inter-quartile range from 223 to 1,154 days.

To model the duration of each of the 122 major uses of force since World War II, the subsequent analysis employs a weibull hazard model.[15] Because many scholars believe armed conflicts are negatively duration dependent—the longer a conflict has dragged on, the less likely it is to end at some future time—the weibull model was chosen over other options, such as the exponential hazard model, which assumes no duration dependence, and the cox proportional hazard model, which makes no assumptions about the form of the baseline distribution.[16]

14. Outside values are those that exceed the upper quartile plus 1.5 times the inter-quartile range.

15. The weibull model is a proportional hazard model that assumes a baseline hazard rate operationalized as: $h_o(t) = pt^{p-1}$. To investigate the effect of explanatory variables on the hazard rate, this baseline hazard is coupled with a scaling parameter consisting of a vector of covariates exponentiated to insure a positive value: $\exp(X\beta)$. The resulting hazard function is simply: $h(t|x_i) = pt^{p-1}\exp(X_i\beta)$.

16. I used a weibull hazard model for four primary reasons. First, the weibull model allows researchers to examine whether wars are indeed negatively duration dependent, as many scholars have argued (see Bennett 1999 for a discussion of how parametric models, such as the weibull, can be used to test such hypotheses, whereas the more general cox model cannot). Most of the subsequent models do find strong evidence of negative duration dependence, consistent with prior scholarly expectations and contra a perspective that is common in the media emphasizing American "war weariness." Second, this modeling choice follows many other recent hazard analyses of conflict duration that also employ a weibull model (e.g., Bennett and Stam 1996, Regan and Stam 2000, Regan 2002, Fearon 2004). Third, Box-Steffensmeier and Jones (1997, 1436) acknowledge that when choosing the appropriate duration model, "discrimination between a cox and weibull model is difficult." For models with time-varying covariates, however, they advise "if the standard errors for the weibull are substantially smaller than those for the cox model, the weibull model would be preferred because of its efficiency." Fourth, the STATA module developed by Boehmke, Morey and Shannon (2006) allows for the simultaneous estimation of a binary selection model (the decision to use force) and a weibull hazard model (conflict duration). This analysis, discussed shortly, is key to eliminating concerns about potential bias from non-random selection. To insure that any finding showing a relationship between the partisan composition of Congress and duration is not the result of faulty assumptions

Rather than examining the covariates' effects on the hazard rate itself (interpreted as the probability of observing a failure in the passage of a unit of time t given the observed hazard rate), the subsequent analyses report results using the accelerated failure time metric, which allows us to model the expected time to failure for each conflict at any given moment.[17] The sign of the resulting coefficients gives the direction, but not the magnitude, of each variable's effect on the expected survival time. First differences are used to illustrate the effect of a change in one independent variable while holding the others constant at predetermined values.

Explanatory Variables

CONGRESS. To test whether the composition of Congress ex ante can influence the expected duration of a use of force, the hazard models include three measures of the presidential party's strength in Congress.[18] The first is a simple dummy variable for divided government.[19] The second is the average percentage of the president's party in both chambers of Congress.[20] However, the effect of Congress' partisan composition could be nonlinear. Increases in the strength of the president's party may

---

about the nature of the baseline hazard rate, all models were replicated using a cox proportional hazard model, which produced very similar results.

17. For the weibull model, this expected duration at time t given the observed values of the covariates is the scaling parameter multiplied by the gamma distribution of $1/(p+1)$ (Greene 2003): $E[t|x_i] = \exp(X_i\beta) * \Gamma(1/p+1)$.

18. Only 22 of the 122 major uses of force span shifts in the partisan composition of Congress. Of these, 13 are principal uses of force, for which changes over time are analyzed using a new set of duration models with time-varying covariates in the next chapter. Of the remaining nine, only four involved a change in partisan control of even a single chamber: the 1953–54 Tachen Islands crisis between China and Taiwan; the 1968–69 response to the Soviet invasion of Czechoslovakia; the 1982-to-present Sinai peacekeeping force; and the 1986–87 military exercises in Honduras.

19. Instances of split partisan control of Congress are coded as divided government. The mechanisms described in chapter 2 do not require the opposition in Congress to be able to pass legislation, but only to be able to use the legislative machinery of even a single chamber to raise the costs for the president by publicly debating and voting on legislation to curtail the use of force or by holding high-profile investigative hearings. As a result, control of both chambers is not a prerequisite for congressional influence.

20. As mentioned in chapter 2, because the cohesiveness of the opposition party may matter, all models were also reestimated using Legislative Potential for Policy Change scores with results virtually identical to those presented in this chapter.

mean a great deal to presidential leeway when his party is in the minority or the legislature is roughly evenly divided. For example, the marginal benefit of a 5-percent increase may be much smaller when his party increases in size from, say, 60 to 65 percent of Congress than when it increases from 47 to 52 percent. To account for this possibility, the models also contain a logarithmic transformation of the partisan composition measure.[21] If presidents are truly unconstrained by Congress, its partisan composition should have no influence on the expected duration of a use of force. However, because partisanship shapes the incentives of members of Congress either to support or to oppose the president's military policy, we expect presidents with strong majorities on the Hill to possess greater leeway to use extended overseas deployments to pursue their foreign policy goals. By contrast, presidents facing stiff partisan opposition will be more wary of long-duration military actions.

Yet other scholars in the international relations literature suggest that a member's status as a military veteran, not his or her partisan identification, is the most important factor in determining his or her attitudes toward military action. Christopher Gelpi and Peter Feaver argue that personal experience in the armed services makes veterans less likely to support the use of force to achieve foreign policy goals.[22] The larger the percentage of veterans in the highest ranks of government, the less frequently the United States will use force abroad. While their argument does not directly explore the degree to which the veteran composition of Congress will continue to influence military decision-making once troops are in the field, their logic suggests that the more veterans there are in Congress, the greater the pressure they will place on the president to limit the duration of overseas deployments.[23] Thus, the models also include a measure of the average percentage of members in both chambers that served in the armed forces.[24]

21. To control for the alternative possibility that shifts in partisanship at both tails of the distribution have little effect, a logistic transformation was also used, with virtually identical results.

22. Gelpi and Feaver 2002, Feaver and Gelpi 2004.

23. Echoing the "Powell doctrine," Gelpi and Feaver do argue that once force has been used, veterans favor using substantial force to achieve military objectives. This argument will be discussed in more detail and tested empirically later in this chapter.

24. In their analysis, Gelpi and Feaver use a composite measure of the percentage of male members of the House of Representatives who are veterans and the percentage of all members of the Cabinet with military service. Because the focus here is on Congress, the

Finally, David Clark argues that the level of congruence between presidential and congressional policy preferences, not the partisan distribution of power, influences the duration of postwar U.S. involvement in militarized interstate disputes.[25] The greater the congruence in policy goals and preferences between the two branches, the more likely the government is to be united behind a military venture and the better equipped presidents are to commit American forces to extended foreign deployments. To test for this possibility, the models also include Clark's most direct measure of institutional congruence, the percentage of roll calls in Congress on which the president took a position decided in his favor.[26]

TARGET STATE CHARACTERISTICS. While there are strong theoretical reasons to believe that domestic political institutions, particularly Congress, influence presidential conduct of military affairs, international factors undoubtedly have an important effect on the duration of a military venture. To ensure that any findings for congressional influence are not merely the product of failing to control for the international determinants of conflict duration, the models also include a number of variables to account for the military power of the target state, its importance to American national interests, and the strategic climate in which the president acts.

Drawing on data from the Correlates of War Project's National Material Capabilities database, the hazard models include measures of the target states' military expenditures in billions of dollars and their mil-

---

models include only congressional military veteran composition. Because the Senate traditionally holds a greater interest and more direct power in foreign affairs, while the House certainly retains some power over military actions through its privileged position in the appropriations process, the average of both chambers is used instead of the percentage in the House only. Furthermore, the percentage of all members, not just of men, seems a more appropriate measure, particularly in the modern era, and therefore the exclusive focus on male members is abandoned.

25. Clark 2000.

26. Because *CQ* begins reporting these presidential support scores at the onset of the Eisenhower administration, models including this measure drop nine observations from 1945 to 1952. Clark's other measures of interinstitutional policy congruence are partisan proxies: two dichotomous divided government variables, one for when the president and both houses of Congress are controlled by opposite parties, and the other for when partisan control of Congress is split.

itary personnel in millions.[27] Target states with higher military bud-
gets and larger armed forces may compel the president to employ an extended use of American military might to achieve his aims.

Additionally, the United States clearly attaches varying levels of importance to different states based on their region, strategic importance,
alliance status, and the potential threat they pose to American interests.
Presumably, the president will be more willing to commit the armed
forces to extended operations when the target country is critical to the
national interest than when it is only of marginal importance. To control for this, the models contain three measures drawn from the literature. Geographic proximity is often cited as a proxy for importance, as
closer states may be of more immediate strategic and economic interest
than distant ones. Thus, the models include a measure of the distance
between national capitals.[28]

Since Bruce Bueno de Mesquita's work in the 1970s, scholars of international relations have also examined the correspondence in states'
alliance structures as a proxy for the level of shared security interests
between states and as an indicator of the expected utility derived by
each state from militarily challenging the other.[29] More recently, Signorino and Ritter offered a new measure of the congruence in states' alliance memberships that rectified some of the shortcomings of the Ken-
dall tau-*b* measure employed by earlier analyses. These *S* similarity
scores are now the standard measure in the literature.[30] Existing scholarship has shown that the greater the similarity in the alliance portfolios
of two states, the less likely they are to go to war. Accordingly, military
actions between the United States and a foreign nation with similar al-

27. See Small and Singer 1990. The National Material Capabilities dataset contained
missing data for several of the country-years included in the analysis. In these instances,
available data from the most recent prior year was used. Substituting linearly interpolated
numbers for the missing years yields virtually identical results. For the twenty-five major
uses of force involving two or three target states, the combined totals of their military personnel and expenditures are used.

28. See Gleditsch and Singer 1975; Garnham 1976; Russett, Oneal, and Davis 1998;
Bremer 1992. When a use of force involved two or more target states, the average distance
between their state capitals and Washington, D.C., was used.

29. See Bueno de Mesquita 1975, 1978; Altfeld and Bueno de Mesquita 1979; Lalman
and Newman 1991; Huth, Bennett and Gelpi 1993.

30. See Signorino and Ritter 1999, Gowa and Mansfield 2004, Leeds 2003, Bennett
and Rupert 2003, Mansfield and Snyder 2002, King and Zeng 2001.

liance memberships may be systematically shorter than confrontations with states having dissimilar alliance portfolios.[31]

Finally, a measure more specific to the United States is the size and scope of the economic and military aid relationship between Washington and the target state.[32] States receiving more largesse from the U.S. foreign aid budget are perceived by policymakers as being more important to American interests, and consequently military actions in these nations are likely to be longer than in states that receive less American interest and aid.

Finally, to control for the greater geopolitical environment in which the military action occurs, the models include dummy variables for the years of the two major wars in the postwar era, Korea and Vietnam, and for the Cold War (1945–89).[33] This allows for the possibility that presidents are less likely to risk bogging down troops in lengthy deployments during times of greater ongoing threat than when they are freed from such considerations.

31. Following the literature, the analysis includes regional alliance similarity scores calculated by the computer program EUGene (Bennett and Stam 2000). For the reasons outlined in Signorino and Ritter (1999), scores weighted by states' relative military capabilities were employed. Replicating the subsequent models with unweighted or global S scores (those based on all states in the international system, not just those in the region of the target state) yields virtually identical results. For the twenty-five major uses of force involving two or three target states, the average of the similarity scores for each state with the United States was used. Alternatively, including the lowest similarity score for any of the target states suggests that if anything, the relationship between alliance similarity and duration is positive (though the coefficient is not statistically significant), while all other results remain unchanged.

32. See Meernik 1994, DeRouen and Heo 2004. Following Meernik, the model includes military and economic aid totals from the current year; the probability that aid totals are a result of military action is low because the budget is usually set in the preceding year. All models were replicated using lagged aid figures; results were identical to those presented in the text. Additionally, the *U.S. Overseas Loans and Grants Greenbook*, published by the Agency for International Development, begins its record-keeping in 1946. For the two observations in 1945 (China and Yugoslavia), the model includes 1946 data. Setting these two observations equal to zero to reflect strictly post–World War II aid totals yields identical results. Finally, for the twenty-five major uses of force involving two or more target states, the total amount of aid received by all states is used. All foreign aid figures are reported in constant 2007 U.S. dollars.

33. Subsequent results are virtually identical regardless of the year adopted as the "end" of the Cold War.

OTHER POLITICAL AND ECONOMIC VARIABLES.   Past research has also paid considerable attention to how other domestic political factors, aside from Congress, influence the use of force. Some scholars have posited that popular rallies in the wake of military action create incentives for presidents to use force in presidential election years.[34] To maximize the benefit of such an action, a president may try to ensure that the deployment is long enough to generate a lasting wave of popular support for his handling of the crisis. To control for this possibility, the models include a dummy variable for presidential election years. In a similar vein, an extensive literature on the diversionary use of force suggests that presidents may use military force to bolster sliding approval ratings.[35] A president with low public approval may prefer to clad himself in the mantle of commander in chief for an extended period to revive his political capital; therefore, the models also include average presidential approval from Gallup surveys in the month immediately preceding the initiation of each use of force.[36]

Lastly, the diversionary-war thesis also suggests that presidents may launch a military venture to distract public attention from a slumping economy.[37] To be effective, the military action must capture public attention until the economic situation improves. Thus, the analysis includes monthly measures of unemployment and inflation. Summary statistics for all variables used in the forthcoming analyses are reported in appendix table 3a.1.

A final caveat: because the hazard models presented in this chapter predict conflict duration only from initial conditions, they cannot account for developments over the course of a conflict and their effect on its duration. Undoubtedly, such factors may greatly influence the length of an overseas deployment, and their influence will be tested in the time-varying covariates models of the next chapter.

---

34. For the effect of the electoral cycle on foreign policymaking more generally, see Nincic 1990, Stoll 1984, Gaubatz 1991.

35. See Brace and Hinckley 1992, Russett 1990, Morgan and Bickers 1992, DeRouen 1995; but for a conflicting interpretation, see Ostrom and Job 1986.

36. If no Gallup poll was conducted in the month immediately preceding the start date, the next closest preceding poll was used. If the start date occurred in the first month of a president's term, his first approval polling result was used.

37. See James and Oneal 1991; Fordham 1998a, 2002, 2005.

Results and Discussion

The first three columns in table 3.1 explore the simple bivariate correlations between each congressional partisanship measure and the duration of a major military venture. In each case, the relevant coefficient is in the expected direction and statistically significant. Divided government corresponds with shorter military deployments while, conversely, strong presidential partisan margins in Congress are correlated with longer uses of force.[38] These bivariate relationships strongly support hypothesis 3: the stronger the president's party is in Congress, the less trouble he anticipates from the legislature and, consequently, the more freedom he has to conduct extended military deployments to pursue his foreign policy goals.[39]

The baseline hazard parameter, p, is less than one indicating negative duration dependence. The longer a use of force lasts, the less likely it is to end at any given future moment. While war weariness driven by mounting costs in blood and treasure may pressure governments to end conflicts before the costs become too great in particular types of conflicts, we find little evidence of this dynamic across the gamut of major American military operations.[40] Instead, this result reinforces popular notions of military interventions as quagmires; the longer the troops stay, the harder it is to extricate them.

Models 4 through 7 add the various international, domestic, and economic control variables to each of the three partisan congressional measures. Even after including the controls, the hazard models offer unambiguous support for theoretical expectations regarding Congress. When presidents facing a strong partisan opposition in Congress exercise force abroad, they tend to limit systematically the duration of their deployments. Conversely, presidents buoyed by strong partisan majorities in Congress face fewer political pressures to end military operations expe-

38. Replicating all models in table 3.1 using the percentage of the president's party in the House and Senate separately, or the lower of the two instead of the average measure, yields virtually indistinguishable results.

39. Adding presidential fixed effects also yields identical results for all three congressional measures. None of the presidential dummies are consistently significant, except for the highly positive coefficient for George W. Bush, whose two major uses of force were still ongoing when the analysis concluded.

40. See Russett 1990.

TABLE 3.1. **Factors influencing the duration of major uses of force, 1945–2004**

Independent variables	(1)	(2)	(3)	(4)	(5)	(6)	(7)
Congress							
% president's party in Congress	6.47*** (2.34)	—	—	4.25** (2.13)	—	—	5.42** (2.94)
Ln (% president's party in Congress)	—	3.42*** (1.08)	—	—	2.09** (1.02)	—	—
Divided government	—	—	−.76** (.47)	—	—	−.71** (.40)	—
% veterans in Congress	—	—	—	−3.79 (3.92)	−3.56 (3.95)	−4.08 (3.92)	—
Presidential support scores in Congress	—	—	—		—	—	−1.19 (1.64)
Target state characteristics							
Military expenditures	—	—	—	−.05 (.23)	−.05 (.23)	−.00 (.23)	.33 (.29)
Military personnel	—	—	—	.27* (.18)	.27* (.18)	.23 (.18)	−.25 (.20)
Distance from United States	—	—	—	−.00 (.09)	−.00 (.09)	−.00 (.09)	−.05 (.08)
Similarity of alliances				.31 (.48)	.31 (.48)	.33 (.48)	−.02 (.48)
U.S. economic and military aid	—	—	—	.55*** (.15)	.55*** (.15)	.57*** (.15)	.65*** (.15)
Strategic climate							
Ongoing war	—	—	—	.03 (.56)	.02 (.57)	.11 (.56)	−.63* (.43)
Cold War	—	—	—	−1.68** (.86)	−1.71** (.87)	−1.64** (.87)	−2.23*** (.54)
Other political variables							
Election year	—	—	—	−.13 (.35)	−.12 (.35)	−.19 (.34)	−.26 (.30)
Presidential approval	—	—	—	.01 (.02)	.01 (.02)	.02* (.01)	.02* (.01)
Economy							
Unemployment	—	—	—	−.00 (.12)	−.01 (.13)	.03 (.12)	−.16 (.13)
Inflation	—	—	—	.01 (.05)	.01 (.05)	.02 (.06)	.04 (.05)
Constant	1.54* (1.15)	7.20*** (.83)	5.26*** (.34)	5.06** (2.32)	8.59*** (2.25)	7.30*** (2.13)	4.43** (1.82)
p	.52 (.05)	.52 (.05)	.51 (.05)	.68 (.04)	.68 (.04)	.68 (.04)	.73 (.05)
Log-likelihood	−263.05	−262.54	−264.60	−234.68	−234.70	−235.14	−210.29
n	122	122	122	122	122	122	113

Note: * $p < .10$; ** $p < .05$; *** $p < .01$. All significance tests are one-tailed; all models report robust standard errors.

ditiously, and as a result the expected durations of their military actions are substantially longer.

Model 7 also adds Clark's measure of the congruence in policy preferences between the executive and legislative branches; however, the resulting coefficient is the wrong sign and statistically insignificant. Preference convergence is only one reason why the partisan composition of Congress should help the president anticipate the likely response of Congress to his military policies. Instead, this model suggests that the partisan incentives members of Congress stand to gain by supporting or opposing the president's military policies are more important. As a result, the partisan composition of Congress remains the dominant ex ante domestic political determinant of the duration of major postwar military actions.[41]

Similarly, none of the models offer much support for Gelpi and Feaver's alternative perspective that the number of military veterans in Congress, not its partisan composition, drives interbranch dynamics over the conduct of military action. The relevant coefficients are consistently negative across specifications; however, in no instance do they reach conventional levels of statistical significance. Although Gelpi and Feaver find that large numbers of House veterans seem to diminish the frequency with which presidents use force, the hazard models offer only modest evidence that the veteran composition of Congress influences the duration of military deployments in the post–World War II era.

Turning to the realpolitik explanations, all of the models offer strong support for the logical contention that the military capabilities of the tar-

---

41. Although this model is temporally truncated because presidential support scores are not available for the immediate post–World War II era, most of the other explanatory variables retain their sign and level of statistical significance. Perhaps a better measure of the congruence of preferences between the president and the legislature is the distance between the common space scores of the president and the median of each chamber. A growing body of congressional scholarship has emphasized the polarization of Congress in recent decades and its significant effects on public policy (McCarty, Poole, and Rosenthal 2006; Hetherington 2001; Jones 2001; though see also Roberts and Smith 2003). In the use-of-force context, as polarization in Congress moves the chamber medians more to the extremes, the gulf widens between presumably more centrist presidents and Congress; this widening may in turn increase interbranch conflict over the conduct of military affairs. Including measures of the average distance between the president's first-dimension common space score and the average of the two chamber medians or the most distant chamber median yields null results, while leaving the findings for the partisan composition of Congress and other control variables virtually unchanged.

get states and the international strategic environment influence the duration of American military actions. While none of the models show any correlation between target state military expenditures and the duration of American military deployments, models 4 and 5 show a significant positive relationship between the size of a target state's military and a conflict's duration. As expected, the larger the target state's military, the longer American forces must be deployed to achieve their goals.

The models also support contentions that the strategic importance of a country to American interests is a strong determinant of a president's willingness to use extended military deployments to pursue his policy objectives there. While the rough measure of strategic importance, the distance between the target state's capital and Washington, and the similarity between U.S. and target state alliance portfolios had no impact in any of the models, each specification shows a statistically significant positive relationship between foreign aid and the duration of military actions.[42] Uses of force involving states that receive substantial sums of American foreign aid are significantly longer than those involving states that receive little or no assistance from Washington.

With respect to the importance of the strategic climate in which the use of force occurs, the models offer little evidence that military actions begun in periods when the United States was engaged in Korea or Vietnam were any shorter or longer than other comparable actions. However, all four specifications reveal strong evidence for the influence of the Cold War. Previous research has found that the United States used force more frequently in the Cold War era, but the majority of these actions were, on average, shorter than comparable post-1989 ventures. A possible explanation for this pattern is that while containing communist expansion prompted presidents to deploy American military might actively across the globe, many of these actions were consciously limited in duration to mitigate the possibility of triggering a serious conflagration between the two superpowers. Additionally, the fall of the Soviet

42. A number of scholars have drawn attention to the limitations of examining only alliance memberships to gauge the similarity of two states' foreign policies (Bueno de Mesquita 1981, Signorino and Ritter 1999). A common suggestion is to augment alliance measures with measures of the similarity in states' voting patterns in the United Nations (Voeten 2000). Including similarity S scores for U.S. and target state UN voting from 1946 to 1996, drawn from Gartzke and Jo 2002, yields a statistically insignificant relationship for the alternative measure and duration across specifications while leaving all other relationships virtually unchanged.

Union itself directly contributed to two of the longest post–Cold War military deployments in Bosnia and Kosovo. Finally, because U.S. forces no longer must stand ready to repel a Soviet invasion of Western Europe, American military assets in the current period are more readily available for peacekeeping and other extended missions—deployments that in the Cold War years could have threatened America's capacity to respond to a direct Soviet threat.

Lastly, the models offer little support for any of the domestic political factors emphasized by diversionary-war theories. Election-year uses of force appear to be no longer on average than non-election-year actions, and presidents with low approval ratings do not launch longer military actions than those with higher levels of public standing. If anything, models 6 and 7 present modest evidence that presidents with higher levels of public support engage in lengthier military endeavors. This echoes Ostrom and Job's finding that presidents are risk-averse and use force more frequently when they possess a "popularity buffer" and are thus better equipped to bear any losses from an unsuccessful venture.[43] Similarly, the models find no evidence supporting theories that presidents wage sustained military actions to divert public attention from a flagging economy. Neither unemployment nor inflation has any systematic relationship with the duration of military actions.[44] Normatively, this is an encouraging result, as it suggests that presidents do not adjust their conduct of military actions from Machiavellian motivations.

Collectively, the duration models presented in table 3.1 found consistent, statistically significant effects for the partisan composition of Congress on the duration of post–World War II military actions. However, although statistically significant, the effects may be substantively small, in which case the models would offer little evidence of congressional power and influence over the president's conduct of military affairs.

Figure 3.3 graphically illustrates the effect of each independent variable in model 4 of table 3.1 on the predicted duration of a major military deployment. Because the influence of a change in any of the independent variables on the expected number of days of a deployment depends on the values of all of the other independent variables, figure 3.3 instead presents percent changes in the expected duration due to a

43. See Ostrom and Job 1986.

44. All models were also reestimated using a misery index of inflation plus unemployment; all results were substantively identical.

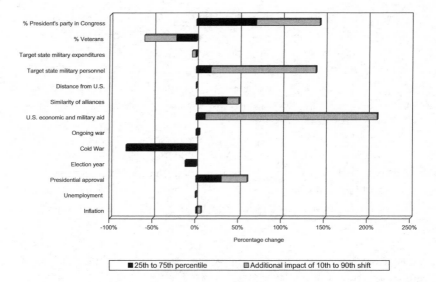

FIGURE 3.3. Predicted effects of variables on conflict duration in major uses of force, 1945–2004. First differences for the following variables are statistically significant: percentage of seats held by the president's party in Congress, target state military personnel, U.S. economic and military aid, Cold War.

shift in each variable. The solid portion of each bar represents the percentage increase or decrease in expected duration resulting from a shift in each independent variable from its 25th to its 75th percentile (or from 0 to 1 for dummy variables), while holding all other variables constant at their means or medians. The dotted portions show the additional effect on duration caused by a further shift from the 10th to the 90th percentile.

In figure 3.3 we see that the influence of Congress's partisan composition on the duration of a military deployment is substantively as well as statistically significant. Increasing the presidential party's power in the halls of Congress from 45 to 58 percent increases the expected duration of a military engagement by 70 percent, while a further increase from 41 to 62 percent more than doubles the predicted duration of a military action.[45]

45. A thirteen-percentage-point swing in congressional partisanship is certainly large, but it is not uncommon. A swing this large or larger has occurred in more than 20 percent of the elections since 1945.

Indeed, the effect of Congress's partisan composition on conflict duration is considerable even when compared to the influence of the statistically significant realpolitik control variables. An increase in the size of the target state's military from its 25th to its 75th percentile (from 46,000 to 652,000 men in uniform) increases the American deployment's expected duration by less than 20 percent. A similar-sized shift in foreign aid from $0 to $176 million increases the expected duration of a conflict by less than 15 percent. Only very large shifts in these variables, from the 10th to the 90th percentiles, produce substantial increases in the predicted length of an American military engagement.

Finally, the Cold War dummy variable has a strong negative impact on the expected duration of a major use of force. Despite comprising the two largest American military actions of the post-1945 era, the average Cold War use of force was significantly shorter than post-1991 ventures. Holding all other variables constant at their means or medians and changing only the Cold War indicator variable from 0 to 1 reduces the expected duration of a military deployment by 80 percent.

A lingering objection some might levy against assertions of congressional power over the conduct of American military actions since the conclusion of World War II is that any such influence is timebound to the post-Vietnam era. Many scholars contend that the Vietnam War unraveled the Cold War consensus and rejuvenated congressional efforts to assert its authority over war-making.[46] Frustration with the Johnson and Nixon administrations' conduct of the war and repeated failure to engage Congress in its planning and execution spurred members on both sides of the aisle to reenergize congressional checks on the executive; the end result of this resurgence was the passage of the War Powers Resolution in 1973. This purported erosion of the bipartisan consensus in foreign policy, coupled with the emergence of a new formal legislative tool for checking the president in military affairs, may have rendered Congress better equipped and more eager to wage partisan attacks on presidential discretion in military affairs after the early 1970s. If so, then the partisan composition of Congress may only affect the duration of military engagements in the post-Vietnam era; accordingly, failing to differentiate between prewar and postwar years may give the false impression

---

46. See Blechman 1990; Destler, Gelb, and Lake 1984; Peppers 1975; Holsti and Rosenau 1984, 1990; but see McCormick and Wittkopf 1990.

that partisan dynamics influenced the duration of military deployments in the entire period since World War II.

To test for this possibility, an additional set of models in table 3.2 divides the congressional partisan measures into pre- and post-1974 components.[47] Across specifications, the partisan composition of Congress in both the prewar and postwar periods remains a statistically significant predictor of a military engagement's expected direction. Furthermore, Wald tests show that there is not even a statistically significant difference in the size of any of the pre- and post-1974 coefficients. Even before Vietnam fractured the parties along hawkish and dovish lines and supposedly reenergized partisan conflict in foreign policy, partisan interbranch struggle greatly influenced the duration of presidential military ventures.[48]

As a final robustness check, the models in tables 3.1 and 3.2 were reestimated using militarized interstate disputes (MIDs) data from 1945 to 2000.[49] Although the Blechman and Kaplan data were specifically designed to study postwar American uses of force—and consequently have advantages over the MIDs dataset, which is the standard for crossnational analyses—several studies of American force dynamics have relied on MIDs data.[50] To ensure that the observed relationship between the partisan composition of Congress and the duration of military deployments is not an artifact of the data set used, all of the models were replicated using the MIDs 3.0 data.[51] Across specifications, the MIDs

47. The choice of year is inconsequential. All models were also replicated with pre- and post-1964 congressional measures to compare the pre-Vietnam era with the years after it began; all results remained virtually identical.

48. Including Clark's measure of *CQ* presidential support scores in Congress yields results virtually identical to those reported in table 3.2 across specifications. The support-scores measure itself is of the wrong sign and is statistically insignificant in every specification.

49. See Jones, Bremer, and Singer 1996; Ghosn, Palmer, and Bremer 2004.

50. For the advantages of the Blechman and Kaplan data, see Fordham and Sarver 2001. For an additional description of limitations in the MIDs data as a measure of uses of force, see Mitchell and Prins 1999. For studies using MIDs, inter alia see Gowa 1998, Clark 2000, Gelpi and Feaver 2002.

51. Fifteen MIDs lacked a definite start date or end date, though every MID had its beginning and ending month specified. All models in these robustness checks were estimated using the maximum duration value provided in the MIDs data. Substituting the minimum duration value or the average of the two yields virtually identical results.

TABLE 3.2. **Influence of congressional partisanship, before and after the Vietnam War, on the duration of major uses of force, 1945–2004**

Independent variables	(1)	(2)	(3)
Congress			
Pre-1974 % president's party in Congress	4.01** (2.13)	—	—
Post-1973 % president's party in Congress	5.43*** (2.19)	—	—
Pre-1974 ln (% president's party in Congress)	—	2.47*** (.99)	—
Post-1973 ln (% president's party in Congress)	—	1.73* (1.10)	—
Pre-1974 divided government	—	—	−.89** (.42)
Post-1973 divided government	—	—	−.52 (.48)
% veterans in Congress	−2.88 (3.68)	−2.58 (3.87)	−3.19 (4.02)
Target state characteristics			
Military expenditures	−.08 (.23)	−.04 (.23)	.01 (.01)
Military personnel	.30** (.18)	.28** (.18)	.22 (.18)
Distance from United States	.01 (.09)	.00 (.09)	.00 (.09)
Similarity of alliances	.15 (.48)	.23 (.46)	.27 (.47)
U.S. economic and military aid	.56*** (.14)	.56*** (.14)	.57*** (.14)
Strategic climate			
Ongoing war	.23 (.57)	.11 (.57)	.09 (.55)
Cold War	−1.40** (.81)	−1.61** (.86)	−1.69** (.88)
Other political variables			
Election year	−.17 (.35)	−.23 (.36)	−.27 (.35)
Presidential approval	.02 (.02)	.02 (.02)	.02* (.01)
Economy			
Unemployment	−.09 (.14)	−.09 (.13)	−.02 (.13)
Independent variables	(1)	(2)	(3)
Inflation	−.04 (.06)	−.02 (.06)	.00 (.06)
Constant	4.45** (2.23)	8.32*** (2.21)	7.08*** (2.12)
p	.69 (.04)	.69 (.04)	.68 (.04)
Log-likelihood	−233.78	−233.92	−234.81
n	122	122	122

Note: * $p < .10$; ** $p < .05$; *** $p < .01$. All significance tests are one-tailed; all models report robust standard errors.

models offer compelling corroborating evidence that the partisan composition of Congress is one of the most important predictors of the duration of a military venture.[52] The stronger the president's partisan cohort in Congress, the more free he is to engage in protracted military actions to pursue his policy goals.[53]

Thus, across multiple data sets, operationalizations of congressional partisanship, and model specifications, the hazard models offer very strong support for hypothesis 3 derived from the theoretical model of military policymaking. Both the president and the leader of the target state look to Congress's partisan composition when anticipating its likely reactions to various military policy options. This affects the strategic cost-benefit calculations of both actors, and the end result is that presidents facing a strong partisan opposition in Congress employ systematically shorter-duration military actions, on average, than do their peers who enjoy strong co-partisan support on Capitol Hill.[54]

52. In her analysis of the factors driving the frequency of American involvement in MIDs from 1945 to 1992, Gowa (1999) found no effect for divided government. Interestingly, even when limiting the sample to these years, the models find a significant effect for divided government on the duration of American military actions, even if it did not influence their frequency.

53. A few of the findings for the control variables are surprising. The positive relationship between unemployment and duration accords with diversionary-war hypotheses that presidents will employ lengthy military engagements to distract public attention from an ailing economy. However, the positive coefficients for alliance similarities and distance between state capitals both cut against theoretical expectations. Yet neither coefficient is significant if MIDs with low hostility levels that do not involve the display of force, use of force, or war are excluded from the analysis. Moreover, even in this truncated MIDs sample, the relationships between congressional partisanship and the duration of a military conflict remain robust across specifications.

54. The theoretical model in chapter 2 suggests two mechanisms through which a strong partisan opposition could decrease the duration of a use of force. First, presidents look to congressional partisanship when anticipating the legislature's likely reaction. A president who anticipates trouble from a Congress controlled by his partisan opponents will consciously avoid lengthy foreign entanglements that could prove politically costly. Alternatively, presidents may not limit the expected duration of their military plans ex ante, but they may be quick to pull out as soon as conditions on the ground begin to sour, for fear of congressional reprisals. Second, in addition to this anticipatory mechanism, congressional partisanship can also influence the duration of a conflict by setting the stage for tangible congressional actions during the course of a military venture that can raise or lower the costs of continuing the use of force beyond what the president initially anticipated. These mechanisms are not mutually exclusive, and indeed both are likely in play. The time-varying

Modeling the Decision to Use Force and Conflict Duration Simultaneously

As the theoretical discussion in the preceding chapter has made clear, decisions about the initiation of major military actions and resulting conflict durations are inextricably linked. When making their cost-benefit calculations, presidents look to the partisan balance of power in Congress to anticipate its likely reaction both when deciding whether or not to respond to an opportunity that arises in the international arena and when crafting the desired duration of the resulting military venture. Because these strategic calculations are so closely intertwined, concerns arise about the possibility of selection bias. The duration models in tables 3.1 and 3.2 included a wide range of controls to account for other military, strategic, and domestic political factors that might influence the duration of major American military actions. However, no model can include all of the necessary controls. If an omitted variable influences both conflict duration and the initial decision of whether or not to use force, then the coefficients from the foregoing duration models are biased and the estimates of the effect of congressional partisanship on conflict duration are misleading.[55]

The best solution to the selection bias problem is to model the two processes—the initiation of military action and the resulting duration of the conflict—simultaneously. Not only does this serve the critically important methodological purpose of correcting for potential selection bias in our estimates, but it also builds on existing research and affords the best possible test of hypothesis 1: that anticipations of congressional reactions based on the strength of the opposition party on Capitol Hill also influence the president's decision of whether or not to adopt a military response to an overseas opportunity in the first place.

---

covariates models in chapter 4 will test the second mechanism directly by demonstrating strong correlations between actions taken during the course of a military venture and changes in its expected duration.

55. Boehmke, Morey, and Shannon (2006, 194) address this issue specifically in their recent *American Journal of Political Science* article. They note that "the problem does not arise because the occurrence of war and the outcome or duration of the war are influenced by the same factors. Nonrandom selection is only a problem when the unobserved factors are related." More generally, see also Achen 1986.

Accordingly, the analyses in table 3.3 employ a selection model to estimate two equations simultaneously. The first-stage equation is a binary choice model in which the dependent variable is whether the president uses force in response to an opportunity that arises in the international environment. The second-stage equation is again a weibull hazard model of the duration of the resulting overseas deployment.[56]

To model the factors leading the president to use force in some cases and to forego a military response in others, we first need to identify a universe of potential opportunities to use force that arise in the international arena. Toward this end, I employ Howell and Pevehouse's database, which catalogues more than 10,000 opportunities to use force between 1945 and 2000. Each "opportunity" represents a front-page *New York Times* article reporting on a major international event that could potentially provoke an American military response, such as a civil war, interstate armed clash, coup d'état, or attack on American military or diplomatic personnel.[57] For each opportunity to use force, the dependent variable is whether the president responded to that opportunity with one of the 122 major uses of force identified above.[58]

---

56. This selection model with a binary first-stage model and second-stage hazard model was developed by Boehmke, Morey, and Shannon (2006). The models in table 3.3 were estimated using their DURSEL module for STATA. This selection model builds on the pioneering work of Heckman (1979).

57. For a complete description of this data set and its construction, see Howell and Pevehouse (2007), appendix B.

58. Howell and Pevehouse's dependent variable is coded 1 for all opportunities to which the United States responded militarily within thirty days. As such, the same use of force from the Blechman and Kaplan data could, and often did, produce multiple 1s in the dependent variable. Here, I have coded the dependent variable as 1 if the opportunity is the last one involving an incident and target state to which the United States has responded militarily within sixty days. (The sixty-day window keeps three uses of force within the sample whose last opportunity occurred outside of a thirty-day window. Re-estimating the models excluding these uses of force yields virtually identical results.) In this operationalization, each major use of force in the opportunities data yields one positive realization of the dependent variable and one observation for the conflict's subsequent duration. Alternatively, following Howell and Pevehouse I reestimated my models coding the first-stage equation's dependent variable 1 for every opportunity within thirty days of a use of force (with the duration only observed for the last positive realization of the dependent variable before each use of force) with virtually identical results. Because in both operationalizations the use of force is relatively rare, I reestimated the first-stage equations separately using rare events logit (King and Zeng 2001; Tomz, King, and Zeng 2003), which yields results virtually identical to those reported in the first stage of the se-

To test hypothesis 1, I construct three models of presidential deployment decisions, with each including one of the three measures of presidential party strength in Congress. Each model also employs all of the same military, strategic, and domestic political control variables from the duration models above.[59] Finally, each model includes two additional variables, commonly called exclusion restrictions, that help identify the selection model equation: the number of additional opportunities in other countries to which the president could conceivably respond on that day, and a measure of how democratic or autocratic the government of the potential target state is.[60]

There are strong theoretical reasons to believe that both of these variables should influence the initial decision of whether or not to use force, but there is little reason to expect these variables to influence the duration of a military action once launched. When simultaneously confronted with multiple opportunities to use force, the president may be less likely to use force in reaction to a given opportunity than when it is the only major international crisis to which he might respond. Once the president has decided to use force, however, it is unlikely that the number of other opportunities to which he did not respond when the use

---

lection models below. Finally, in most of their reported models, Howell and Pevehouse include all uses of force—both major and minor—in their dependent variable. Here, because the duration analyses only examine major uses of force, minor uses of force (those receiving a 4 or 5 on the Blechman and Kaplan scale) are excluded. This analysis thus provides an important additional test of whether congressional partisanship affects the initiation of the most intense group of American military actions. All three models in table 3.3 suggest unequivocally that it does.

59. Following Howell and Pevehouse, the model also includes a series of regional dummy variables and presidential fixed effects. Although unreported in the tables, the effects of both series are jointly significant. I also reestimated these selection models with a first-stage equation specification identical to that used by Howell and Pevehouse. Most importantly, in each case the congressional variables have a strong, statistically significant impact on conflict duration. For a full presentation and discussion of these alternate results, see the appendix to this chapter.

60. Unlike an instrumental variable analysis, which accounts for endogeneity between a regressor in the second-stage equation and the dependent variable, Heckman-type selection models can be estimated without an exclusion restriction (i.e., a variable that predicts the outcome variable in the first-stage equation, but is otherwise uncorrelated with the dependent variable of the second-stage equation). However, without an exclusion restriction, these models rely heavily on the untestable assumption that the error terms of the two equations are jointly normally distributed. See Sartori 2003 for a helpful discussion.

of force began will have much influence on the subsequent duration of that military action. Instead, the strategic and political imperatives of the case at hand should govern this calculation. Similarly, an extensive literature in international relations argues that democracies are very unlikely to enter military conflicts with one another.[61] However, once the United States has decided to use force, it is not clear why the nature of the target state's government should affect its conduct and the resulting duration of the military venture.[62] The number of contemporaneous opportunities to use force is drawn from the Howell and Pevehouse data set, while the target state's democratic governance variable is from the Polity IV database.[63] Empirically, neither variable has a substantively or

61. Among others, see Kant 1983 [1795], Ray 1995, Russett 1990, Russett and Oneal 2001, Maoz and Russett 1993, Gartzke 1998.

62. Bennett and Stam (1996) do argue that regime type can influence conflict duration. To test their hypothesis, Bennett and Stam include an additive measure of both the initiating and target states' Polity democracy scores in a duration model, and they find that more democratic dyads wage shorter wars. Slantchev (2004), however, argues that the level of democracy in the initiating state, not the target state, is the significant predictor of conflict duration. Democratic states tend to anticipate problems at home and wage shorter, easier wars. According to this logic, the United States may be more reluctant to attack a democratic state than a more autocratic one, but once the decision has been made (and the target state has resisted and not capitulated to American demands to ward off an attack), then the target state's democracy level should not affect the duration of the conflict. To test between these two competing perspectives, I reestimated Bennett and Stam's model with separate variables for the democracy level of both the initiating state and the target state (I thank the authors for generously providing their data for replication purposes). When separating the two democracy measures, neither coefficient is statistically significant. The coefficient for the variable measuring the level of democracy in the *initiating* state is negative, consistent with both Bennett and Stam's and Slantchev's theory. However, the coefficient for the variable measuring the level of democracy in the *target* state is actually positive. Moreover, because the Polity data was missing for one or more states for twenty-one of the seventy-seven wars in their sample, Bennett and Stam replaced missing observations with the mean democracy score for all observations. Reestimating their analysis after dropping these observations yields virtually identical results for every other substantive variable of interest, but the coefficient for their additive democracy measure is now substantively and statistically insignificant. As a result, there are strong reasons to believe that the target state's democracy level should influence the probability with which the United States acts militarily, but should have little influence on the subsequent duration of an American use of force.

63. The polity2 index codes each state's government structures on a scale of increasing democratization from –10 to 10. Employing a democracy dummy variable coding states with polity2 scores of 6 and higher or 7 and higher (both are commonly used in the liter-

statistically significant effect if included in any of the duration models presented in table 3.2.[64]

In the second-stage duration equation, not all of the 122 major uses of force analyzed in tables 3.1 and 3.2 are represented in the Howell and Pevehouse opportunities data set. In some cases, the precipitating event may have simply missed the front page. In others, the American military response was so quick that the first *Times* report covered both the triggering event and the American response. And still other uses of force were responses to events not captured in the coding criteria. As a result, the number of observations in the second-stage duration equation is significantly smaller, just under 70. Accordingly, each duration model employs a reduced-form model specification including only the four variables that had consistent, statistically significant effects on conflict duration in the models from table 3.1: one of the three measures of congressional partisanship, the size of the target state's military, the amount of foreign economic and military aid given to the target state, and a dummy variable for the Cold War.[65] Results for both the selection and duration models are presented in table 3.3.

The results from the first-stage equations of the selection models strongly support hypothesis 1. All three models offer robust evidence that the stronger the president's party in Congress, the more likely he is to respond militarily to an opportunity to use force in the international arena. First differences show that an increase in presidential partisanship from its 25th to its 75th percentile more than doubles the predicted probability of a military response to an opportunity. Similarly, first differences calculated from model 3 suggest that presidents in divided governments are almost 75 percent less likely to use force in response to an opportunity than are presidents in unified governments, holding all other variables constant at their means or medians.

---

ature) yields virtually identical results across specifications. For the latest update to this data, see Marshall and Jaggers (2007).

64. Including the polity2 democracy variable in model 4 of table 3.2 yields a p-value of .98. Including the number of ongoing opportunities variable in model 4 of table 3.2 yields a negative coefficient, but one that is statistically insignificant ($p = .33$).

65. Including presidential approval, which was statistically significant in model 6 of table 3.1, in the second-stage equation yields a positive but insignificant coefficient estimate for approval's effect on conflict duration and virtually identical results for all other variables across specifications.

TABLE 3.3. **Factors influencing the initiation and duration of major military actions**

Independent variables	(1)	(2)	(3)
Selection model			
% president's party in Congress	1.32** (.70)	—	—
Ln (% president's party in Congress)	—	.55** (.34)	—
Divided government	—	—	−.19** (.10)
% veterans in Congress	−.86 (1.44)	−.84 (1.47)	−.60 (1.44)
Military expenditures	.48 (.69)	.48 (.69)	.47 (.70)
Military personnel	−.05 (.06)	−.05 (.06)	−.05 (.06)
Distance from United States	.02 (.05)	.02 (.05)	.03 (.05)
Similarity in alliances	−.03 (.12)	−.03 (.12)	−.03 (.12)
U.S. economic and military aid	−.00 (.03)	−.00 (.03)	−.00 (.03)
Ongoing war	−.05 (.11)	−.05 (.11)	−.10 (.11)
Cold War	.09 (.28)	.09 (.29)	.08 (.29)
Contemporaneous opportunities	−.09*** (.04)	−.09*** (.04)	−.09*** (.04)
Target state democracy score	−.02*** (.01)	−.02*** (.01)	−.02*** (.01)
Election year	.05 (.06)	.04 (.06)	.03 (.05)
Presidential approval	−.05 (.32)	−.04 (.33)	.04 (.33)
Unemployment	.03 (.03)	.03 (.03)	.03 (.03)
Inflation	−.00 (.01)	−.00 (.01)	−.00 (.01)
n	12,594	12,594	12,594
Duration model			
% president's party in Congress	5.76*** (2.91)	—	—
Ln (% president's party in Congress)	—	2.84** (1.33)	—
Divided government	—	—	−.85** (.49)
Military personnel	.09 (.13)	.09 (.13)	.07 (.13)
U.S. economic and military aid	.49*** (.14)	.48*** (.14)	.49*** (.14)
Cold War	−1.99*** (.80)	−1.96*** (.80)	−1.78** (.87)

(*continued*)

TABLE 3.3. (*continued*)

Independent variables	(1)	(2)	(3)
Constant	3.61**	−4.56	5.60
	(1.90)	(5.48)	(.83)
n (uncensored)	68	68	68
Rho (error correlation)	−.07	−.07	.25
	(.16)	(.13)	(.00)
Log-likelihood	−781.59	−781.87	−781.93

Note: * $p < .10$; ** $p < .05$; *** $p < .01$. All significance tests are one-tailed; all models report Hubert/White/sandwich clustered standard errors on country-president combinations. The selection models also include fixed effects for each presidential administration, as well as dummy variables for geographic regions.

The coefficients for many of the control variables are in the expected direction. For example, all three models suggest a modest positive correlation between unemployment and the probability of a military response. This is consistent with diversionary-war theories, and in some alternate model specifications the coefficient does reach conventional levels of statistical significance. However, none of the controls included from the duration models in table 3.1 are statistically significant in the first-stage models presented here. As a further robustness check, each model was reestimated with a different set of control variables taken from Howell and Pevehouse's model of the factors governing the decision to use force in response to an opportunity arising in the international environment. These results are presented and discussed in full in the appendix to this chapter. While these alternative specifications yield a number of additional statistically significant findings, most importantly they also consistently show strong evidence that congressional partisanship has a substantively and statistically significant effect on both the initiation and duration of American military actions.

Finally, in accordance with theoretical expectations, the coefficients for both the number of contemporaneous opportunities and the level of democratic governance in the target state are negative and statistically significant. Multiple competing opportunities to use force decrease the probability of the president seeking a military solution to any one specific crisis. And consistent with an extensive literature on the democratic peace, the more democratic is the target state, the less likely the president is to use force against it.[66]

66. The only statistically significant regional effect suggests that the United States is less likely to respond militarily to opportunities that arise in Africa. Otherwise, the regional and presidential state fixed effects are jointly significant.

Consistent with the earlier duration analyses, the results from the second-stage duration models also strongly support hypothesis 3. Even after correcting for potential selection bias and estimating the models of conflict initiation and duration simultaneously, all three specifications provide compelling evidence that the strength of the opposition party in Congress significantly influences presidential conduct of military affairs.[67] In each specification, the relationship between congressional partisanship and conflict duration is both statistically and substantively significant. Moreover, these relationships hold even in the truncated sample of military actions whose precipitating event was captured in the opportunities database. The predicted duration of a military action increases significantly as the strength of the president's party in the legislature grows. By contrast, when the president's partisan opponents hold the reins of power on Capitol Hill, the model suggests that he employs systematically shorter military ventures than he would if his co-partisans controlled Congress.

To illustrate the effects of opposition control of Congress graphically, figure 3.4 plots two survival functions estimated from model 3. The difference between the solid and dashed curves represents the estimated effect of divided government on a conflict's predicted duration. For example, the model suggests that a major military action in unified government has approximately a 40-percent chance of lasting at least 100 days. By contrast, the model estimates only a 20-percent chance of a major military action reaching or exceeding 100 days in duration in divided government.

The other control variables also largely behaved as they did in the full duration models in table 3.1. In all three models, the coefficient for target state military personnel is positive as expected, but it fails to meet conventional levels of statistical significance. Military ventures involving states more critical to the American national interest, as measured by their aid relationship with the United States, tended to be significantly longer than uses of force involving target states that received little U.S. aid. And, as in the previous models, Cold War uses of force again appear to be systematically shorter on average than military ventures begun after the fall of the Soviet Union.

---

67. These strong, statistically significant relationships hold even if each congressional partisanship measure is the only variable included in the duration equation.

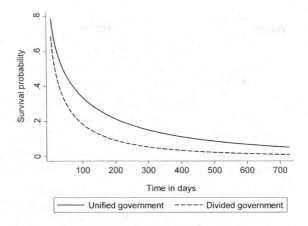

FIGURE 3.4. Influence of divided government on conflict duration

Finally, the rho parameter represents the correlation between the error terms from the selection and duration equations. In two of the three
model specifications, the estimate of rho is not statistically significantly
different from zero. This suggests that the error terms of the selection
and duration models are not significantly correlated with one another.
In other words, in two of the three specifications, the unobserved factors
that influence the initiation of military action are not significantly correlated with the unobserved factors that shape conflict duration. As a result, the estimates from the full duration models of all uses of force in
tables 3.1 and 3.2 likely do not suffer from selection bias and should provide the best picture of the full dynamics driving the duration of major
American military actions in the post–World War II era.

In sum, simultaneously modeling the initial decision of whether to use
force in response to an opportunity abroad and the subsequent duration
of a military action once commenced provides strong support for both
hypotheses 1 and 3 drawn from the theory presented in the preceding
chapter. Both the president and the leader of the target state look to the
partisan composition of Congress when anticipating its likely reaction
to various policy options. As a result, the president is both less likely to
use force when confronted with a strong partisan opposition on Capitol
Hill and, when he does use force, more likely to employ a systematically
shorter-duration mission in pursuit of his policy goals.

The Duration of American Militarized Interstate Disputes, 1877–1945

Like the vast majority of scholarship on the forces driving American military policymaking, the models in the preceding sections focused exclusively on the post–World War II era. Perhaps surprisingly, the statistical evidence shows that, even in this period of alleged bipartisan consensus, foreign policy was actually characterized by considerable partisan interbranch struggle over the conduct of military affairs. But did politics ever stop at the water's edge? The theory in chapter 2 predicts that this relationship between congressional partisanship and the duration of military actions should continue to hold as long as the president and his co-partisans in Congress share ideological preferences and electoral incentives. The late nineteenth century, after the reemergence of a genuine two-party system following the end of Reconstruction in 1877, was an era of intense partisan polarization and heightened partisan electoral competition. Moreover, it was during this period that the agenda powers of the majority party grew considerably, particularly in the House under the iron fists of Speakers Thomas Reed and Joseph Cannon.[68] In this strongest period of congressional party government in American history, partisan conflict over military affairs should have been particularly acute.[69] Thus, conducting duration analyses similar to those presented in tables 3.1 and 3.2 with pre-1945 data affords a test of a further observable implication of the theory articulated in the previous chapter.

Data and Model

While the Blechman and Kaplan data used previously are not available for the pre-1945 era, the Correlates of War Project's militarized interstate dispute dataset provides a record of U.S. military interventions

68. For trends in polarization, see McCarty, Poole, and Rosenthal 2006. On party government in Congress from the late nineteenth century to the revolt against Cannon, see Schickler 2001, Rohde 1991, Zelizer 2004.

69. An alternative perspective, however, could emphasize that the pre-1945 era predates the advent of the imperial presidency and the alleged usurpation of congressional war powers by the executive branch. In this different political and institutional environment, Congress may have possessed a stronger voice in military affairs across the board, and its influence may not have waxed and waned as intensely with its partisan composition. The empirical analyses in this chapter will test between these two competing hypotheses.

beginning in 1816. Although several prominent international relations scholars have noted the significant advantages that the Blechman and Kaplan data afford for analyses specifically focused on the U.S. use of force, a number of recent scholarly works continue to employ the MIDs data.[70] Moreover, as a robustness check, all models from tables 3.1 and 3.2 that used the Blechman and Kaplan data were reestimated using U.S. involvement in MIDs from 1945 to 2000 with virtually identical results. Therefore, to test whether the same partisan dynamics governing interbranch struggle over the conduct of major military actions in the post–World War II era also characterized interbranch relations in earlier periods, this section examines the duration of U.S. involvement in militarized interstate disputes from 1877 to 1945.[71]

The United States was involved in seventy-four militarized interstate disputes during this period, of which forty-nine involved the display of force, use of force, or full-scale war—criteria more akin to the definitions of the types of actions constituting use of force for Blechman and Kaplan. Figure 3.5 illustrates the frequency of American involvement in all MIDs and in the subset of disputes directly involving the use or display of military forces. The distribution of events is relatively uniform across the period, with two small spikes in martial activity surrounding World Wars I and II. Figure 3.6 summarizes the distribution of the durations of U.S. involvement in these militarized disputes. The median duration of a dispute was relatively short, only 61 days. However, the duration of the median MID involving the use of force was considerably longer, 143 days. More than a quarter of MIDs involving the United States lasted 200 days or more.

The main independent variables of interest are again the three measures of Congress's partisan composition: the average percentage of both chambers controlled by the president's party, the logarithmic transformation of this percentage, and a divided government dummy variable.

70. See Fordham and Sarver 2001 for an overview of the MIDs–versus–Blechman and Kaplan data debate. For recent works using MIDs, see Gowa 1998, Clark 2000.

71. For eighteen of the seventy-four MIDs during the period, precise starts or end dates are unknown, though for each MID a starting or ending month is identified. For each of these disputes, the MIDs data provided both a maximum and minimum possible duration for the conflict (for each of the MIDs whose precise start and end dates were known, the two are equivalent). In the models presented below, the dependent variable reports the maximum duration of each MID. Replicating the models using the minimum duration or the median between the maximum and minimum yields virtually identical results.

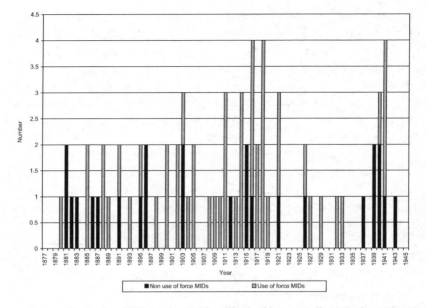

FIGURE 3.5. Frequency of U.S. involvement in militarized interstate disputes, 1877–1945

The models also include all of the control variables from the preceding analyses that were available for this earlier period: the percentage
of Congress that served in the military; a presidential election dummy
variable; the number of men in the armed forces arrayed against the
United States in the militarized dispute; the similarity scores between
the United States and the target state's regional alliance memberships;
and the average distance in miles between Washington and the opposing state's capital.

Weibull hazard models are again used to assess the effect of each
variable on conflict duration. First differences illustrate the effect of a
change in each independent variable on duration while holding the others constant at predetermined values.

Results and Discussion

The first three columns of table 3.4 report simple bivariate regressions
for each of the three congressional composition measures on the duration of all seventy-four militarized interstate disputes in which the
United States was a party from 1877 to 1945. Consistent with the re-

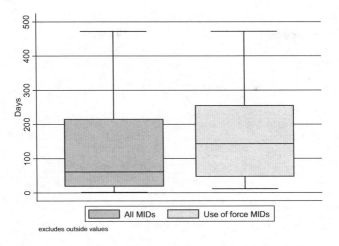

FIGURE 3.6. Durations of U.S. involvement in militarized interstate disputes, 1877–1945

sults in chapter 3, the partisan composition of Congress had a substantial impact on the duration of American military ventures, even prior to World War II. The stronger the president's party in Congress, the longer is the expected duration of a militarized dispute. Conversely, MIDs begun in periods of divided government are systematically shorter than those initiated when the president's party also controls both houses of Congress.

To insure that the relationship between partisanship and duration observed in the bivariate regressions is not the spurious result of omitted variable bias, models 4 though 6 add the domestic political and realpolitik controls discussed above. Even after including the control variables, the relationships for the three congressional partisanship measures and duration remain in the expected direction, and only the coefficient for average partisanship in model 4 fails narrowly to meet conventional levels of statistical significance.

Several of the control variables also had a statistically significant relationship with MID duration in the pre–World War II era, including Congress's veteran composition, the presidential election dummy variable, and the size of the opposing state's military. However, before discussing any of these relationships in depth, the analysis next examines whether these relationships continue to hold among the critical subset of MIDs involving the display of force, use of force, or full-scale war.

TABLE 3.4. **Factors influencing the duration of all U.S. militarized interstate disputes 1877–1945**

Independent variables	(1)	(2)	(3)	(4)	(5)	(6)
Congress						
% president's party in Congress	4.55** (2.76)	—	—	3.14 (2.60)	—	—
Ln (% president's party in Congress)	—	2.66** (1.29)	—	—	1.81* (1.22)	—
Divided government	—	—	−1.08*** (.41)	—	—	−.64** (.39)
% veterans in Congress	—	—	—	−1.52* (1.00)	−1.46* (.98)	−1.36* (.97)
Election year	—	—	—	−.65* (.39)	−.65** (.39)	−.75** (.43)
Target state characteristics						
Military personnel	—	—	—	.11** (.06)	.11** (.06)	.09* (.05)
Similarity of alliances	—	—	—	−.49 (.62)	−.48 (.61)	−.55 (.69)
Distance from United States	—	—	—	.05 (.11)	.05 (.11)	.05 (.10)
Constant	2.28* (1.49)	6.41*** (.09)	5.04*** (.24)	3.58** (1.63)	6.38*** (.73)	5.43*** (.45)
p	.60 (.06)	.60 (.06)	.61 (.06)	.67 (.07)	.67 (.07)	.66 (.07)
Log-likelihood	−155.31	−154.93	−154.28	−148.99	−148.80	−148.85
n	74	74	74	74	74	74

Note: * $p < .10$; ** $p < .05$; *** $p < .01$. All significance tests are one-tailed; all models report robust standard errors.

This first set of models analyzed the duration of all militarized interstate disputes to which the United States was a party from 1877 to 1945. However, this universe of cases includes some categories of events, such as threats to use force and other lesser state actions, that do not meet Blechman and Kaplan's criteria for coding as a use of force; this divergence brings into question the comparability of these results with the primary findings of the post-1945 analyses.[72] To insure that the relation-

72. However, the replications of the Blechman and Kaplan models in chapter 3 on all U.S. MIDs from the post-1945 era reveal virtually identical political and international dynamics governing the duration of U.S. actions.

ship between the partisan composition of Congress and the duration of American MID involvement is not being driven solely by low-hostility-level actions involving no direct use of U.S. military forces, the second set of models presented in table 3.5 replicates the earlier specifications including only the 49 MIDs involving the display of force, use of force, or war in the analysis.[73]

Most importantly, consistent with theory even in this truncated sample, the core relationships between congressional partisanship and duration hold. The three bivariate regressions again confirm expectations that the stronger the president's party is in Congress, the more latitude the commander in chief has to use extended military engagements to pursue his foreign policy goals. Conversely, presidents acting in the more politically perilous environment of divided government employ shorter military actions than their peers operating in eras of unified partisan control of the White House and Congress.

Even after adding the political and realpolitik controls in models 4 through 6, the coefficients for each of the partisan congressional measures remain strong and statistically and substantively significant. Drawing on the results from model 4, figure 3.7 presents a series of first differences analogous to those presented previously for post-1945 uses of force. The top bar shows that increasing the strength of the president's party in Congress from 51 to 61 percent increases the expected duration of a military action by more than 40 percent. A further shift from 47 to 65 percent almost doubles the expected duration of a military action. Thus, even when limiting the scope of analysis strictly to actions involving the display of force, use of force, or full-scale war, the partisan composition of Congress is one of the most important predictors of the duration of the American military response.

As in the preceding analysis of all MIDs, the restricted models also show a negative relationship between the number of veterans in Congress and the duration of American military actions before 1945. However, the

73. Gowa (1998) narrows her focus even further to include only those MIDs involving the use of force or war (hostility level 4 or 5 in the MID coding system). Because many displays of force (hostility level 3 actions) in the post-1945 period also appeared in the Blechman and Kaplan data, I have also included all hostility level 3 events here. Replicating the models in table 3.5 on only uses of force and wars (hostility level 4 and 5 events) yields virtually identical results for all congressional partisan measures.

TABLE 3.5. **Factors influencing the duration of U.S. militarized interstate disputes involving the display of force, use of force, or war, 1877–1945**

Independent variables	(1)	(2)	(3)	(4)	(5)	(6)
Congress						
% president's party in Congress	4.84**	—	—	3.76*	—	—
	(2.70)			(2.54)		
Ln (% president's party in Congress)	—	2.62**	—	—	2.00*	—
		(1.29)			(1.27)	
Divided government	—	—	−1.12***	—	—	−.66**
			(.44)			(.37)
% veterans in Congress	—	—	—	−1.14	−1.07	−.80
				(.97)	(.99)	(1.03)
Election year	—	—	—	−.48*	−.49**	−.61**
				(.30)	(.30)	(.33)
Target state characteristics						
Military personnel	—	—	—	.07*	.07*	.04
				(.06)	(.05)	(.05)
Similarity of alliances	—	—	—	−1.27***	−1.32***	−1.47***
				(.56)	(.55)	(.60)
Distance from United States	—	—	—	.09	.08	.08
				(.12)	(.12)	(.10)
Constant	2.74**	6.99***	5.65***	3.51***	6.78**	5.69***
	(1.51)	(.80)	(.21)	(1.46)	(.86)	(.41)
p	.82	.82	.84	1.02	1.02	1.02
	(.07)	(.07)	(.08)	(.09)	(.09)	(.10)
Log-likelihood	−84.15	−84.10	−83.00	−74.35	−74.33	−74.29
n	49	49	49	49	49	49

Note: * $p < .10$; ** $p < .05$; *** $p < .01$. All significance tests are one-tailed; all models report robust standard errors.

estimated size of the effect is smaller when only MIDs directly involving force are used, and the standard errors surrounding each estimate are considerably higher. These results parallel those of the post-1945 models in tables 3.1 and 3.2; those models also consistently showed negative relationships between the veteran composition of Congress and the duration of American military actions, but in each case the estimated coefficient failed to reach conventional levels of statistical significance. Ultimately, Gelpi and Feaver's theory emphasizing the importance of Congress's veteran composition in shaping military policymaking may indeed capture a part of the interbranch dynamics over the duration and conduct of military actions. However, the data strongly suggests that, at least since the end of Reconstruction, partisanship has been the dominant factor driv-

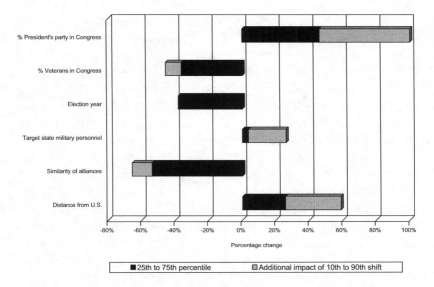

FIGURE 3.7. Predicted effects of variables on conflict duration in U.S. militarized inter-state disputes involving the display of force, use of force, or war, 1877–1945. First differences for the following variables are statistically significant: percentage of seats held by the president's party in Congress, election year, target state military personnel, similarity of alliances.

ing struggle between the legislative and executive branches over conduct of major American military operations abroad.

As in the previous models of all MIDs, models 4, 5, and 6 in table 3.5 find that uses of force initiated during presidential election years are systematically shorter (on average by 40 percent) than those begun in off-years. The robustness of this relationship across specifications and operationalizations of the dependent variable is puzzling in contrast to the absence of any evidence for a relationship between the election cycle and duration of military actions in the post-1945 era. However, it is consistent with prior research by Stoll, who finds that presidents launch fewer military interventions in peacetime presidential election years, and cross-national research by Gaubatz, who finds that democracies are less likely to initiate wars at the end of the electoral cycle throughout the nineteenth and twentieth centuries.[74]

74. See Stoll 1984, Gaubatz 1991. One possible explanation for the declining importance of this dynamic over time is the ultimate defeat of isolationism as a viable political

Turning to the realpolitik determinants of the conduct of military affairs, the directional thrust of each variable remains the same as in the preceding models using all MIDs. Models 4, 5, and 6 all show a positive relationship between the size of a target state's military and the duration of American military actions. Yet, the substantive size of this estimated effect is exceedingly modest. First differences in figure 3.7 show that a 25th to 75th-percentile increase in the size of the target state's military increases a MID's expected duration by only 3 percent.

The models also find a robust negative relationship between the similarity of alliances held by the United States and the target state and a military operation's duration. The all-MIDs models of table 3.4 also yielded negative coefficients across specifications, but none of the three reached conventional levels of statistical significance. When limiting the scope of analysis only to those actions directly involving the display or use of force, the hazard models suggest that the stronger the level of alliance congruence between the United States and its adversaries, the shorter the duration of the American military action. Figure 3.7 demon-

---

force in the aftermath of World War II and the inauguration of the Cold War (Mandelbaum and Schneider 1978, Wildavsky and Oldfield 1991). As late as the end of World War I, American isolationism, an ideology whose pedigree extends back to Washington's Farewell Address of 1796, reemerged and scuttled Woodrow Wilson's plan for active American diplomatic and military engagement in the world. The strength and breadth of isolationist beliefs throughout the American public in the 1930s and early 1940s kept America on the sidelines even as Germany invaded first Czechoslovakia, then Poland, and then France. So great was the perceived political peril of actively joining Britain in the war that even after the Japanese attack at Pearl Harbor, Franklin Roosevelt could not promise Winston Churchill that the United States would also declare war on Japan's ally Germany unless the Nazis first declared war on the United States (Meacham 2003, 128–34). In this political environment it was logical for presidents who employed American military might to limit its scope and duration when the judgment of the voters was soon at hand. In the post–1945 era, the defeat of the Axis powers, followed by the immediate rise of a Cold War with the Soviet Union, largely ended the viability of isolationism. Through Harry Truman's courtship of Senator Arthur Vandenberg, and the forging of bipartisan support for the Truman Doctrine's military and economic engagement of communist expansion around the world, the power of the old guard of the Republican Party led by Senator Robert Taft and other isolationists quickly diminished. On the left, opponents of the active containment of communism and American military interventionism, such as Henry Wallace, were branded reds and politically marginalized. With the end of isolationism, presidents faced fewer ex ante political risks for beginning potentially lengthy military actions in election years than their predecessors who had done so against a background of widespread distrust of active American military engagement in the world.

strates that an increase in the similarity score of U.S. and target state alliances from its 25th to its 75th percentile significantly decreases the expected duration of a military action between the two by more than 50 percent. Finally, as in table 3.4, none of the specifications in table 3.5 finds a significant relationship between duration and the distance between national capitals.

Regardless of whether the hazard models analyze the duration of all MIDs or just those directly involving the use of American military forces, the empirical evidence for a connection between the partisan composition of Congress and the duration of American military actions from 1877 to 1945 is unambiguous across specifications. Strongly consistent with hypothesis 3, the larger the ranks of the president's party in Congress, the longer the military actions he tends to employ in pursuit of his foreign policy goals, even in this earlier epoch of American history.

Congressional Influence over the Scope of Military Action

The final set of analyses tests the central claim of hypothesis 2: that presidents with strong partisan support in Congress should be freer to launch large-scale military ventures than their peers who are confronted by a strong opposition party. Just as the major uses of force from the Blechman and Kaplan series appear qualitatively different in their dynamics from more minor military actions, in the same way not all "major" uses of force are created equal. For example, a brief series of joint exercises to signify improved relations with Morocco in 1982 and the 1991 Persian Gulf War are both coded as major uses of force on the Blechman and Kaplan scale.[75] While members of Congress may have few incentives to concern themselves with the largely invisible former action, they should possess considerable motivations to seek influence over the conduct of the latter.

Examining the list of 122 "major" post–World War II uses of force, three classes of military action encompassing twenty uses of force stand out from the rest: deployments of ground troops to countries or regions

---

75. As a further comparison, the U.S. invasion of the Dominican Republic in 1965 and the dispatch of naval ships to the Mediterranean after the killing of Colonel William Higgins in Lebanon in 1989 are both coded as level 2 uses of force.

where they were not already stationed, sustained uses of American fire-power, and extended military operations involving American air or na-val vessels in hostile zones. For clarity, military actions meeting one or more of these criteria will be designated "principal" uses of force to dis-tinguish them as a subset of the "major" uses of force identified by Blech-man and Kaplan. The twenty principal uses of force with their start and end dates are listed in appendix table 3a.2. Because operations such as these have the greatest potential for significant economic, human, and political costs, ascertaining the degree of congressional influence over the initiation and conduct of these principal military actions is critical to establishing the relevance and importance of domestic institutional con-cerns in presidential military decision-making.

Military actions meeting one or more of these criteria offer presidents the greatest levels of risk and reward. On the positive side of the ledger, because this class of military action is highly salient even to an inatten-tive public, the president stands to reap considerable political rewards and public accolades for his foreign policy crisis management. Yet pre-cisely because of the public engagement and political stakes involved, these types of actions also entail the greatest risks. The often steep mon-etary costs and possibility for American casualties inherent in this type of military action create the potential for a political backlash against the president if the operation falters. Moreover, these tangible costs also af-ford the president's would-be opponents in Congress a window of oppor-tunity to engage the policymaking process and challenge executive dis-cretion in war-making. If such congressional actions can further affect the political and military costs the president stands to incur during the course of a military venture, as the theoretical model of the preceding chapter suggests, then presidents possess strong incentives to anticipate this reaction and adjust the scope of their military response accordingly. As a result, a president should be more wary of launching a highly vis-ible principal use of force when his party's ranks in Congress are weak, even when he has already decided on some form of military response to a foreign crisis.

Data and Methodology

The majority of incidents from the Blechman and Kaplan list either clearly met or failed to meet the principal use-of-force coding criteria. For example, the requirement that any deployment of ground forces be to a region where American troops did not already have a permanent presence included events such as the dispatch of troops to Haiti to restore Jean Bertrand Aristide in 1994, while it excluded actions in which the United States merely bolstered an existing force in the region, such as the addition of troops to South Korea after the 1976 tree-cutting incident that killed three American servicemen. Similarly, the temporal requirement for the use of firepower or exposing American military aircraft and vessels to threats included extended engagements, such as the bombing of Kosovo or the U.S. reflagging of Kuwaiti tankers during the Iran-Iraq War, while it excluded quick surgical strikes such as the attacks on Chinese aircraft in the days following the downing of a British airliner in 1954, or the 1986 bombing of Tripoli.

There were, however, several close calls. U.S. participation in the Sinai peacekeeping force is coded by Zelikow as a level 3 use of force; however, the American contingent was almost indistinguishable in size from that of a similar peacekeeping mission in Macedonia in the 1990s that was coded a level 4 use of force. As a result, this instance was excluded from the list.[76]

Finally, to justify the inclusion of the Berlin airlift and the 1987–88 re-flagging of Kuwaiti oil tankers in the Iran-Iraq War, it was necessary to create a third category: extended military operations of American air or naval vessels in hostile zones. While this category may seem qualitatively different from the classes of events that involve ground troops or sustained firepower, the reasons for its inclusion become clear when the strong potential in each of these cases for triggering a wider conflict and incurring American casualties is considered. With respect to Berlin, the very real possibility of sparking a war between the United States and the Soviet Union, the continual risk to and multiple casualties of Ameri-

76. Replicating the models in table 3.6 including the Sinai peacekeeping force as a principal use of force yields almost identical results. Also with respect to the duration analyses forthcoming in chapter 4, the deployment of the Sinai peacekeeping force is one of the rare instances in which Congress authorized the use of force prior to any military deployment, and there have since been no efforts to curtail American participation. Thus, including it in the analysis would only strengthen the analysis's finding that authorizations and the absence of congressional criticism provide presidents with considerable leeway to continue deployments for long stretches of time.

can airmen, and the enormous cost of the operation all opened the door for a congressional response, and hence the airlift was included in the final set.[77] Similarly, the decision to reflag Kuwaiti tankers and offer them American naval escorts in the middle of the tanker war between Iran and Iraq triggered a firestorm of criticism that the Reagan administration's actions would invariably drag the United States into a war in the Middle East. Additionally, while no Americans were killed in the reflagging operations, several of the escorted tankers did strike mines, and consequently the danger to American naval vessels and personnel was real and acute.[78] For these reasons, both of these actions were included in the final tally.[79]

The subsequent logit models investigate the factors driving the scale of American military operations. Given that the president has decided to respond to a foreign crisis with force, what factors influence the probability that he will dispatch ground troops, use sustained firepower, or send large-scale U.S. air and naval units into hostile zones to achieve his policy goals?

If hypothesis 2 is correct, the partisan composition of Congress should factor strongly into this calculation. To test this proposition, the logit models first include the average partisan composition of Congress. The relationship between the veteran composition of Congress and the scale of American military actions is more complex. While few scholars have studied the scope of American uses of force, Gelpi and Feaver offer

77. Some might also argue that the first two incidents, the American intervention in Manchuria and deployments in Trieste, should be excluded as they stem from the aftermath of World War II. Nevertheless, a review of the two uses of force in contemporary news accounts and *Facts on File* suggests that they were viewed as separate conflicts and involved the United States sending troops into regions it had either never occupied or from which its forces had already withdrawn. Hence, I am inclined to treat them as independent uses of force, albeit begun in the special circumstances arising from the abrupt end of World War II. Excluding them from the analyses in this chapter and the next yields virtually identical results across specifications.

78. Before the re-flagging mission began, thirty-seven American sailors were killed during an Iraqi missile attack on the USS *Stark*.

79. As a robustness check, I reestimated all of the models in table 3.6, but excluded the Berlin airlift and Persian Gulf reflagging from the list of principal uses of force. The results were virtually identical. Additionally, I have reestimated all of the time-varying covariates models run in the next chapter without these two uses of force; all observed relationships remain the same sign and are statistically significant.

theoretical reasons and empirical evidence strongly suggesting that the veteran composition of political elites is an important predictor of the intensity of a use of force.[80] Echoing the "Powell Doctrine," their research on the civil-military gap in opinion on the proper exercise of military force argues that while veterans are less willing to support military responses to foreign crises, once a military action has been decided upon, they prefer decisive large-scale uses of force to achieve the mission's objectives. Gelpi and Feaver argue that the more veterans there are in Congress, the more pressure they will place on the president to use substantial force once the decision to intervene militarily has been made. To test this possibility, the logit model also includes the average percentage of Congress that served in the armed forces.

To insure that any statistical relationship found for Congress's partisan or veteran composition is not merely the result of omitted variable bias, the logit models also include the international and domestic control variables from the previous duration analyses. Theoretical expectations are straightforward. The stronger the target state's military, the less likely the president is to risk triggering a costly escalating military conflict—and consequently the lower the probability of him choosing to use ground troops or sustained firepower to achieve his goals. A target state held to be vital to the national interest, as measured by geographic proximity, similarity in alliance structures, and American foreign aid relationship, should be more likely to elicit a principal military response than a state with less strategic importance. Finally, diversionary-war theories suggest that a president may be more likely to initiate highly visible principal uses of force to bolster his public support when it is low, in an election year, or to distract the public from a sagging economy.

Results and Discussion

The first model in table 3.6 includes only the average percentage of the president's party in Congress measure and a constant. As expected, the bivariate relationship is positive and statistically significant, supporting theoretical expectations that the stronger a president's party is in Con-

---

80. See Gelpi and Feaver 2002. An additional exception is Wang 1996.

TABLE 3.6. **Factors influencing the scale and scope of major uses of force**

Independent variables	(1)	(2)	(3)	(4)
Congress				
% president's party in Congress	4.83**	5.49*	4.96	—
	(2.84)	(4.15)	(4.40)	
Pre-1974 % president's party in Congress	—	—	—	5.54*
				(4.16)
Post-1973 % president's party in Congress	—	—	—	6.48*
				(4.60)
% veterans in Congress	—	—	−7.14	—
			(6.51)	
Target state characteristics				
Military expenditures	—	−1.73**	−1.44**	−1.69**
		(.93)	(.89)	(.92)
Military personnel	—	.35	.23	.35
		(.31)	(.33)	(.31)
Distance from United States	—	−.24	−.17	−.23
		(.20)	(.22)	(.20)
Similarity of alliances		−.21	−.11	−.29
		(.87)	(.90)	(.86)
U.S. economic and military aid	—	.63***	.58***	.64***
		(.24)	(.24)	(.25)
Strategic climate				
Ongoing war	—	−1.74*	−1.17	−1.63*
		(1.21)	(1.26)	(1.22)
Cold War	—	−2.79***	−1.57	−2.48**
		(.84)	(1.69)	(1.14)
Other political variables				
Election year	—	−.32	−.21	−.30
		(.75)	(.80)	(.74)
Presidential approval	—	.02	.02	.02
		(.04)	(.04)	(.04)
Economy				
Unemployment	—	−.27*	−.06	−.32
		(.18)	(.24)	(.25)
Inflation	—	−.12	−.13	−.14
		(.10)	(.11)	(.11)
Constant	−4.07***	−.16	1.59	−.38
	(1.48)	(3.16)	(3.91)	(3.13)
Log-likelihood	−53.12	−36.69	−36.06	−36.61
n	122	122	122	122

Note: * $p < .10$; ** $p < .05$; *** $p < .01$. All significance tests are one-tailed; all models report robust standard errors.

gress, the more political leeway he has to employ large-scale military actions to pursue his foreign policy objectives.[81]

Model 2 adds the target-state, economic, and domestic political control variables, with similar results. The coefficient for the strength of the president's party in Congress remains positive and statistically significant, strengthening confidence that the relationship between congressional partisanship and the scale of a use of force is not spurious.[82]

The expanded logit model also affords strong support for realpolitik contentions that the target state's military strength and importance to the American national interest are powerful predictors of the scale and scope of U.S. military action. Presidents are less likely to risk a major conflict by using large-scale military forces against a target state that invests heavily in its military, while they are more likely to use the most dramatic military actions at their disposal to respond to a crisis in a country toward which the United States has previously demonstrated a strong commitment through economic and military assistance. Also illustrating the importance of international factors in military decision-making, model 2 finds that the strategic climate in which the president acts greatly influences his willingness to launch a principal use of force. Presidents were less willing to deploy ground troops, use sustained firepower, or provocatively endanger American planes or naval vessels in hostile zones during the Cold War, when such actions carried a greater risk of instigating a wider war with the Soviet Union. Similarly, when American forces were already heavily committed in Korea and Vietnam, presidents were less willing to initiate additional major commitments of U.S. forces in other regions of the globe.

With respect to the electoral cycle, presidential approval, and the economy, model 2 offers scant evidence that these factors substantially shape the scale of a military action. While the selection models in table 3.3 suggest that presidents facing high unemployment may be more likely, on average, to respond militarily to an opportunity arising in the

81. Substituting divided government and the logged partisan composition of Congress produces similar results; both coefficients are in the expected direction and statistically significant $p < .05$, one-tailed test.

82. Replicating model 2 with the logged partisan composition of Congress and a divided government dummy produces similar results. However, the coefficient for divided government, though negative as expected, is no longer statistically significant.

international arena, model 2 of table 3.6 suggests that, if anything, such uses of force begun in periods of high unemployment are less likely to involve significant new commitments of ground troops or the sustained use of firepower. Thus, while high unemployment may be an important predictor of the frequency with which presidents use force abroad, on a more normatively assuring note, economic troubles do not make presidents more likely to escalate the scale of these actions by employing ground troops or firepower to distract public attention from domestic woes.[83]

The third logit model adds the veteran composition of Congress measure to test Gelpi and Feaver's hypothesis that once the decision to use force has been made, military veterans in Congress favor and advocate intense, extensive military operations to achieve American objectives. In sharp contrast to Gelpi and Feaver's theoretical claims, the resulting coefficient is actually negative. This relationship suggests that the greater the number of veterans in Congress, the less likely presidents are to launch a principal use of force given that they have already decided on some military response. This result could be evidence not only that veterans frown upon military solutions to foreign crises more than their civilian counterparts in government (though the hazard models in tables 3.1, 3.2 and 3.3 find little evidence that the number of veterans in Congress influences either the initiation or duration of post-1945 military deployments), but also that they may oppose directly placing American ground, air, and naval troops in harm's way even when the president has opted for a military course of action. Alternatively the relationship could merely be spurious; indeed, likelihood ratio tests cannot reject the restricted model 2, excluding the veteran measure, with even 90-percent confidence.

Even in model 3, the coefficients for the partisan composition of Congress, the target state's military expenditures, and the target state's foreign aid receipts remain in the expected directions and of roughly equal magnitudes, though the partisan composition coefficient narrowly misses conventional levels of statistical significance.[84] Coefficients for the on-

---

83. For the role of unemployment as a predictor of the frequency with which presidents use force abroad, see Ostrom and Job 1986, James and Oneal 1991, Fordham 1998a.

84. Because likelihood ratio tests cannot reject the restricted model 2, and because the coefficient for the congressional veteran variable does not accord with prior theoretical expectations, I am inclined to favor the results in model 2 as a more accurate reflection of the relationship between congressional partisanship and the scale of the use of force.

going war, Cold War, and unemployment variables retain their negative sign, but are no longer statistically significant.

As a final robustness check, model 4 replicates the analysis from model 2, but disaggregates the partisan composition of Congress into pre- and post-Vietnam measures. Both coefficients are positive and statistically significant, demonstrating that the strength of the president's allies on Capitol Hill was an important factor in his decisions regarding the scale of American military operations even before the Vietnam War, when the bipartisan consensus in foreign policy supposedly reigned.[85] Wald tests again show no statistically significant difference between the size of the coefficients for pre- and post-Vietnam partisanship.

To illustrate the substantive impact of each variable on the probability that the president launches a principal use of force given that he has already decided on a military course of action, figure 3.8 presents a series of first differences drawn from simulations derived from model 2. The solid portion of each bar represents the change in the predicted probability generated by increasing each variable from its 25th to its 75th percentile, or from zero to one in the case of the three dummies, while holding all other variables constant at their mean, and setting the dichotomous variables equal to zero. The dotted portion reflects the additional impact of a 10th to a 90th percentile shift in each independent variable.

Figure 3.8 demonstrates that, consistent with hypothesis 2, the partisan composition of Congress has a substantial influence on the scale of American military actions. The models suggest that in the years since the fall of the Soviet Union, a shift in the strength of the president's party from 45 to 58 percent increases the probability that the president will use a principal military action to achieve his policy goals by more than 15 percent. A further shift from 41 to 62 percent increases the probability of a principal use of force by almost 30 percent.

Both the importance of a target state to America's national interest and the target state's military capabilities also have some measure of influence over the probability with which presidents exercise extreme military force. A 25th to 75th percentile shift in U.S. foreign aid to the target

85. As in the duration model, replicating the analysis with a 1963/64 cutoff and with the logged partisan composition measure for both cutoff dates yielded virtually identical results. Models including pre- and post-divided government measures yielded the expected negative coefficients, but they failed to reach conventional levels of statistical significance.

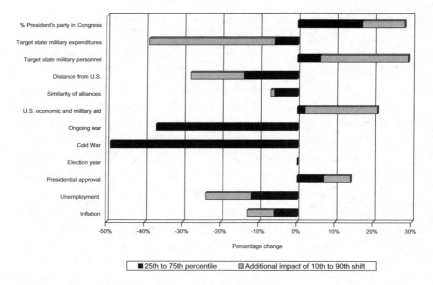

FIGURE 3.8. Predicted effects of variables on the probability of a president responding with a principal use of force. First differences for the following variables are statistically significant: percentage of seats held by the president's party in Congress, target state military expenditures, U.S. economic and military aid, ongoing war, Cold War, unemployment.

state produces a marginal 2-percent increase in the likelihood that the president decides upon a principal use of force. However, a more dramatic increase in aid, from its 10th to 90th percentile, yields a 20-percent increase. Similarly, a 25th to 75th-percentile increase in target state military expenditures generates a modest 5-percent decrease in the likelihood of a principal military response. Only a dramatic increase in target-state military spending from the 10th to the 90th percentile yields a major change in the probability of observing a principal use of force.

The first differences also make clear that the broader political and strategic climate in which the president reacts to world events also significantly influences the scope of his military actions. The perilous geopolitical climate of the Cold War and the strains on military resources applied by contemporary American involvement in Vietnam or Korea decrease the probability of a principal military response by more than 45 and 35 percent respectively. Finally, an increase in unemployment from its 25th to its 75th percentile also decreases the estimated probability of the president choosing to use ground troops or sustained firepower by approximately 15 percent.

Conclusion

Consistent both with theoretical expectations and recent research, the empirical analysis of this chapter provides strong evidence that the partisan composition of Congress influences presidential decisions of whether or not to use force in response to foreign crises. Yet, perhaps even more importantly, the analyses also show that congressional influence in military policymaking does not end once presidents dispatch American armed forces abroad. Across a range of statistical models, this chapter demonstrates that Congress has exerted considerable influence over the scope and duration of major military actions since the end of Reconstruction in 1877. Consistent with theory and hypotheses 2 and 3, throughout this period the partisan composition of Congress emerges as the best predictor of legislative influence over the conduct of military operations. The stronger the president's party in Congress, the less likely he is to face costly institutional challenges to his conduct of foreign policy. Consequently, presidents with strong partisan support in Congress are free to deploy American forces overseas for significantly longer periods to achieve their policy goals than their counterparts who cannot rely on strong support in the legislature. Moreover, the partisan control of Congress also influences the scale of postwar uses of force. Anticipating greater legislative support, presidents with large majorities on Capitol Hill are more likely to use ground troops, employ sustained firepower, or commit American air and naval vessels to hostile areas than presidents with less partisan support in Congress.

These results reinforce and build on the foundations of recent scholarship emphasizing the importance of domestic political institutions in military policymaking. But they also break new ground by moving beyond the almost exclusive focus on the factors influencing the initiation of military actions to explore the dynamics—both domestic and international—that drive presidential conduct of military action. Both the hazard and logit models provide strong evidence that the importance of partisan institutional conflict does not end once American troops are in the field; rather, interbranch politics continue to influence presidential decision-making concerning the scale and duration of overseas deployments.

However, an implicit assumption underlying this and previous research claiming congressional influence over the initiation of the use of force is that Congress can take action during the course of a military venture to raise the costs of continuing it for the executive. To test this assumption and, more specifically, hypotheses 4a and 4b from chapter 2, the next chapter examines the influence of a range of congressional actions launched during the course of a major military venture on its duration.

Appendix to Chapter Three

To model the decision of whether to use force in response to an opportunity arising in the international environment, the first-stage equations of the selection models estimated in table 3.3 included the three congressional partisanship measures and all of the control variables from the models in table 3.1, as well the two exclusionary restrictions discussed in the text: the number of other contemporaneous opportunities to use force at the time of the decision, and the level of democratic governance in the target state. These variables were hypothesized to affect the probability with which the president used force abroad, but not the resulting duration of the military action. However, in these model specifications, only the three congressional partisanship measures and the two exclusionary restrictions had a statistically significant influence on the probability with which the president decided upon a military response.

As a robustness check, each model was reestimated with all of the control variables from Howell and Pevehouse's model of the factors governing the initiation of military action.[1] Several of the background controls overlapped across the two sets of models, including unemployment, inflation, presidential approval, the election year dummy variable, and the two exclusionary restrictions: the number of contemporaneous opportunities and the target state's polity2 democracy score. The Howell and Pevehouse model also included two additional variables capturing the broader international environment at the time of an opportunity to use force: the first summarizes the level of American hegemony (mea-

---

1. For more complete discussions of these model specifications, see Howell and Pevehouse 2007, 62–63, 94–95.

TABLE 3A.1. **Summary statistics for hazard models of major uses of force**

	Mean or median	Standard deviation	Minimum value	Maximum value
Dependent variable				
Duration	272.25	899.43	1	8319
Independent variables				
% president's party in Congress	.50	.08	.35	.68
Divided government	1	.47	0	1
% veterans in Congress	.61	.09	.28	.73
CQ presidential support scores in Congress	.69	.14	.36	.93
Military expenditures (in hundreds of billions of dollars)	.36	.98	0	4.62
Military personnel in millions of dollars	.84	1.38	0	5.19
Distance from United States (in thousands of miles)	5.23	2.21	1.13	10.19
Similarity in alliances	−0.00	.48	−.76	1
U.S. foreign aid to target state (in billions of dollars)	.54	1.28	0	7.77
Ongoing war	0	.34	0	1
Cold War	1	.32	0	1
Election year	0	.41	0	1
Presidential approval	55.92	12.74	26	87
Unemployment	6.15	1.83	.9	10.80
Inflation	4.18	3.77	−.7	18.80

sured as the percentage of the total international military capabilities held by the United States), and the second reports the number of ongoing world disputes not involving the United States. Additional controls included a variable capturing an additional characteristic of the target state—namely, whether it was a major power—as well as four measures of the United States' relationship with the target state: the number of shared alliances between the two states, a military capabilities ratio

TABLE 3A.2. **Twenty post–World War II principal uses of force, with start and end dates**

	Start	End
Chinese Civil War	12/29/1945	6/20/1947
Trieste	5/21/1945	9/15/1947
Berlin airlift	6/26/1948	9/30/1949
Korea	6/26/1950	7/27/1953
Lebanon	7/15/1958	10/25/1958
Thailand	5/17/1962	8/7/1962
Vietnam	8/4/1964	3/29/1973
Dominican Republic	4/28/1965	9/26/1966
Lebanon[1]	8/25/1982	2/26/1984
Grenada	10/25/1983	12/15/1983
Persian Gulf reflagging	7/21/1987	9/25/1988
Panama	12/21/1989	2/13/1990
Persian Gulf War	8/7/1990	5/9/1991
Somalia	12/9/1992	3/25/1994
Haiti	9/19/1994	2/29/1996
Rwanda	7/31/1994	9/30/1994
Bosnia	2/28/1994	12/2/2004
Kosovo	3/24/1999	—
Afghanistan	10/7/2001	—
Iraq	3/19/2003	—

[1] The American use of force in Lebanon consisted of two separate deployments. The first deployment of Marines as part of the multinational force in Lebanon began on August 25, 1982, and concluded on September 10, 1982. On September 29, 1982, the Marines returned to Lebanon and remained there until February 26, 1984.

summarizing the relative military strengths of the United States and the target state, a dummy variable indicating whether the Soviet Union was a direct participant in the crisis or an ally to the target state, and the volume of trade between the United States and the target state. Finally, the Howell and Pevehouse models also accounted for two additional factors: the number of opportunities that the target state had produced in the preceding thirty days, and the number of U.S. troops deployed within the target state's borders at the time the opportunity arose. Results from these alternative model specifications are presented in table 3a.3.[2]

Most importantly, even when using this alternative model specification, I continue to find strong relationships between congressional partisanship and both the probability with which presidents use force in response to an opportunity and the duration of such military ventures once launched. The coefficients for both the average percentage of the president's party in Congress and the logarithmic transformation of this

2. Like the models in table 3.3, these models also follow Howell and Pevehouse by including a series of unreported regional and presidential fixed effects.

TABLE 3A.3. **Selection model replicating Howell and Pevehouse equation for conflict initiation**

Independent variables	(1)	(2)	(3)
Selection model			
% president's party in Congress	1.23**	—	—
	(.63)		
Ln (% president's party in Congress)	—	.56**	—
		(.31)	
Divided government	—	—	−.12
			(.11)
Unemployment	.02	.02	.02
	(.02)	(.02)	(.02)
Inflation	.00	.00	.00
	(.01)	(.01)	(.01)
Presidential approval	−.24	−.23	−.18
	(.31)	(.31)	(.31)
Election year	.06	.06	.04
	(.06)	(.06)	(.06)
Hegemony	−2.70**	−2.94**	−1.81
	(1.68)	(1.66)	(1.94)
World disputes	.00	.00	.00
	(.01)	(.01)	(.01)
Major power	.11	.10	.08
	(.19)	(.18)	(.19)
Target state democracy score	−.24**	−.24**	−.24***
	(.11)	(.11)	(.11)
Alliances	−.20**	−.20**	−.19**
	(.12)	(.12)	(.12)
Trade	−.02	−.02	−.02
	(.02)	(.02)	(.02)
Soviet involvement	−.28***	−.28***	−.28***
	(.11)	(.11)	(.10)
Capability ratio	.01	.01	.01
	(.04)	(.04)	(.04)
Previous opportunities	−.01***	−.01***	−.01***
	(.00)	(.00)	(.00)
Contemporaneous opportunities	−.08***	−.08***	−.08***
	(.04)	(.04)	(.04)
Troops deployed	−.00	−.00	.00
	(.02)	(.02)	(.02)
n	12,984	12,984	12,984
Duration model			
% president's party in Congress	5.68**	—	—
	(2.95)		
Ln (% president's party in Congress)	—	2.63**	—
		(1.37)	
Divided government	—	—	−1.00**
			(.57)
Military personnel	.08	.09	.04
	(.13)	(.13)	(.13)
U.S. economic and military aid	.47***	.45***	.49***
	(.15)	(.14)	(.14)

TABLE 3A.3 *(continued)*

Independent variables	(1)	(2)	(3)
Cold War	−1.95***	−1.80**	−1.70**
	(.81)	(.83)	(.88)
Constant	3.76**	−5.14	5.72
	(1.85)	(5.48)	(.84)
n (uncensored)	64	64	64
Rho (error correlation)	−.10	.25	.25
	(.12)	(.00)	(.00)
Log-likelihood	−733.48	−733.32	−734.07

Note: * $p < .10$; ** $p < .05$; *** $p < .01$. All significance tests are one-tailed; all models report robust standard errors clustered on country-president combinations. The selection models also included fixed effects for each presidential administration, as well as dummy variables for geographic regions.

measure were positive, as expected, and were statistically significant in the selection model.[3] The coefficient for divided government in the first-stage equation is negative, as expected—though, as in Howell and Pevehouse's analyses, it fails to meet conventional levels of statistical significance. In the second-stage duration models, the coefficient for each operationalization of congressional partisanship is in the expected direction and statistically significant.

The control variables in this alternative specification of the duration model behave exactly as they did in the models of table 3.3. Uses of force involving target states with a stronger aid relationship to the United States are longer on average than those involving states of less strategic importance to the United States, and Cold War uses of force are shorter on average than those that began after the collapse of the Soviet Union.

Finally, in the selection model the results both confirm several relationships observed in the models in table 3.3 and reveal a number of new statistically significant findings. Consistent with prior results, each model in table 3a.3 suggests that the president is less likely to respond militarily to an opportunity arising abroad when the target state is a democracy and when the number of contemporaneous opportunities is high. The models also suggest that presidents were less likely to respond militarily to an opportunity in which the Soviet Union was a direct participant

3. Replicating this model using Legislative Potential for Policy Change (LPPC) scores, which take into account both the size of the partisan majority and its ideological cohesion, also yields strong, statistically significant coefficients in both the selection and duration models.

or an ally to the target state, and, interestingly, that they are less likely
to resort to force when the level of American hegemony is high. The latter result may be surprising, but both results are consistent with Howell
and Pevehouse's findings after they adjusted their analysis to account for
potential strategic avoidance behavior by other state actors.[4] In the alternative specifications, we also see the expected relationship between
alliances and the use of force; presidents are significantly less likely to
adopt a military response to a crisis involving a target state with which
the United States shares strong alliance memberships. Finally, contra
Howell and Pevehouse, each specification in table 3a.3 finds a small, statistically significant inverse relationship between the number of previous
opportunities a target state has generated in the preceding month and
the probability that the president responds militarily.[5]

4. See Howell and Pevehouse 2007, 99–102.
5. In their first set of analyses, Howell and Pevehouse find a statistically significant
positive coefficient for this variable. Once they account for strategic avoidance behavior,
however, the coefficient is negative but statistically insignificant.

CHAPTER FOUR

Congressional Actions
and the Conduct of War

Congressional influence over military policymaking does not end once American troops are deployed abroad. Despite the radically transformed political and strategic environment in which Congress and its members must operate once American soldiers are in the field, there is robust empirical evidence that interbranch politics continue to influence the scope and duration of major military ventures. When presidents confronted by a strong partisan opposition in Congress use force, they systematically employ missions of smaller scale and shorter duration than do their peers who are backed by strong co-partisan majorities on Capitol Hill.

Yet while the statistical analyses of the preceding chapter do demonstrate Congress's continued influence over the conduct of major military actions, they share the same fundamental limitation as prior studies that focus exclusively on the dynamics driving the initial decision to intervene. The observed correlations are robust and certainly suggestive of a strong congressional role in shaping the scope and duration of major military actions; however, the evidence in the preceding chapter tells us virtually nothing about the levers through which Congress exerts its influence on presidential strategic decision-making.

As hypothesized in the existing literature on conflict initiation, much of the action may be anticipatory. Presidents facing a strong partisan opposition at the other end of Pennsylvania Avenue may logically expect more trouble from Congress should a military action not proceed exactly according to plan than presidents who are backed by a Congress led by their partisan allies. However, for the anticipatory mechanism to work, Congress must possess the capacity and tools to raise the costs of waging a large-scale, long-duration military action for the president. Congress certainly has the constitutional and statutory power to terminate a military action of which it disapproves. However, in none of the 122 major uses of force analyzed in the preceding chapter did Congress successfully exercise its power of the purse or the War Powers Resolution to compel the president to end a military engagement against his will.

Yet Congress's repeated failure to terminate military engagements legislatively does not mean that Congress and its members are always passive actors at the margins of military policymaking. Consider, for example, the dramatic reversal in congressional engagement over the conduct of the war in Iraq. After authorizing the use of force against Iraq in October of 2002, Congress initially receded from the public eye and remained virtually silent on major questions regarding the war's conduct. However, a series of events—from the kindling of a Sunni insurgency against American forces to the 9/11 Commission report's finding that there was no operational relationship between Saddam Hussein and Al Qaeda, to the inability of team after team of experts to find any evidence of Iraq's alleged weapons of mass destruction—fueled critiques of the administration's decision to invade and its conduct of the war.

In January of 2005, several prominent Democrats in both the House and Senate fired the opening salvoes in what would become an intense interbranch struggle for influence over the war's conduct. In a speech at Johns Hopkins University, Senator Edward Kennedy argued that the war in Iraq had morphed from one of liberation into one of occupation, and warned that the continued presence of American troops in the Middle East was "fanning the flames of violence." Kennedy concluded with a call for an immediate withdrawal of 12,000 troops after the Iraqi elections and a complete withdrawal by early 2006. "There will be more serious violence if we continue our present dangerous and reckless course. It will not be easy to extricate ourselves from Iraq, but we must begin."[1] That same week, California Congressman Lynn Woolsey and thirty-three fellow Democrats introduced H Con Res 35 expressing the sense of Congress that President Bush should develop and implement a plan for withdrawing American forces from Iraq.

While Kennedy's and Woolsey's position initially gained few converts, even among Democrats, June 2005 proved to be a turning point in

1. Stephen Dinan, "Kennedy Says U.S. Presence in Iraq is Fueling Insurgency." *Washington Times*, January 28, 2005, 1.

congressional assertiveness in Iraq policy when a key House Republican, Walter Jones of North Carolina, broke party ranks and co-sponsored a new Democratic initiative, HJ Res 55, which sought to compel President Bush to set a timetable for withdrawing American forces from Iraq. The impact of HJ Res 55 on the political debate surrounding the Iraq War was twofold. First, as a joint resolution, the June initiative, which quickly gained the support of over fifty cosponsors, was the first legally binding measure introduced in Congress that, if passed, would formally compel the president to change the course of Operation Iraqi Freedom. As such, the action was the first genuine institutional challenge to presidential prerogatives in the conduct of operational military affairs in Iraq. It also had significant implications for public opinion, as the visual of Congressman Jones—the noted hawk who had led the fight for "freedom fries" in the House cafeteria to protest France's refusal to support the war—standing on the same podium with Ohio Democrat and leading antiwar crusader Dennis Kucinich to advocate withdrawal sent shock waves through the political arena. Discussions of the measure and Jones's defection filled the nation's op-ed pages while Jones himself appeared on ABC's *This Week* and publicly disclosed the reasons for his dramatic about-face: "When I look at the number of men and women who have been killed, it's almost 1700 now, in addition, close to 12,000 have been severely wounded and I just feel that, you know, the reason of going in for weapons of mass destruction, the ability of the Iraqis to make a nuclear weapon, that's all been proven that it was never there. I voted for the resolution to commit the troops and I feel that we've done about as much as we can do."[2]

By August, Senator Chuck Hagel (R-Nebraska), a decorated combat veteran who had long criticized the administration's rush to war and failure to send adequate forces, publicly compared Iraq to Vietnam and declared the need for an exit strategy. Hagel warned, "Now we're locked into a bogged down problem, not . . . dissimilar to where we were in Vietnam. The longer we stay, the more problems we're going to have . . . the longer we stay there, the more similarities are going to come together."[3] Less than a year after securing his reelection, in large part due to his perceived steadfastness and resolve in Iraq and the war on terror, Presi-

2. Walter Jones, ABC News, *This Week with George Stephanopoulos*, June 12, 2005.
3. Chuck Hagel, ABC News, *This Week with George Stephanopoulos*, August 21, 2005.

dent Bush began to face increasingly assertive challenges to his policies in Congress, even from members of his own party.

These rising tensions came to a head in November when, in the span of a single week, Democrats in both the House and Senate attempted to embarrass the president through legislation calling for withdrawal from Iraq. Senate Democrats struck first by introducing an amendment to a Department of Defense authorization bill calling on the president to reduce American troop levels in Iraq gradually. Two days later, noted Democratic hawk and Vietnam veteran John Murtha of Pennsylvania publicly chastised the administration's conduct of the war as "a failed policy wrapped in illusion" and introduced another binding resolution, HJ Res 73, calling for the immediate withdrawal of American forces from Iraq within six months.[4] While both resolutions were soundly defeated, they set the stage for even more aggressive legislative and investigatory attacks on Bush's war policies when the Democrats seized the reins of the 110th Congress in 2007.

The concluding chapter discusses these and other developments in the Iraq War and their consequences for the conduct of the American military venture in the Middle East in more detail. However, to assess more generally the effect of such actions on the president's conduct of military operations, a large-n approach is needed. Since the United States emerged as a superpower in the wake of World War II, have these sorts of actions—introducing and voting on high-profile legislative initiatives to curtail the scope and duration of a military action, holding committee investigations into alleged executive misconduct of a war, and making rhetorical appeals in the public sphere advocating a change in course— had any effect on the duration of major military engagements?

Chapter 2 proposed two mechanisms through which such congressional actions could have real ramifications for presidents' decision-making calculus. First, these actions may dramatically affect the political costs of staying the course for the president. Legislative initiatives authorizing military action, even ex post facto, and vocal support for the president's military policies provide the White House considerable leeway and po-

---

4. After a heated exchange on the House floor, Republicans introduced H Res 571, expressing the sense of the chamber favoring immediate withdrawal from Iraq, to try to force Democrats to take a stand supporting a radical shift in policy. The measure was soundly defeated, 3–403, though in subsequent months more Democrats shifted toward the Murtha position.

litical cover when prosecuting military operations. Conversely, formal debates and floor votes on legislative initiatives to curtail an ongoing operation, high-profile congressional hearings investigating the administration's conduct of a war, and public calls from members for a change in course withdraw political cover and can significantly raise the political costs of staying the course for the president.

Such actions may also affect the strategic costs of continuing the military status quo on the ground through the signals they send to foreign actors. Legislative authorizations and vocal expressions of congressional support for the administration's policies signal American unity and resolve, and may dissuade the target state from escalating its resistance in the hopes of outlasting the domestic political will to fight in Washington. This in turn may lower the costs in the field of continuing the administration's chosen course of action. By contrast, legislative initiatives to curtail a use of force, investigatory oversight hearings, and public calls for a change in course may embolden the target state and raise the military costs of staying the course.

To test empirically whether these actions can affect the conduct of major military ventures as proposed in hypotheses 4a and 4b (see table 2.1), this chapter analyzes the influence of such congressional maneuvers on the duration of the twenty most intense military ventures of the post-1945 era. Employing hazard models that allow the values of the explanatory variables to change over time, the analysis demonstrates that congressional actions during the course of each conflict significantly influenced the probability of a military engagement ending at a given moment in time.

Data and Methodology

To explore how developments in Congress and in the overarching political and strategic environment more generally influence the duration of American military ventures, this chapter focuses on the twenty principal uses of force since World War II identified in chapter 3—those involving deployments of ground troops to countries or regions where they were not already stationed, the sustained use of firepower, or significant commitments of American air or naval vessels to hostile zones. The duration analysis in chapter 3 only examined the impact of initial conditions on a use of force's expected duration. These static models found evidence of a strong link between the partisan composition of Congress and the length of American military engagements, but they offered little insight into the means through which Congress as an institution or individual members of Congress raised or lowered the costs of an extended foreign deployment for the president. This chapter employs weibull hazard models with time-varying covariates to investigate how the hazard rate for each military action changes as new developments arise on the ground and political actors grapple with these changes and each other in the public sphere.[5] As in chapter 3, to ease interpretation of the effects various factors have on duration, the models report coefficients in the accelerated-failure time metric, which allows us to model the expected time to failure for each conflict at any given moment.[6]

The dependent variable comprises the twenty principal uses of force since World War II and the unit of analysis is the conflict-month. Because these "principal" uses of force were the most publicly and politically salient of postwar American military ventures, they provide the greatest opportunities for assessing the impact of the two proposed mechanisms of congressional influence on the president's conduct of military affairs.

Explanatory Variables

Because theory suggests that Congress can raise or lower the political and strategic costs of continuing a chosen military course for the president through a variety of formal and informal actions, the duration models begin by including measures of formal legislative activity, investigative congressional oversight, and the informal maneuverings of individual members of Congress in the public sphere.

Formal Legislative Actions

Congressional Quarterly and Congressional Research Service publications reveal a host of successful and attempted legislative initiatives to

---

5. To allow the value of the explanatory variables to change over the course of each military action, the time-varying covariates (TVC) weibull model makes a small adjustment. It assumes the same baseline hazard: $h_o(t) = pt^{p-1}$. However, the vector of explanatory variables X now varies with time yielding: $h(t|x(t)) = pt^{p-1}\exp(X(t)\beta)$.

6. The expected duration at time t given the observed values of the covariates is the scaling parameter multiplied by the gamma distribution of $1/(p+1)$ (Greene 2003): $E[t|x_i(t)] = \exp(X_i(t)\beta) * \Gamma(1/p+1)$.

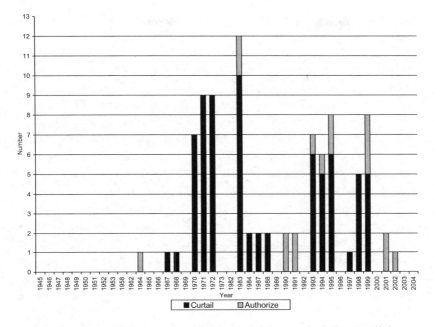

FIGURE 4.1. Frequency of congressional legislative actions to authorize or curtail the use of force

influence the conduct of the twenty principal presidential uses of force in the postwar era.[7] The frequency with which Congress considered legislation to authorize or curtail a use of force is presented in figure 4.1.[8]

Consistent with accounts of congressional deference and the Cold War consensus, figure 4.1 shows few direct legislative challenges to the president's conduct of military affairs in the seven pre-Vietnam principal uses of force. For example, in the wake of American casualties and a lack of Nationalist success against Chinese communist insurgents in Manchuria, Congress considered a resolution (H Res 80) asking Secretary of State George C. Marshall for information on the timetable for withdrawal of U.S. forces, but took no further action. Perhaps more emblematic of congressional wariness to challenge the president formally, Democratic Speaker Sam Rayburn in 1958 actually refused to recognize any

7. For example, see Brown 2003.

8. Figures 4.1 and 4.2 include only the years in which one or more principal use of force was ongoing, not every year from 1945 to 2004.

member of the House intending to speak against President Eisenhower's deployment of U.S. Marines to Lebanon.[9] If Congress influenced the duration of pre-Vietnam interventions—which the static duration models of the preceding chapter strongly suggest it did—such influence was likely exerted through other means.[10]

The Vietnam War proved to be a watershed in Congress's willingness to challenge legislatively the president's preeminence in foreign affairs. With increasing U.S. engagement in Vietnam, Congress began to assert itself more forcefully in foreign policy. The protracted conflict prompted numerous congressional attempts to curtail military operations in Southeast Asia, including enacted legislation banning funding for American ground troops in Cambodia and Laos. This wave of congressional assertiveness continued even after the fall of Saigon. Of the nine principal uses of force occurring between the end of the Vietnam War and the conclusion of President Bill Clinton's first term, members of Congress formally attempted to curtail the use of force on eight occasions. Only President George H. W. Bush's swift invasion of Panama escaped efforts at congressional intervention.

The majority of the actions to curtail the use of force were launched in periods of divided government; however, opposition party control of even one chamber was not a necessary condition for legislative challenges to presidential discretion to occur. Although scholars have long documented the majority party's capacity to manipulate procedural rules to control the legislative agenda, the myriad of appropriations bills and other legislation not often subject to restricted or closed rules afford opportunities for the minority to attach provisions constraining military action as amendments.[11] Indeed, virtually every effort to rein in presidential discretion in military affairs introduced in periods of unified government was done via amendment, not via stand-alone legislation. The lone exceptions were three resolutions attacking the Clinton administration's policies in Haiti in the run-up to the 1994 midterm election when

9. *CQ Weekly*, 1958, 930.

10. There are, however, several prominent examples of legislative initiatives to curtail ongoing military actions in the pre–World War II era. This list includes efforts to cut off funding for U.S. troops in Russia during World War I and in Nicaragua in the 1920s. See Johnson 1995.

11. Inter alia, Aldrich and Rohde 1998, 2001; Cox and McCubbins 1993, 2005; Den Hartog and Monroe 2008.

Democratic lawmakers, eager to distance themselves from an unpopular president, allowed Republicans to bring their measures to the floor.[12]

While the number and types of formal actions Congress has undertaken to exert its influence over major military operations vary considerably across cases, the descriptive data in figure 4.1 show unambiguously that congressional actions in military affairs in the post-Vietnam era were not rare, isolated events.

The time-varying covariates (TVC) models below include measures of two classes of formal legislative activity: legislative authorizations to use force and efforts to curtail an ongoing military action. The first measure is a dummy variable denoting whether Congress had previously taken steps to authorize a foreign deployment. It is coded one beginning in the month during which a majority of one chamber of Congress first authorized the use of force; the variable is coded one from this month to the end of the conflict and zero for all months for which there was no prior authorization. Presumably, congressional authorizations, even if passed by a single chamber, provide presidents with at least a modicum of political cover to sustain an extended engagement of military resources abroad. In the expected survival time framework, the coefficient for this authorization variable should be positive, as the estimated duration of the use of force should be larger if at least one chamber of Congress has authorized the action.

The models also investigate the effect of legislative actions to curtail presidential discretion in the conduct of military affairs on a venture's expected duration. However, not all legislative actions to curtail an ongoing operation have equal legal or political weight. To capture some of this variance in the types of actions members introduce, the analysis divides all congressional challenges into two categories based on whether or not the demands they place on the president are legally binding. Concurrent resolutions or provisions expressing the sense of Congress are primarily vehicles for position taking and public posturing, not substantive assertions of congressional influence over the conduct of military

12. The limited yet significant number of challenges to the president, even in periods of unified government, dovetails with the results of the preceding chapter, suggesting that when estimated in the same model, the average percentage of the president's party in Congress, not divided government, is the best predictor of the duration of a use of force. Formal control of a chamber is not vital to checking the president, though it certainly helps. Rather, what is essential is that the minority party in Congress be strong and cohesive enough for its attacks on the president to have political bite.

affairs. Through these nonbinding actions, the president's opponents in Congress can criticize the executive's deployment of troops, call for their return home, or saddle the president with reporting and other requirements while avoiding the costs associated with legally binding actions, such as exposing members to countercharges of failing to support the troops in the field or triggering the interbranch constitutional struggle inevitably touched off by an effort to invoke the War Powers Resolution.

These open expressions of congressional criticism may have some effect on raising the political costs to the president. However, because such actions fail to carry any concrete consequences for the president and hence are often seen as hollow rhetoric, their impact should be limited. Nonbinding resolutions do not put new alternatives to the administration's policy onto the national agenda, and therefore they do not represent serious institutional challenges to the president's preeminence in military affairs. Similarly, the signals nonbinding actions send to foreign actors are also ambiguous. On the one hand, such actions are publicly visible signs of congressional unease over the administration's conduct of a use of force; on the other, they demonstrate Congress's unwillingness to use the formal legislative means at its disposal to rein in presidential conduct of which it does not approve. Consequently, the effects of nonbinding actions to curtail a conflict should be limited, if they have any influence at all.

Conversely, binding legislative actions to cut off funding for an operation, invoke the War Powers Resolution, or mandate a timetable for withdrawal have greater repercussions for the president and are more serious challenges to perceived presidential prerogatives as commander in chief.[13] They clearly signal to the president that he is perilously close to the limits of what Congress will accept, and they encourage him to adjust his conduct of military affairs accordingly to avoid a potentially costly showdown with the legislature. Legally binding congressional

13. As early as 1917, legal scholar Edward Corwin emphasized the difference between legally binding and nonbinding legislative constraints on presidential foreign policy power. When describing President Ulysses S. Grant's resentment of congressional resolutions expressing the legislature's beliefs on what the proper foreign policy of the United States should be with respect to French aggressions in Mexico, Corwin wrote: "His attitude is probably accounted for by the fact that the resolutions were joint (i.e., binding) resolutions. This fact brought before him, he evidently believed, the question whether the national legislature had any legislative power in the premises, and this he very warrantably denied" (1970 [1917], 45).

challenges to presidential authority remove any political cover the president may have previously enjoyed from congressional silence. Such actions also send unambiguous signals of American disunity to the targets of a military venture. They encourage the target state to continue to resist and thereby raise the tangible costs of continued military action. Because binding actions represent genuine institutional challenges to presidential power over the conduct of military operations, the coefficient on this variable is expected to be strongly negative, as binding actions to constrain the executive should decrease the expected duration of the use of force.[14]

Two remaining difficulties in operationalizing the congressional action variables are deciding upon the proper threshold of support an action must attain to qualify as a viable challenge to the president's conduct of military affairs, and determining how long the effects of such an action are expected to last. For example, should all proposed legislative actions, even those that fail to receive committee hearings, be included as formal legislative challenges to presidential discretion, or should only those meeting certain criteria be included? Treading a narrow middle ground between being too exclusive and too inclusive, both the binding and nonbinding variables include all legislative actions to curtail the use of force that came to the floor for a vote and received the support of at least 40 percent of one chamber of Congress. This operationalization is narrow enough to exclude trivial actions that either never made it to the floor or garnered but a modicum of support among either chamber, while not being so exclusive as to drop serious challenges to the president that gained the support of a substantial proportion of one or both chambers of Congress, but failed to curry a majority vote in either.[15] Alternatively, the critical factor could be the public visibility of a legislative challenge, not the raw level of support it received in the roll call. To account for this, the models include an alternative measure of the number

14. As an example of the greater political consequence and newsworthiness of a binding action, contrast the vehement presidential response to, and deluge of media coverage of, HJ Res 55, which would have compelled the president to set a fixed timetable for withdrawal from Iraq, with the more subdued administration and press reaction to nonbinding initiatives expressing similar sentiments, such as H Con Res 35.

15. To insure that any findings are not an artifact of the 40-percent threshold, other thresholds for floor support, including none at all, were also tested in the models with virtually identical results.

of front-page *New York Times* articles mentioning a congressional action to curtail the use of force in a given period.[16]

Finally, we must decide how long the effects of such actions are expected to last. Clearly it is not reasonable to expect congressional efforts to curtail the use of force in Bosnia in 1995 to still influence the hazard rate of the deployment in 2004. Nor does the impact of even an unsuccessful challenge to presidential discretion in directing military policy dissipate within a month. As a compromise, the models incorporate measures for each observation of the number of binding and nonbinding legislative actions to curtail a given use of force in the past year.[17] The expectation, again, is that binding actions that received at least 40-percent support in one chamber of Congress should decrease a conflict's duration (i.e., increase the hazard rate), while nonbinding actions should have no systematic effect.

Investigative Oversight

While legislative initiatives to authorize or curtail the use of force may be the most dramatic means at Congress's disposal to influence presidential conduct of major military actions, they are not the only munitions in the legislature's strategic arsenal. Another powerful way in which Congress can seek to shape the political debate surrounding military policymaking and influence the scope and duration of the use of force is through its capacity to launch high-profile investigations into the executive branch's conduct of military affairs.[18]

To construct a measure of congressional investigatory activity over time throughout each principal use of force, I first used Congressional Information Service publications to identify all 484 hearings related to the military engagements. However, much congressional oversight is merely routine and unlikely to have any effect on the conduct of military operations. Thus, I made a second sweep through the hearing data and examined each hearing's summary and testimony-specific descriptions

16. The *Times* rarely distinguished between binding and nonbinding actions; therefore, the mention of any congressional initiative to constrain the president's conduct of foreign affairs was coded in the construction of this measure.

17. Biannual counts were also used with virtually identical results.

18. For research on the forces driving high-profile investigations and their political ramifications, see Mayhew 1991; Kriner and Schwartz 2008; Fowler and Hill 2006; Ginsberg and Shefter 1995, 2003; Aberbach 1990, 2002; Parker and Dull 2009.

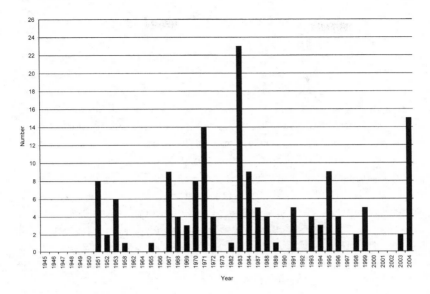

FIGURE 4.2. Frequency of investigative hearings on the use of force

to identify only those hearings containing specific allegations of executive misconduct or overtly critical attacks on the administration's handling of military operations. This second sweep identified 152 investigatory oversight hearings on the twenty principal uses of force. Figure 4.2 summarizes the frequency of these congressional inquests into major ongoing military operations during the post–World War II era.[19]

While formal legislative challenges to presidential conduct of major military operations only emerged toward the end of the war in Vietnam, before the 1970s congressional opponents of administration policies were considerably more aggressive in the committee room. The Korean War prompted a number of highly critical investigations into President Truman's conduct of the conflict, including the high-profile inquest into his firing of commanding General Douglas MacArthur and alleged strategic blunders that resulted in Chinese intervention and the interminable stalemate on the ground.

19. Each "hearing" given a unique identification number by CIS could unfold over a number of days. For example, from May 9 to 11, 1972, the Senate Foreign Relations Committee held a hearing entitled "Causes, Origins, and Lessons of the Vietnam War," CIS hearing number 73-S381-3. Employing an alternative measure of investigatory activity weighting each hearing by its number of days yields similar results.

Less than fifteen years later, Senator William Fulbright (D-Arkansas) used the power of the gavel to open a series of executive-session hearings on the Johnson administration's 1965 invasion of the Dominican Republic.[20] Fulbright avoided blaming Johnson directly for alleged policy missteps, and instead decried faulty advice given to the president. Nevertheless, the Senate Foreign Relations Committee's inquiry and Fulbright's own words foreshadowed the age of increased open interbranch conflict over military policy that was to come: "The concept of the president being permitted to do anything he likes in the field of foreign relations is . . . a misguided concept. It is true that [the president] has the power . . . [but] once that power has been exercised by the president, it is our duty to call him to account."[21] Since the Korean conflict, every principal use of force save one—President Clinton's modest dispatch of troops for Rwandan relief efforts—has attracted at least some investigatory inquiries from Congress, though as figure 4.2 clearly demonstrates, the intensity of this scrutiny has varied considerably from case to case.

By holding high-profile investigatory hearings into the president's conduct of military operations, Congress can expose administration failings in the conduct of military operations and raise the political costs for the president of staying the course. Moreover, the public nature of these hearings and the media spectacle that often ensues allows members to send important signals of domestic dissension to foreign actors. Accordingly, the expectation is that as congressional investigatory activity in the last year grows, the expected duration of a major military action will decrease.[22]

Congressional Activity in the Media

A final, more informal means through which Congress can affect the political and strategic costs of continuing a military action for the president is through individual members' statements and policy recommendations

20. Executive sessions are difficult to code because they are given but a single CIS number and are thus counted as a single hearing. Replacing the Fulbright hearings with a higher value on the critical hearings measure would only strengthen the statistical results finding a strong impact for investigatory oversight on the duration of major military actions.

21. *CQ Weekly*, September 30, 1965, 2058.

22. As with the legislative initiatives measures, reestimating all models with biannual instead of annual counts yielded similar results.

in the public sphere. Vocal support for or opposition to the president's policies in the mass media can both mold public opinion and, more generally, raise or lower the political pressures on the White House to change course and adjust its conduct of military operations. Congressional actions can also send signals of American unity or resolve to foreign actors which influence the military costs of staying the course. To gauge members' rhetoric on military issues as reported in the mass media, I conducted an extensive content analysis of *New York Times* coverage for each of the twenty postwar principal uses of force.[23]

Because only the most prominent news coverage is likely to influence mass public opinion, this analysis focuses exclusively on front-page articles. For each of the twenty principal uses of force except Vietnam and Korea, I began by downloading from the Proquest Research Library service every front-page article mentioning the target country or region of each military action. This initial search returned over 5,200 articles. I then made a first sweep through the articles to exclude those unrelated to military operations. The remaining 3,225 were then content-coded for mentions of legislative action to authorize or curtail the use of force; reports of congressional investigations into the administration's handling of a military venture; public evaluations of the conduct of military action by the administration, members of Congress, and other domestic and international political actors; and a number of developments on the ground that chart the course of each operation as it progressed.[24]

23. Although many studies of the media's impact on public opinion focus on the elite print and network broadcasting media, the proliferation of alternative news sources to traditional stalwarts such as the *Times* brings into question the extent of the influence that it and similar sources have on the general public. However, recent research suggests that such concerns are probably overstated. Graber (1989), Mermin (1999), and others contend that even in the age of new media, elite media including the *Times* continue to be an influential source of news for most Americans. More importantly, a study of coverage of the lead-up to the Iraq War in local and national television broadcasts and in the *New York Times* shows that all three sources seem to adhere to the basic tenets of the indexing framework and pay considerable attention to the opinions and policy proscriptions of members of Congress (Howell and Pevehouse 2007). If all news sources index their coverage of military actions to the level of debate in Washington, particularly within Congress, then the balance of congressional support for and against the president and his policies reported in the *Times* should be largely representative of media coverage more generally.

24. The sheer volume of news coverage of the Vietnam and Korean wars precluded a similar approach for these two conflicts. Instead, I focused only on those articles containing congressional statements on American military involvement. Adjusting the search pro-

TABLE 4.1. **Percentage of front-page *New York Times* articles on principal uses of force 1945–2004 reporting policy recommendations of various actors**

Political actors	Percentage of stories
President	37
Administration officials	47
Congress	27
Members of Congress	22
Ex-administration officials	2
Presidential candidates	6
Congressional candidates	1
Military commanders	28

For public congressional policy recommendations to have a significant influence on presidential conduct of a use of force, members must be active enough in the public sphere, and their statements portrayed frequently enough in the mass media, to seep into the popular consciousness. Fortunately, a survey of front-page *Times* coverage summarized in table 4.1 alleviates such concerns. Almost a third of the 3,225 articles for the eighteen non-Korea and non-Vietnam uses of force referenced one or more political actors offering a recommendation for the future conduct of an ongoing military action. Consistent with research by Robert Entman, the White House is indeed the most prominent source of policy judgments and arguments reported in the mass media.[25] Presidential statements on the proper course of military affairs appeared in 37 percent of the 975 articles offering a recommendation for the conduct of an operation, while almost half (47 percent) featured the opinion of an administration official. However, the opinions of Congress also receive substantial media attention. More than a quarter of the articles reported the views of Congress, and 22 percent contained policy recommendations specifically attributed to individual members. While members of Congress received slightly less attention than the president, they still garnered considerably more attention than any other political actors received, including officials from previous administrations and candidates for national office, and their policy proscriptions achieved a level of sa-

---

tocols to capture only articles potentially containing congressional actions or evaluation of the conflicts yielded 2,030 articles, which were then content-coded for public congressional statements on the military presence and course of each action as well as for mentions of legislative actions to authorize or curtail the use of force.

25. Entman (2004).

lience on par with the recommendations of military commanders in the Pentagon and in the field.[26]

This cursory glance at *New York Times* coverage of the twenty principal postwar uses of force unambiguously supports previous research asserting Congress's privileged position as the chief source of foreign policy positions outside of the White House. However, public congressional comments on the exercise of force can take many forms. For example, in the wake of a military action members of Congress frequently weigh in on whether the initial decision to intervene militarily was warranted. However, the effects of such statements on public opinion concerning the proper conduct of an ongoing deployment may be limited.[27] Expressions of support for the decision to intervene do not necessarily connote support for an extended deployment. Similarly, public condemnations of a president's rush to use force alone may generate little pressure for withdrawal. Indeed, members frequently temper their opposition to a military venture by admitting that because a commitment has been made, the troops cannot simply be withdrawn. For years this was the pattern of most Democratic congressional statements on the war in Iraq. While they criticized the premises on which President Bush had misled the country into war, congressional Democrats readily acknowledged that American forces could not cut and run from the Middle East, even in the face of mounting costs in lives and treasure. Even as of August 2007, a number of Democrats continued to espouse this logic in their public pronouncements; these public statements in turn undercut efforts by the Democratic leadership to mobilize the party caucus behind legislative initiatives to mandate a timetable for withdrawal.[28]

26. Although comparable figures cannot be compiled for Vietnam and Korea, the policy recommendations of Congress also received substantial media attention in the two largest conflicts of the post–World War II era. More than 330 front-page articles reported congressional preferences for escalation, the status quo, deescalation, or withdrawal from Korea and Vietnam, and 292 articles attributed policy recommendations to individual members of Congress.

27. Including measures of statements of support for or opposition to the initial decision to intervene militarily from the president's partisan supporters and adversaries in the subsequent TVC models (particularly table 4.2, model 4) yields variable results that are highly sensitive to specification.

28. See, for example, the statements of Brian Baird (D-Washington), Tim Mahoney (D-Florida) and Jerry McNerney (D-California), all of whom returned from a 2007 trip to Baghdad affirming the need to maintain the surge and continue the American military presence in Iraq, despite their belief that the initial decision to intervene had been a mis-

Of far greater potential import are explicit congressional policy recommendations for the conduct of an ongoing military venture. When
members of Congress publicly acknowledge that the troops must stay,
even if they decry the initial decision to intervene, they provide the
president with political cover to continue a deployment. Moreover, the
absence of official voices articulating policy alternatives largely keeps
policy options opposed to the president's default position off the political agenda. Public calls for de-escalation or withdrawal, however, should
rally public opinion against the president and prompt a national debate
on the proper course of military affairs. In the face of open congressional dissension, the president must respond to pressures to terminate military actions more expeditiously than he would in the absence of vocal
congressional challenges.

To test for the importance of public congressional policy proscriptions
on the duration of postwar military ventures, I content-coded each front-
page *New York Times* article for any statement or statements in which
members of Congress advocated escalating American military involvement, maintaining the status quo, de-escalating the American presence,
or withdrawing altogether from the region. The frequency with which
members made such policy recommendations reported in the mass media is summarized in figure 4.3.[29]

Finally, past scholarship emphasizes that the identity of the actor
making the policy recommendation may be critically important in determining the credibility of the signal it sends and its influence on public opinion. Indeed, Howell and Kriner's experimental results discussed
in chapter 2 strongly suggested that the influence of a congressional cue
supporting or opposing the president's military policies critically de-
pended on both the content of the message and the partisan identity of
the sender. Consistent with a lengthy literature on the greater influence
of "costly" signals (i.e., those that clearly conflict with the sender's immediate political self-interest), Howell and Kriner found that experimental
cues supporting President Bush's policies from congressional Democrats

---

take. Jonathan Weisman, "Senator Calls for Maliki's Ouster." *Washington Post*, August 21,
2007, A1.

29. Articles that reported conflicting views from members of a single party are included in both the escalate/status quo and de-escalate/withdraw tallies.

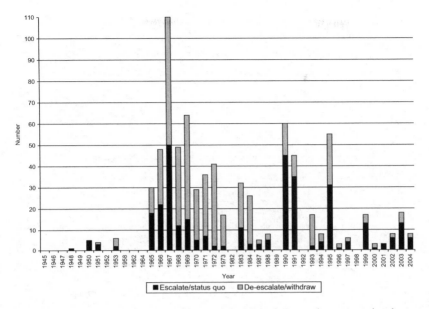

FIGURE 4.3. Frequency of front-page *New York Times* stories reporting congressional recommendations concerning the conduct of a use of force

and cues opposing Bush from congressional Republicans had the largest and most consistent effects on public opinion.[30]

To assess the impact of congressional policy statements in the public sphere on the duration of military deployments, the TVC models include monthly measures of both congressional parties' public proposals for a venture's conduct. As with formal legislative actions to curtail a use of force, the influence of such statements is finite; year-old congressional

30. Howell and Kriner 2007, Kriner and Howell n.d. For additional observational evidence on the importance of costly signals in driving support for war, see Baum and Groeling 2008. For source effects and public opinion, see Asch 1987 [1952]; Koeseke and Crano 1968; Dutton 1973; Eagly, Wood, and Chaiken 1978; Lupia and McCubbins 1998; Sniderman, Brody, and Tetlock 1991; Tomz and Sniderman 2004; Baum 2002; Baum and Groeling 2005. For the importance of costly signals in the international context, see Fearon 1994; Schultz 1998, 1999, 2001; Auerswald 2000. Such costly signals may also introduce conflicting considerations into different partisan groups' support for the president's policies. Prior research has shown that conflicting considerations may generate greater ambivalence or uncertainty (Alvarez and Brehm 1995, 2002; Gronke and Brehm 2002) that can produce shifts in opinion, particularly in matters of foreign policy (Kriner 2006).

calls for withdrawal are unlikely to weigh heavily on a president's mind
in the absence of continued criticism of his policies. To account for this,
the TVC models include six-month moving average measures of congressional and other actors' judgments and recommendations for the conduct of each use of force.[31]

Political, Military and Economic Controls

A major advantage of the time-varying models is that they afford an opportunity to control for changes in the political and strategic environment that develop over the course of a military operation. Accordingly,
the TVC models begin by including monthly and annual measures for
many of the political and military control variables included in the non-
TVC duration models of the preceding chapter. On the international side
of the equation, as the target state's military strength in dollars spent
and men in uniform increases or decreases over time, the duration of the
American military presence may also vary accordingly.[32] Weaker target
states may require shorter deployments of ground troops or uses of firepower than operations targeted at more formidable military opponents.
Similarly, the strategic environment created by the Cold War or the extended American involvement in Korea or Vietnam may also influence
the duration of an American military action. Confronted with the exigencies of perceived Soviet threats and preexisting troop commitments,
presidents in these periods may face increased incentives to terminate
military actions expeditiously.

The TVC models also enable a more nuanced test of diversionary-war
theories by examining how changes in the domestic political situation
over the course of an operation—not just the political conditions at a
conflict's outset—influence the conduct of military action. For example,
the electoral cycle may factor into presidential decisions about the conduct of a use of force. Scholars have theorized that presidents may initiate uses of force in election years to give themselves and their party the
advantage of a popular rally around the flag in support of a military ven-

31. All models were also reestimated using quarterly measures with very similar
results.

32. The relationship between the target state's military capacity and the duration of an
American military operation is likely endogenous; however, the models find no statistically
significant relationship.

ture.[33] Yet presidents may also try to end these military actions before Election Day to reap the political benefits of proclaiming mission accomplished and bringing the troops home. To test for this possibility, the models also include a dummy variable for presidential election years.

Many diversionary-war theories also emphasize presidential desire to distract public attention from a flagging economy when launching military actions abroad.[34] By extension, presidents should be unlikely to end a military action until economic conditions have rebounded to politically acceptable levels. To control for this possibility, the models include an additive misery index of monthly unemployment and inflation figures obtained from the Bureau of Labor Statistics. If diversionary-war theories are correct, the higher the misery index, the longer the duration of a use of force.

Conflict Developments

An acknowledged weakness of the duration models presented in the previous chapter was their inability to control for developments on the ground as each conflict progressed. Conditions in the field, not congressional actions or criticism in Washington, may solely determine the length of military operations. If members of Congress only act to raise the political costs of continuing military action for the president in the wake of American casualties or deteriorating conditions in the target country, the legislature may not have any independent role in influencing presidential decisions. Because the preceding hazard models predicted duration using only initial conditions, they could not test these competing possibilities.[35] However, by including monthly and cumulative measures of American casualties, the TVC models can assess whether Congress has an influence on the duration of military actions independent of the necessities dictated by changes in the military situation on the ground.

Theoretically, casualties could affect the presidential decision to ter-

33. Stoll 1984, Gaubatz 1991.

34. James and Oneal 1991, Fordham 1998b, Russett 1990, Richards et al. 1993, Levy 1989, Levy and Vakili 1992.

35. However, for the positive, statistically significant coefficients for the partisan composition of Congress to be merely the products of omitted variable bias, partisanship in Congress and combat casualties or other developments on the ground would have to be correlated. There is little reason to expect this to be the case.

minate a use of force in at least two ways. First, as hypothesized by John Mueller and others, the cumulative effect of casualties may be what matters most; as American deaths mount, so too does the political pressure on the president to bring the troops home.[36] Alternatively, what may be more important to the president when deciding whether or not to continue a use of force at time t is not the number of casualties sustained over the entire course of the operation, but only those inflicted on American forces in recent months.[37] To account for these contrasting possibilities, the TVC models include both a measure of cumulative American casualties in each operation up to the month at hand and a measure of U.S. casualties in the last quarter.[38]

Public Opinion

Finally, the time-varying models alleviate additional concerns about the independence of any observed effects for Congress's formal and informal actions on duration by also controling for changes in public support for both the president and the military operation itself throughout each conflict. A number of prior studies strongly suggest that actions in Congress and public opinion are inextricably linked. When deciding whether and how to respond to presidential military policies, members of Congress surely look to the state of public opinion, and in turn the public updates its assessments of a military action and of the commander in chief in light of maneuverings in Congress. Untangling the full complexities of this relationship is beyond the scope of this analysis. However, by including a number of public opinion measures and tracking changes in them over time, the TVC models attempt to insure that any observed relationship between congressional actions and conflict duration is not the re-

---

36. Inter alia, Mueller 1973, Russett 1990.

37. E.g., Gartner and Segura 1998; Gartner, Segura, and Wilekning 1997.

38. Monthly casualty counts for the six pre–1970 uses of force were compiled by the author from media sources. Casualty totals for the Vietnam and Korean conflicts were generated from the Korean War Casualty File and the Combat Area Current Casualty Southeast Asia files available from the National Archives. Casualty totals for operations conducted between 1980 and 2000 were taken from Department of Defense DIOR records and updated through 2004 (for Bosnia and Kosovo) from media reports. Casualty totals for the ongoing wars in Iraq and Afghanistan were obtained from http://www.icasualties.org. Substituting counts of casualties from the last six months yields virtually identical results.

sult of omitted variable bias and the failure to control for shifts in public opinion.

One readily available, highly salient measure of public opinion is presidential approval. Diversionary-war scholars have long speculated that presidential incentives first to initiate and then, by extension, to continue a military venture may vary with levels of public approval.[39] Specifically, a president with poor public standing may seek to extend a military engagement in the hopes of rallying public opinion around the troops and their commander in chief. Alternatively, recent changes in public support may matter as much as its raw level at a given moment. Accordingly, the TVC models include two Gallup approval measures. The first captures the president's average standing among the public in the last quarter; the second reports the change in presidential support over the preceding six months.

In addition to presidential approval, popular support for the military mission itself may also significantly affect the duration of a conflict. To construct more conflict-specific measures of public support for ongoing military actions, I searched the Roper Center's public opinion archive to identify every poll in the database on each of the twenty principal uses of force. Unfortunately, polling on specific military actions is often sporadic, and the wording of questions can vary considerably across time and polling organizations. One possible solution to these problems is to use Kalman filtering and smoothing. Not only can Kalman filtering impute missing data points by drawing on information from all available polls in the sample, but it can also smooth data variations in question wording, sample sizes, and uneven spacing between polls to produce a roughly uniform series across multiple data sources.[40] Employing this technique yielded imputed opinion series for eighteen of the twenty principal uses of force. For the two remaining military actions for which no conflict-specific public opinion information was available—Trieste and Thailand—approval data was used as the best available alternative to complete the time series. Paralleling the approval measures, the analysis includes two measures of popular support for a military engagement. The first reports the level of popular support for the military action in

39. Ostrom and Job 1986; Marra, Ostrom, and Simon 1990; Brace and Hinckley 1992; DeRouen 1995.

40. See Green, Gerber, and de Boef 1999; Hamilton 1994.

the preceding quarter; the second captures the change in support for the
military action over the preceding six months.

Results and Discussion

Results for the TVC analyses of the durations of the twenty principal
postwar uses of force are reported in table 4.2 below. Model 1 includes
the four congressional legislative action variables culled from *CQ* and
CIS sources and a constant.[41] Strongly consistent with hypothesis 4a, the
coefficient for congressional authorizations is positive and statistically
significant. Once Congress has authorized a use of force, it extends political cover to the president and frees him to pursue a longer military
campaign to achieve his policy goals. Also according to theoretical expectations and consistent with hypothesis 4b, the coefficient for binding
legislative actions to cut off funding for a deployment or set an explicit
timetable for withdrawal is strongly negative and statistically significant.
The more actively Congress challenges the president's conduct of a military operation legislatively, the shorter the expected duration of the deployment. By contrast, the coefficient for nonbinding actions to curtail a
use of force is statistically insignificant, as expected. Nonbinding actions
lack the force of law and are less formidable political assaults on presidential discretion than binding joint resolutions or legislative provisions.
As a result, these nonbinding actions seem to have little influence on the
president, who presumably sees them as empty rhetoric, not legitimate
signals of congressional resolve to challenge his discretion in the conduct

41. The preceding chapter focuses on the effect of the partisan composition of Congress on the duration of military action. Yet the theoretical mechanisms for congressional influence described in chapter 2 suggest that the most important means through which
the partisan balance of power in Congress affects duration is through its influence on the
likelihood with which Congress or individual members act to raise the political costs to the
president though formal or informal means. Estimating models including just the average
percentage of the president's party in Congress yields the expected positive relationship
between presidential party strength and the expected duration of military action; however,
after the congressional action variables are included in the model, the relationship for partisanship disappears. The party composition of Congress surely affects the duration of the
twenty principal uses of force, but as we will see in chapter 6, it primarily does so indirectly
by influencing the extent to which Congress acts to rein in the president legislatively or
through investigative oversight.

TABLE 4.2. **Factors influencing conflict duration, time-varying covariates models**

Independent variables	(1)	(2)	(3)	(4)	(5)
Congressional actions					
Authorizations	1.93***	2.12***	2.26**	2.83***	2.84***
	(.52)	(.52)	(.49)	(.45)	(.53)
Binding actions to curtail	−.42***	—	−.54***	−.64***	—
	(.12)		(.22)	(.22)	
Nonbinding actions to curtail	.45	—	—	—	—
	(.45)				
Investigative hearings	−.10**	—	−.13***	−.14**	—
	(.05)		(.02)	(.07)	
Curtailing actions reported in media	—	−.11***	—	—	−.19**
		(.04)			(.09)
Investigative hearings reported in media	—	−.06**	—	—	−.07***
		(.02)			(.03)
International factors					
Military expenditures	—	—	−.61	−.63	−.22
			(.46)	(.68)	(.66)
Military personnel	—	—	.03	−.03	−.06
			(.09)	(.09)	(.10)
Ongoing war	—	—	−.66	−.77	−.48
			(.47)	(.51)	(.52)
Cold War	—	—	.56	1.13**	1.16**
			(.42)	(.56)	(.60)
Casualties last quarter	—	—	.04	.33	.14
			(.13)	(.24)	(.30)
Cumulative casualties	—	—	.02*	.03**	.02
			(.01)	(.01)	(.02)
Domestic variables					
Election year	—	—	.07	−.12	−.25
			(.47)	(.42)	(.38)
Misery index			−.07***	−.08	−.05
			(.03)	(.05)	(.05)
Public opinion					
Presidential approval last quarter			−.03	−.03	−.03
			(.02)	(.02)	(.03)
Support for war last quarter			−.02	−.02	−.02
			(.02)	(.02)	(.02)
Change in presidential approval			.01	.01	.00
			(.02)	(.02)	(.01)
Change in support for war			.00	−.00	.00
			(.02)	(.02)	(.01)
Congressional rhetoric					
President's party escalate or status quo			—	−.26	−.08
				(.19)	(.21)
President's party de-escalate or withdraw			—	−.23***	−.15***
				(.05)	(.06)
Opposition party escalate or status quo			—	.22**	.24***
				(.09)	(.09)

(continued)

TABLE 4.2. (*continued*)

Independent variables	(1)	(2)	(3)	(4)	(5)
Opposition party de-escalate or withdraw			—	.07 (.08)	.08 (.06)
Constant	3.06*** (.28)	3.08*** (.20)	6.00*** (.70)	6.27*** (1.34)	5.45*** (1.20)
p	1.15 (.17)	1.28 (.22)	1.80 (.40)	2.00 (.43)	2.03 (.45)
Log-likelihood	−23.27	−22.72	−16.82	−11.72	−12.61
n	583	583	583	583	583

Note: * $p < .10$; ** $p < .05$; *** $p < .01$. All significance tests are two-tailed; all models report robust standard errors clustered on conflict.

of military affairs.[42] Finally, the first model shows considerable evidence that members' maneuverings in the committee room can also influence the duration of a major military engagement. Again consistent with hypothesis 4b, as the intensity of congressional investigative oversight of the president's conduct of military operations increases, the duration of the American deployment decreases.

The measures of congressional efforts to rein in presidential discretion in the conduct of military policymaking in model 1 included every legislative challenge that received the support of at least 40 percent of one chamber of Congress and every investigative hearing identified in the Congressional Information Service abstracts. However, the media coverage that such efforts to challenge the president generate may

42. Alternatively, nonbinding actions may impose fewer political costs because they receive substantially less media coverage than more serious binding challenges to presidential policies. The *New York Times* content coding strongly supports this assessment of relative media attention. Moreover, model 2 shows a strong negative correlation between media reports of congressional legislative challenges to the president and conflict duration, even though the media measure does not differentiate between binding and nonbinding legislative initiatives. Model 1 was also replicated using biannual tallies of the number of binding and nonbinding actions to curtail a use of force and of the number of investigative hearings with similar results. The distinction between the effects of binding versus nonbinding legislative initiatives on conflict duration foreshadows the one that emerges between various recommendations made by Congress members in the public sphere. Whereas "costly" signals of support from the president's partisan opponents or opposition from his co-partisans in Congress have a significant influence on conflict duration, less "costly" speeches (i.e., support from co-partisans and calls for withdrawal from the partisan opposition) have no statistically significant effect.

be a better indicator of Congress's ability to raise the political costs of staying the course for the president or to send signals to foreign actors. If such actions receive scant attention from the popular press, they are unlikely to influence domestic or foreign audiences as posited in the theoretical mechanisms described in chapter 2. Accordingly, model 2 replaces the binding and nonbinding action tallies compiled from *Congressional Quarterly* with the number of front-page *New York Times* stories that discuss legislative efforts to curtail military actions in the preceding year. In the same way, model 2 replaces the tally of congressional hearings coded from CIS abstracts with the number of front-page *New York Times* articles mentioning congressional hearings critical of a military engagement. The results are virtually identical to those reported in model 1. Congressional authorizations continue to increase the expected duration of a military action while the volume of media coverage highlighting congressional challenges to the president decreases the expected length of an overseas deployment.[43] The coefficients for media measures of formal legislative challenges to the president and of congressional committee inquiries into the conduct of a military action are both negative and statistically significant.[44]

Model 3 adds the international and domestic political controls described above, many of which were also used in the duration models of the preceding chapter, as well as four measures of public support for

43. The baseline hazard parameter p in models 1 and 2 is greater than one, but in each specification one lies within the 95-percent confidence interval, so we cannot reject the null of no duration dependence. This suggests that the baseline hazard rate for the twenty principal uses of force does not systematically increase or decrease over time. As subsequent models add more explanatory and control variables, the baseline parameter increases and is significantly greater than one in multiple specifications. This may indicate that unlike all major uses of force, for which the baseline hazard rate appears to decrease over time, for the twenty principal uses of force involving ground troops or firepower the baseline hazard rate—or the probability of an action terminating at a given point independent of any change in the explanatory variables—increases slightly with time. The contrast between the baseline hazard rates for all of the major uses of force and this subset of principal uses of force may be due to the more precise specifications of the TVC models, which are able to incorporate the effect of changes in the political and tactical situation on the ground as an operation progresses.

44. As a final robustness check, models 1 and 2 were reestimated excluding data from the Vietnam and Korean wars. Doing so yields results virtually identical to those reported in table 4.2, except that the coefficient for the media investigative hearings variable, while still negative, fails to reach conventional levels of statistical significance.

the president and the military engagement at hand. Most importantly, even in this expanded specification, the sign and statistical significance of the coefficients for the three congressional action variables remain unchanged. Congressional authorizations yield longer conflict durations, while both binding legislative initiatives to curtail the military action and committee investigations into a use of force's conduct produce shorter conflict durations.

Turning to the international variables, for the twenty principal uses of force, changes in the target state's military expenditures and in the size of its armed forces have no systematic impact on the duration of the American deployment. This null result is perhaps unsurprising when considering the peacekeeping nature of many of these actions. Large, technologically sophisticated armies are not a prerequisite to fuel the ethnic and factional violence American forces were repeatedly dispatched to quell. Thus, states with small, ill-equipped militaries can be just as troublesome and require as long an American military commitment as target states with greater formal military capabilities.

Similarly, model 3 offers scant evidence that the presence of an ongoing war or the strategic environment of the Cold War produced shorter uses of force among the subset of principal military actions. The coefficient for the Cold War period is positive while that for an ongoing war is negative; however, neither coefficient meets conventional levels of statistical significance.

Finally, one of the most significant limitations of the non-TVC duration models in the preceding chapter was their inability to account for the influence of developments on the ground in the course of an operation on a deployment's duration. Perhaps the most important of these developments to presidential decision-making is the toll a military venture exacts in lives of American servicemen. Casualties are a highly visible and easily interpreted indicator of a conflict's progress that may send important signals to foreign actors, other domestic politicians, and the general public alike.[45] As a result, rightly or wrongly, they are the terms on which many military actions are ultimately judged.

To control for the influence of American casualties on the duration of a military action, model 3 adds measures of both recent and cumulative

45. See Morgan and Campbell 1991, Ray 1995, Stam 1996, Gartner and Segura 1998, Kriner and Shen 2010; but see also Berinsky 2007.

casualties to the analysis with mixed results.[46] Examining first the impact of marginal casualties—those suffered in the last quarter—the model yields a positive coefficient, but one that is statistically indistinguishable from zero. Replacing the quarterly casualties specification with current-month and biannual casualty counts also yields positive but statistically insignificant coefficients. This null result strongly suggests that American policymakers are not so casualty-phobic that they instinctively pull the plug on a military venture in the immediate aftermath of a burst of combat casualties.

To test for the alternative possibility that the total number of casualties incurred, not recent casualty rates, drives presidential decisions to stay in or pull out, model 3 also includes a monthly measure of cumulative casualties for each operation. The results are inconclusive. The coefficient is positive and statistically significant, suggesting that as casualties mount, the American commitment becomes intractable and the prospects for withdrawal more remote.[47] However, the abnormally high cumulative casualty totals for two of the longer postwar U.S. military operations, Vietnam and Korea, may be driving the finding. To account for this possibility and to smooth the cumulative casualty distribution, model 3 was reestimated using the log of cumulative casualties.[48] Under this specification, the relevant coefficient is still positive, but is statistically indistinguishable from zero ($p = .53$). Alternatively, replicating model 3 without Vietnam and Korea yields a negative coefficient for cumulative casualties, suggesting the opposite relationship to that reported in model 3: that as American war deaths rose in the smaller-scale principal uses of force, the expected duration of a military action decreased. However, this coefficient is also statistically insignificant.[49]

46. All marginal and cumulative casualty measures include casualties sustained in the month of each observation. This allows current-month casualties to influence the probability that the conflict ends in that same month.

47. Estimating two separate models—the first including only casualties in the last quarter and the second only cumulative casualties—yields virtually identical results. The coefficient for quarterly casualties remains positive and insignificant, while the coefficient for cumulative casualties is positive and significant.

48. Logging the measure of marginal casualties (regardless of whether it is for the current month, the most recent quarter, or the most recent six months) also yields statistically insignificant results.

49. The previous chapter raised one possible explanation for the absence of a consistent relationship between casualties and the duration of a military venture: the influence of casualties on presidential conduct of military affairs may be conditional on whether the

Taken together, the inconsistent results across model specifications offer little evidence that casualties have any direct impact on the conduct of military operations. This is not to say that casualties do not enter into decisions of whether to continue a military commitment or end it. Indeed, chapter 6 will show that casualties do play some role in shaping Congress's willingness to act legislatively to constrain the president's free hand in military affairs. Certainly the bombing of the Beirut Marine barracks in 1983 and the downing of a Black Hawk helicopter over Mogadishu ten years later played at least an indirect role in precipitating presidential decisions to withdraw. However, independent of other circumstances and political pressures, such as congressional actions or major shifts in public opinion, casualties seem to have little uniform influence on decisions regarding the length of military operations.

On the domestic side of the ledger, model 3 finds some evidence that political and economic factors influence conflict duration. In contrast to the expectations of diversionary-war theories, the model suggests an inverse relationship between the health of the economy and the duration of a major military engagement. Far from prolonging a military action to distract from a poor economy, the negative coefficient for the additive misery index of inflation and unemployment suggests that presidents facing economic turmoil at home are more likely to terminate their military ventures expeditiously than presidents who are freed from economic

---

president's partisan opponents control Congress. Presidents may anticipate an opposition Congress acting to raise the political costs of continuing a military action in the wake of casualties on the ground. As a result, they may respond to casualties by shortening the duration of a military deployment in periods of divided government, but stay the course even in the face of rising casualties when their co-partisans hold sway on Capitol Hill. A final alternative specification interacted the quarterly casualties measure with divided government, but the results offered no support for the theoretical contention. The resulting coefficient for quarterly casualties in divided government is positive and statistically significant ($p = .10$) suggesting that far from contemplating immediate withdrawal, presidents are more likely to keep U.S. troops on the ground in the aftermath of recent casualties when the opposition party controls one or more houses of Congress. Yet this relationship is likely spurious. No results are found when the six-month casualty tally is interacted with divided government for all observations; similarly, when the sample excludes Vietnam and Korea, the coefficients for both the quarterly and biannual casualty counts are negative. Finally, in these alternate specifications, the cumulative casualties coefficient varies considerably, even flipping signs. Yet in every case, the relationships for congressional actions remain unchanged.

concerns. This negative relationship parallels results from the preceding chapter suggesting that presidents saddled with high unemployment are less likely to use ground troops or firepower as their military response to a crisis than are presidents facing more politically palatable economic conditions.

There are at least two plausible explanations for this finding. First, a weak economy may signify greater domestic demands for government resources; burdened with a greater need to confront economic problems on the home front, presidents may seek to end costly overseas ventures more expeditiously. Second, it is not clear that diversionary war theories actually predict that presidents will extend ongoing military engagements in times of economic trouble to distract attention from the domestic front. Rather, a president saddled with a flagging economy may look for a short military action with a high probability of quick success, such as the invasion of Grenada in 1983, to generate a quick boost in public approval. Extending an existing engagement may be unlikely to generate this same surge in support.

Also inconsistent with diversionary-war theories, model 3 offers little evidence that the electoral cycle influences expected duration. This null result mirrors the findings reported in chapter 3 showing no relationship between an election year and the initiation or duration of any major use of force in the post-1945 era.

Finally, model 3 includes four measures of public opinion: quarterly measures of both presidential approval and support for the military action itself, as well as measures of the change in each over the preceding six months. Across the board, model 3 finds little evidence that public opinion dynamics directly influence the duration of a major military action. The coefficients for both quarterly public support variables are actually negative, though neither is statistically significant. This negative relationship reflects the fact that, throughout the post-1945 era, presidents have repeatedly persisted in maintaining American military commitments abroad in the face of low public support for such actions or even for themselves personally. Korea and Vietnam are the most prominent examples, yet the dynamic also characterizes more minor engagements, such as President Clinton's decision to keep American troops in Bosnia for the last six years of his administration, despite little public support for the mission in the Balkans. In some cases, low levels of popular support do appear to contribute to presidential decisions to withdraw American forces. In other cases, however, presidents assiduously stay the course and appear wholly undeterred by low approval ratings. Levels of public support alone cannot explain presidential conduct of military actions.

Turning to the two change-in-opinion variables, both coefficients are positive, as we would expect; however, both are substantively small and statistically insignificant. Collectively, the null results for all four opinion variables in model 3 suggest that in the absence of official opposition to the president's military policies in Washington, particularly on Capitol Hill, public opinion has little direct, systematic influence on the duration of major military engagements. Only when a souring public mood is coupled with concrete political pressure in Washington do presidents appear to reconsider their military policy course and adjust the duration of ongoing military operations accordingly.

Each of the first three model specifications in table 4.2 offers strong evidence that by formally attempting to authorize or curtail a use of force legislatively, or by holding high-profile investigative hearings in the committee room, members of Congress can significantly influence the cost-benefit calculations of the president and, ultimately, the expected duration of a military deployment. The next set of models (4 and 5) explores an alternative, more informal means through which Congress might shape the conduct of military affairs: the pressure that individual members of Congress exert on the president through their actions and statements in the public sphere as reported in the mass media.

Model 4 adds four media measures of explicit congressional recommendations for the proper conduct of the use of force. Because congressional judgments supporting the president's conduct of military affairs by his partisan opponents and calls for de-escalation or withdrawal from members of the president's own party may be more credible signals both to foreign leaders and the American public, the policy recommendations were coded for the partisanship of their sources. The results strongly accord with theoretical expectations. As the number of public calls for de-escalation or withdrawal from the president's co-partisans increased, the conflict's predicted duration decreased. Presidents facing public breaches in the ranks of their partisan base appear to adjust their conduct of a military operation accordingly and pursue a more timely withdrawal of American forces. Conversely, support from the president's partisan opponents emboldens the commander in chief to employ a more protracted military operation to pursue his policy goals. Opposition-party recommendations for escalation or maintaining the status quo produce longer expected durations.[50] And finally, general support for the president's course of action among his partisan supporters and calls for a change in course from his partisan opponents have little impact on the duration of military deployments.

Even after controlling for the potential of individual members of Congress to influence the duration of a military engagement through informal means, model 4 still shows strong relationships between formal congressional actions and changes in expected duration. Authorizations continue to increase the expected duration of uses of force, while binding legislative initiatives to curtail military operations and committee investigations into their conduct decrease the duration of conflicts. The results for all of the control variables remain very similar to those observed in model 3.

Finally, model 5 replicates the specification in model 4, but it substitutes the two media measures of congressional legislative and investigative activity from model 2 for the objective measures drawn from *CQ* and CIS reports. All results remain virtually identical to those reported in model 4.

Even after controlling for American casualties, public opinion, and a host of international and domestic political control variables, the models in table 4.2 all provide strong evidence that the formal and informal actions of members of Congress continue to influence the conduct of military affairs. Through legislative efforts to authorize or curtail the use of force, as well as committee investigations into the conduct of military affairs and vocal critiques of presidential policy in the mass media, members of Congress are able to serve as an important check on the executive, even after troops have been committed to the field.[51] The

50. Replicating model 4 with quarterly statement tallies instead of biannual measures yields virtually identical results. Again, the coefficients for calls by the president's own party for de-escalation or withdrawal and recommendations by the president's partisan adversaries to escalate or maintain the military commitment are in the expected direction and are statistically significant.

51. A final concern is that factors unique to each use of force not captured in the domestic or international control variables included in the model are truly driving the military action's duration, not congressional actions. For example, the brief two-month duration of American involvement in Grenada may be the result of specific factors relating to the engagement itself, not any congressional response to the invasion. As a final robustness check, a cox proportional hazard model reestimated a reduced-form model including the two legislative action measures to curtail the use of force (binding legislative actions and committee investigations), the two informal congressional action measures (public calls

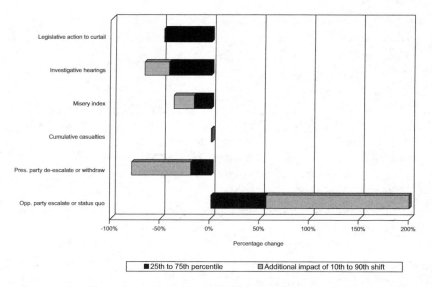

FIGURE 4.4. Predicted effects of variables on conflict duration in principal uses of force, 1945–2004. All first differences presented are statistically significant.

first differences presented in figure 4.4 demonstrate just how steep the political and strategic costs the legislature can impose on the president may be.

Across specifications, the time-varying covariate models strongly suggest that the factor with the greatest influence on the duration of a principal military deployment is whether one or more chambers of Congress have previously authorized the action. The influence of congressional authorizations is so large that it moves the expected temporal scope of a military action from the realm of two to three months to almost a year, if all other variables are held at their means or medians. The effect

---

for escalation or the status quo by the president's partisan opponents and recommendations for de-escalation or withdrawal from the president's co-partisans in Congress), and dummy variables for each conflict to control for idiosyncratic factors. Even after controlling for fixed effects for each conflict, all relationships between formal and informal congressional actions and conflict duration continue to hold (though the coefficient for calls for de-escalation or withdrawal from members of the president's party is statistically insignificant). As a final robustness check, I reestimated an identical model using a discrete-time duration model; results for all four congressional variables remained in the expected direction and statistically significant.

is strikingly large, but it accords with a quick comparison of the principal uses of force that did enjoy some form of congressional authorization with those that did not. The lengthy American military commitments in Vietnam, Bosnia, Kosovo, Afghanistan, and Iraq all received at least some authorization from one or more chambers of Congress. Similarly, while some of the non-authorized interventions were indeed quite lengthy, such as American involvement in Trieste, Manchuria, Korea, and the Dominican Republic, most of these deployments were considerably shorter than the authorized ventures.

To assess the substantive impact of the remaining statistically significant independent variables on a deployment's length, figure 4.4 presents a series of first differences drawn from model 4 in table 4.2.[52] The solid portion of each bar represents the percent change in an action's expected duration produced by increasing each variable from its 25th to its 75th percentile (or from zero to one in the case of the legislative actions to curtail the use of force variable) while holding all other explanatory variables constant at their means or medians. The dotted portion illustrates the additional impact on duration of a shift from the 10th to the 90th percentile of each independent variable.

The first bar shows that for each binding legislative action to curtail a use of force in the preceding twelve months, the expected duration of a military deployment decreases by 50 percent. What Congress gives legislatively it can also, to a great extent, take away. For example, although it had authorized the Marine peacekeeping presence in Lebanon, the legislature subsequently changed course and repeatedly called for withdrawal both formally through legislative initiatives and informally in the media in the wake of the October bombing of the Marine barracks in Beirut. As we will see in the next chapter, this congressional pressure played a critical role in effecting President Reagan's abrupt reversal and the withdrawal of U.S. Marines from Lebanon in February 1984.

In a similar vein, the second bar shows that politically damaging

52. All first differences report shifts from the 25th to 75th and 10th to 90th percentiles for each variable that was statistically significant in models 3 or 4, for all twenty principal uses of force. For the cumulative casualties measure, however, the anomalously large totals from Vietnam and Korea were excluded when calculating percentiles. To preserve the scale of the graph, the very large effects for legislative authorizations and for the Cold War are omitted.

congressional investigations of the administration's conduct of a military engagement can also significantly influence its expected duration. Increasing the level of congressional investigative activity from its 25th to its 75th percentile decreases the predicted duration by more than 40 percent, while a shift from the 10th to the 90th percentile produces almost a 70-percent reduction.[53] While high-profile committee investigations of a military venture or attempted congressional actions to cut off funding or set a withdrawal date for a military action do not bring the operation to a screeching halt, the models suggest that these congressional maneuvers do have a significant influence on the president and encourage him to end a deployment more quickly than he would in the absence of a formal legislative challenge.

The first differences also reveal that Congress wields considerable influence over the president's decision calculus in the conduct of military affairs through more informal channels—its members' actions in the public sphere. An increase from the 25th to the 75th percentile in the number of front-page articles citing members of the president's party in Congress speaking out against his military policies and calling for de-escalation or withdrawal decreases the deployment's expected duration by 20 percent. At the extremes of the distribution, the effect of these calls for de-escalation is considerably stronger, as an increase from the 10th to the 90th percentile in the number of articles citing these concerns slashes the expected duration by almost 80 percent. Conversely, public statements of support for escalating the American military commitment or staying the course by the opposition provide the president with considerable political cover to continue a deployment. An increase from the 25th to the 75th percentile in the level of opposition-party support for the president's handling of military actions in the preceding six months increases the expected duration of a military action by more than 50 percent, while a more dramatic shift from the 10th to the 90th percentile in vocal opposition party support more than doubles the expected duration.[54]

---

53. An increase from the 25th to the 75th percentile represents a shift from zero to four critical investigative hearings in the preceding twelve months. An increase from the 10th to the 90th percentile represents a shift from zero to eight.

54. Increases from the 25th to the 75th percentile in opposition support for staying the course and in co-partisan calls for de-escalation or withdrawal represent shifts from zero to two and from zero to one front-page articles, respectively. Increases from the 10th to the 90th percentile represent shifts of zero to five and from zero to seven, respectively.

Turning to the statistically significant control variables, predicted durations for Cold War uses of force were more than three times as long, on average, as for post–Cold War uses of force with identical values on the other independent variables.[55] As with legislative authorizations, this first difference is omitted from figure 4.4 to maintain the scale. The domestic economy also has a substantial effect on conflict duration. The models suggest that a sagging economy can decrease the predicted duration of a use of force by up to 40 percent. Finally, while the cumulative casualties coefficient was statistically significant, the first differences confirm that only very large shifts have any effect on expected conflict duration. A shift from the 10th to the 90th percentile shift in non-Vietnam, non-Korea cumulative casualties produced a decrease of only one percentage point in the predicted duration of a use of force.

Three Potential Limitations

Endogeneity

While the results in table 4.2 strongly support the theoretical contention that Congress, by engaging the military policymaking process through a variety of formal and informal actions, can influence the president's strategic calculus and, in turn, his conduct of military affairs, at least three difficulties remain in ascertaining the true extent of congressional influence. The first concern is that congressional actions to authorize or curtail the use of force may be endogenous and that the causal arrow may not run from congressional actions to changes in expected duration, but from expected duration to congressional actions.

Legislative authorizations to use force are quite likely partially endogenous. Congress may only act to authorize military engagements that it expects from the outset will be long in duration and that therefore require congressional action. Military ventures that are anticipated to be limited in scope and short in duration may not attract enough congressional attention to warrant debate over whether to authorize them. If this is the case, the models may falsely ascribe influence to congressional

---

55. Post–Cold War principal uses of force have, on average, been longer in duration than their predecessors. However, the significant positive coefficient suggests that Cold War uses of force are significantly longer than we would have expected given the values of the other independent variables in the analysis.

authorizations when Congress is merely ratifying the preexisting state of affairs.

It is certainly possible and perhaps even probable that Congress is unlikely to act to formally authorize military actions that it perceives will be short in duration—although there are prominent counterexamples. For instance, Congress did take steps to authorize the humanitarian aid mission to Somalia in early 1993, despite widespread belief that the American commitment they were sanctioning would not be extended. However, if the causal arrow ran only in one direction, from anticipated duration to congressional action, we would expect Congress to authorize every military action that had the potential to be a protracted deployment. The historical record, however, suggests otherwise. For example, Congress authorized the Johnson administration's escalation in Vietnam with the Gulf of Tonkin Resolution in 1964, but remained silent with regards to the same president's invasion of the Dominican Republic in the next year. Similarly, the Senate tacitly authorized the Clinton administration's dispatch of American peacekeepers to Bosnia in 1995, though it had refused to authorize the deployment of almost the same number of peacekeepers to civil war–torn Haiti a year earlier. Even when confronted with operations of similar character on commensurate scales, Congress has chosen to authorize some and not to authorize others.

Moreover, recent experience strongly suggests that legislative authorizations have buoyed presidents' willingness to use extended military operations to pursue their foreign policy goals, and have hindered subsequent legislative actions to pressure the administrations to change course. Republican efforts to rein in the Clinton administration's peacekeeping missions in the Balkans, which had long overrun the initial duration estimates, were hampered by prior congressional votes to support, albeit reluctantly, the administration's commitments. Similarly, many Democrats' 2002 votes to authorize the war in Iraq undoubtedly blunted their initial willingness to challenge President Bush's conduct of the war in late 2003 and early 2004, even in the face of rising human and financial costs and spiraling violence on the ground.

Because the causal relationship between legislative authorization and the duration of a military engagement is likely reciprocal, the statistical analyses may overestimate the magnitude of an authorization's true influence on the duration of a use of force. Nevertheless, the empirical evidence does support the theoretical contention that congressional authorizations to use force affect the course of policymaking by granting presidents greater leeway to use extended engagements of American military forces abroad to pursue their foreign policy goals than they would have without prior congressional approval.

A greater concern for the argument that Congress retains and exercises a check on presidential conduct of major military operations is the possibility that legislative actions to constrain the president and curtail a use of force are also endogenous. Members of Congress may have information about when a use of force is likely to end that is not captured in the variables included in the preceding hazard models. If members know when an unpopular venture is likely to conclude, they may use the formal tools at their disposal, such as legislative proposals or committee investigations, as vehicles to pander to public opinion and to claim credit for taking steps to end a military engagement that the president was already about to terminate absent any congressional action. The models themselves provide some evidence to minimize these concerns. If legislative actions were merely mechanisms for public posturing, there would be no theoretical reason to find a correlation only between legally binding congressional initiatives and decreased conflict duration. For the purposes of position taking and publicly claiming credit, nonbinding actions should be just as effective as binding actions.

To account for the possibility of endogeneity more formally, however, an instrumental variable approach is needed. To move toward a two-stage model, the analysis in table 4.3 employs a discrete-time duration model instead of the weibull hazard models used previously. The discrete-time method re-parameterizes the duration of each principal use of force as a series of monthly binary observations, coded 0 if the American military action did not end in the specified month and 1 if it did.[56] The first column in table 4.3 presents a reduced-form model including all of the variables from model 4 in table 4.2 that had a statistically significant impact on the duration of a military deployment, as well as the ongoing-war dummy variable which only narrowly missed conventional levels of statistical significance.[57]

---

56. For a more extended discussion of discrete-time duration analysis, see Box-Steffensmeier and Jones 1997, Allison 1982, Yamaguchi 1990, and Singer and Willet 1993.

57. Replicating all of the models in table 4.3 without the ongoing-war dummy variable yields virtually identical results.

TABLE 4.3. **Instrumental variable analyses of factors influencing conflict duration**

Independent variables	(1)	(2)	(3)
Congressional actions			
Authorizations	−1.10***	−.95**	−1.22***
	(.39)	(.39)	(.44)
Binding actions to curtail	.33***	—	—
	(.13)		
Investigative hearings	.07***	—	—
	(.01)		
Congressional challenges*	—	.24**	—
		(.10)	
Congressional challenges reported	—	—	.17***
in media*			(.05)
Congressional rhetoric			
President's party de-escalate or	.08**	.06*	.11***
withdraw	(.03)	(.04)	(.03)
Opposition party escalate	−.10*	−.13*	−.21***
or status quo	(.05)	(.08)	(.06)
Control variables			
Ongoing war	.52**	.57**	−.32
	(.21)	(.27)	(.45)
Cold War	−.25	−.38	−.28
	(.31)	(.44)	(.41)
Misery index	.02	.01	−.03
	(.02)	(.02)	(.03)
Cumulative casualties	−.02***	−.03*	−.03**
	(.01)	(.02)	(.01)
Constant	−1.67***	−1.43***	−.74
	(.33)	(.44)	(.61)
n	583	583	583

Note: * $p < .10$; ** $p < .05$; *** $p < .01$. Variables with asterisks are predicted values using average partisan composition of Congress as an instrumental variable. All significance tests are two-tailed; all models report robust standard errors clustered on conflict.

The results are substantively identical to those in the hazard analysis. An authorization to use force decreases the probability of a military action ending at a given moment, while a legally binding initiative to curtail a military engagement and congressional hearings investigating the use of force significantly increase the probability of the president terminating a foreign deployment. Members of Congress can also influence the likelihood of an action ending through their informal statements in the public sphere. Specifically, public calls by the president's co-partisans for de-escalation of the American military commitment or withdrawal increase the probability of an action ending, while vocal support for the president's course of action by his partisan opponents decrease the likelihood of termination.

A two-stage instrumental variable probit model is then used to account for potential endogeneity in the relationship between congressional actions to curtail a use of force and a conflict's expected duration.[58] To avoid the theoretical and practical complexities of including two endogenous variables in the probit equation, the analysis combines the legislative and investigative measures into a single additive index capturing the cumulative number of legislative and investigatory challenges to the president's conduct of military affairs.

A valid instrument must be highly correlated with the likelihood of Congress exercising its legislative and investigatory powers to challenge the president, while simultaneously being uncorrelated with the error term of the main equation. In other words, the instrumental variable's sole impact on the dependent variable must be through its influence on the instrumented factor. Fortunately, the partisan composition of Congress provides such an instrument. As chapter 6 will demonstrate, the strength of the opposition party in Congress is the single greatest predictor of congressional willingness to challenge the president legislatively. Equally important, there is little theoretical reason to expect Congress's partisan composition to influence an ongoing military engagement's duration, except through its impact on the likelihood of legislative challenges to presidential discretion.[59]

The first-stage equation producing estimated values of congressional legislative challenges to the president, independent of a conflict's duration, is

58. The resulting coefficient estimate for the effect of legislative actions on conflict duration is unbiased and consistent. See Heckman 1978.

59. Indeed, as discussed previously in the notes, once congressional actions are accounted for in the model, including the partisan composition measure in the hazard models has no effect. Nevertheless, the instrument is not perfect. As chapter 3 argues, presidents look to Congress's partisan composition to anticipate its likely reaction when crafting the goals and initial intended duration of a military response to a foreign crisis. Thus, the partisan composition of Congress may affect conflict duration by causing the president to narrow the scope of a military action ex ante, not just by raising the probability of a legislative response during the course of a venture.

Congressional challenges* = $fn[\beta_1(\text{authorization}) + \beta_2(\text{war})$
$+ \beta_3(\text{Cold War}) + \beta_4(\text{misery index}) + \beta_5(\text{cumulative casualties})$
$+ \beta_6(\text{de-escalation or withdrawal by own party}) + \beta_7(\text{escalation or}$
support of status quo by opposition party) $+ \beta_8(\text{partisan composition}$
of Congress)]

The second-stage equation, which explores the effect of these predicted values on the duration of a military deployment, is simply

Probability of an action ending = $fn[\beta_1(\text{authorization}) + \beta_2(\text{war})$
$+ \beta_3(\text{Cold War}) + \beta_4(\text{misery index}) + \beta_5(\text{cumulative casualties})$
$+ \beta_6(\text{de-escalation or withdrawal by own party}) + \beta_7(\text{escalation}$
or support of status quo by opposition party) $+ \beta_8(\text{congressional}$
challenges*)]

Results from the second-stage equation are presented in column 2 of table 4.3.

Even in this instrumental variable analysis, the statistical results strongly suggest that binding legislative initiatives to curtail a military action and high-profile congressional investigations into the president's conduct of military affairs have a substantial effect on the duration of a military engagement. While Wald tests cannot reject the possibility that the relationship between legislative actions and duration is endogenous ($p = .23$), the positive coefficient for the predicted values of the congressional challenges index strongly suggests that, through its legislative and investigative powers, Congress can have a significant, independent impact on the probability of a president terminating an ongoing military venture.

Finally, model 3 in table 4.3 replicates an identical instrumental variable analysis, but it uses predicted values of media reports of legislative and investigative challenges to the president's conduct of military affairs, instead of the objective count measures used in model 2. Even using this alternative operationalization of congressional challenges to the president, the resulting coefficient is positive and statistically significant while all other relationships remain unchanged. Thus, although the relationships between congressional actions and a military operation's duration may be partly reciprocal, the empirical analyses provide compelling evidence across model types and specifications that Congress's formal legislative actions and committee-led investigatory activity can influence the president's strategic calculus when deciding the scope and duration of American military action.

Leadership or Pandering?

The question "Who is leading whom?" is a second possible objection to the statistical analysis's assertion of congressional influence. When members of Congress make policy recommendations in the public sphere, are they merely pandering to public opinion or truly leading it? American politics scholars across subfields have long wrestled with the question of whether political elites, including legislators, lead or lag public opinion.[60] While the relationship undoubtedly cuts both ways, most scholars of public opinion in foreign policy argue that the causal arrow runs primarily from elite action to the general public.[61] Precisely because the public is least informed on matters of foreign affairs, popular opinion should be more receptive to elite cues on questions of foreign policy than on domestic issues for which other cues or heuristics are more readily accessible.[62] If Congress ever has the capacity to influence public opinion, it should be at its highest in the realm of foreign affairs, where popular beliefs are most malleable.[63] Moreover, a growing number of experimental studies reviewed in chapter 2 complement these survey-based approaches and offer compelling evidence that the public positions taken by members of Congress can dramatically influence popular opinion on questions of war and its conduct.

Thus, although members of Congress may look to public opinion when crafting both their actions on the floor and their public recommendations for the proper conduct of military policy, a growing body

---

60. See Phillips 1949; Levy 1989; Margolis and Mauser 1989; Lindsay 1994; Jacobs and Shapiro 2000; Sobel 2001; Canes-Wrone, Herron, and Shotts 2001; Canes-Wrone 2005; Hetherington 2001. For detailed historical analyses of the complicated relationships between foreign policy, public opinion, and congressional action see Foyle 1999, Sobel 2001, Sobel and Shiraev 2003.

61. See Bennett 1990; Page and Shapiro 1992; Zaller 1992; Zaller and Chiu 1996; Berinsky 2007, 2009; Jacobs and Page 2005.

62. On the public's lack of information in foreign affairs, see also Almond 1960, Lippman 1972. For its reliance on heuristics, see Popkin 1991, Neuman et al. 1992, Lupia and McCubbins 1998.

63. For parallel reasoning, see Canes-Wrone's (2005) argument that presidents have greater success going public in foreign than in domestic policy matters.

of survey and experimental research suggests that Congress possesses a significant capacity to alter and mold popular beliefs on major questions of foreign affairs. By shaping public opinion on a military engagement or planting the seeds of potential future opinion shifts, members of Congress can greatly change the political incentives that presidents face when plotting the course of military policy.

The Independence of Congressional Influence

A related final concern is the extent to which Congress's influence on presidential decision-making is an independent force, as opposed to the degree to which it merely reflects domestic political pressures more generally. When deciding whether to act formally or informally to leave its mark on the conduct of military policy, Congress does not do so in a political vacuum. As the analyses in chapter 6 will show, levels of and changes in popular support for a war and for the commander in chief, as well as developments on the ground in the field, all influence whether and when Congress acts to confront the president's handling of military affairs. Because members of Congress consider the greater domestic political climate when deciding whether to act to authorize or curtail an ongoing deployment, or to call publicly for its continuation or termination, it is intrinsically difficult to untangle the precise degree of influence Congress wields independent of all other domestic political considerations. Indeed, it is a question perhaps better suited for case study analysis like that presented in the next chapter.

It would be wrong, however, to conclude that Congress simply follows public opinion and that its actions have no independent influence on presidents' strategic calculus. Shifts in public opinion alone have little explanatory power in the statistical analyses above; it is only when public opposition is coupled with tangible opposition within the government itself that presidents appear willing to alter their chosen policy course. Instead, the relationship between congressional engagement with military policymaking and more general domestic political pressures is undoubtedly reciprocal. Congress can serve as both an activator of domestic concern and an outlet through which general domestic discontent with a president's handling of military affairs is transformed into institutional pressure to change course. Its members' statements and arguments in the public sphere can trigger real or anticipated changes in support for or opposition to the president's policies among the general public, and its formal actions can serve as concrete expressions of those sentiments that either strengthen political support for staying the course or raise the stakes for noncompliance.

Conclusion

This chapter empirically establishes Congress's capacity to influence the duration of major military actions through a range of formal and informal tools. It presents consistent and compelling empirical evidence that congressional authorizations provide the president with valuable political cover to pursue an extended commitment of U.S. forces to pursue his foreign policy goals. By contrast, even an unsuccessful legislative initiative to curtail a use of force and committee investigations into the executive's conduct of military affairs affect the president's strategic calculations and decrease an operation's predicted duration. In the same way, the maneuverings of individual members of Congress in the public sphere have significant ramifications for the president's conduct of ongoing military operations. Public support from his partisan opponents enables the president to employ a longer-duration military venture in pursuit of his policy goals, while vocal opposition from his partisan opponents encourages him to curtail the length of an overseas deployment.

The empirical demonstration of strong relationships between these congressional actions—none of which formally compel the president to change course—and changes in the duration of military conflict is critically important. Indeed, that Congress possesses this power is the core assumption underlying both previous scholarship and the analysis of the preceding chapter, which asserts that partisan dynamics influence the scope and duration of American military actions. Even if presidents primarily anticipate congressional responses when deciding how to act, adjusting their conduct of military affairs based on the partisan composition of Congress is only rational if Congress has the means at its disposal to impose costs on the president if he strays too far from its preferred policy. The TVC models confirm that Congress does have this capacity and indeed frequently exercises it.

The next chapter explicitly links the congressional actions shown here to affect conflict duration to the two mechanisms of congressional influence identified in chapter 2: raising or lowering the political and military costs of staying the course for the president. Chapter 6 then investigates the indirect impact of broader domestic political concerns on the duration of military deployments through their influence on congressional behavior.

CHAPTER FIVE

"Sitting Ducks":
Marines in Beirut, 1982–84

The statistical analyses of the preceding chapter demonstrated strong correlations between congressional actions and the durations of major military operations since World War II. When the administration's opponents in Congress speak out against a military venture's conduct, hold investigative hearings, or introduce and bring to the floor legislative initiatives to curtail the use of force, presidents have routinely adjusted their conduct of military operations accordingly and decreased their duration. As such, these analyses provide strong support for hypotheses 4a and 4b, which link congressional actions and changes in tangible military policy outcomes as developed in chapter 2.

However, these statistical correlations offer little insight into the causal mechanisms through which these congressional actions effected the observed changes in policy. The theory in chapter 2 argued that congressional support for or opposition to a use of force can affect its duration by raising or lowering both the political and military costs that the president stands to incur from continuing a military venture. Because many of these costs are all but impossible to quantify, the proposed mechanisms are difficult to assess statistically. However, in-depth qualitative analysis drawing on archival evidence and historical data to trace the causal chains leading from actions in Congress to changes in policy outcomes is particularly well suited to testing theoretical claims about mechanisms. In this way, case study research offers perhaps the best and most direct test of the political costs and signaling mechanisms posited in chapter 2.

Moreover, supplementary qualitative analysis can help further address concerns about endogeneity and omitted variable bias in the statistical analyses that complicate the task of making definitive causal arguments. To address the endogeneity concerns, the last chapter concluded with an instrumental variable analysis, which offered strong evidence that the causal arrow does indeed run in the hypothesized direction: from congressional actions to changes in presidential decision-making and conflicts of shorter duration. Qualitative analysis can further address this concern by showing the precise pathways through which actions in Congress shaped major policy decisions in key cases. Similarly, while the statistical analyses of the preceding chapters controlled for a host of factors that might be correlated both with Congress's willingness to act and with conflict duration—such as public support for the president and for the military action itself, American casualties, and other changes in the situation on the ground—all such measures are necessarily imperfect. If some factor not captured in the model is correlated with both congressional actions and changes in conflict duration, this factor and not congressional maneuverings, may be driving the observed relationships.[1] By illuminating the precise mechanisms through which congressional actions effect changes in policy, qualitative case study analysis can also address such concerns about either spurious correlation or the independence of Congress's influence on the conduct of military affairs.

Thus, to bolster the statistical evidence from the preceding chapters and directly test the causal mechanisms by which congressional actions can effect changes in policy outcomes, this chapter presents an in-depth historical case study of the politics precipitating the withdrawal of U.S. Marines from Lebanon in February 1984. The historical narrative, which draws heavily on archival evidence from the Ronald Reagan Presidential Library, makes plain that in this case concerns about endogeneity are ill-founded. When Congress spurred itself to action in late 1983 and early 1984 and called for a withdrawal of American forces from Beirut, Reagan and many of his top advisors had no intention of doing so if left strictly to their own devices. Indeed, for months following the Marine

---

1. If this omitted factor is not causally related to congressional actions, then the correlation between congressional actions and duration is spurious. If, however, the omitted factor is an unmeasured cause of congressional actions, then although those actions would still be part of a causal chain leading to changes in policy outcomes, their effect would not be independent.

barracks bombing in October of 1983 the president personally raised the stakes involved in Lebanon and emphasized that pulling back from Beirut would entail a capitulation to the terrorists.

The historical data also shows that actions in Congress had a strong, independent effect on the administration's decision calculus. Congressional challenges to the administration's policies were not mere proxies for shifts in public opinion or changes in the situation on the ground in Lebanon. Rather, internal memoranda from the Reagan administration make clear that actions within Congress played a pivotal role in precipitating the abrupt policy reversal and redeployment of the Marines offshore. At multiple points, high-ranking officials within the administration lamented that the increased congressional pressure arose at a time when the public was not demanding withdrawal of American forces from Beirut and when the situation on the ground was not deteriorating to the point that the mission no longer could achieve its goals.

Finally and perhaps most importantly, the Lebanon case study also shows *how* the congressional actions examined statistically in the preceding chapter—legislative initiatives, investigations, and public calls for a change in policy—affected the administration's cost-benefit calculations through the two mechanisms posited in chapter 2. Congressional opposition raised both the political and the military costs that administration officials perceived they would have to pay if they continued the Lebanon deployment. Archival records reveal top administration officials ruminating on the political ramifications of continuing the Beirut mission in the face of virulent, sustained congressional opposition both for the Republican Party's electoral fortunes in the November elections and for the president's own re-election prospects. Similarly, consistent with signaling hypotheses, the evidence also demonstrates that, both publicly and privately, top administration officials believed that congressional opposition was closely watched in Damascus and that it emboldened the Syrians and their allies in Lebanon. This heightened intransigence, administration officials warned, undermined the United States' position and caused even ardent supporters of the U.S. mission in Lebanon to concede that only an expanded, more aggressive, and more costly military mission could achieve American goals in the region.

In addition to the analytic advantages that a qualitative approach affords for tracing causal processes and identifying the precise mechanisms by which congressional actions have effected shifts in administration military policy, a case study of U.S. military involvement in Lebanon is also of considerable intrinsic interest because it represents perhaps the opening salvos in the United States' ongoing struggle against the forces of international terrorism. In the immediate aftermath of September 11, 2001, a host of governmental analysts and academics searching for the genesis of the terrorist threat began reexamining recent American history through a new lens. Scholars dutifully recounted the immediately shocking but oft-forgotten early blows in this new global struggle: the first World Trade Center attack in 1993, the 1998 bombing of the American embassies in Kenya and Tanzania, and the strike against the USS *Cole* in October 2000. The sudden emergence of the terrorist threat in the early 1990s and its escalating warning signs leading up to the 9/11 attacks seemed, in retrospect, all too obvious.

However, now almost a decade removed from the tragic events that have so altered the American political landscape, it is clear that American engagement with global terrorism and religious extremists extends even further into our history. On March 12, 2007, veteran journalist Ted Koppel appeared on NBC's *Meet the Press* and reminded audiences that President George W. Bush's war on terror was actually a very old idea, a conflict that had begun almost a quarter-century earlier when Islamic terrorists, believed to be precursors to Hezbollah, launched a suicide attack against American Marines stationed at Beirut International Airport as part of the multinational peacekeeping force in Lebanon. The October 23, 1983, attack claimed the lives of 241 American Marines and served notice that America now faced a new threat, one different from that posed by traditional nation-states and their formal armies. Observers at the time also presciently saw Lebanon as a striking departure from the foreign policy challenges of the past. Secretary of State George Shultz in his memoirs called the Lebanese action one of "state-sponsored terrorism" perpetrated by non-state actors—something that would become a "new worldwide phenomenon" with which the United States would have to grapple.[2]

Thus, an analysis of the politics governing the initiation, continuation, and withdrawal of the American military commitment in Lebanon may shed important insights into the politics governing subsequent American confrontations with the radically new threat posed by global terror fueled by non-state actors.

---

2. Shultz 1993, 230. See also Shultz 2006.

The Genesis of American Involvement in Lebanon

The United States' history of military involvement in Lebanon dates back to President Eisenhower's dispatch of American forces to the region in 1958 at the request of Lebanese President Camille Chamoun to quell internal unrest from Syrian and Nasserist elements and stabilize the country. Eisenhower ordered fourteen thousand Marines to the small Middle Eastern nation to secure Beirut International Airport and other vital infrastructure while the government consolidated its position. In a little over three months, the United States persuaded Chamoun to resign, a new election was held, and U.S. troops withdrew from the country.

Yet Lebanon's position in the volatile region was always vulnerable to foreign forces. The "Black September" attempted coup against the king of Jordan in 1970 by Palestinian Liberation Organization (PLO) militants prompted their exile from Jordan into southern Lebanon. The PLO quickly came to dominate that region, which they used as a staging ground for attacks on Israel. In addition to the increased tensions with Israel, sectarian violence between Christians and Muslims also grew and eventually compelled Lebanon's Christian government to invite the Syrian army into the country to quell the fighting. After brokering an uneasy truce, Syrian forces declined to leave.

By early 1982, tensions between the PLO guerrillas in southern Lebanon and Israel had risen so much that Israeli Defense Minister Ariel Sharon decided to invade his country's northern neighbor in the hopes of eliminating the PLO threat once and for all. Deep internal divisions plagued the Reagan administration over how to respond to these mounting tensions in the Middle East. Secretary of State Alexander Haig adopted a staunchly pro-Israel position, while Secretary of Defense Caspar Weinberger and others advocated a more balanced approach.[3] In addition to courting support from Haig, Sharon also struck a deal with Christian Phalange militia leader Bashir Gemayel for cooperation against the PLO and Syrian occupiers: Israel would be rid of the PLO, and Gemayel left in control of Lebanon.[4]

On June 3, 1982, Sharon was presented with his fait accompli: the assassination of Israel's Ambassador Shlomo Argov in London, allegedly

---

3. For a discussion of the extent of Haig's support for Sharon, see Weinberger 1990, 144.

4. Reeves 2005, 102.

by PLO militants. With troops already massed on the border, he commenced the invasion of Lebanon three days later. The Reagan administration's official response to the invasion was initially mixed, reflecting the range of views within the circle of the president's foreign policy
advisors. Yet the ferocity of the Israeli assault, particularly the use of
American-made cluster bombs against civilian targets in Beirut, swung
the balance in favor of those urging Reagan to pressure Israeli Prime
Minister Menachem Begin to halt the advance and break the siege of
the Lebanese capital. After Haig's abrupt resignation, newly installed
Secretary of State George Shultz, National Security Advisor William
Clark, and Reagan's special envoy Phillip Habib, who for months had
attempted to broker a cease-fire, pleaded with Reagan to intervene personally. Deputy Chief of Staff Michael Deaver even threatened to resign if the president did not act. On August 16, 1982, Reagan acquiesced.
Calling Begin, he told the prime minister that the slaughter in Beirut
was another "holocaust" and insisted that it must stop.

To encourage the Israelis to come to the table, the Reagan administration had long debated the merits of American participation in a multinational force (MNF) that could oversee the implementation of any
agreement. Absent an agreement by all parties to withdraw their forces,
Weinberger and the Joint Chiefs of Staff strongly opposed any deployment of American forces to Lebanon.[5] Wariness of an American deployment was not limited to the Pentagon or even the administration; in consultations with the executive branch, Senate Majority Leader Howard
Baker (R-Tennessee) also expressed reservations and took his concerns
directly to the president.[6] Yet Habib desired a firm American commitment as bargaining leverage to bring the Israelis and Syrians to the table.
By July, Habib had won at least a tentative commitment from Reagan
that U.S. troops would help implement any deal, despite the objections
of Weinberger and the Joint Chiefs. Three days after Reagan's telephone
call to Begin, Israel signed a Habib-brokered deal to halt its offensive if
the United States, France, and Italy would form an MNF to evacuate the
PLO guerrillas for resettlement in other Muslim countries.

On August 20, 1982, Reagan informed the nation that he had authorized the dispatch of eight hundred U.S. Marines to participate in the
MNF overseeing PLO withdrawal. The first Marines went ashore on

5. Weinberger 1990, 144.
6. Cannon 2000, 400.

August 24, 1982, and began supervising and facilitating the PLO withdrawal. Less than three weeks later, with the evacuation complete, the Marines redeployed to their ships and left Lebanon on September 10. Although he had opposed the engagement, Weinberger judged it a complete success that saved countless lives. He was equally pleased by its short duration: "I felt, as President Eisenhower had felt twenty-five years earlier, that we should not have a permanent presence in Lebanon."[7]

The Second MNF

No sooner had the Marines departed Lebanon than violence upset the fragile peace. On September 14, 1982, President-elect Bashir Gemayel was assassinated in a bombing of his Phalange Party headquarters. Seizing on the unrest, Sharon ordered the Israel Defense Forces (IDF) forward into West Beirut, where they engaged Muslim fighters. By September 17, the IDF controlled much of Beirut and had encircled the two largest Palestinian refugee camps, Sabra and Shatila. Under cover of night, the Israeli military secretly authorized Christian Phalange forces to enter the camps and root out remaining PLO fighters. Once inside, however, for almost three days the Phalange militia slaughtered hundreds of Palestinian civilians as reprisals for Gemayel's assassination while the IDF did nothing to stop the attacks.

Reagan publicly condemned the attacks, and a new debate arose about a second American force for Lebanon. On the hawkish end of the spectrum, special envoy Robert McFarlane and many on the National Security Council backed by Secretary of State Shultz favored dispatching to the region a sizeable American force of several divisions, bolstered by a large French contingent to compel both the Israelis and the Syrians to withdraw. Only this breathing space, they reasoned, would give new President-elect Amin Gemayel, Bashir's older brother, the chance to stabilize the political situation on the ground. However, the idea of a larger, potentially longer-term commitment of U.S. forces in uncertain conditions was anathema to Defense and the Joint Chiefs. Weinberger derided the NSC proposals as wholly "in keeping with their passionate desire to use our military," and emphasized his vigorous opposition to any deployment unless there was a firm agreement in place for both sides

7. Weinberger 1990, 150.

to withdraw their forces, subject to MNF monitoring.[8] This fundamental cleavage within the administration—Weinberger and the Joint Chiefs on one end, Shultz, McFarlane, and the NSC on the other—stubbornly persisted through the entire course of the Marine mission in Lebanon.

Convinced of the value of an American military presence in Lebanon, President Reagan quickly dispatched a new contingent of Marines to patrol Beirut International Airport. The first soldiers reentered Lebanon on September 29, 1982, with the limited mission of keeping the airport open and maintaining an American presence in the area; toward this end, they were under strict rules of engagement that authorized action only in self-defense.

Mirroring the divisions within Reagan's own administration, public and congressional reaction to the deployment was also mixed. Within a month and-a-half of the Marines' return to Beirut, polling outfits conducted five surveys with similarly worded questions querying public support for the new American peacekeeping contingent. On average, a little less than half of Americans, 47 percent, supported the president's decision, with the results of individual surveys ranging from a maximum of 56 percent to a minimum of 40 percent supporting the action. While tepid, the support for Reagan's handling of the situation in Lebanon was actually higher than overall popular evaluations of his job performance, as his approval rating hovered at 43 percent in the fall of 1982.

Reaction in Congress was also somewhat ambivalent. In addition to Baker's wariness over a military presence in Lebanon, the chairmen of the House Foreign Affairs Committee (HFAC) and Senate Foreign Relations Committee (SFRC), Clement Zablocki (D-Wisconsin) and Charles Percy (R-Illinois), both raised the specter of the War Powers Resolution and demanded that the president comply with its provisions.[9] At issue was the discretion that the compromise language in section 4(a) of the resolution afforded the president to report his dispatch of troops to Congress under one of three conditions. If the president reported under the first condition, section 4(a)(1)—certifying that he had deployed American troops "into hostilities or into situations where imminent involvement in hostilities is clearly indicated by the circumstances"—the

8. Weinberger 1990, 151; Shultz 1993, 107–9.

9. Letter, Percy and Pell to Ronald Reagan, September 24, 1982, folder ND 016 100931, WHORM; letter, Zablocki to RR, July 6, 1982, folder ND007 092396, WHORM, Ronald Reagan Library.

report would automatically trigger the War Powers Resolution's ninety-day withdrawal clock, absent congressional authorization for the deployment. Instead, Reagan reported the Lebanon action "consistent with the War Powers Resolution" and cited the second condition: that troops had been deployed "into the territory, airspace or waters of a foreign nation, while equipped for combat." Under this provision, the withdrawal clock was not automatically triggered; that would require a congressional resolution directing the president to terminate the action.[10]

Zablocki and Percy, joined by SFRC ranking member Claiborne Pell (D–Rhode Island), had formally appealed to Reagan in writing as far back as July and August 1982 and argued that any U.S. military deployment to Lebanon would by definition be a deployment into a "zone of hostility" that must trigger the War Powers Resolution's automatic withdrawal clock. Indeed, Percy insisted that the ninety-day clock had already begun ticking from the moment the troops returned to their posts. Yet the administration assured Congress that the Marines were in no imminent danger. Reagan himself replied, "I want to emphasize that there is no intention or expectation that U.S. Armed Forces will become involved in hostilities. Our agreement with the government of Lebanon expressly rules out any combat responsibilities for the U.S. forces."[11]

The mission's first casualties occurred on September 30, 1982, when one Marine was killed and three wounded by unexploded ordinance at the airport—U.S.-made cluster bombs that the IDF had promised to use only in self-defense. Two more Marines lost their lives in October and December of that year. Yet these incidents prompted little outcry in Congress or among the public.[12]

Despite turf battles between the Foreign Relations and Foreign Affairs committees and the White House over each branch's institutional prerogatives in war powers, the defining character of the initial congres-

10. Whether this can be done through a concurrent resolution as specified in Section 5(c) of the War Powers Resolution or whether *INS v. Chadha* requires a joint resolution is a matter of considerable debate. See Grimmett 2004.

11. *Congressional Quarterly Almanac* 1982, 169.

12. The September 30, 1982, casualties were the first casualties from the MNF. Two other American soldiers serving as part of the UN monitoring force in southern Lebanon were killed by a landmine five days earlier. Detailed casualty information for all soldiers killed in Lebanon during this period is available from the Department of Defense Statistical Information Analysis Division.

sional reaction to the second MNF deployment was neither one of enthu-
siastic support nor of acrimonious opposition. Yet there was sufficient
unease and displeasure with the deployment that one HFAC aide predicted, "If a few [more] Marines come back in bags, the concern will be
a lot greater."[13]

Mounting Storm

The Marines maintained their position at the airport throughout the
end of 1982 and into 1983 while Shultz and American envoys in the Middle East struggled in vain to reach an agreement with Israel and Syria
to withdraw their forces from Lebanon. As Weinberger had feared, the
Marines had become a small contingent of allegedly neutral troops inter-
posed between two armies. Indeed, the close proximity of IDF and U.S.
forces produced several near clashes between the two, most famously
the showdown between Marine Captain Charles Johnson and an Israeli
tank in March of 1983. During this period the American forces also took
small but significant steps toward shedding their reputation as a neutral
party by training small units of the Lebanese Armed Forces (LAF).[14]
This expansion of the Marine force's role would eventually lead militias
opposed to the Lebanese government to view the Marines as a party to
the conflict, allied with the LAF.[15]

The stakes for the American mission in Lebanon suddenly grew considerably on April 18, 1983, when a suicide bomber crashed his van into
the U.S. Embassy in Beirut, killing sixty-three people, seventeen of
them Americans. Among the Americans killed were five members of
the armed forces and eight CIA employees, including the agency's Near
East director Robert Ames. At the time, the blast was the deadliest attack on an American diplomatic mission in history.

If casualties alone are enough to spur presidents to terminate American military deployments hastily, the embassy bombing may well have
precipitated an expeditious withdrawal. After all, public support for
the mission had always been tepid, and congressional enthusiasm for
the MNF, even among the president's own party, was modest. Moreover,

13. *Congressional Quarterly Almanac* 1982, 169.
14. Shultz 1993, 225–26.
15. Reeves 2005, 164.

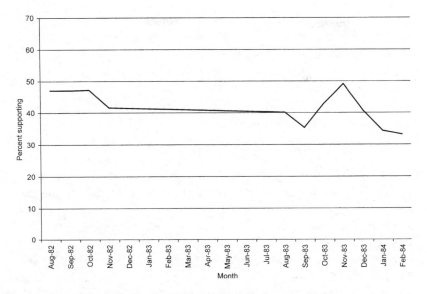

FIGURE 5.1. Public support for the Marine mission in Lebanon, 1982–84

the Reagan administration had assured Congress and the public that the costs of the mission would be low. Yet figure 5.1, which traces popular support for the Lebanon mission from 1982 through 1984, clearly shows that the embassy bombing had little effect on the public or the White House. Although opinion polls on the question were conducted infrequently during this period, they show no real evidence of any significant drop-off in popular support for the MNF mission in Lebanon. Indeed, what is most striking about the polling data is how consistent popular support for the mission was over time. A majority of the public never supported the Marine mission, even in 1982, and approval for MNF participation remained virtually flat throughout its duration. Moreover, Reagan's personal job approval rating was the same or even slightly higher in May, after the bombing, than it had been immediately before the attack.

The reaction in Congress was muted as well. Echoing the Senate Foreign Relations Committee's call in the winter of 1982, HFAC attached a rider to the Lebanon aid bill (S 639) demanding prior congressional assent to any expansion of the Marine presence in Beirut. In the Senate, Claiborne Pell and Paul Sarbanes (D-Maryland) again raised the issue of the War Powers Resolution and demanded that the administration invoke section 4(a)(1) and seek congressional authorization for a continued presence. Yet the Republican leadership bowed to administration pressure and kept the Pell-Sarbanes initiative at bay while agreeing with the House position as a compromise.[16] With the aid bill passed, congressional attention to Lebanon quickly waned and the mission again receded from the public spotlight.

While conditions on the ground worsened throughout 1983—the American ambassador's residence itself became the target of artillery attacks—the situation facing the Marines changed most dramatically in the wake of an apparent diplomatic victory for the administration. With Bud McFarlane, who replaced Phillip Habib as the administration's special envoy to the region, and Secretary of State Shultz directly engaged in the diplomatic efforts, the Israeli and Lebanese governments reached a tentative agreement for an IDF withdrawal, but with an important caveat: Israel would only withdraw when Syria agreed to do so as well, something Syria's President Hafez al-Assad had no intention of doing. The administration continued to step up pressure on the Israelis to withdraw, in the hopes that it would stabilize Lebanon and in turn compel Syria to pull back.

During the summer of 1983, conditions on the ground worsened and violence grew. Reevaluating their position, the Israelis decided to withdraw their forces from the Shouf Mountains, where the Druze militia was growing increasingly troublesome and engaging LAF forces, to defensive positions south of the Awali River. Without the IDF in place on the hills to keep the peace, the Marines at the airport became increasingly vulnerable to shelling from Druze and other antigovernment forces.

As attacks on the Marine positions escalated, the Reagan administration debated a change in course. McFarlane, convinced that a greater show of U.S. strength on the ground could turn the diplomatic tables, again advocated an augmented American force with a greatly expanded mission. Shultz refused to back McFarlane's plan, but strongly supported continuing U.S. participation in the MNF, as did National Security Advisor Bill Clark. The Joint Chiefs and Weinberger again countenanced terminating the MNF. Having taken his advisors' counsel, Reagan continued to support steadfastly the American presence in Lebanon.

While publicly calling on the IDF to withdraw, privately the Reagan administration pleaded with the Israelis to stay. On August 28, the pres-

---

16. *Congressional Quarterly Almanac 1983*, 116–17.

ident called Prime Minister Begin and asked him to keep IDF troops in the Shouf until the Syrians, who had been stepping up activity there to pressure the Israelis to leave, also withdrew. However, Begin unexpectedly resigned and the new government began a withdrawal within the week. The very next day, two American Marines, the first to die from hostile fire, were killed by Druze artillery; the Marines returned fire with artillery, small arms, and a helicopter gunship. Fourteen American soldiers were wounded in the attack. Two more Americans were killed on September 6, but fortunately for the White House, the casualties were overshadowed by news of the Soviet downing of a commercial airliner, KAL 007.

Faced with these mounting attacks on U.S. positions, the Reagan administration confronted a difficult choice: maintain the status quo, withdraw, or escalate the American commitment beyond its limited peacekeeping role. From an increasingly war-torn Beirut, McFarlane requested naval gunfire in support of LAF forces battling the Druze in the Shouf Mountains. He reasoned that naval support, including from the recently dispatched battleship *New Jersey* and its sixteen-inch guns, would back the fledgling LAF force, protect the Marines by silencing Druze artillery, and serve as a strong signal to the Syrians of American resolve in Lebanon. Shultz and Clark both supported McFarlane's ploy, while Weinberger and the Marine commanders on the ground opposed the idea.[17]

Reagan again sided with the hawks and amended National Security Decision Directive 103, which set the parameters for the Marine mission, to allow for naval gunfire support. On September 16, 1983, frigates were ordered to fire in support of LAF forces battling Druze positions in the Shouf.

Congressional Authorization

The attacks on Marine positions and American escalation prompted renewed calls from within Congress for the president to invoke the War Powers Resolution. Yet while Reagan dutifully reported the developments in Lebanon to Congress, consistent with section 4 of the War Powers Resolution, he refused to admit that the Marines were engaged

17. McFarlane 1994; Reeves 2005, 172–73.

in a zone of hostilities, which would trigger the ninety-day withdrawal clock.[18] To add an air of military legitimacy to the president's dubious contention, the administration sent General P. X. Kelley to testify before Congress that the Marines were not in immediate danger and were not being targeted by warring factions.[19]

Many in Congress vehemently disagreed. SFRC Chairman Percy lamented, "We have people in helicopters, we're shooting rockets and artillery—if that isn't imminent hostilities, I don't know what is." Echoing Percy, House Foreign Operations Appropriations Subcommittee Chairman Clarence Long (D-Maryland) called the Marines "sitting duck targets in an undeclared war" and announced his intention to introduce an amendment to the pending FY1984 Department of Defense appropriations bill (HR 4185) that would cut off funding for the operation within thirty days unless Reagan invoked section 4(a)(1) of the War Powers Resolution, automatically triggering the withdrawal clock.

Fortunately for the administration, it had allies in the leadership of both chambers. Despite his misgivings about the deployment, Howard Baker rallied his troops to the party's banner in the Senate. And, surprisingly, Speaker Tip O'Neill (D-Massachusetts) championed the president's cause in the House. O'Neill was genuinely torn by the situation in Lebanon. On the one hand, he fervently believed that Reagan was in strict violation of the spirit of the War Powers Resolution and that action was needed to assert Congress's institutional prerogatives in questions of military policymaking. Yet on the other, he was sensitive to the signal an American withdrawal in the face of enemy fire would send to the rest of the world, and he publicly proclaimed that "it would be unwise for the United States ever to cut and run."[20] Seeking some middle ground, O'Neill pushed for a compromise: Congress would invoke the War Powers Resolution as required when American troops are placed in hostile zones, but it would also simultaneously authorize the continued presence of those troops in Lebanon for at least an additional eighteen months.

The compromise (HJ Res 364) immediately encountered resistance in HFAC, even from some committee Republicans. Toby Roth

18. Ronald Reagan, "Letter to the Speaker of the House and the President Pro Tempore of the Senate Reporting on United States Participation in the Multinational Force in Lebanon." *Public Papers of the President*, August 30, 1983.

19. *Congressional Quarterly Almanac 1983*, 173.

20. Reeves 2005, 174.

(R-Wisconsin) was most vehement, and indeed prescient, in his objections to the bill, and warned, "If [we] keep the Marines in Lebanon, we're just waiting for a tragedy to happen." Of the compromise eighteen-month authorization, Roth lamented, "The Marines can no more keep peace than you can bring back the dead . . . [if the eighteen-month authorization passes,] there will be many Americans killed, it's a cinch."[21] Many committee Democrats shared Roth's concerns, and some introduced amendments attempting to cut off funding for the Marine mission altogether. Yet HFAC chairman and O'Neill ally Clement Zablocki assured doubters that the legislation did represent some concessions from the president, who actually preferred "an open-ended commitment."Zablocki eventually prevailed.

As HJ Res 364 moved to the floor, O'Neill took advantage of congressional procedures to secure a restrictive rule from the Rules Committee that greatly circumscribed the number and nature of permissible amendments. Both the speaker and Lee Hamilton (D-Indiana) worked the Democratic ranks, with O'Neill making the vote a matter of party loyalty. Concerned about the eventual result, Democratic leaders at one point considered decreasing the authorization from eighteen months to a year; however, the leadership held firm, beating back an amendment by Clarence Long and David Obey (D-Wisconsin) to add further restrictions to the authorization, and the speaker himself addressed the chamber immediately before the final vote. O'Neill emphasized to his colleagues that this authorization was not another Gulf of Tonkin Resolution, and he made a final appeal to wavering Democrats that a vote for this authorization in no way precluded congressional action in the future: "I believe the president of the United States when he says to me head-to-head he has no plans to change the peacekeeping role of the marines . . . if at any time I have reason to believe that the spirit and the letter of this resolution is not being lived up to, I will do . . . whatever is necessary concerning Lebanon to get our men back."[22] The joint resolution carried on a 270–161 vote.

For the administration, the vote was a significant triumph. Secretary of State Shultz, in particular, believed that it not only was essential to avoiding a constitutional interbranch showdown over war powers, but more importantly was a tremendous boost to the U.S. bargaining posi-

21. *Congressional Quarterly Almanac* 1983, 118–19.
22. *Congressional Quarterly Almanac* 1983, 119.

tion in the region. "The vote was of immense importance," Shultz wrote. "It let everyone know that the United States had staying power."[23]

However, the president faced even stauncher initial opposition, ironically, in the Republican-controlled Senate. Whereas O'Neill had been able to mute his troops' calls for tougher action, the Senate Democratic caucus voted unanimously to introduce an alternative resolution (SJ Res 163) invoking the War Powers Resolution retroactively to August 28, 1983, with no extended authorization for the Marine presence. The Senate Foreign Relations Committee took up both this proposal and a substitute by member Charles Mathias (R-Maryland) invoking the War Powers Resolution with a six-month authorization (SJ Res 159). When committee consideration began, the Republicans substituted Mathias's language with the eighteen-month authorization from the House. The committee was sharply divided as most of the majority Republicans attempted to toe the line for the president, though even the chairman, Charles Percy, openly expressed reservations: "I don't think any of us knows where this is leading."[24] For a time, Democrats succeeded in restoring Mathias's original formulation for a six-month authorization. Finally, however, after a heavy round of pressure from Majority Leader Baker, who himself was ambivalent about the wisdom of the mission, committee Republicans succeeded in reporting the eighteen-month formula. Although he agreed to "carry the banner for the president," the majority leader warned Shultz that "if things go badly and we do pull out, we've written the script for the Democrats."[25]

Despite tepid support even from Republican members for the compromise in the floor debate, the Senate defeated a Democratic attempt to place more restrictions on the deployment by a party-line 55–45 vote; the eighteen-month authorization passed and was signed into law (PL 98–119). However, as O'Neill reminded his colleagues in his floor speech advocating passage, the authorization contained explicit language for Congress to consider any proposed changes to the authorization through expedited procedures. The terrorist bombing of the Marine barracks only eleven days after the authorization became the law of the land quickly provided the mission's myriad opponents with an opportunity to exploit this open door.

23. Shultz 1993, 226.
24. *Congressional Quarterly Almanac* 1983, 118.
25. Shultz 1993, 226.

Barracks Bombing and Aftermath

On October 23, 1983, the Marine mission at Beirut International Airport suffered the deadliest terrorist attack against American troops in history. A suicide bomber crashed through the outer perimeter of the Marine barracks in an explosives-laden truck and plowed into the building, killing 241 American servicemen. The worst fears of the Reagan administration's congressional opponents—and of Secretary of Defense Weinberger, who five days earlier had warned that the troops were "sitting on a bull's eye" at the airport and proposed redeploying them to ships offshore (a plan that garnered little support and was not even put to a vote at the National Security Planning Group meeting)—had been realized, and quickly.[26]

Fearing public backlash, Reagan could have announced his intentions to withdraw the Marines to safer positions in ships offshore, or at the very least to review immediately the basis for their continued presence at the airport. Instead, he upped the political ante. Shultz later described the mood in the White House in the bombing's immediate aftermath as somber, yet resolute: "We were shocked and grieved. But the president was determined not to be driven out of Lebanon by this terrorist attack." On October 24, the president met with reporters to reiterate his determination not to waver in the wake of the bombing. Giving voice to the nation's concerns, he began, "Many Americans are wondering why we must keep our forces in Lebanon. Well, the reason they must stay there until the situation is under control is quite clear: We have vital interests in Lebanon, and our actions in Lebanon are in the cause of world peace." But in addition to the justness of the mission, Reagan offered another reason for his determination not to yield: the struggle in Lebanon could not be separated from its broader Cold War context, and any sign of American weakness here would have repercussions elsewhere. "The struggle for peace is indivisible," he said. "We cannot pick and choose where we will support freedom; we can only determine how. If it's lost in one place, all of us lose. If others feel confident that they can intimidate us and our allies in Lebanon, they will become more bold

---

26. Agenda for NSPG meeting, October 23, 1983, folder NSPG 0075, 23 Oct 1983, box 91306, Executive Secretariat, NSC: Records NSPG, Ronald Reagan Library; memo, Weinberger to McFarlane, November 7, 1983, folder "Lebanon Chronology (1)," box 91354, Executive Secretariat, NSC: country file, Ronald Reagan Library.

elsewhere."[27] Three days later, Reagan addressed the nation on prime-time television and reiterated his determination not to withdraw. "Let me ask those who say we should get out of Lebanon: If we were to leave Lebanon now, what message would that send to those who foment instability and terrorism?" Withdrawal, he argued, was not an option, and to make his case he appealed to the legacy of the fallen. "Brave young men have been taken from us. Many others have been grievously wounded. Are we to tell them their sacrifice was wasted? They gave their lives in defense of our national security every bit as much as any man who ever died fighting in a war. We must not strip every ounce of meaning and purpose from their courageous sacrifice."[28]

Reagan had clearly thrown down the gauntlet at the feet of any political opponents who would countenance withdrawal, and he was backed in this endeavor by key members of his administration and the military. The day after the bombing, Secretary of State Shultz testified before Congress, "We are in Lebanon because the outcome in Lebanon will affect our position in the whole Middle East. . . . To ask why Lebanon is important is to ask why the whole Middle East is important—because the answer is the same."[29] Perhaps even more interestingly, the military commanders, many of whom had long opposed the mission privately, came out publicly in support of continuing U.S. participation in the MNF. Echoing testimony given by Naval Chief James Watkins in September before the bombing that withdrawing from the MNF could "plunge Lebanon into anarchy," Marine General Kelley vociferously and bluntly put the case for staying to would-be congressional proponents of withdrawal in a public hearing: "I don't think the United States of America, the greatest country in the free world, should back off from some damn terrorist attack."[30]

27. Ronald Reagan, "Remarks and a Question-and-Answer Session with Regional Editors and Broadcasters on the Situation in Lebanon." *Public Papers of the President*, October 24, 1983. See also Ed Meese, "Outlines of Points on Lebanon," October 23, 1983, folder "Lebanon Bombing/Airport," box 41, Executive Secretariat, NSC, country file, Ronald Reagan Library.

28. Ronald Reagan, "Address to the Nation on Events in Lebanon and Grenada." *Public Papers of the President*, October 27, 1983.

29. Cannon 2000, 444.

30. Senate Armed Services Committee, 84-S201–22, October 31, 1983. *CQ Weekly*, November 5, 1983, 2288.

However, despite the unified White House–Pentagon front, reaction on Capitol Hill was decidedly more mixed. Many members on both sides of the aisle vehemently criticized the administration's reckless foreign policy and demanded the Marines' withdrawal. While the president's prime-time speech rallied popular support for the mission, many in Congress expressed sharp skepticism. Oregon Republican Slade Gorton bluntly told White House officials, "the president's wrong on Lebanon." Idaho Republican Steve Symms also expressed concern, while Pete Domenici (R–New Mexico) relayed that although "on Grenada, [I'm] with you 100% . . . Lebanon is a tough issue."[31] O'Neill, however, again tempered the congressional opposition by adamantly opposing withdrawal, which he claimed "would say to the fanatics and the terrorists of the world that they have achieved what they set out to do." When the Democratic rank and file demanded a caucus meeting to protest his standing behind Reagan, O'Neill launched into a vigorous defense of his position, allegedly concluding with the remark that he stood by the president in the wake of disaster because "I am a patriot!"[32]

Complicating the political arena in the immediate aftermath of the barracks bombing was the Reagan administration's October 25 invasion of the small Caribbean island nation of Grenada. O'Neill learned of the invasion the day following the barracks bombing, after a long session of his House Lebanon Task Force's meetings with Secretaries Weinberger and Shultz. The president secretly requested to meet with congressional leaders that night. When asked by his aide Kirk O'Donnell whether he believed the president had major plans for Lebanon, O'Neill replied that he figured the target was Grenada. "I just have a feeling about it," he recalled saying. "The administration has been wanting to go in there for a long time. . . . Besides, the Prime Minister down there has been killed, so they have the perfect excuse." O'Donnell asked, "Then you don't think the meeting is about Lebanon?" "Sure I do," O'Neill replied. "They're invading Grenada so people will forget what happened yesterday in Beirut."[33]

O'Neill may have been wrong in part; according to some adminis-

31. Typescript, "Senate Reaction," folder "Lebanon/Grenada, RR's speech 10/28[1983] (1 of 5)," box 4, Michael Baroody files, Ronald Reagan Library.

32. *CQ Weekly*, October 29, 1983, 2217; *Congressional Quarterly Almanac*, 1983, 121.

33. O'Neill 1987, 365.

tration records, Reagan had made the decision to invade Grenada even before learning of the Beirut bombing.[34] Yet on the other count, the speaker was correct; the rally effect generated by the Marines storming the shores of Grenada muted any popular backlash against the administration from the horrific events in Lebanon. *Washington Post* journalist Lou Cannon notes that while Reagan did not launch the Grenada invasion as a diversionary tactic as many commentators have assumed, "the president and his White House staff were shameless and successful in using the easy victory in Grenada to wipe away the stain of the unnecessary disaster in Beirut."[35] Indeed, as figure 5.2 illustrates, Reagan's approval rating, which had hovered at 47 percent in September 1983 before the bombing, jumped six percentage points in the first poll after the Beirut blast. Similarly, when asked in November of 1983 whether the events in Lebanon and Grenada would make respondents more or less likely to vote for Reagan in 1984, respondents answered more likely by almost a two to one margin![36] Critically, as figure 5.2 shows, the president's public approval rating actually increased over the remaining months of the deployment.

Moreover, apart from the boost in support for Reagan following the Grenada invasion, there is little evidence that the Beirut bombing and the loss of 241 Marines had any major effect on public support for the mission in Lebanon specifically.[37] Public support for the Lebanon deployment in September was already low, averaging in the upper thirties across several polls. Indeed, Reagan acknowledged the low level of public support for his Lebanon policy in his personal diary in September of 1983, almost a month before the barracks bombing.[38] The lack of support did not deter him from his course, though it may explain his fre-

34. Yet a chronology in *Congressional Quarterly* given to reporters by Secretary of State Shultz suggests that the president made the "tentative" decision to invade Grenada only after he returned to Washington from a golfing outing in Georgia after learning of the attacks in Beirut. See Richard Whittle, "Questions, Praise Follow Grenada Invasion." *CQ Weekly,* October 29, 1983, 2221–24.

35. Cannon 2000, 441–442, 448–449. Interestingly, only 6 percent of the public reported believing the action was a diversionary strike in a November, 1983, poll. *Los Angeles Times* poll # 1983–073: November 12–17, 1983.

36. *Los Angeles Times* poll # 1983–073: November 12–17, 1983.

37. *Los Angeles Times* poll [USLAT1983-073], November 12–17, 1983. Burk (1999) reaches a similar conclusion.

38. In his diary for September 30, 1983, Reagan (1990, 447) wrote: "[Latest opinion polls] show I'm up on job rating, the economy. But on foreign policy—Lebanon—I'm way

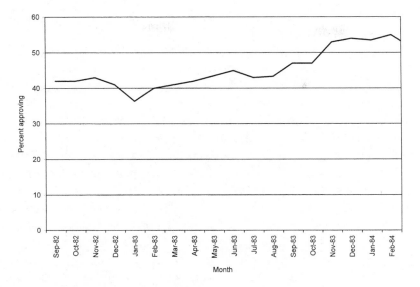

FIGURE 5.2. President Ronald Reagan's approval rating, 1982–84

quent public pronouncements on the justness of the American cause in Lebanon—he discussed the American presence there more than twenty times in September and October, before the bombing—as an attempt to court popular support. If anything, the bombing may have yielded a short-term rally in popular support for the president's Lebanon policies, as shown in figure 5.1.

The administration's efforts paid immediate dividends in shaping public opinion. Far from collapsing in the wake of the barracks bombing, support for the administration's handling of the situation in Lebanon actually increased.[39] In the days immediately following the bomb-

---

down. The people just don't know why we're there. There is deeply buried isolationist sentiment in our land."

39. The administration's pollsters kept a close eye on the multiple polls conducted in the days following the explosion and noted a rally even before the president's speech. "Despite the differences between the Lebanon and Grenada issues, both are currently subject to the rally-round-the-president effect . . . . furthermore, the public was shown to be less supportive of Lebanon policy weeks ago, *before* the Beirut explosion, than it was last night *before* the president spoke. This suggests one or more circumstances favored the President, independent of his speech." Memo, Bernard Roshao to John Hughes, folder "Lebanon/ Grenada, RR's speech, 10/27[1983] (2 of 5)," box OA 11244, box 4, Michael Baroody files, Ronald Reagan Library.

ing, four polls queried the public on its support for the Marine presence in Beirut; ironically, support ran a little stronger in the wake of the attack, with an average of 45 percent approving of the mission and the administration's handling of it. Support peaked after Reagan's prime-time address. An ABC split-sample poll taken immediately before and after the speech suggested an enormous bounce for the administration. Before the speech, 50 percent of those sampled approved of the administration's handling of the situation in Lebanon, while 45 percent disapproved. After the speech, 80 percent said they approved, with only 20 percent disapproving. Seeking to exploit the poll, the White House included the results in its talking points for administration officials and allies.[40]

Perhaps even more telling was a question asked three weeks after the bombing on public support for the deployment's duration. From November 12 to 17, the *Los Angeles Times* asked more than two thousand Americans whether the Marine deployment should last for the full eighteen months requested by Reagan and authorized by Congress. A startling 53 percent of Americans favored a deployment lasting the full eighteen months or longer, while only 33 percent supported a shorter mission.[41]

Thus, the bombing alone did not precipitate the Marine withdrawal. Reagan and key members of his staff emerged from the tragedy defiant, and they publicly proclaimed the necessity of staying the course. Similarly, there is no evidence that the bombing triggered an avalanche of popular pressure on Reagan to change course. On the contrary, in the weeks immediately following the bombing, support for the president and for the mission itself increased. The combination of domestic political and international strategic factors that compelled the dramatic policy reversal in February 1984 would emerge gradually in the weeks and months following the attack, and in both cases Congress would play a critical role in generating the changes that precipitated the withdrawal.

40. "Memorandum for Administration Spokesmen," folder "Lebanon/Grenada, RR's speech, 10/27[1983] (2 of 5)" box OA 11244, box 4, Michael Baroody files, Ronald Reagan Library. Also forwarded to White House spokesman Larry Speakes were tallies of comments to the White House switchboard, which were overwhelmingly positive. Memo, Peter Roussel to Larry Speakes, October 31, 1983, folder "Lebanon/Grenada, RR's speech, 10/27[1983] (3 of 5)." box OA 11244, box 4, Michael Baroody files, Ronald Reagan Library.
41. *Los Angeles Times* poll [USLAT1983-073], November 12–17, 1983.

The Interbranch Conflict Intensifies

Despite the absence of any popular outcry for withdrawing U.S. Marines from Lebanon, many members in both chambers of Congress, who had fought against the eighteen-month authorization only weeks before, began a new round of attacks on the president's military policies in Lebanon. To counter Reagan's rosy rhetoric on Lebanon—in his October 27 prime-time address, he even argued paradoxically that the attack was a signal of the mission's overall success—both the House and Senate launched extensive hearings into the bombing and the mission more generally.[42] The House Armed Services Committee held extensive hearings on the failures that had led to the bombing in November and December 1983, while the Senate Armed Services and Foreign Relations committees, as well as the House Appropriations and Foreign Affairs committees, also held public inquiries into various aspects of Lebanon policy.[43]

Proponents of ending the engagement also began to move forward on the legislative front. In the House, however, they continued to face an implacable obstacle in the form of Speaker O'Neill. When Clarence Long offered a new amendment to the DOD appropriations bill cutting off funding for the Marine mission after March 1, 1984, the effort encountered stiff resistance from the Democratic leader. Using procedural powers, O'Neill had part of the amendment's moderating language ruled out of order, leaving the chamber with a stark choice between an absolute and unconditional funding cutoff and a clean bill. The House struck the amendment, though many who voted for it took to the floor to express their sincere desire to find a way out of Lebanon.[44]

Senate Democrats followed a similar course by introducing SJ Res

---

42. Ronald Reagan, "Address to the Nation on Events in Lebanon and Grenada." *Public Papers of the President*, October 27, 1983.

43. House Committee on Armed Services, "Full Committee Hearings on the Use of U.S. Military Personnel in Lebanon and Consideration of Report from Sept. 24–25 Committee Delegation to Lebanon," 84-H201-26; Senate Committee on Armed Services, "Situation in Lebanon," 84-S201-22; House Committee on Armed Services, "Review of Adequacy of Security Arrangements for Marines in Lebanon and Plans for Improving That Security," 85-H201-26; House Committee on Appropriations, "Department of Defense Appropriations, Situation in Lebanon and Grenada," 84-H181-1; Senate Committee on Foreign Relations, "Authorization for U.S. Marines in Lebanon," 84-S381-5; House Committee on Foreign Affairs, "Developments in the Middle East, Nov. 1983," 84-H381-36.

44. *CQ Weekly*, November 5, 1983, 2289.

190, which would slash the MNF authorization from eighteen to three months. Even though these initiatives had little chance of ever becoming law, consistent with the theory articulated in chapter 2, many members nevertheless believed that such efforts had considerable bite through raising the political costs of staying the course for the president. For example, acknowledging that any joint resolution faced an uphill battle as it would have to survive a presidential veto, cosponsor Alan Dixon (D-Illinois) argued that the action was not merely an empty gesture but actually a tangible political tool because even committee approval of the bill would bring the issue firmly onto the public agenda and put "real pressure" on Reagan to change course.[45]

While Majority Leader Baker was able to bottle up an earlier proposal calling for Reagan to replace the Marines with troops from neutral countries, the provisions of PL 98–119, which had authorized the MNF participation, required expedited action on any proposal, such as SJ Res 190, which sought to amend the authorization. The bill was dutifully referred to the Foreign Relations Committee, on which the GOP held a one-seat advantage, for consideration, but Chairman Percy was forced to stall committee action on the proposal when Charles Mathias broke party lines and agreed to vote with the Democrats if they would amend the bill's authorization to reflect his earlier proposal for a six-month authorization retroactive to August 29. When Democrats signaled their willingness to compromise, Percy halted a November 15, 1983, markup session and successfully pushed the process over into the next session of Congress.[46] The first session of the ninety-eighth Congress adjourned on November 18, which gave the Reagan administration a temporary reprieve from overt congressional action against its Lebanon policies.

In the immediate aftermath of the bombing, the political fault lines within the White House remained virtually the same as they had been before the bombing. Weinberger and many in the military continued privately to advocate redeployment while Shultz, McFarlane—now national security advisor after Bill Clark's move to the Department of the Interior—and the NSC remained strongly supportive of a continued presence and a more aggressive posture. Indeed, Shultz fervently believed that the reactions of Syria and other opponents of the LAF in

45. *CQ Weekly*, November 12, 1983, 2359. On a parallel track, Senator John Melcher (D-MT) introduced a resolution to repeal PL 98–119.

46. *Congressional Quarterly Almanac* 1983, 122–23.

the wake of the augmented U.S. naval shelling and aerial actions justified a more aggressive approach: "As the strife-filled days [following the
bombing] went by, we observed that when our forces were aggressive in
reconnaissance and reacted sharply when fired on, the Syrians stepped
back and sounded more accommodating."[47] Weinberger would later lament that the State Department and the NSC "played to that worry of
the President's by telling him that it would always appear that we had
'cut and run,' that we had been 'driven out,' and similar phrases designed
to encourage the belief that only if we stayed out of Lebanon could we
demonstrate our manhood or secure any of the objectives we wanted."[48]
However, the positioning of some key players in the Reagan court began
to shift as developments on the ground played out, and as political pressure built with ominous signs of renewed energy on Capitol Hill.

As the United States became more directly engaged militarily in the
conflict through the shelling and air patrols authorized by the president
in National Security Decision Directives 103 and 111, the danger to U.S.
troops remained high. December 4, 1983, was another bloody day for
U.S. forces. Shelling from the Shouf Mountains killed eight Marines at
the airport, while two Navy fighter jets were downed on a bombing raid
against Syrian antiaircraft positions. One of the pilots died in the crash,
one was rescued, and one was captured by the Syrians. Syria later released the downed airman after personal diplomacy by the Reverend
Jesse Jackson, himself a presidential candidate in 1984.

Back in Washington, December brought the final reports of two investigations into the barracks bombing, one by the House Foreign Affairs Commmittee and the other by a Department of Defense–appointed
independent inquiry led by retired Admiral Robert Long. To preempt
criticism of the administration's overall policy in Lebanon and to keep
the public narrowly focused on the lapses of security at the barracks, the
White House strategically leaked the report's security-related findings
ahead of its release. Additionally, immediately after the report's publication, Reagan himself took full responsibility for the lapses in security
and declared that there would be no courts-martial for the officers on
the ground. The action served both to portray Reagan as a commander
in charge and to keep the media focus on security lapses rather than on
the commission's call to reexamine the basis for the American presence

47. Shultz 1993, 229.
48. Weinberger 1990, 160.

in Lebanon.[49] An examination of major national print and television broadcast media from the period show that the effort was largely successful. In his national radio address on December 10, Reagan affirmed his determination to hold fast, and emphasized that the Marines would leave only "once internal stability is established and withdrawal of all foreign forces is assured."[50]

Yet, the Long and HFAC reports, coupled with the continued attacks on American forces, only emboldened those in Congress who for months had sought to end the American military commitment in Lebanon, and strengthened their ranks. By December 9, 1983, Bill Alexander (D-Arkansas), the chairman of Speaker O'Neill's ad hoc Lebanon Oversight Committee, publicly reported that the Lebanon compromise embodied in PL 98–119 no longer enjoyed much support in the House: "I do not believe that the president can count on the support of a majority in the Congress for continuation of his present policies in the region."[51] By mid-December, even two Democrats who had been stalwart supporters of the administration's policies, Lee Hamilton of Indiana and Les Aspin of Wisconsin, wrote the president recommending a reduction of the use of force in Lebanon. And on December 19, the House Armed Services Committee released the results of its own investigation into the Marine deployment and urged the president "in the strongest terms" to reevaluate its policy. In a letter to Reagan and Vice President Bush that was also released to the public, Representative William Nichols (D-Alabama) warned, "Failure of the administration to adequately reexamine its policy and relate it to present conditions will only mean that such reexamination will have to be done by Congress." The committee expressed its belief that "the solution to Lebanon's problems will only be found at the bargaining table," and rejected the idea that it could "be found on the battlefield with the participation of U.S. armed forces."[52]

49. Ronald Reagan, "Remarks and a Question-and-Answer Session with Reporters on the Pentagon Report on the Security of United States Marines in Lebanon." *Public Papers of the President*, December 27, 1983. *CQ Weekly*, December 17, 1983, 2671–72; Cannon 2000, 452.

50. Ronald Reagan, "Radio Address to the Nation on the Situation in Lebanon." *Public Papers of the President*, December 10, 1983.

51. *CQ Weekly*, December 17, 1983, 2671.

52. Letter, Nichols to Reagan, December 21, 1983, folder ND016 186262, WHORM, Ronald Reagan Library.

Perhaps even more importantly, O'Neill also showed signs of wavering. On December 22, 1983, seventy House members urged the speaker in a letter to make a review of the nation's military policy in Lebanon a matter of the highest priority when the second session of the ninety-eighth Congress began in early 1984. Copies of the letter circulated throughout the NSC and the White House, leading to the inescapable conclusion that "it is clear from the attached that Lebanon will be high on the agenda when Congress returns in January."[53] Two weeks later, on January 3, 1984, the speaker convened another meeting of his Lebanon Oversight Committee for personal discussions with Reagan administration officials who were trying to convince Congress to stay the course. After the meeting, O'Neill's reversal was complete. The speaker, who had been pivotal in passing the eighteen-month authorization the previous September, now publicly proclaimed the need for a radical change in Lebanon: "I will join with many others in Congress in reconsidering congressional authorization for the Marine presence in Lebanon . . . [the status quo] is unacceptable . . . patience in Congress is wearing very thin."[54]

On the same day, Percy—the Republican committee chairman who in November had postponed a vote on the Democratic effort to slash the authorization for the Marine force (SJ Res 190)—also switched course. Facing stiff competition in the upcoming primary and general election, he now openly called for a phased withdrawal: "It is my feeling that we are no longer really a constructive part of the peacekeeping force there. We are a target and we are causing hostile actions in Lebanon."[55] Toward this end, Percy scheduled intersession hearings to consider the Democratic legislation to compel withdrawal. Even before Percy's move in the Senate, House Minority Leader Robert Michel (R-Illinois) on December 27, 1983, recommended redeploying the troops offshore and asked, "Can the presence of the Marines any longer be defended?"[56] After a briefing for Republican members by Weinberger and McFarlane

53. Memo, Everett to Fortier, folder "Lebanon III (5 of 5)," box 90753, Donald Fortier files, Ronald Reagan Library.

54. *CQ Weekly*, January 7, 1984, 3.

55. *CQ Weekly*, January 7, 1984, 6. For Percy's precarious electoral circumstances, see memo, Rollins to Baker III, April 6, 1983, folder "WH Staff Memoranda—Political Affairs [2 of 3]," box 5, James Baker III files, Ronald Reagan Library.

56. *CQ Weekly*, January 7, 1984, 5.

on January 4, 1984, Michel conceded that concern and doubt among his troops was growing. Indeed, the Reagan administration was later stung by private calls for ending the Marine deployment from Trent Lott (R-Mississippi) and Dick Cheney (R-Wyoming), both of whom had been stalwart administration supporters.[57]

Although Reagan and his policies had emerged relatively unscathed from the immediate aftermath of the barracks bombing, many in the administration were deeply concerned about the gathering storm in Congress. In preparation for a January 3, 1984, meeting of the National Security Policy Group, officials at both the Department of Defense and the National Security Council warned of the perilous environment on the Hill and its ramifications for the endeavor in Lebanon. "[Before] the reassembly of Congress on January 23, we need to look open-mindedly at our Lebanon policy with a view toward demonstrating fresh progress and the emergence of milestones of success. Time is short." The NSC and DOD officials made it perfectly clear that this reevaluation was necessary not because the situation on the ground was deteriorating, but because of the changed political realities created by an increasingly assertive congressional opposition. "Ironically, we find our domestic support unraveling . . . *at the very moment certain conditions on the ground begin to improve*—e.g., Soviets urging caution on Syria, uncertainty about internal Syrian leadership capacity for initiative, the strengthening of U.S. ties, and the sobering impact of U.S. military action on affected Lebanese factions." Despite these positive developments on the ground, the report warned against escalating the American engagement and even of staying the course because "further casualties to the MNF will only accelerate demands in the Congress and the European capitals to bring home the MNF."[58]

The newly minted national security advisor, Bud McFarlane, echoed many of the same concerns in a January 3 memorandum to the president:

> We can expect a growing crescendo of criticism from both liberals and conservatives when Congress reassembles on January 23. The growth in domes-

57. Reeves 2005, 203. *CQ Weekly*, February 11, 1984, 239.

58. "NSC Summary of Defense Department Comments on Non Paper: Next Steps in Lebanon," folder "Lebanon Chronology (2)," box 41, Executive Secretariat, NSC, country file, Ronald Reagan Library. Emphasis added.

tic opposition comes at a time when the situation on the ground in Lebanon has not deteriorated significantly . . . [we] need to develop a legislative strategy for dealing with the Congress.[59]

For Weinberger and many at Defense, raising such concerns about congressional pressures served their longstanding desire to end the MNF mission and redeploy the Marines offshore. For others more intimately concerned with political issues, such as White House Chief of Staff James Baker III and Vice President Bush, the alarm bells from Capitol Hill served gradually to shift their position from general support of staying the course in Lebanon toward joining those advocating withdrawal.

As the administration white paper warned, the legislative attacks on Reagan's policies only intensified when Congress returned from its recess on January 23. The Senate Foreign Relations Committee scheduled a final markup on the binding SJ Res 190 for January 31. In the House, Samuel Stratton (D-New York) introduced HJ Res 459, which would require offshore redeployment of the Marines by April 1, 1984. Others pursued a less direct nonbinding path. House Foreign Affairs Committee chairman Dante Fascell (D-Florida) acknowledged that it was "very difficult to pick a time certain" for withdrawal, but was confident that Congress would pass a resolution "built around something that says, 'Let's get these guys out as soon as possible.'"[60] Indeed, O'Neill provided the spark for just such an approach when he cleared the way for a nonbinding resolution (H Con Res 248 and S Con Res 92) that called for a "prompt and orderly withdrawal" of the Marines from Lebanon and directed the president to report to Congress within thirty days on the steps he was taking toward implementing a change in policy.[61] Furthermore, O'Neill made it clear that he wanted the resolution passed by Congress's

59. Memo, McFarlane to Reagan, January 3, 1984, folder "CPPG Meeting, January 30, 1984, Lebanon," box 91834, William Burns files, Ronald Reagan Library.

60. *CQ Weekly*, January 28, 1984, 126.

61. In the statistical models of chapter 4, nonbinding resolutions had no systematic effect on conflict duration. In the current context, however, it is important to remember that there were binding initiatives pending in Congress, particularly in the Senate. If H Con Res 248 were the only expression of congressional discontent, its influence might have been minimal. However, in the Lebanon case the resolution was not just a nonbinding critique of administration policy introduced on a whim. Instead, it served as a concrete ex-

recess on February 2. The Democrats and even their Republican allies understood the difficult of formally compelling the president, with veto pen in hand, to change course. Yet, they clung to the idea that their actions carried considerable political weight even if they did not become law. "What it comes down to is pressure; that's the whole point of this," Senator Joseph Biden (D-Delaware) argued.[62]

Publicly, the Reagan administration refused to back down. High-ranking officials lobbied Republican senators in both the Foreign Relations Committee and in the caucus as a whole in an attempt to stem the tide of defections. In the House, the president sent to Lee Hamilton and Les Aspin, erstwhile supporters of the MNF, personal notes arguing the continued merits of maintaining the Marine presence in Beirut.[63] Furthermore, in his January 25 State of the Union address Reagan reiterated the justness of America's cause in Lebanon and the need to stay the course: "Your joint resolution [authorizing] the multinational peace-keeping force in Lebanon is also serving the cause of peace [PL 98–119]. . . . We must have the courage to give peace a chance. And we must not be driven from our objectives for peace in Lebanon by state-sponsored terrorism."[64]

Privately, however, administration officials acknowledged that political pressure from Congress was mounting. Interestingly, they perceived this pressure even though popular support for Reagan remained higher than it had been in years and support for the Lebanon mission itself remained relatively constant. Donald Fortier, the senior director for political-military affairs on the NSC, emphasized to National Security Director McFarlane, who still favored a more aggressive American posture in Beirut, that Congress and not the public posed the biggest obstacle:

> Our basic problem is the disjunction between what I perceive to be the basic sentiment of the American people and the likely attitudes of the House leaders we will have to convince. The former are essentially of the view that we

pression of O'Neill's conversion from general support for the mission to open opposition to its continuation.

62. *CQ Weekly*, February 4, 1984, 227–28.

63. *CQ Weekly* January 28, 1984, 152.

64. Ronald Reagan, "Address Before a Joint Session of the Congress on the State of the Union." *Public Papers of the President*, January 25, 1984.

should either do something serious or get out. The latter are more concerned with getting out than doing something serious, and, in fact, doing something serious is likely to frighten them more than our current untenable position.[65]

In a similar vein, Secretary of State Shultz, emphasizing the Democrats' shift in strategy, pointed to Congress as the major source of the political pressure: "Congressional support was eroding, and Democratic strategy, led by House Speaker Tip O'Neill, focused on actual withdrawal of U.S. forces rather than on reducing the duration of the mandate voted for in September."[66] McFarlane, despite his ardent advocacy of a more aggressive military role in Lebanon, concurred and acknowledged that political concerns were paramount, noting that a presidential election year "does concentrate your mind."[67]

Perhaps the most important change within the administration itself that precipitated the dramatic reversal in policy was the conversion of both White House Chief of Staff Baker and Vice President Bush to the cause of redeployment. By late 1983 to early 1984, Baker, renowned for his political skills and cunning, reassessed the stakes in Lebanon and came to the conclusion that continuing the Marine presence had the potential to become a major political liability in the 1984 election cycle.[68] He had long had his finger on the pulse of opposition to the administration's Lebanon policy within the Republican congressional ranks. Indeed, Baker had helped direct the administration's lobbying of Congress for the eighteen-month authorization in September, and he also knew firsthand that support for the Lebanon mission within the Republican caucus, even from the majority leader, was fragile.[69] The administration had dodged a bullet thus far in terms of maintaining public support, but

65. Memo, Fortier to McFarlane, "Overcoming Congressional Reservations on the New Lebanon NSDD," February 1, 1984, folder "Lebanon III (1 of 5)," box 90753, Donald Fortier files, Ronald Reagan Library.

66. Shultz 1993, 229.

67. Cannon 2000, 435.

68. Cannon 2000, 451–53.

69. See Clark to NSPG, cc: Bush, Meese, Baker, and Deaver, September 3, 1983, folder NSPG 0068 & 0068A (1) 03 Sep 1983, box 91306, Executive Secretariat, NSC, Ronald Reagan Library: NSPGs; memo, Duberstein to Baker III, Meese, Deaver, et al., October 7, 1983, folder "W.H. Staff Memoranda—Legislative Affairs 7/83–12/83 [2 of 3]," box 5, James Baker III files, Ronald Reagan Library; memo, Duberstein to Baker III and Darman, October 29, 1983, folder "W.H. Staff Memoranda: Legislative Affairs 7/83–12/83 [1 of 3]," box 5, James Baker III files, Ronald Reagan Library; agenda for NSPG meeting, October 23,

sustained criticism from a hostile Congress threatened to erode this support quickly. In Baker, Weinberger and other longtime opponents of the deployment now had a powerful ally, and they would gain another one with the reversal of Vice President Bush. As late as January 9, 1984, Bush did not support withdrawing the Marines at a National Security Planning Group meeting. However, after consultations with Baker and others, and after his own reevaluation of the stakes in Lebanon, by early February he had become a leading proponent of withdrawal.[70]

Thus, the evidence is insurmountable that officials across all branches of the Reagan administration were keenly aware of the political costs they stood to incur by defying congressional opposition and staying the course in Lebanon. They feared the effects of congressional criticism on anticipated changes in public opinion, as well as the tangible electoral consequences such a shift would have for the president himself and for his party in congressional races.

Yet the archival records also show strong evidence for the second hypothesized mechanism of congressional influence: Congress's ability to raise—albeit inadvertently, through the signals its actions send to foreign actors—the military costs the president perceives he must pay to continue a military engagement. While it is exceedingly difficult to ascertain whether congressional signals actually affected the calculus of the Syrians and other factions hostile to the American presence within Lebanon, archival documents make clear that administration officials *believed* it did, and that the anticipated military costs of attaining American objectives in Lebanon rose accordingly. Both in their public pronouncements and in their private correspondence, a diverse range of officials within the Reagan policymaking team voiced concerns that vociferous opposition to the MNF in Congress emboldened the Syrians and their Lebanese proxies, exacerbated the difficulties the MNF faced, and thereby raised the costs of staying the course in Beirut.

In a cable from the field back to Washington, Donald Rumsfeld, McFarlane's successor as special envoy to the Middle East and former defense secretary under Gerald Ford, lamented that "the Syrians were watching the debate [in Congress] and drawing their own conclusions about the sustainability of [United States government] support for the

---

1983, folder NSPG 0075, 23 Oct 1983, box 91306, Executive Secretariat, NSC: Records NSPG, Ronald Reagan Library.

70. Shultz 1993, 230–31; Cannon 2005, 454–55.

[government of Lebanon]." Rumsfeld warned that even the September authorization was a source of problems for the administration because it "was worded in a way which allowed our presence in Lebanon to be scrutinized at any time and made priority business of the Congress. . . . This creates perpetual uncertainty emanating from the U.S. and affecting the situation in Lebanon."[71] Secretary of State Shultz echoed these concerns when lamenting the legislative measures to curtail the Marine mission in Lebanon that were pending before Congress. Although the president still retained the veto, Shultz noted, the mere presence of such legislative initiatives on the agenda then and for the foreseeable future caused real problems for the White House, particularly with Syria.[72]

Shultz shared Rumsfeld's concerns that actions in Congress were sending unintended signals to Damascus that raised the costs of staying the course in Lebanon.[73] "I was convinced that Syria and the Lebanese opposition now believed that Congress would eventually force a pullout and that this had been a primary factor in Syrian intransigence during December," he would later write in his memoirs.[74] When the Marines were still in Lebanon, Shultz claimed in a television interview that the Syrian foreign minister had openly boasted to his Lebanese counterpart that the United States would withdraw from Beirut in the face of domestic political pressure as soon as it lost a few Marines.[75] His deputy Law-

---

71. Cable, Rumsfeld to McFarlane, Weinberger, Vessey, Casey, and Shultz, January 29, 1984, folder "Lebanon I (1 of 5)," box 90753, Donald Fortier files, Ronald Reagan Library. Rumsfeld's assessment was also shared by the CIA: "These Shia and Palestinian groups, as well as their Iranian and Syrian sponsors, almost certainly believe that the bombing at the Marine compound in October has influenced U.S. public opinion and put pressure on U.S. policymakers to withdraw from Lebanon. They are therefore convinced that an intensifying campaign of terrorist violence against the MNF will advance their objective." Directorate of Intelligence, "The Terrorist Threat to US Personnel in Beirut," January 12, 1984, folder "Lebanon (11/30/1983)," box 43, Executive Secretariat, NSC, country file, Ronald Reagan Library. For a similar assessment, see: "Foreign Intelligence and National Security Policy Developments, October–December 1983," folder "Foreign Intelligence and National Security Policy Developments, October– December 1983, (1)," box 91129, Crisis Management Center (CMC), NSC Records, Ronald Reagan Library.

72. Cable, Shultz to McFaralane, Weinberger, Vessey, and Casey, February 5, 1984, folder "Lebanon I (4 of 5)," box 90753, Donald Fortier files, Ronald Reagan Library.

73. Cable, Shultz to McFarlane, Weinberger, Vessey, and Casey, February 2, 1984, folder "Lebanon I (2 of 5)," box 90753, Donald Fortier files, Ronald Reagan Library.

74. Shultz 1993, 229.

75. Cannon 2000, 415.

rence Eagleburger also expressed these views publicly, testifying before the House Foreign Affairs Committee in January that Syria and its allies in Lebanon drew strength from "the obvious weakening of will" in Washington."[76]

This view was even shared by many members of Congress. Georgia Republican Newt Gingrich wrote in a memo to the Office of Legislative Affairs: "Our allies and even our opponents have grown remarkably sophisticated at watching the U.S. Congress and the news media. Thus, seemingly secondary actions on television or in Congressional Committees can play a key role in leading foreign governments and movements to decide how to respond to our initiatives."[77] Pennsylvania Republican Robert Walker echoed Gingrich's concerns, lamenting, "I think that some of what is taking place in Lebanon today can be ascribed to the policies that have been enunciated in this House by leaders, who, in my opinion, should have known better."[78]

As a result, by late January 1984 almost every top administration official acknowledged that congressional actions had raised both the political and the military costs of staying the course in Lebanon. This dramatically changed domestic political environment precipitated the stunning policy reversal of February 7.

Endgame

Throughout early 1984, the administration wrestled with three possible military options in Lebanon. The most hawkish officials, including McFarlane and Shultz, instinctively favored an even more aggressive approach. However, even the hawks readily conceded that while the attacks on American troops justified a more aggressive military intervention, "there is no U.S. congressional or domestic support for wider military involvement."[79] Faced with these realities, McFarlane proposed a hybrid option: while yielding to pressures for a drawdown in the size of

76. *CQ Weekly*, February 4, 1984, 227.

77. Memo, Duberstein to Meese, Baker, Deaver, McFarlane, Gergen, Darman, and Elliott, October 26, 1983, folder NDo16 183642, WHORM, Ronald Reagan Library.

78. *CQ Weekly*, February 18, 1984, 302. Ironically, Dick Cheney, who supported withdrawing the Marines, openly disputed Walker's view.

79. Memo, Hill to McFarlane, folder "Lebanon II (4 of 4)," box 90753, Donald Fortier files, Ronald Reagan Library.

the American forces in Lebanon, he favored compensating for any re-
ductions with greatly strengthened rules of engagement that would allow
U.S. forces on land, sea, and air to take a more active role in responding
to attacks and stabilizing the country. Beginning to redeploy some forces
offshore, McFarlane argued, was "indispensable for regaining the initiative with Congress, and thus, for securing backing for expanded rules of
engagement."[80] President Reagan agreed to these expanded rules of engagement and codified them in the February 1, 1984, National Security
Decision Directive 123, which among other changes authorized the use
of air and naval gunfire against any Syrian position firing into greater
Beirut, not just in response to attacks on Marine positions. Yet, even as
the directive went into effect, a cable citing the "explosive situation on
the Hill" warned Rumsfeld to prepare President Gemayel for a reduced
American footprint on the ground in Lebanon.[81]

The final option was withdrawing all American forces from Beirut,
and as late as February 2, Reagan publicly proclaimed that he would
have none of it. "[Tip O'Neill] may be ready to surrender, but I'm not,"
he chided, in response to a question by *Wall Street Journal* reporter Al
Hunt. "As long as there is a chance for peace, the mission remains the
same."[82] And in his national radio address on February 4, the president
acknowledged difficulties in Lebanon but maintained that they were "no
reason to turn our backs on friends and to cut and run. If we do, we'll
be sending one signal to terrorists everywhere: They can gain by waging
war against innocent people."[83]

Yet even as Reagan reiterated his determination—and despite the
pleas of Donald Rumsfeld, Bud McFarlane, and George Shultz for re-
taining a residual force on the ground—others in the administration

80. Memo, McFarlane to Rumsfeld, February 5, 1984, folder "Lebanon II (1 of 4),"
box 90753, Donald Fortier files, Ronald Reagan Library.

81. Cable, Rumsfeld to Eagleburger, folder "Lebanon I (3 of 5)," box 90753, Donald
Fortier files, Ronald Reagan Library.

82. Ronald Reagan, "Interview with Robert L. Bartley and Albert R. Hunt of the *Wall
Street Journal* on Foreign and Domestic Issues." *Public Papers of the President*, February 2,
1984. Some accounts have questioned whether the decision to withdraw from Lebanon had
already been made before Reagan attacked O'Neill. While there may well have been an
agreement in principle among some of the key players, there is considerable evidence that
the final decision was not made until February 7, 1984.

83. Ronald Reagan, "Radio Address to the Nation on the Budget Deficit, Central
America, and Lebanon." *Public Papers of the President*, February 4, 1983.

were preparing to withdraw the Marines.[84] On February 7, 1984, with both Reagan and Shultz out of Washington, Vice President Bush presided over a meeting of the National Security Planning Group. The vice president, and now McFarlane as well, crossed over to Weinberger's camp and supported redeploying the troops offshore. Undersecretary of State Eagleburger was the lone remaining dissenter. After the meeting, Bush spoke with Reagan over a secure call and the president quietly approved the decision.[85] The vice president himself then went to Capitol Hill to explain the reversal to a relieved congressional leadership.[86]

The decision met with approval and calls for an expedited redeployment on both sides of the aisle.[87] Republican members of Congress, many of whom feared Lebanon would hurt their reelection campaigns, almost unanimously expressed relief. According to *Congressional Quarterly*, "indicative of the Republican attitude was a headline on a press release issued by Sen. Larry Pressler of South Dakota: 'Pressler—first Republican Senator to oppose troops to Lebanon—supports withdrawal.[88] The last U.S. Marine serving as part of the MNF left Lebanon on February 25, 1984.

Conclusion

The sequence of events leading up to the sudden reversal of administration policy and the dramatic withdrawal of U.S. Marines from Lebanon clearly demonstrates that open congressional opposition to Reagan's conduct of the mission in Beirut was critically important in precipitating the change in course. By tracing the pathways of congressional in-

84. For the views of McFarlane, Shultz, and Rumsfeld, see memo, McFarlane to Reagan, February 7, 1984, folder "Lebanon II (2 of 4)," box 90753, Donald Fortier files, Ronald Reagan Library.

85. Cannon 2000, 454–55.

86. McFarlane, "Steps," folder "Lebanon Documents (26 Jan 1984)," box 90929, Ronald Reagan Library.

87. For example, when Deputy Secretary of State Kenneth Dam told Republican members on February 9 that the Marines could remain on the ground for up to several more months, there was open revolt. In the words of Henry Hyde, "that went over like the proverbial lead balloon." *CQ Weekly*, February 11, 1984, 240.

88. *CQ Weekly*, February 11, 1984, 239.

fluence, the case study achieves two important objectives. First, it vividly illustrates Congress's capacity to influence the scope and duration of a use of force independent of major shifts in public opinion and changing conditions on the ground. The analysis makes clear that there was no dramatic shift in public opinion after the Beirut barracks bombing that compelled the Reagan administration to withdraw the Marines; in fact, in the wake of the attack the public rallied behind the president. As such, opponents of Reagan's policies in Congress initially fought against the tide of public opinion, and the modest decline in popular support for the president's handling of the Lebanon mission occurred only after a sustained campaign against the deployment on Capitol Hill.[89] Similarly, the administration's own internal analysis of the situation in early January 1984 makes clear that changing conditions on the ground did not necessitate a dramatic change in the nature of the Marine mission. Indeed, by the National Security Council's own estimate, some conditions in the region were actually improving. Instead, administration officials repeatedly emphasized domestic pressures to curtail the scope and duration of the Marine mission.[90] Moreover, as the political and military situation in Lebanon worsened in late January and early February 1984, it is interesting that a number of key administration officials publicly and privately believed that there was a direct link between congressional opposition at home and the deterioration of the situation on the ground in the Middle East.

Second, the case study illustrates how the formal and informal congressional actions examined in the statistical analyses of chapter 4 affected presidential decision-making through the proposed theoretical mechanisms for congressional influence over presidential conduct of military affairs developed in chapter 2. Vocal opposition to the president in Congress—expressed through hearings and legislative initiatives to

89. However, as the David Gergen quote in chapter 2 illustrated, the White House was very concerned about anticipated future public opinion. Many feared that, in part because of the open opposition to the mission in Congress, popular support for the Marine mission could quickly wane.

90. "NSC Summary of Defense Department Comments on Non Paper: Next Steps in Lebanon," folder "Lebanon Chronology (2)," box 41, Executive Secretariat, NSC, country file, Ronald Reagan Library; memo, McFarlane to Reagan, January 3, 1984, folder "CPPG Meeting, January 30, 1984, Lebanon," box 91834, William Burns files, Ronald Reagan Library.

curtail presidential authority, and the visible defection from the White House of a number of prominent Republicans and erstwhile Democratic allies—raised the political stakes of staying the course in Lebanon. Nothing shook Reagan's basic belief in the benefits to be gained from a strong, defiant stand in Beirut. But the political pressure generated by congressional opposition to his policies on both sides of the aisle raised the likely political costs of obtaining these policy benefits. Congressional opposition also influenced the Reagan administration's decision-making indirectly by affecting its estimate of the military costs that would have to be paid to achieve American objectives. In the final analysis, through both the domestic political costs and signaling mechanisms discussed in chapter 2, congressional opposition contributed to the administration's ultimate judgment that the benefits the United States might reap by continuing the Marine mission no longer outweighed the heightened political and military costs necessary to obtain them.

Finally, while the Marine mission in Lebanon is admittedly but one case, it is a case that many in the Reagan administration believed had important implications for subsequent military policymaking. In a post-mortem review, Don Fortier of the National Security Council and Steve Sestanovich at the State Department warned that the debacle in Lebanon raised the possibility that, in the future, the decision to use force might be akin to an all-or-nothing decision. "If the public and Congress reject any prolonged U.S. role (even when the number of troops is small)," the administration analysts lamented, "we will always be under pressure to resolve problems through briefer, but more massive involvements—or to do nothing at all." Thus, from the administration's "conspicuously losing to the Congress" over Lebanon policy, Fortier and Sestanovich argued that the White House would have to anticipate costly congressional opposition if similar actions were launched in the future and adjust its conduct of military operations accordingly, with the end result being a "narrowing of options" on the table and more "limited flexibility" when deploying major contingents of American military might abroad.[91]

This last point echoes the first anticipatory mechanism posited in

91. Memo, Fortier (NSC staff) to McFarlane, March 7, 1984, folder "Lebanon II (4 of 4)," box 90753, Donald Fortier files, Ronald Reagan Library; memo, Fortier to McFarlane, "Lebanon Implications Memo," folder "Lebanon II (4 of 4)," box 90753, Donald Fortier files, Ronald Reagan Library.

chapter 2, and reminds us that Congress need not overtly act to rein in a military action of which it disapproves for it to have an important influence on the scope and duration of a major military endeavor. Rather, presidents, having observed Congress's capacity to raise the political and tangible costs of a given course of military action, may anticipate the likelihood of congressional opposition and adjust their conduct of military operations accordingly.

CHAPTER SIX

The Logic of Congressional Action

The statistical and archival data of the previous two chapters plainly demonstrate that when Congress acts in the military arena, it has tangible consequences for the conduct of military policymaking. Even if Congress cannot enact legislation formally compelling the president to abandon his preferred policy course, when momentum builds behind legislative initiatives to curtail an ongoing use of force or when congressional committees hold hearings investigating the administration's conduct of military operations, these actions shape presidential cost-benefit calculations and influence the duration of major military ventures. However, to understand fully the extent of congressional influence over the conduct of military actions, we must ascertain under what conditions members of Congress are willing and able to use these tools at their disposal.

The theory presented in chapter 2 focused almost exclusively on partisanship as the key force driving congressional willingness to confront the executive in the military arena. It posited that the president and the target state's leader anticipated greater legislative pressure from a Congress dominated by opposition partisans than from one controlled by the president's partisan allies. Consistent with this hypothesis, the analyses in chapter 3 found robust relationships between the strength of the president's party, the initiation of major military actions, and the scale and duration of those actions once launched. By extension, theory suggests that the partisan composition of Congress should be the strongest predictor of the number and intensity of the legislative and investigative challenges to the administration's handling of military affairs that arise during a use of force. However, even an opposition-controlled Congress is aware of the potential costs its members might incur by attacking the policies of the commander in chief after U.S. troops are deployed abroad. Thus, the frequency and timing of congressional challenges to presidential conduct of military operations are a function both of baseline partisan incentives and of the emergence of windows of opportunity in the political and strategic environment.

The goals of this chapter are twofold. First, it tests the simple hypothesis derived from chapter 2 that the partisan composition of Congress should be one of the most important and consistent predictors of the frequency and intensity of congressional challenges to the president's conduct of military affairs. Second, the chapter pushes the theory further to explore in more detail how this baseline partisan incentive is conditioned by the nature and contours of the political and strategic environment in which members of Congress act.

Partisanship and Windows of Opportunity for Congressional Challenges

The theory presented in chapter 2 suggests that the partisan composition of Congress should be the most important predictor of variance in its willingness to assert its institutional prerogatives and challenge presidential discretion in the conduct of military affairs. Because members of the opposition party are significantly more likely than presidential co-partisans to possess ideological and partisan electoral incentives to oppose the administration's military policies, the strength of the partisan opposition's ranks in Congress should greatly influence the legislature's willingness to confront the president and seek to influence the direction of major military operations. However, while partisanship provides a strong baseline predictor of the level of interbranch conflict over military affairs, other forces also surely drive variance in congressional assertiveness in military policymaking. Members of Congress do not operate in a political vacuum. They do not blindly attack the president's policies simply because they possess the requisite tools to do so. Instead, they conduct their own cost-benefit calculations and weigh the benefits they stand to gain against the very real potential costs of publicly confronting the commander in chief. Chapter 2 described the policy and electoral benefits that members of the opposition party may gain by opposing the president's conduct of a major military venture. However, such opposition is subject to the damaging countercharge of failing to support or even undercutting American troops in the field. Moreover, to the extent that congressional actions send important signals to foreign actors, would-be congressional critics are also concerned about the policy costs of open opposition. In many cases, particularly if the intervention enjoys wide public support and good prospects for success, the costs may exceed any electoral, policy, or ideological benefits that may come from confronting the president's handling of military affairs.

Indeed, even the earliest history of the republic testifies to the electoral ramifications of opposing a mostly popular and ultimately successful war, through the demise of the Federalists after the War of 1812.[1] In such cases, the costs of a direct attack on the president's commitment of American forces abroad are steep enough to ward off congressional challenges, even from a strong partisan opposition.[2] Only when the expected benefits outweigh the likely costs should even the staunchest of partisan opponents openly battle the president and seek to alter his military policy course. Accordingly, while the partisan composition of Congress provides a strong baseline prediction for the level of interbranch conflict in the military arena, the degree to which members of Congress challenge presidential conduct of major military operations is also strongly

1. While precisely who "won" the War of 1812 is still a matter of debate, Andrew Jackson's decisive victory at New Orleans—although it occurred after the peace treaty had been signed—made Federalist opposition to the war ring particularly hollow after its conclusion.

2. Instead, in such political circumstances the opposition may continue to attack the president's actions, but only at the margins, while consistently recognizing the need and even desirability of maintaining the American military commitment. For example, consider the Democratic critiques of the Bush administration's conduct of military actions in Afghanistan. As the clear centerpiece in the war on terror, Operation Enduring Freedom enjoyed consistently strong support among the general public through 2008. Despite continued casualties, escalating costs, and the failure to bring large segments of the country under government control—all factors that the Democrats have pointed to as signs of failure in Iraq—Democratic attacks on the administration's Afghanistan policy called primarily for an escalation, not a de-escalation, of the American military presence. John Kerry made the administration's failure to use American troops to hunt Osama bin Laden at Tora Bora a centerpiece of his 2004 presidential campaign, and in the 2006 midterm elections many Democratic candidates ran on a platform of drawing down American involvement in Iraq, in part so that critical resources could be redirected to Afghanistan. Partisan interbranch conflict in World War II followed a similar pattern: while Republican leaders remained solidly behind Franklin Roosevelt's military efforts against the Axis, which enjoyed steady, cross-partisan support among the general public (Berinsky 2009), they took aim at FDR's handling of the war effort on the domestic front.

influenced by the political and strategic environment in which the president's opponents must act.

In the political realm, whether the anticipated benefits of challenging the president's military policies outweigh the costs of doing so is a function of both the strength of his standing among the public and the level of popular support for the ongoing military engagement. Presidency scholars have long noted that the president's job approval rating among the public is an important indicator of his political capital in Washington.[3] A president shielded by a strong approval rating is an unattractive target for would-be congressional opponents who are reticent to confront a popular commander in chief. Even members of Congress who oppose the president's military policies on ideological grounds may be reticent to attack him when his public support remains strong. However, a president with only ambivalent support among the general public is considerably more vulnerable to congressional attacks. Sensing political weakness, his opponents in Congress may seize on his handling of military operations as a new, highly salient dimension on which to confront him in the hopes of further weakening his—and by extension his party's— political fortunes and electoral clout.

In a similar vein, congressional opponents of the president's policies surely gauge popular support for the military action itself when calculating the costs and benefits of an institutional challenge to presidential discretion. Even a Congress stacked with the president's partisan opponents should be unlikely to challenge openly his conduct of a popular war.[4] However, when the public is ambivalent toward or even predisposed against the administration's military policies, the political environment

3. Inter alia Neustadt 1990, Kernell 1997.

4. For example, despite the sharp divisions among Democrats during the lead-up to the first Gulf War in the autumn of 1990 and the considerable public opposition many displayed in the debate to authorize the use of force, the war's critics became virtually silent once Operation Desert Storm began. Public support remained high throughout the weeks of sustained bombings, even as civilian casualties began to mount and inevitably some Coalition planes and pilots failed to return to their bases. Given this well of popular good will for the president, most Democrats viewed attacking the war as tantamount to political suicide. As a result, few decried the war vocally and none challenged it legislatively, despite considerable ex ante opposition. At times, critiques of the administration did arise, such as Democratic calls for an expansion of the U.S. military role to protect the Kurds in northern Iraq and even to aid the Shiite uprisings against Saddam's rule in the south. However, at no time did the opposition rank and file, despite its numerical strength, question the fundamental decision to maintain the American commitment in Iraq.

is much more conducive to congressional challenges. As the Lebanon case study in the preceding chapter makes clear, Congress can act with great effect even in the absence of a major change in popular support for a military mission. Nevertheless, shifts in popular support for a war and its prosecution may open significant windows of opportunity for strategic congressional opponents to attack the president's policies and attempt to turn military policymaking to their political advantage.

In addition to considering the contours of the domestic political environment, would-be opponents in Congress also look for opportunities in the strategic environment. Even if public support for the president or for the military engagement itself has not waned, adverse developments in the field may provide the impetus for congressional attacks on the administration's policies. Setbacks on the ground may heighten policy doubts about the president's handling of military affairs and exacerbate ideological and substantive policy disagreements between the administration and its congressional opponents. From a more political perspective, they may provide an opportunity to turn domestic public opinion against the president and his policies through vigorous signs of congressional opposition. In both ways, the emergence of adverse developments in the field makes potential administration opponents more likely to judge that the benefits of challenging the president's conduct of military affairs outweigh the potential costs of doing so.

Thus, although the balance of partisan power in Congress is a powerful predictor of the overall level of interbranch conflict over the conduct of military affairs, it alone cannot explain the full dynamics of when and how vigorously Congress will act to challenge the president's conduct of military affairs. These dynamics are also a function of strategic opportunities for action in the domestic and international environment. The stronger the ranks of the president's partisan opponents, the more likely Congress is to hold investigative hearings or introduce legislation to curtail an ongoing use of force, and the more likely such initiatives are to garner substantial support on the chamber floors. However, even the president's partisan opponents must consider the likely reaction of the public and other actors in the specific political and strategic context of the moment. If the prospective costs of challenging the president outweigh the potential benefits, even an opposition-dominated Congress should remain silent. Conversely, when popular support for the president and his policies begins to wane, or when developments on the ground, such as mounting American casualties or an unanticipated strategic setback, open a window of opportunity for Congress to seize the initiative, the expected costs of attacking the president's policies decrease and his partisan opponents in Congress should be poised to act.

Model

Because most scholars have long dismissed failed legislative challenges to the president's discretion in military affairs and investigations of his conduct of military operations as mere public posturing of little tangible consequence, the existing literature has paid scant attention to the factors that drive Congress's willingness to use these tools.[5] An important exception, however, is a 1995 analysis by James Meernik. Although Meernik remained skeptical that such actions had any influence over the course of military policymaking, he endeavored to explain why Congress attempted to invoke the War Powers Resolution in response to some uses of force but not others.[6]

Recognizing the potential importance of partisan dynamics and the president's political capital in explaining the likelihood of a legislative challenge, Meernik's statistical analysis included a divided government dummy variable, the president's Gallup approval rating at the outset of each use of force, and a number of control variables. Yet the static approach of his analysis severely limits its ability to illuminate the complexities driving the frequency and timing of congressional challenges during the course of a military operation. The unit of observation was not some measure of time within each military engagement, but each major use of force itself. All explanatory variables were measured at the initiation of each conflict. However, Congress need not invoke the War Powers Resolution, exercise its power of the purse, or convene a committee investigation into administration conduct of a military venture only at the outset of an engagement. Indeed, most such legislative efforts occur months or even years after American combat forces first arrived in

5. Katzmann 1990, Mann 1990, Nathan 1993; but see Reveley 1981, Crabb and Holt 1988, Auerswald 2000.

6. To reiterate, Meernik does not believe Congress exerts genuine influence through such actions. Rather, through these attempts to invoke the War Powers Resolution, according to Meernik, (1995, 377) Congress demonstrates its willingness "to speak, but not to act against the president in [military] matters."

theater. The situation on the ground, public opinion, the partisan balance of power, and even the occupant of the Oval Office can change dramatically in the interim.

To better understand why Congress spurs itself to action in some types of conflicts but not others—and why, even with regard to the same use of force, it sometimes aggressively challenges the commander in chief and at other times remains quiescent—requires a dynamic model that can account for changes in the political and strategic environment over the course of a conflict. Therefore, this chapter first employs a series of negative binomial event-count models to explore the factors that influence the number of binding legislative initiatives and the number of investigative hearings that Congress launches challenging the president's conduct of military affairs in a given month. In these models, the unit of analysis is the conflict-month for each of the twenty principal uses of force involving the deployment of ground troops, sustained use of firepower, or significant deployment of American air or naval vessels to hostile zones in the postwar era examined in chapter 4. The second half of the chapter then models the factors that influence individual members' votes on these initiatives.

To test the theoretical prediction that partisan incentives critically influence members' decisions about whether or not to challenge legislatively the president's handling of military operations, the models first include a measure of the average percentage of Congress controlled by the president's party in each month. This figure changes throughout the course of a conflict in twelve of the twenty principal uses of force, and the partisan control of at least one house of the legislature switches in ten cases. Given the resulting dramatic shifts in partisan incentives for congressional action to check the executive, a dynamic, not static modeling approach, is clearly needed.

Similarly, popular support for an ongoing military action and the commander in chief—which critically moderates the costs and benefits Congress stands to reap from challenging the president's policies—can also vary considerably throughout the course of each overseas deployment. For example, Harry Truman's approval rating varied from a high of 87 percent to a low of 33 percent over the duration of the American garrisoning of Trieste in the wake of World War II. While less dramatic, the variance in popular support for Lyndon Johnson during the 1965–66 invasion and occupation of the Dominican Republic (70 to 47 percent) and for Bill Clinton during the humanitarian operations in Somalia

(56 to 41 percent) was still substantial and representative of similar fluctuations during the other principal uses of force. Because both the overall level of support for the president, or for the military action itself, and recent changes in each may be important predictors of congressional willingness to challenge the president, the event count models employ all four public opinion variables from chapter 4. These comprise quarterly measures of presidential approval and public support specifically for each of the twenty principal uses of force, as well as the change in both of those variables over the preceding six months. When the president enjoys strong approval ratings and the public supports his conduct of a foreign military venture, even an opposition-controlled Congress should be wary of launching a legislative or investigatory challenge to the administration's conduct of military affairs. Similarly, increasing short-term support for the president and his handling of military affairs should decrease the expected number of legislative challenges.

When contemplating a formal challenge to presidential conduct of military affairs, members of Congress also surely respond to developments on the ground in the target state, as these, too, can affect their cost-benefit calculations. Major events or increases in casualties can inject greater variance and instability into public opinion and enable Congress to seize the initiative from the president and reframe the policy debate.[7] As such, adverse developments can activate the latent partisan incentives of opposition members to attack the president by decreasing the likely political costs they risk incurring by doing so.

Accordingly, the models include two sets of controls to measure changes in the military situation in the field. First are the quarterly and logged cumulative American casualties for each observation.[8] Spikes in casualties may galvanize public attention, inject greater instability into public support for military action, and precipitate growing dissent toward the administration's policies. These shifts can considerably weaken the president's political position, reduce the expected costs of challenging him for his partisan opponents, and lower the benefits for his co-

---

7. Gronke and Brehm 2002, Kriner 2006, Kriner and Schwartz 2009.

8. Logged cumulative casualties were used to smooth the anomalously high casualty totals in Vietnam and Korea. Instead, employing the unlogged measure yields a positive coefficient for the cumulative casualties variable in models of both dependent variables, though in the investigatory hearings model it is statistically insignificant. All other results are virtually unchanged.

partisans of remaining steadfastly behind his policies. Therefore, a surge in casualties may open the door for a congressional challenge. Alternatively, the cumulative number of American casualties may be a better predictor of when Congress rises up to challenge the president through its legislative and investigatory powers. Instead of responding to small spikes in casualties, there may be a threshold of tolerance that, once exceeded, prompts a congressional reaction. For example, the media frenzy surrounding the two-thousandth American casualty in Iraq in the fall of 2005 heightened public awareness of the seemingly intractable situation in the Middle East. This, in turn, made public advocacy of withdrawal more politically palatable, and indeed congressional challenges to President Bush's handling of the war intensified in the wake of this milestone. Thus, cumulative casualties may increase the probability that Congress will challenge the president legislatively.

Additionally, for all the principal uses of force excluding Vietnam and Korea, the models include an alternative measure of the course of each conflict: the number of front-page *New York Times* articles mentioning the military making progress toward or suffering setbacks from achieving its goals in the previous quarter. Congress may limit its formal challenges to presidential discretion in military affairs when the situation on the ground, or at least the media's portrayal of it, is improving. As the military situation on the ground improves, even opposition members of Congress may perceive fewer political gains and greater political costs from challenging the president legislatively. Conversely, when the media paint a grimmer picture of matters on the ground, opposition members may sense a heightened opportunity to attack the president.[9]

Finally, the models also include two additional domestic political controls that may influence congressional decisions to investigate or legislatively challenge the president at a given time: a simple additive misery index of unemployment and inflation, as well as a dummy variable for

---

9. The indexing literature suggests that the media look to Congress when crafting the tone of their coverage. As a result, this relationship is potentially endogenous. However, content analysis of *New York Times* coverage suggests that the *Times*'s own evaluations of the military situation on the ground were largely independent of vocal congressional opinions on both the initial decision to intervene and the proper course for an ongoing venture. Opposition party criticism of the initial decision to use force is correlated with media reports of deteriorating conditions on the ground at $r = .43$, but every other correlation between media reports of conditions in the field and congressional evaluations of the conflict and recommendations for its conduct are correlated at $r < .10$.

presidential election years. The theory presented in chapter 2 offers few specific expectations about either variable's influence on the frequency and timing of congressional action. A poor economy might well increase the president's political vulnerability, however, making him more susceptible to congressional attacks in general, including challenges to his handling of foreign affairs.

The fully specified event-count models are summarized in this equation:

Expected number of congressional challenges $= \beta_0 + \beta_1(\%$ pres. party$) + \beta_2($quarterly approval$_{t-1}) + \beta_3($quarterly support for conflict$_{t-1}) + \beta_4(\Delta$ approval$) + \beta_5(\Delta$ support for conflict$)$
$+ \beta_6($election year$) + \beta_7($misery index$) + \beta_8($quarterly casualties$_{t-1})$
$+ \beta_9($cumulative casualties$) + \beta_{10}($reports of military progress$)$
$+ \beta_{11}($reports of military setbacks$)$

All models report standard errors clustered on conflict.[10]

Results and Discussion

The first set of models (1–3) in table 6.1 assesses the impact of each factor on the expected number of binding initiatives to curtail the use of force brought to the floor in a given month.[11] Model 1 begins by adding only the partisan composition of Congress and the four measures of domestic public opinion. As expected, the coefficient for the partisan composition of Congress variable is negative and statistically significant. The stronger the president's party in Congress, the less likely Congress is to challenge the president legislatively.[12]

10. Because the presence of multiple binding congressional actions to challenge the president's conduct of military affairs in a single month was a relatively rare phenomenon, the models in table 6.1 were also replicated with a binary version of the dependent variable using a logit model. All results remain virtually identical to those presented.

11. All of the models in table 6.1 were also reestimated including a lagged dependent variable, with results virtually identical to those presented.

12. Although the historical record documents several examples of congressional attempts to curtail a use of force in unified government, and although the duration models in chapter 3 suggest that partisan strength was a better predictor of duration than a divided government dummy variable, divided government is an even stronger predictor of whether or

TABLE 6.1 **Factors influencing the number of formal congressional challenges to the use of force**

Independent variables	Legislative Initiatives			Investigative Hearings		
	(1)	(2)	(3)	(4)	(5)	(6)
Congress						
% president's party in Congress	−.22*** (.07)	−.19*** (.09)	−.24*** (.08)	−.11*** (.02)	−.10*** (.03)	−.19*** (.07)
Public opinion						
Presidential approval last quarter	−.03* (.02)	−.04* (.03)	−.10*** (.03)	−.04** (.02)	−.04* (.02)	−.08*** (.03)
Support for war last quarter	−.04 (.03)	−.03 (.03)	.02 (.03)	−.04** (.02)	−.03** (.01)	−.03 (.02)
Change in presidential approval	−.00 (.02)	.00 (.02)	.00 (.02)	.01 (.02)	.01 (.02)	.02 (.02)
Change in support for war	−.04 (.02)	−.03 (.02)	−.05*** (.02)	−.04*** (.01)	−.04*** (.01)	−.06*** (.02)
Domestic variables						
Election year	—	−.75 (.82)	−2.66*** (1.01)	—	−.11 (.30)	−.19 (.37)
Misery index	—	−.06 (.09)	−.18** (.09)	—	−.01 (.08)	−.10 (.07)
Conflict variables						
Casualties last quarter	—	−.37 (.24)	9.57** (4.09)	—	−.04 (.16)	4.39 (4.68)
Ln (cumulative casualties)	—	.12** (.06)	−.26 (.24)	—	.12** (.06)	.20 (.23)
Military making progress	—	—	−.07** (.04)	—	—	.01 (.02)
Military meeting setbacks	—	—	.12* (.07)	—	—	−.00 (.05)
Constant	11.29*** (4.04)	10.51* (5.69)	15.28*** (5.30)	7.90*** (1.14)	7.17*** (2.61)	13.85*** (4.13)
Log-likelihood	−148.63	−145.62	−80.79	−324.35	−317.87	−195.46
n	583	583	441	583	583	441

Note: * $p < .10$; ** $p < .05$; *** $p < .01$. All significance tests are two-tailed; all models report robust standard errors clustered on conflict.

In a similar vein, the coefficients for each of the four variables measuring public support for the president and his handling of a military action are also negative, and the coefficient for presidential approval in the last quarter is statistically significant. Thus, high levels of public support

not a formal legislative challenge to the president is brought to the floor. Substituting divided government for the partisan composition measure across specifications yields the expected strong positive coefficient and leaves all other relationships unchanged. Similarly, substituting the log of the partisan composition measure leaves all results substantively unchanged.

as well as recent increases in it appear to reduce the expected number of predicted legislative challenges in a given month. This confirms theoretical expectations that the president's standing among the general public critically moderates congressional willingness to constrain his handling of an ongoing military operation. Presidents enjoying strong reserves of popular support are less appealing political targets for congressional attacks than chief executives bereft of widespread public approval. Even for members of Congress with latent partisan incentives to challenge the president, the benefits of doing so are smaller and the potential risks are higher when the president remains strong in the polls. As such, opposition members appear to wait for a more favorable political climate before throwing down the gauntlet at the foot of the commander in chief.

The models in column 2 add two measures of conditions in the strategic environment—recent and cumulative American casualties—as well as two additional domestic political controls. Even in this expanded specification, the results for the partisan composition of Congress and public opinion variables remain virtually identical to those observed in model 1. While model 2 provides little evidence that Congress responds to more recent spikes in casualties, the coefficient for logged cumulative casualties is positive and statistically significant. This suggests that as the number of American war dead mounts, so, too, does congressional willingness to seek to curtail the use of force legislatively. Finally, the coefficients for the election-year dummy variable and the misery index both failed to reach conventional levels of statistical significance.

Finally, to insure that the relationships observed in models 1 and 2 are not driven merely by American experience in the Vietnam and Korean wars, model 3 drops these two conflicts from the analysis. Also, because changes in the military situation on the ground should also moderate partisan incentives and strongly influence members' calculations when contemplating a formal challenge to the president's conduct of an ongoing campaign, model 3 includes two additional measures: the numbers of front-page *New York Times* articles citing military progress or setbacks on the ground in the target state.

Even after the exclusion of Vietnam and Korea from the sample and the inclusion of the additional controls, the partisan composition of Congress and public opinion remain significant predictors of the expected number of legislative challenges to the president's conduct of military affairs. Strong co-partisan majorities on Capitol Hill, high levels of pres-

idential approval, and increasing support for the war itself all significantly reduce the frequency of congressional challenges.

Furthermore, model 3 offers strong evidence that congressional willingness to challenge the president legislatively in the military arena is influenced by conditions on the ground. When Vietnam and Korea are excluded from the sample, only recent casualties appear to increase the
likelihood of a congressional response. As first differences will demonstrate, however, the substantive effect of even a large increase in marginal casualties is minimal. Turning to the two media measures of the
military situation in the target state, the results from model 3 again accord with theoretical expectations. The predicted number of legislative challenges to a use of force increases with the number of *New York
Times* front-page articles citing military setbacks on the ground, and decreases with the number of media reports of military progress in the target state.

Finally, the negative coefficients for both the election-year and
misery-index variables, which were statistically insignificant in model 2,
are now statistically significant in model 3. At first blush, the negative
correlation between economic health and congressional challenges to
the president in the military arena appears counterintuitive. Theory suggests that congressional willingness to attack the president should increase as the costs of doing so decline. Presumably, the likely political
costs of attacking a vulnerable president presiding over a weak economy
are less than those of attacking a president who can wrap himself in the
mantle of a strong economy.

However, these empirical results remind us of the opportunity costs
that opposition members incur by attacking the president on military affairs and shifting public attention to foreign policy when the president
is already beset by economic difficulties. Although a growing number
of scholars have documented the relevance of foreign policy concerns
in voters' decision calculus in national elections, economic concerns
remain foremost on the minds of voters at the ballot box.[13] As a result,
in poor economic times, opposition members of Congress may have little to gain politically by attacking the president and shifting the focus

13. Aldrich, Sullivan, and Borgida 1989; Nincic and Hinckley 1991; Hurwitz and Peffley 1987. For the dominance of economic concerns, see Kiewiet 1983; MacKuen, Erikson,
and Stimson 1992; Wlezien and Erikson 1996; Hibbs 2000; Campbell 2000; Lewis-Beck
and Rice 1992.

of national attention from the weak economy, where they stand to benefit the most, to military policy, where their prospects for political gain are less certain. Conversely, when the economy is strong, opposition members possess considerable incentives to introduce a new policy dimension on which voters might judge the president and his party less favorably.

To illustrate this dynamic further, consider the strategies of congressional Democrats in the lead-up to the 2004 election. Despite mounting American casualties and spiraling violence in Iraq, most Democrats, even many who voted against the war, were puzzlingly reluctant to challenge President Bush over the war's conduct in the general election campaign. Instead, the main emphasis of their strategy was to focus squarely on the slumping economy. The Democratic leadership believed, perhaps incorrectly, that they stood to gain more ground by hammering the president for his poor performance in the economic realm than for policy debacles in Iraq.

Finally, model 3 also yields a statistically significant negative coefficient for the election-year dummy variable. Superficially, this negative relationship is also counterintuitive. Logically, we might expect Congress to be more active in challenging the president in an election year when the political consequences of its actions are potentially the most severe. One possible explanation for the unexpected result is that the president's opponents in Congress consciously refrain from challenging the incumbent in an election year to defer to their party's presidential candidate. An interinstitutional showdown over war powers could both distract attention from the opposition party's candidate and potentially conflict with his or her campaign strategy in the national election. While the correlation is puzzling, the consequences for the analysis are rather small. First differences presented in figure 6.1 show that the substantive effects of the electoral-cycle variable and the misery index on the likelihood of a congressional challenge are quite limited.

To explore the relative impact of each of these various factors on the expected number of legally binding legislative challenges to the president in a given month, figure 6.1 presents a series of first differences from one thousand simulations derived from model 3 in table 6.1. The solid portion of each bar in the graph represents the change in the predicted number of legislative initiatives to curtail the use of force that is produced by a shift in each variable from its 25th to its 75th percentile while holding all other variables constant at their means or medians. The dotted

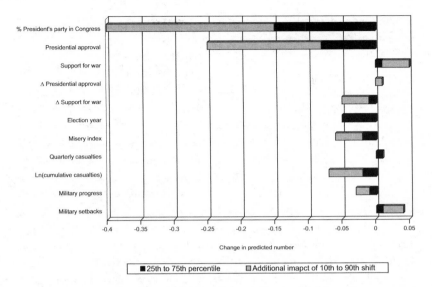

FIGURE 6.1. Predicted effects of variables on the number of binding congressional actions to curtail the use of force. First differences for the following variables are statistically significant: percentage of seats held by the president's party in Congress, presidential approval, change in support for war, election year, misery index, quarterly casualties, military progress, military setbacks.

portion illustrates the additional impact of increasing each independent variable from its 10th to its 90th percentile.

Consistent with theoretical expectations, the partisan composition of Congress is by far the single most important predictor of the legislature's willingness to act. To put the size of the effect in perspective, legislative initiatives occurred in only 36 of the 583 conflict-months in the analysis. Thus, the average number of binding congressional actions in a month was slightly more than .06. Holding all other variables constant at their means and medians, the expected number of congressional actions in a month increases more than tenfold from .01 to .16 when the strength of the president's party in Congress decreases from 57 to 47 percent. As figure 6.1 shows, the effect of a 10th to 90th percentile shift is even greater. Thus, the models suggest that presidents with strong partisan majorities in Congress are not totally immune from congressional challenges, but they can rest assured that only in extraordinary circumstances will they face formal legislative affronts to their prerogatives in the conduct of military affairs. Conversely, presidents facing opposition-dominated legislatures operate under the very real threat that Congress may seek to challenge their military leadership should an opportunity for political gain arise.

The first differences also make clear that the president's level of support among the public is the second most important determinant of the likelihood of congressional challenges. A popular president with an approval rating in the sixties is very unlikely to face a legislative challenge from Congress (expected number: .02). By contrast, an unpopular president with a 40-percent approval rating faces a very real possibility of a legislative challenge (expected number: .26). A weakened president lacking a stable base of public support is a more attractive target for opposition-party legislators eager to reap political gains from challenging the executive. The only other public opinion variable to achieve statistical significance in model 3 was for the change in support for the military campaign. However, the first differences in figure 6.1 show that while increasing support for a military engagement does decrease the expected number of legislative challenges, the substantive effect is modest even at the extreme ends of the distribution. Similarly, the coefficients for both the election-year dummy variable and the misery index were both negative and statistically significant; however, substantively their effects are quite limited, particularly in comparison to the effects generated by identical shifts in the partisan composition of Congress or in presidential approval. Finally, figure 6.1 illustrates the effects of marginal casualties and media reports of military progress or setbacks, all of which were statistically significant in model 3, on the predicted number of congressional legislative challenges to the president. These effects, too, are comparatively quite small. Clearly, the partisan composition of Congress and the president's level of political capital are the most important factors driving Congress's willingness to exercise its formal powers to confront the president legislatively.

The next set of models (4–6) in table 6.1 investigates the influence of the same variables on the number of investigative hearings Congress launches into the president's conduct of a military action in a given conflict-month. Across specifications, the observed dynamics driving congressional investigatory activity closely mirror those influencing the frequency and timing of legislative challenges to presidential military policies.

The partisan composition of Congress and public support for the president and the use of force are by far the most important predictors of the timing and intensity of congressional investigations into military operations. In all three specifications, the partisan composition of Congress, presidential approval, and the change in public support for the war are inversely and significantly correlated with the number of investigative hearings. In models 4 and 5, the coefficient for the level of popular support for the military engagement is also negative and statistically significant. Thus, consistent with theory, the models suggest that Congress is most likely to use its investigative powers when it is controlled by the opposition party. However, this eagerness to use the committee gavel is conditional on the president's standing among the public and on the level of and changes in popular support for the military action.

The only coefficient among the control variables that reaches conventional levels of statistical significance is for the logged cumulative casualties variable in model 5. This suggests that as the American death toll mounts, congressional investigatory activity increases. However, when Vietnam and Korea are excluded from the sample, this relationship, while still positive, is no longer statistically significant.

To illustrate the substantive size of each variable's effect on the predicted number of investigative hearings in a given month, figure 6.2 presents another series of first differences holding all other variables

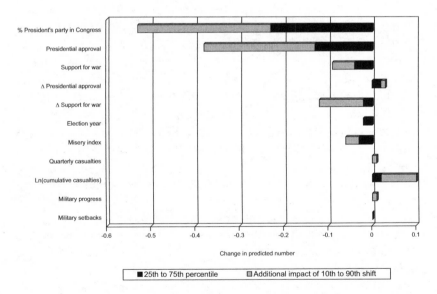

FIGURE 6.2. Predicted effects of variables on the number of congressional investigations into the use of force. First differences for the following variables are statistically significant: percentage of seats held by the president's party in Congress, presidential approval, change in support for war.

constant at their means or medians. The estimated effects of each variable on investigate activity largely mirror the predicted effects of each variable on legislative activity shown in figure 6.1. The partisan composition of Congress and the degree of presidential approval have by far the largest influence on the predicted number of investigative hearings in a given month. Strong levels of popular support for a military venture and increases in it also can depress Congress's incentives to confront the president through its investigatory powers. By contrast, large cumulative numbers of American casualties may open a window of opportunity for congressional challenges, though the estimated coefficient is not statistically significant.

Summary

Consistent with theoretical expectations, the models presented in table 6.1 confirm that Congress's partisan composition is the most important predictor of its willingness to use the formal legislative and investigative tools at its disposal to challenge the president's conduct of ongoing military operations. However, the models also show that changes in the domestic political environment and in the strategic situation on the ground are also important components of such calculations. By shaping the potential costs and benefits that members of Congress stand to reap from attacking the president's handling of military affairs, public opinion, American casualties, and media reports of military developments on the ground all influence the likelihood of a formal congressional challenge to the president. When deciding whether to act to curtail a use of force legislatively or to confront the president in front of television cameras in the committee room, members of Congress, even of the opposition party, pay close attention to the opportunities afforded by the domestic political environment. They refrain from attacking a commander in chief with formidable levels of public support, but smell blood in the water when the public has begun to drift away from the president. Similarly, developments in theater play an important role in opening windows of opportunity for congressional action. Mounting U.S. casualties and reports of setbacks on the ground may also activate opposition members' preexisting incentives to challenge the president, while public reports of progress may dissuade congressional action.

The above analyses provide considerable evidence for the critical importance of partisanship, moderated by opportunities in the domestic and strategic environment, in driving congressional behavior at the aggregate level. The next section of this chapter shifts the level of analysis to the motivations underlying the votes of individual members of Congress and examines the relative influence of a member's party affiliation, role within the institution, specific electoral circumstances, and district characteristics on his or her willingness to support initiatives to check executive discretion in foreign affairs.

Partisan Dynamics and Roll Call Voting

Although a variety of incentives clearly influence congressional behavior, on politically explosive votes—such as efforts to override the president and curtail the use of force—partisan dynamics should dominate individual vote choices. Members of the president's party face strong incentives to support their ally in the White House in all but the most extreme circumstances. Even when conditions on the ground begin to deteriorate and public support for a military engagement wanes, congressional co-partisans vocally rebuke the president and his conduct of foreign policy only at great political risk. A swift reversal of position would expose them to charges of flip-flopping for political expediency, while undermining their party's titular leader could spill over into an electoral disaster for their party across levels of government.[14]

Occasionally, members of the president's party do become leaders of the opposition to his military policy. William Fulbright was a lone voice in the wilderness throughout the mid-1960s when even the vast majority of Republicans refused to criticize the failings of Lyndon Johnson's Vietnam policy. Similarly, as early as 2005 a small but growing number of Republicans, including North Carolina's Walter Jones and Nebraska's Chuck Hagel, began criticizing the Bush administration's efforts in the Middle East and calling for an accelerated exit strategy. However, the

---

14. Moreover, as discussed in chapter 2, if presidents share the ideological orientations of their party's mean member on the proper use of military force, then presidents of different parties should pursue fundamentally different types of military actions. If so, then members of the opposition party may also have ideological reasons to oppose the current president's military actions, yet may support the different kinds of actions pursued by a partisan ally in the White House—and vice versa for members of the other party.

strong partisan incentives not to oppose openly a co-partisan president on critical votes in military affairs should encourage the vast majority of members to toe the party line.

Members of the opposition, conversely, have few partisan incentives to support the president. If a military action succeeds in quickly meeting expectations and goals, members of the opposition, even if they have supported the venture, stand to gain little at the polls. Instead, the president and members of his party will reap the lion's share of the electoral reward. If a military action fails, however, opposition party support will only help provide the president with political cover and diminish the opposition's ability to exploit the White House's errors in judgment for political gain. Rather, visible opposition to the president's policies—particularly when it is calculated to coincide with opportunities in the political and strategic environment, as the models in the preceding section suggest most legislative actions consciously are—can pay dividends by damaging the electoral prospects of the president and, in turn, those of his party. Thus, members of the opposition share a common incentive to vote to curtail presidential discretion in the conduct of military affairs.

This baseline orientation may be tempered by individual members' unique electoral situations. For opposition members whose districts the president has carried in the most recent election, the risks of opposing the president may outweigh any potential benefit that would accrue to their party as a whole. However, for the vast majority of opposition members, politically damaging attacks on the president and his administration serve both broader partisan and narrower individual electoral interests.

In addition to partisanship and personal electoral circumstances, many other factors may influence congressional voting behavior on major questions of military policy. For example, an extensive literature on the civil-military gap suggests that members who have served in the military have significantly different preferences on military policy than their civilian peers.[15] This body of research suggests that members' military experience or lack thereof may influence how they interpret and ultimately vote on legislative initiatives to curtail a use of force. Many veterans may interpret congressional efforts to constrain an ongoing military action as interfering with the judgment of the commanders in the

---

15. Holsti 1998, 2001; Feaver and Gelpi 2004; Sarkesian, Williams, and Bryant 1995.

field—or, worse, as undermining the troops on the ground. If so, veterans may be less likely to vote in favor of an action to curtail the use of force, independent of their partisan identification.

Individual members' institutional positions within Congress may also factor into their vote choices on military affairs. Members of both chambers' foreign relations and armed services committees have the greatest expertise and institutional interest in foreign affairs. While the debate between distributive and informational theories of legislative organization rages on, the possibilities for self-selection onto these committees and the expertise these members subsequently acquire may shape their preferences in military policy and influence their willingness to challenge presidential discretion in foreign affairs.[16] The precise expectation for this influence, however, is unclear. From one perspective, members of these committees are the logical defenders of congressional prerogatives in military affairs. As such, they may be more willing than other members, ceteris paribus, to defend Congress's war powers and vote to constrain executive discretion. On the other hand, members of these committees may be the most sensitive to the foreign policy ramifications of open congressional dissent. Moreover, augmented briefings and consultations with administration officials may shape these committee members' military preferences, which in turn may make them wary of publicly rebuking the White House.[17] The subsequent models will test these competing theoretical perspectives.

Finally, although constituency pressures usually reinforce partisan incentives for opposition members to oppose the president's policies and vice versa, on occasion they may conflict with partisan motives. In his study of congressional votes on defense spending bills in the early 1980s, Larry Bartels found that "safe" Democrats in the House, who routinely ran unchallenged, responded to constituent preferences for greater defense spending at the beginning of the 1980s by voting to appropriate almost as much money for defense as comparable "vulnerable" Democrats, who won by much smaller margins and hence should have been more sensitive to local electoral pressures.[18] One potential measure of district-level preferences on military matters is the number of active-

---

16. For distributive theories, see Ferejohn 1986, Shepsle and Weingast 1987, Weingast and Marshall 1988. For informational theories, see Krehbiel 1990, 1991.

17. Huntington 1961.

18. Bartels 1991.

duty military personnel residing in each state or district. For the same reasons that members of Congress who served in the military may be less likely to vote to curtail an ongoing use of force, constituent opinion in districts with higher numbers of military personnel may run stronger against votes to constrain the executive's hand in foreign policy than it does in districts with lower concentrations of soldiers.

All of these factors—an individual member's unique electoral circumstances, veteran status, committee memberships, and constituency characteristics—likely influence his or her vote choices on legislative actions to constrain the president's free hand in the conduct of military operations. However, the strong partisan electoral incentives in play suggest that these factors should influence voting decisions only at the margin. The subsequent roll call analyses will test for the relative influence of each factor on congressional decision-making.

Finally, the only factor raised in the theoretical discussion of chapter 2 that might rival partisanship as a predictor of a member's willingness to vote to curtail a use of force is whether he or she had previously voted to authorize the military action. Having previously voted to authorize a use of force might dissuade many members from voting to curtail it at a later date, even if conditions on the ground have changed. The relative importance of such prior votes, partisan affiliation, and the other factors discussed previously will also be assessed in the pooled roll call analyses with which this chapter concludes.

Model

A series of logit models explores the dynamics driving congressional roll-call voting on all twenty-one binding legislative challenges to the president's conduct of military affairs during the Reagan and Clinton presidencies. To test for the importance of partisanship in members' voting calculus, the models include a dummy variable for whether or not each member is a Republican. A member's party identification could influence his or her vote choice in one of two ways. First, as posited in chapter 2, a member's partisan relationship to the president provides strong incentives for him or her to support or oppose the administration's handling of military affairs. If party ties to the president are most responsible for determining members' vote choices, Republicans should have been considerably less likely than Democrats to vote to curtail military actions during Ronald Reagan's presidency, and significantly more likely to do so when Bill Clinton held office.

Alternatively, the driving factor may not be the parties' different political incentives but rather their divergent ideological beliefs concerning the use of military force. If Republicans are more hawkish on military matters and less likely to rein in ongoing military operations, then the sign of the coefficient should be the same, regardless of whether Clinton or Reagan was president at the time of the vote.

Electoral factors—most importantly the president's previous success in a state or congressional district—may moderate the importance of partisanship and also significantly influence members' decision calculus when they are faced with a vote to constrain the executive's conduct of military action. Consequently, the logit models include a measure of the president's percentage of the two-party vote in each state or congressional district in the previous election. The stronger the president's track record of success in a state or district, the more wary members, even of the opposition, will be to challenge him. As an additional electoral control, the models also include each member's share of the vote in the preceding election as a rough gauge of electoral safety. "Safe" members, with partisan or policy motivations to attack the president's handling of military affairs, may feel freer to do so than less "safe" members with similar dispositions who nonetheless might view any such action as a politically risky gambit.[19]

To test for the importance of a member's military veteran status and committee memberships on his or her likelihood of voting to curtail a use of force, the models also include dummy variables for whether he or she served in the military, and for whether that member was currently serving on either chamber's foreign relations or armed services committees at the time of the vote.[20]

Finally, to account for possible variations in district preferences, the models include measures of the number of military personnel residing in each state or district, which have been drawn from the decennial

<hr />

19. Bianco 1994.

20. The names for these committees changed slightly over time, but their memberships and duties remained virtually identical. When Republicans assumed control of Congress in 1995, they renamed the House Armed Services Committee the House National Security Committee, and the Foreign Affairs Committee the International Relations Committee.

census.[21] States or districts with large populations of military personnel may generate strong constituent pressure to oppose congressional efforts to constrain a use of force, which many in the military might view as undermining the morale of the troops in the field. As an additional proxy for constituent preferences, the models also include a dummy variable for the states of the former Confederacy. Traditionally, the South has been more hawkish and supportive of military endeavors than other regions of the country, regardless of the partisan composition of its congressional delegation. As such, Southern legislators may face stronger pressures than other members, even of the same party, to oppose any congressional efforts potentially seen as hampering military flexibility or failing to support the troops

The fully specified logit model is summarized in this equation:

Pr (voting to curtail the use of force) = β_0 + β_1 (Republican)
+ β_2 (presidential vote) + β_3 (congressional vote) + β_4 (veteran)
+ β_5 (Foreign Affairs/Relations) + β_6 (Armed Services)
+ β_7 (military personnel in district) + β_8 (Southern state)

Results and Discussion

The first set of models in table 6.2 presents the logit results from roll call analyses of nine binding legislative actions to curtail the use of force during the Reagan administration. The House votes focused on efforts to limit U.S. involvement in the Lebanon peacekeeping force and the invasion of Grenada in 1983, while the Senate votes also dealt with the reflagging of Kuwaiti tankers during the Iran-Iraq War in 1987–88. The results largely accord with theoretical expectations.

Republicans were considerably less likely to rebuke a president of their own party and curtail his military actions, even though all three engagements involved considerable American casualties.[22] Holding all

21. Data drawn from Adler 2003. All models were also reestimated including a measure of the percentage of veterans in a state or congressional district. In none of the models did the resulting coefficient reach conventional levels of statistical significance.

22. However, the attack on the USS *Stark* in 1987 preceded the beginning of the reflagging operation. The numbers are small, of course, in comparison to other major military actions, but considerably larger than those for any military action initiated by President Clinton.

TABLE 6.2 **Factors influencing roll call votes on binding initiatives to curtail the use of force during the presidencies of Ronald Reagan and Bill Clinton**

Independent variables	Reagan		Clinton	
	House	Senate	House	Senate
Republican	−1.24**	−2.93***	3.29***	2.03***
	(.52)	(1.01)	(.44)	(.19)
Presidential vote in district	−2.18***	−10.75***	−2.50***	−6.70***
	(.60)	(1.68)	(.95)	(1.25)
Congressional vote	−.16	−.71	.37	−5.82***
	(.31)	(1.60)	(.63)	(1.53)
Veteran	−.12***	.21	−.22**	−.63**
	(.02)	(.15)	(.09)	(.29)
Foreign Affairs/Relations Committee	−.48*	−.09	−.37***	.13
	(.25)	(.15)	(.12)	(.32)
Armed Services Committee	−.56***	−.59**	−.09	.35
	(.15)	(.28)	(.19)	(.32)
Military personnel in district	−7.63	.06	−7.39	−.80
	(5.15)	(2.10)	(5.75)	(1.92)
South	−.67**	−.91***	−.27***	−.05
	(.30)	(.17)	(.10)	(.24)
Constant	2.29***	7.73***	−.61	5.14***
	(.51)	(1.43)	(.83)	(1.38)
n	1,282	465	2,960	490
Log-likelihood	−788.91	−206.17	−1,198.45	−246.51
% correctly predicted	68	81	86	76

Note: * $p < .10$; ** $p < .05$; *** $p < .01$; All significance tests are two-tailed; all models report robust standard errors clustered on vote number.

other variables constant at their means or medians, Republican House members were almost 30 percent less likely to vote to curtail the use of force than were Democrats with identical electoral and constituent pressures.[23] However, whether this Republican propensity to vote against curtailing the use of force is a result of co-partisan ties with an incumbent president or symptomatic of a more general willingness to use military force abroad cannot be determined from the Reagan data alone. If the latter is the case, then the coefficient for Republicans in the Clinton vote models should also be negative, or at least not positive. However, if partisan incentives primarily drive vote choice, then the sign of the Republican coefficient should switch in the Clinton models.[24]

23. Put in other words, the predicted probability of voting to curtail the use of force for two individual members with identical characteristics aside from their party affiliation was .45 for the Republican, and .74 for the Democrat.

24. Members' ideological orientations may also strongly influence their vote choices on major questions of military policy. However, because partisanship and ideology as mea-

While partisanship was the most important predictor of a member's vote choice, this baseline incentive was moderated by his or her unique electoral situation. The statistically significant negative coefficient for presidential vote share corresponds with theoretical expectations. The stronger the president's showing in a member's district, the higher are the risks of opposing him and, consequently, the less likely that the member is to oppose the president on such a highly salient issue as a vote to curtail the use of force. First differences suggest that a Democrat, predisposed for partisan reasons to vote against the president, and in whose district Ronald Reagan had snared 76 percent of the two-party vote (90th percentile) was 17 percent less likely to vote to curtail a use of force than a comparable Democrat in whose district Reagan had received only 42 percent (10th percentile). However, the coefficient for each member's vote share in his or her last election is statistically insignificant, suggesting that "safe" members were no more or less likely to vote to constrain presidential discretion in military affairs than were "vulnerable" members.

The House model offers some evidence that members' individual characteristics influence their military votes. For example, the coefficient for whether a representative served in the military is in the expected negative direction and is statistically significant. However, the magnitude of the effect is rather small. First differences suggest that congressional veterans were only 3 percent less likely to vote to curtail a use of force than their civilian peers with equivalent partisan and electoral backgrounds. This echoes recent work by William Bianco, who finds that military veterans do appear to vote differently than other members of Congress on a range of foreign policy issues, but that these differences are quite small in comparison with the influence of other traditional predictors of congressional vote choice, particularly partisanship.[25]

The House model also suggests that representatives serving on the Foreign Affairs and Armed Services committees were considerably less likely to vote to curtail the use of force than their peers, by margins of 11 and 13 percent respectively. These findings contradict hypotheses that members of these committees, the institutional loci of foreign policy ex-

---

sured by NOMINATE scores correlate so highly throughout this period, I have included only partisan measures. When members' first-dimension NOMINATE scores are added, the results remain substantively similar across specifications.

25. Bianco 2005.

pertise within Congress, should be the most ardent defenders of congressional prerogatives in directing foreign affairs. Instead, these members were even less likely than others to vote to constrain the executive. This negative relationship echoes David Rohde's finding of greater support for the administration in the foreign policy committees than among the rank and file throughout the Reagan era.[26] It also complements Gary Cox and Matthew McCubbins' analysis showing that Democrats on the Armed Services committee were significantly more conservative on foreign policy issues than other Democrats during this period.[27]

Finally, the Reagan House model suggests that constituency preferences may have influenced members' vote choices. Southern representatives, on average, were 15 percent less likely to vote to curtail a use of force than were members with similar characteristics from other regions of the country. Moreover, the coefficient for the number of military personnel in a representative's district is negative, as expected. However, it fails to meet conventional levels of statistical significance, and substantively its estimated influence is rather small. First differences show that an increase from the 10th to the 90th percentile in the number of military personnel in a district only decreases the predicted probability of voting to curtail a use of force by roughly 2 percent.

Column 2 in table 6.2 replicates the same model specification on roll call data from the five binding initiatives to curtail the use of force that reached the Senate floor in the Reagan era. The results across chambers are quite similar, suggesting that the same dynamics influenced the votes of representatives and senators alike. As in the House models, the dominant factor again was partisanship. Republicans in the Senate were almost 60 percent less likely to vote to constrain Reagan than were Democrats. Senators from states that had gone heavily for Reagan in the last election, like their peers in the House, were again much less likely to cross the president in the military realm than were similar senators in other states. Individual characteristics also continued to influence vote choice. The coefficient for the Foreign Relations Committee dummy is negative as in the House model, albeit statistically insignificant—yet the model does show strong evidence that members of the Armed Services Committee were less likely to vote to curtail an ongoing action than were other members. Finally, the Senate model also offers modest evidence

26. Rohde 1991, 1994.
27. Cox and McCubbins 1993.

for the influence of constituency pressures. While the model shows no relationship between the number of military personnel in a state and a senator's vote choice, it continues to show a strong Southern bias against voting to curtail ongoing military actions.

The only irregularity is the positively signed, though statistically insignificant, coefficient for a member's military veteran status. Contra the House, veterans in the Senate appear to have been, if anything, more likely to support binding legislative actions to curtail the use of force during the Reagan era than their civilian peers. It is possible that, in the 1980s, Senate veterans had service experiences that differed from those of their peers in the House and that might account for their starkly different voting behavior on measures involving the use of force. However, the finding could also be spurious given the relatively small number of observations, and the coefficient does fail to reach conventional levels of statistical significance. By the 1990s, as the second set of models in table 6.2 will demonstrate, veterans in the Senate, like their compatriots in the House, were less likely to vote to curtail ongoing military actions than were their peers.

The second set of models in table 6.2 extends the analysis to seven votes in the House and six in the Senate from the Clinton era that covered American military involvement in Somalia, Bosnia, and Kosovo. In sharp contrast to the negative relationship observed between being a Republican and the probability of voting to curtail an ongoing use of force during the Reagan era, the positive coefficient in the Clinton years suggests that Republicans were on average almost 70 percent more likely to vote against the use of force than were their Democratic peers. This dramatic change provides strong evidence that Republicans do not, as a general principle, oppose legislative constraints on executive discretion in military affairs. Rather, when Bill Clinton settled into the Oval Office, the incentives for Republican members of Congress fundamentally changed. To maximize their potential political gains, they now formed the bulk of support for efforts to constrain presidential discretion in foreign affairs while Democrats, who had vehemently opposed President Reagan's peacekeeping mission in Lebanon and other military endeavors, also shifted roles and now voted en masse against efforts to curtail U.S. military commitments in Somalia and the Balkans.

Admittedly, even this dramatic shift in voting behavior is not ironclad proof that divergent preferences alone are not driving the observed patterns. If presidents simply share the military policy preferences of their co-partisans in Congress and consequently pursue different types of military actions than presidents of the other party, then shared preferences alone could explain the reversal in voting behavior between the Reagan and Clinton eras.

However, diverging party preferences over the proper exercise of military force cannot explain variations in partisan support within Congress for the same military intervention when the party in the White House changes. For example, if Republican ideals about the proper role of military action in American foreign policy drove congressional Republicans' opposition to U.S. interventions in Somalia and Kosovo under President Clinton, they should have vigorously opposed the former intervention when George H. W. Bush began it before leaving office in the winter of 1992, and they should have continued to criticize the latter intervention after George W. Bush came to power in 2001.[28] Yet, the Republican rank and file heartily supported the elder Bush's decision to send troops to Somalia, and reserved their criticism of the operation until Clinton took office. Conversely, grumbling by Republicans on Kosovo and the need to end the American commitment there dissipated overnight when a Republican commander in chief entered the White House and decided to keep the troops in the Balkans. Thus, the dramatic reversals in Republican and Democratic positions on initiatives to curtail the use of force provide convincing, if not indisputable, evidence that partisan dynamics—and particularly partisan electoral incentives—are the motive force governing voting behavior in military policy.

While partisanship continues to account for the vast majority of the variance in voting patterns, the other dynamics observed in the Reagan era also appear to drive congressional voting behavior in the Clinton years. Representatives from districts where Clinton had performed strongly in the most recent election were considerably more wary of opposing his military policies than were representatives from other districts. Veterans in the House were again less likely to vote to curtail an ongoing deployment than were other representatives. Members of the Foreign Affairs Committee, too, were less likely to support efforts to constrain the executive. Finally, district characteristics also appear to

28. Furthermore, many military operations begun by Democratic and Republican presidents (e.g., U.S. participation in the 1982–84 Lebanon peacekeeping force versus U.S. participation in the UN force a decade later in Bosnia), are so similar in scope and mission that it renders the first assumption all but untenable.

have influenced members' voting calculus. The negative coefficient for military personnel in the district is in the expected direction, though it again fails to meet conventional levels of statistical significance. However, the House model suggests that Southern representatives remained less likely to support curtailing a use of force when troops were in the field, though the magnitude of this effect was considerably smaller in the 1990s than in the previous decade (an estimated decrease of 3 percent, as opposed to 15 percent in the 1980s). In the Senate, the effect for the Southern dummy variable disappears entirely. The diminishing size of Southern exceptionalism in military policy voting patterns is almost certainly due to the continued partisan realignment of the South and its congressional delegations toward the Republican Party throughout the period, which brought constituency and partisan incentives into closer alignment.[29]

The Senate results closely mirror those in the House. However, the largest surprise is the statistically significant negative coefficient for a senator's vote share in the last election. Presumably, senators who secured large margins of victory in their previous electoral contests might have greater political leeway to vote for legislative actions challenging the president's handling of military affairs if they had partisan, policy, or institutional incentives for doing so. However, the Clinton Senate results suggest that the "safest" senators from an electoral standpoint were considerably less likely than their peers to vote to constrain military operations. Re-estimating the model with partisan interactions shows that the result holds for senators of both parties. Republicans and Democrats who had enjoyed resounding victories in their most recent electoral contests were substantially less likely to support the binding initiatives than were their peers. The reasons for this relationship are not immediately obvious, and the correlation may be spurious.[30]

29. Rohde 1991, Carmines and Stimson 1989.

30. If the military actions were unpopular (as each operation was at some point in its course), this unpopularity could explain "safe" Democrats' greater propensity to vote with Clinton, as they would be most insulated from any electoral backlash. A similar logic could also begin to explain why "safe" Republicans were less likely to attack Clinton and his military policies than were other Republicans with more tenuous holds on their seats. Electorally vulnerable Republicans may have held even stronger incentives to attack Clinton's policies for personal gain than their peers from safer seats who shared partisan incentives to challenge Clinton but did not possess strong personal electoral imperatives to do so. As a robustness check to ensure that the results for the other variables are not artifacts

TABLE 6.3 **Factors influencing roll call votes on binding initiatives to curtail the use of force, 1981–2000**

Independent variables	House (1)	Senate (2)	House (3)	Senate (4)	House (5)	Senate (6)
Member of opposition party	2.44***	2.44***	2.47***	2.28***	2.36***	1.38***
	(.47)	(.51)	(.45)	(.56)	(.45)	(.43)
Presidential vote in district	−3.19***	−7.48***	−2.88***	−7.23***	−2.06***	−4.76***
	(.64)	(1.76)	(.67)	(1.98)	(.42)	(.87)
Congressional vote	−.20	−2.59*	−.09	−2.30	−.61	−3.77
	(.47)	(1.42)	(.56)	(1.57)	(.98)	(2.86)
Veteran	−.12**	−.24	−.12***	−.21	−.15	−.71***
	(.05)	(.21)	(.04)	(.19)	(.20)	(.21)
Foreign Affairs/ Relations	−.36***	.10	−.31***	.00	−.11	.09
	(.11)	(.19)	(.12)	(.16)	(.15)	(.40)
Armed Services	−.29**	−.11	−.29**	−.19	−.43***	.55*
	(.13)	(.25)	(.14)	(.25)	(.12)	(.33)
Military personnel in district	−7.11**	.51	−6.64**	1.03	−3.93	−1.11
	(3.28)	(1.58)	(3.21)	(1.66)	(13.01)	(1.68)
South	−.48***	−.39**	−.46***	−.51***	−.71***	−.36
	(.12)	(.18)	(.11)	(.15)	(.06)	(.33)
Clinton	−.10	−1.10*	−.36	−.51	2.02***	—
	(1.05)	(.61)	(1.13)	(.58)	(.04)	
Previously voted to authorize	—	—	−1.71	−1.69***	−2.58***	−1.84***
			(1.32)	(.29)	(.62)	(.29)
Constant	.77	4.42**	.85	4.21**	.76	4.15***
	(1.34)	(1.83)	(1.43)	(1.97)	(1.66)	(1.62)
n	4,242	955	4,242	955	855	392
Log-likelihood	−2,077.98	−469.44	−2,003.56	−448.71	−307.43	−173.84
% correctly predicted	80	75	81	78	85	81

Note: * $p < .10$; ** $p < .05$; *** $p < .01$. All significance tests are two-tailed; all models report robust standard errors clustered on vote number.

Finally, the models in table 6.3 pool all of the votes in each chamber across administrations to produce estimates of each variable's effect on vote choice over the entire time period. The results for the House almost perfectly accord with theoretical expectations. Representatives from the opposition party were considerably more likely to challenge the president and vote to curtail a military venture. Individual members' specific electoral circumstances also strongly influenced their votes. The stronger the president had performed in a representative's district in the previous election, the less likely that representative was to vote against the

---

of this potentially spurious correlation between vote choice and past congressional vote shares, the model was reestimated omitting the congressional vote measure. The relationships between party affiliation, presidential vote share, military veteran status, and committee memberships remain the same even in this restricted specification.

administration in military affairs. Military veterans and members of the
Foreign Affairs and Armed Services committees were also less likely
to vote to constrain the commander in chief than were non–committee
members. District characteristics also had significant effects, as representatives with higher shares of military personnel in their districts and
representatives from the South were less likely to vote to curtail a use of
force than were their peers.

Figure 6.3 graphically illustrates the relative magnitudes of each variable's effect on vote choice in the House through a series of first differences. The solid portion of each bar represents the increase or decrease
in the predicted probability of voting to curtail a use of force, generated
by shifting the given variable from its 25th to its 75th percentile, or from
zero to one in the case of dummy variables, while holding all other variables constant at their means or medians. The dotted portions reflect the
additional impact that a shift from the 10th to the 90th percentile in each
explanatory factor has on the probability of a given member voting to
constrain the president. As figure 6.3 plainly shows, partisanship dom-

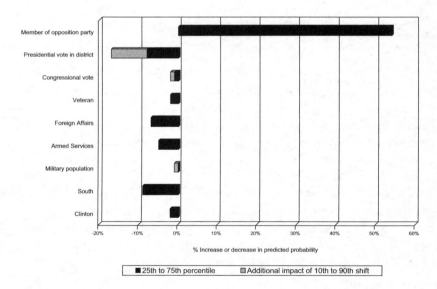

FIGURE 6.3. Predicted effects of variables on the probability of legislators voting to curtail the use of force. First differences for the following variables are statistically significant:
status as member of opposition party, presidential vote in home district, status as miltary
veteran, membership in Foreign Affairs Committee, membership in Armed Service Com-
nittee; military population in home district; location of home district in the South.

inates congressional vote choices. Switching a hypothetical member's partisanship from the same party as the president to the opposition increases his or her probability of voting to curtail the use of force by over 50 percent. This effect is moderated somewhat by the president's electoral strength in the district, as well as by a member's veteran status, institutional position as measured by committee assignments, and constituency pressures. However, the estimated size of these factors' influence on vote choice clearly pales in comparison to that of party affiliation.

The second model in table 6.3 shows the findings for all roll calls in the Senate. Again, the results largely parallel those for the House. Partisanship continues to dominate vote choice, even in the upper chamber. Similarly, the better the president fared in a given state in the most recent election, the less likely the senators of that state are to buck the president and vote to curtail a use of force. The coefficient for military veterans is negative, as in the House model, but for the Senate it fails to reach conventional levels of statistical significance. The model shows no correlation between a senator's assignment to the Foreign Relations or Armed Services committees and his or her vote choice. It also finds no evidence of any influence for the number of military personnel in his or her state. Southern senators are, on average, slightly less likely to vote to constrain presidential discretion in military affairs. And finally, the dummy variable identifying votes in the Clinton era suggests that the Senate as a whole was less likely to vote to curtail an ongoing military action in the 1990s than it was in the 1980s under Reagan.

Finally, both the House and Senate models were reestimated including one additional variable: whether each member had previously voted to authorize the use of force in question (models 3 and 4). The theory presented in chapter 2 speculated that presidents value legislative authorizations not because they desire the constitutional sanction for their actions, but because they want the political cover that an authorization affords. One reason that authorizations may prove politically valuable is that, once having voted to authorize a military action, members of Congress might think twice before voting to curtail the use of force in that same action. The data provides strong support for this additional observable implication of the theory. In both the House and Senate models, the relevant coefficient is negative, substantively large, and—in the Senate model—statistically significant. First differences calculated from model 4 suggest that having previously voted to authorize a use of force decreases the estimated probability of a senator from the opposition party voting to curtail that same action from 61 to 24 percent. Further, when narrowing the universe of cases to the legislative efforts to curtail uses of force that Congress had previously voted to authorize (models 5 and 6), we see statistically significant negative relationships in both chambers. Even after controlling for partisanship, institutional position, and constituency characteristics, members of Congress who had previously voted to authorize the use of force were significantly less likely to vote to constrain the president's conduct of that mission at a later date.

Conclusion

Consistent with the theory articulated in chapter 2, the models in this chapter show that partisanship is indeed the dominant factor influencing whether and when Congress uses the legislative and investigative tools at its disposal to challenge the president's military policies. As the ranks of the president's partisan opponents increase on Capitol Hill, so, too, do the frequency and intensity with which the legislature challenges his military policies both on the floor and in the committee room. In a similar vein, the models show that once a curtailing legislative initiative is brought to the floor, the partisan relationship of each member to the president is the most important factor influencing his or her vote on the pending action.

The models also show, however, that even an opposition Congress treads carefully when calculating whether its interests are best served by confronting the commander in chief in the politically perilous environment that emerges once American troops are deployed in the field. Because the potential costs of criticizing an ongoing military mission are high, congressional opponents look for windows of opportunity to open either in the domestic political environment or in the strategic environment in theater. Similarly, while a member's partisan relationship to the president is the most important predictor of his or her voting behavior, other factors, such as the strength of support for the president within his or her state or district, also enter into the decision calculus.

Thus, the analyses in this chapter yield important information about the limits of congressional influence in the military arena. The quantitative and qualitative analyses in the preceding two chapters have demonstrated that Congress can influence the president's conduct and the duration of military operations when it considers legislation to curtail the use of force or when it investigates the administration's conduct of military operations. However, members of Congress only use these institutional tools when they judge that the benefits of challenging the president outweigh the costs they might incur from doing so. The contours of the political environment in Washington and the strategic situation on the ground, although they play little direct role in the duration models described in chapter 4, strongly influence these calculations.

CHAPTER SEVEN

Conclusion: Congressional Constraints and the War on Terror

As a final examination of the nature and limits of congressional influence over the conduct of American military policymaking, this chapter traces congressional reactions to the ongoing war in Iraq and assesses the consequences of these congressional maneuvers for politics and policy. Despite considerable reasons to question the administration's claims and oppose its proposed military action against the Iraqi regime of Saddam Hussein, Congress at the conflict initiation phase readily acquiesced to the president's demands and authorized the use of force. However, as the political and strategic environment changed dramatically over the months and years following the initial invasion, opponents of President George W. Bush's policies in Congress increasingly began to challenge his conduct of the war on the floor, in the committee room, and over the airwaves.

Theory suggests that such actions should raise both the political and the military costs that Bush stood to incur by maintaining the status quo in the Middle East. Consistent with this expectation, the statistical analyses in chapter 4 demonstrate that such actions historically have decreased the expected duration of a major military venture. Yet in the Iraq case, Bush remained undeterred in the face of intense congressional challenges to his military policies and even escalated the scale of the American commitment. Certainly, the effects of congressional opposition on the duration of the Iraq War do not match those predicted by hypothesis 4b. Can such an outcome be reconciled with the theory articulated in chapter 2? Or does the Iraqi case suggest that the dynamics

shown to hold in earlier eras of American history are no longer operative in the new context of the war on terror?

The Iraqi case is subject to multiple interpretations. It is possible that
congressional actions simply did not affect Bush's strategic calculations
at all, and that this is why they failed to produce any observable change
in policy. However, it is also possible that high-profile congressional opposition *did* raise the costs of staying the course in Iraq for the president,
but that the benefits he perceived from staying the course, and the costs
he believed he would incur if he withdrew American troops prematurely,
simply outweighed even these heightened costs. Testing between these
two alternative hypotheses is exceedingly difficult because, in terms of
policy outcomes, they are observationally equivalent. However, if the
available data suggests that the theoretical mechanisms posited in chapter 2 were operative and that congressional actions did increase the political or military costs of staying the course for the president, the Iraq
case would still fit within the theoretical mold even if these actions did
not lead the president to curtail the military commitment. If, however,
we find no evidence that Congress raised the costs of continuing the
war in Iraq for the president, then the case would raise important questions about the capacity of Congress to influence military policymaking
through informal means in contemporary politics.

Congress and the Initiation of the Iraq War

When all one hundred members of the Senate huddled in its well into
the early morning hours of October 11, 2002, to debate and vote on legislation authorizing the use of military force against the Iraqi regime
of Saddam Hussein, there were strong reasons to believe that Congress
might withhold its assent. To begin with, the language of the resolution
itself was almost unprecedented in the scope of the power it delegated
to the president.[1] The resolution was not a declaration of war. It was not
even an explicit authorization to use force in the face of an alleged attack, like the infamous Gulf of Tonkin Resolution passed thirty-eight
years earlier. Instead, it delegated to the president sole authority to de-

---

1. One of the few resolutions to surpass it in the breadth of authority and power delegated to the president was the Authorization for Use of Military Force against the perpe-
trators of the 2001 terrorist attacks, which was passed shortly after September 11.

termine at an unspecified future time that Iraq posed a threat to the United States and to take military action against it at his discretion. This almost wholesale delegation of legislative powers to the president might logically have undermined the resolution's prospects for passage.

Moreover, even as the White House pressed Congress to act immediately, there was great uncertainty over how to proceed against Iraq both at home and abroad. The United Nations continued to pursue a resumption of inspections before considering a new resolution authorizing member nations to take military action against a noncompliant Iraqi regime. While Prime Minister Tony Blair and the United Kingdom remained steadfastly supportive of taking a hard line against Saddam, other NATO allies, including France and Germany as well as Russia, openly questioned the administration's case for war and ardently called for extended diplomacy rather than preemptive military action to address the impasse. Even American public opinion was decidedly split on the question of intervention. A majority of Americans supported military action writ large, but when asked whether Congress should give the president the authority to use force against Iraq whenever he deemed necessary, a clear majority replied in the negative. Similarly, when given the options of imminent military action versus granting UN weapons inspectors more time to discern Iraq's capabilities regarding weapons of mass destruction, a full 57 percent of Americans favored waiting.[2]

With the House of Representatives already having approved the joint resolution, Senator Robert Byrd (D–West Virginia), the unofficial historian of the Senate and inveterate defender of its constitutional prerogatives, rose to oppose the authorization. As was his wont, Byrd reached back into the annals of imperial Roman history and metaphorically alluded to the demise of Tiberius Claudius Nero. Regaling his colleagues, Byrd described how when Nero, huddling in a freedman's villa outside of Rome, heard the thundering hooves of approaching praetorian guards seeking to apprehend him as an enemy of the state, he grasped a knife and drew the blade across his neck. "Mr. President," Byrd thundered, "here in this pernicious resolution on which the Senate will vote soon, we find the dagger that is being held at the throat of the Senate of the United States."[3] Like the last of the Julio-Claudian emperors almost two

2. Gallup/CNN/*USA Today* poll [USAIPOCNUS2002-37], September 20–22, 2002. CBS News poll [USCBS2002-09C], September 22–23, 2002.

3. Robert C. Byrd, *Congressional Record* S10238, October 10, 2002.

millennia earlier, Byrd believed the Senate was about to fall on its own sword.

Despite the legitimate questions raised about the resolution's constitutionality, despite the lingering doubts about the accuracy of the administration's case for war and its legality under international law, and despite considerable uncertainty about when military action would ultimately be commenced and how the nation would grapple with a war's aftermath, seventy-seven senators voted "aye," setting in motion events that in March 2003 would launch what has become one of the longest military conflicts in American history.

In hindsight, Congress's complicity in the headlong rush to war in Iraq seems shocking. However, congressional acquiescence is what would be expected, given the theory developed in chapters 2 and 6. An intensely loyal and ideologically polarized Republican Party controlled the House of Representatives, whose speaker freely described his job as that of being the president's field marshal in the legislature.[4] Because of the polarized rank and file and the majority leadership's iron grasp on the institutional machinery of the chamber, the final outcome in the House was never in doubt. Similarly, despite nominal Democratic control of the Senate (a majority achieved only with the vote of the Senate's lone independent, James Jeffords of Vermont), the political climate in late 2002 was decidedly stacked against any overt challenge to Bush in the military arena. Still riding a post-9/11 tidal wave of popularity, Bush's Gallup approval rating in early October stood at an imposing 67 percent. For Democrats desperately seeking to avoid the label of being soft on terrorism in the impending midterm elections, challenging the president and his mantle of 9/11 leadership was simply out of the question. Moreover, although a number of Republicans expressed misgivings as the vote neared, all but Lincoln Chaffee, a vestigial liberal Republican from Rhode Island, returned to the party fold.

Finally, the course of the national policy debate in the lead-up to the invasion testified to the stark informational asymmetries enjoyed by the president at the conflict initiation phase. Using the bully pulpit to its fullest, Bush presented the nation his assessment of the intelligence data and warned that the country could not wait "for the final proof—the

---

4. On the eve of the 2004 elections, Hastert would famously state that his job was "to pass the president's program." Jonathan Alter, "It's Almost Zero Hour." *Newsweek*, November 3, 2004.

smoking gun—that could come in the form of a mushroom cloud."[5] Congressional opponents of the administration's plans simply lacked the resources and information needed to rebut effectively the president's justifications for war, many of which subsequently proved to be fallacious. Given this state of party power in Congress, the president's strong domestic political position, and his institutional advantages at the conflict initiation stage, the result, as predicted by theory, was presidential ascendance.

Congress and the Conduct of the War in Iraq

As of December 2004, when the empirical analyses in chapters 3 and 4 ended, Congress had done little to assert itself in Iraq policymaking. Democratic criticism in the 2004 reelection contest focused primarily on the Bush administration's initial decision to invade and the dubious intelligence on which it had based its public case for war. While Democrats united around this critique of the war's initiation, they remained considerably more divided about its proper course moving forward. By the end of 2005 the tide in Congress had begun to turn against the administration, as Democrats introduced the first legislative initiatives to curtail the use of force in Iraq and a few prominent Republicans began publicly questioning the administration's policies and calling for a change in course. Momentum in Congress accelerated in 2006 as Democrats, sensing the electoral advantages that challenging the president's handling of the war might afford, grew increasingly assertive in demanding a shift in strategy. Time and again, however, the Republican majority thwarted the efforts of the increasingly vocal Democratic minority. Calls for investigations were rebuffed and legislative initiatives designed to pressure the president were buried in committee as the Republican leadership of both chambers used all of its powers to short-circuit formal affronts to the president's Iraq policy.

However, the 2006 midterms proved to be a watershed change in congressional assertiveness in Iraq policy. Consistent with both theory and the partisan dynamic driving interbranch conflict over the conduct of military affairs observed from the end of Reconstruction into the

5. George W. Bush, "Address to the Nation on Iraq from Cincinnati, Ohio." *Public Papers of the President*, October 7, 2002.

post–Cold War era, the Democratic victories energized congressional challenges to the Bush administration's conduct of the Iraq War. In stark contrast to the record of the 109th Congress, the newly installed Democratic majorities of the 110th Congress quickly used the legislature's institutional machinery to challenge the administration's war policies on several fronts. Speaker Nancy Pelosi declared that the mandate of November had been for Congress to chart "a new direction" in Iraq, and toward this end in 2007 she unleashed a legislative and investigative assault on the administration's conduct of the war.[6] The onslaught culminated in the 2007 appropriations battle, during which Congress passed a funding bill that set a timetable for withdrawing American forces from Iraq. President Bush defiantly vetoed the bill, and war opponents ultimately caved by passing a "clean" appropriation without the timeline. Both chambers considered alternative measures to hamstring Bush's freedom of action in Iraq. For the remainder of Bush's term in office, however, opponents of the war remained thwarted by the presidential veto and the filibuster in the Senate.[7]

In the committee room, where the chairman wields the gavel with little constraint from the minority, congressional opposition also intensified dramatically. In their first fifteen months in power, newly minted Democratic committee chairmen held more critical oversight hearings into the war effort than their Republican predecessors had done in the conflict's first four years. In the first one hundred days alone, Democrats used the forum of the hearing room to question the president's rationale for the surge, investigate continued body armor shortages for troops in the field, highlight abuse by Blackwater, Halliburton, and other private contractors, and—perhaps most detrimental for the administration—

6. For Pelosi's mandate claim, see William Branigin, "Democrats Take Majority in House; Pelosi Poised to Become Speaker." *Washington Post*, November 7, 2006. For evidence of the Iraq War's influence on the 2006 midterms, see Kriner and Shen 2007, Grose and Oppenheimer 2007.

7. See for example, House Armed Services Committee chairman Ike Skelton's bill (HR 2956) requiring that redeployment begin within 120 days, Virginia Republican Senator John Warner's proposal (an amendment to HR 2206) to tie funding for continued U.S. military operations to demonstrated Iraqi progress in meeting established benchmarks (HR 2206), and the proposal by Virginia Democratic Senator Jim Webb (an amendment to HR 1585) to undercut the surge by requiring minimum stateside rest and training periods between foreign deployments.

uncover and publicize evidence of the maltreatment of wounded soldiers at Walter Reed Army Medical Center.[8] Significantly, none of these wartime developments probed by Democrats in early 2007 were new. Most if not all of the specific cases of alleged abuse had been known well before the 2006 midterm, yet it was not until Democrats seized control that Congress aggressively turned its investigative eye on these wartime failures. Contrasting the flurry of investigation under the Democrats with the more lethargic pace of the preceding two Congresses, Illinois Democrat Rahm Emanuel perhaps put it best: "What a difference a year makes."[9]

This exponential increase in legislative challenges to the Bush administration's war policies following the partisan sea change of 2006 is strongly consistent with theory and past precedents.[10] However, subsequent events make it plain that this congressional opposition had few if any tangible effects on the Bush administration's war plans. In response to congressional efforts to force a phased withdrawal of U.S. forces from Iraq, the president audaciously countered with a plan to *increase* the number of troops to stabilize the security situation on the ground and provide breathing space for the fledgling Iraqi government to reach a political solution to the nation's ills. While the troop "surge" provoked outright opposition from most congressional Democrats and public skepticism even from some leading Republican lawmakers, Bush pressed on undeterred and raised American troop levels from 130,000 to 170,000. When Bush left office on January 20, 2009, he did so with more troops on the ground in Iraq than had been there when the Democrats seized power in the November 2006 elections. Plainly, the intense institutional challenges to presidential conduct of the war in Iraq failed to produce a major shift in the conflict's conduct.

This result could suggest that the "new imperial presidency," as Andrew Rudalevige has called it, is simply so strong in the contemporary context of the war on terror that the informal mechanisms of congressional influence that shaped the courses of major military ventures in pre-

8. For a more thorough discussion and analysis of this investigations data, see Howell and Kriner 2009, Kriner 2009.

9. Peter Baker, "Libby Verdict Brings Moment of Accountability." *Washington Post*, March 7, 2007, A1.

10. See Kriner and Schwartz 2008.

vious times no longer exert any meaningful check over the commander in chief.[11] Alternatively, congressional opposition may have raised both the political and the military costs of continuing the war. However, these heightened costs may simply have been exceeded by the benefits that President Bush perceived from staying the course in Iraq. Because these two interpretations are observationally equivalent in terms of policy outcomes, to test between them we must instead endeavor to determine whether congressional opposition to the war raised the costs of staying the course in Iraq for Bush. On this metric, the evidence for congressional influence through informal means, while not conclusive, is strong indeed.

Congress and the Political Costs of Staying the Course in Iraq

One of the mechanisms by which congressional opposition influences presidential cost-benefit calculations is by sending signals of American disunity to the target state. Measuring the effects of such congressional signals on the calculations of the target state is always difficult. In the case of Iraq it is exceedingly so, given the lack of data on the non-state insurgent actors who were the true "target" of the American occupation after the fall of the Hussein regime. Similarly, in the absence of archival documents, such as those from the Reagan Presidential Library presented in chapter 5, it is all but impossible to measure the effects of congressional signals on the administration's perceptions of the military costs it would have to pay to achieve its objectives militarily.

By contrast, measuring the domestic political costs of congressional opposition, while still difficult, is at least a tractable endeavor. Chapter 2 posited two primary pathways through which congressional opposition could raise the political costs of staying the course militarily for the president. First, high-profile congressional challenges to a use of force can affect real or anticipated public opinion and bring popular pressures to bear on the president to change course. Second, congressional opposition to the president's conduct of military affairs can compel him to spend considerable political capital in the military arena to the detriment of other major items on his programmatic agenda. On both of these

11. See Rudalevige 2005.

dimensions, congressional opposition to the war in Iraq appears to have had the predicted effect.

Congressional Influence on Public Opinion

Previous chapters have discussed the difficulties of assessing with certainty Congress's influence on public opinion. These relationships are undoubtedly reciprocal. For example, growing public opposition to the war played a key role in bringing the Democrats to power in the 2006 midterms, and this victory led in turn to the exponential expansion of legislative challenges to the Bush administration's conduct of the war in Iraq.[12] Chapter 2 reviewed a number of recent studies that have employed a range of statistical and experimental techniques to assess the influence of congressional actions on popular support for war.[13] A comprehensive analysis of the effects of specific actions taken in Congress on public wartime opinions is beyond the scope of this chapter. However, the remainder of this section seeks preliminary insight on this question by considering the following counterfactual: If Republicans had narrowly retained control of the 110th Congress and had used their powers of agenda control to clamp down on legislative dissent and politically damaging investigative oversight, would the public have responded differently to the administration's troop surge? There are strong reasons to think that it might well have done so.

After being beleaguered for much of the summer of 2007, Bush administration officials hit the airwaves en masse in late 2007 and early 2008 to trumpet the success of the troop surge. The president, the secretaries of state and defense, military commanders, and even Republican presidential candidates all emphasized the decreasing violence in trouble spots across Iraq, modest progress toward political benchmarks, and—most importantly—a substantial reduction in the casualty rate of American forces. On this last metric, consider the data presented in figure 7.1. The early spring of 2007 was a period of intense fighting and significant American military losses. The 126 American soldiers killed

12. For the influence of the Iraq War on the 2006 midterms, see Kriner and Shen 2007, Grose and Oppenheimer 2007, Gartner and Segura 2008.

13. In the current context, see also Kriner's analysis (2009), which employs an instrumental variable model to assess the influence of congressional investigations on popular support for the war in Iraq.

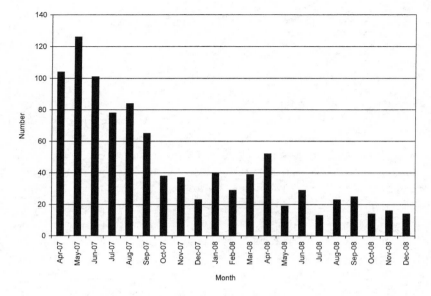

FIGURE 7.1. American military casualties in Iraq, April 2007–December 2008

in May were the highest tally since 2004; it was the third deadliest month for U.S. forces in the entire conflict to date. After that spring, however, American casualty rates declined considerably. Indeed, the 92 American soldiers killed in Iraq during December 2007 and the first two months of 2008 was the fewest in any three-month period in the war's five-year history, and casualty rates continued to decline through the remaining months of the Bush presidency.

An extensive literature has linked changes in casualty rates to shifts in public opinion.[14] Yet throughout 2007 and into 2008, most polls of American attitudes on the war showed little signs of any movement. For example, figure 7.2 traces changes in the percentage of Americans responding that they opposed the war in CNN/Opinion Research Corporation surveys from May 2007 to December 2008.[15] Support for the war did not rebound at all in the wake of alleged progress under the surge. In fact, the line tracking support is essentially flat, with virtually the same

14. Inter alia, Garner and Segura 1998; Klarevas 2002; Eichenberg 2005; Eichenberg, Stoll, and Lebo 2006.

15. The precise wording of the question was: "Do you favor or oppose the U.S. war in Iraq?"

percentage of Americans disapproving of the war in December 2008 as in April 2007. Similarly, there is little systematic polling evidence to suggest that the significant decrease in casualty tallies after the summer of 2007 improved the public's outlook for the war's prospects for success. Figure 7.3 traces the percentage of the public responding that "achieving victory in Iraq is still possible" from NBC/*Wall Street Journal* polls from April 2007 to June 2008, the last time the question was asked. Despite the dramatic decline in American casualty rates during this period, the data suggests strikingly little movement in popular attitudes. As of June 2008, the vast majority of Americans still believed that military success was unachievable in Iraq, despite recent gains in stabilizing the situation on the ground.

Finally, and perhaps most importantly, the surge's trumpeted success failed to sap much strength from public demands for a withdrawal of U.S. forces from Iraq. Figure 7.4 reports data from Pew Research Center polls between June 2007 and June 2008 querying respondents whether they believed "the U.S. should keep military troops in Iraq until the situation has stabilized" or whether they thought "the U.S. should bring its troops home as soon as possible." On this metric, again, we see virtually no evidence of any change in popular support for the war. Despite the

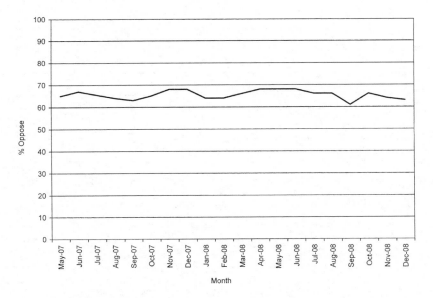

FIGURE 7.2. Percentage of Americans opposing the Iraq War, May 2007–December 2008

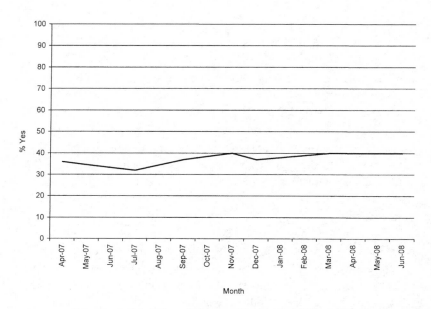

FIGURE 7.3. Percentage of Americans believing victory in Iraq still possible, April 2007–June 2008

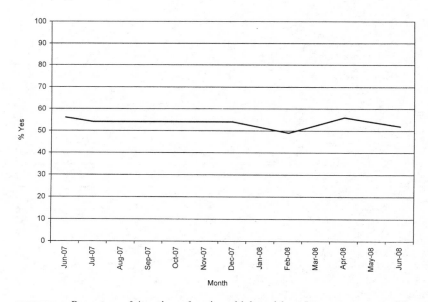

FIGURE 7.4. Percentage of Americans favoring withdrawal from Iraq as soon as possible, June 2007–June 2008

surge's success on many metrics, virtually the same percentage of Americans favored the expeditious withdrawal of American troops in June of 2008 as had done so a year earlier.

It may be that after more than four years of war the public was simply ready for it to end, regardless of any improvement in conditions on the ground. In 2005 John Mueller, a pioneer of the study of war casualties and public opinion, predicted in *Foreign Affairs* that even if declining casualty rates materialized, they would be more likely to "cause the erosion in public support to slow or even cease rather than trigger a large upsurge in support."[16]

However, another possible reason for the lack of a rally around the flag was that every time the administration tried to shift the frame in Iraq, congressional Democrats opened a new front of attack against the president's policies. When the Bush administration emphasized increasing stability in Iraq, Democrats focused on contractor fraud and the war's staggering financial cost to the taxpayer. When the president pointed to new alliances between U.S. troops and Sunni militias that had previously tried to kill them, congressional opponents reminded Americans of the toll the war had taken on U.S. readiness in Afghanistan and of its stark human costs, including those who survived Iraq only to suffer neglect at Walter Reed. In April of 2008 the administration dispatched General David Petraeus and Ambassador Ryan Crocker to trumpet the gains made in the security situation on the ground. On the day before the hearings began, Senator Sheldon Whitehouse (D–Rhode Island) told reporters that while security gains were "nice to have . . . essentially they're meaningless" if they could not tell policymakers anything about when the Iraqi regime would be ready to stand up so that American forces could stand down. Even several Republican senators undercut the administration's message. First-term Senator Bob Corker of Tennessee acknowledged in a hearing, "I think all of us realize we're disappointed at where we are," and vulnerable incumbent Norm Coleman of Minnesota asked, "How do we get out of this mess?"[17]

From extant data alone, it is impossible to conclude with certainty

16. Mueller 2005. Mueller notes that because dissatisfaction was so strong, for support to rise many Americans would have to shift their opinions from outright opposition (as opposed to uncertainty) to support—an unlikely scenario.

17. Karen DeYoung, "Petraeus, Crocker Testify before Impatient Lawmakers." *Washington Post*, April 8, 2008.

that congressional opposition was the decisive factor forestalling a rally in popular support for the war and the president. Nevertheless, this interpretation is consistent with an extensive literature emphasizing the importance of open criticism of Washington elites, particularly in Congress, in blocking the emergence of rally-around-the-flag effects.[18] In the Iraq context, emboldened congressional opposition to the White House in the Democratic-controlled 110th Congress provided such open opposition in spades. The significant gains made by American forces on the ground, dramatically decreased U.S. casualty rates, and tenuous signs of political progress all should have redounded to the president's advantage. Yet support for the war failed to rebound and the administration continued to face stiff public resistance to its policies until its final days in office. While the absence of any rally in popular support for the war is not conclusive proof of the effects of congressional opposition on public opinion, it is strongly consistent with theoretical expectations.

The Costs of Congressional Wartime Opposition to the Bush Agenda

There is also considerable circumstantial evidence suggesting that the intense congressional opposition to Bush's Iraq War policies imposed an additional, significant political cost on the president: it brought action on virtually every other issue on his domestic and international agendas to a grinding halt. With an approval rating mired in the low thirties throughout his final year in office and with more than twice that figure *disapproving* of his job performance, Bush devoted every bit of his political capital to insuring continued funding for the war in Iraq.

Measuring the costs that congressional wartime opposition exacts on other presidential agenda items is perhaps even more difficult than conclusively showing its influence on public opinion. However, on several metrics the data strongly suggests that Bush failed to achieve almost all of his non-Iraq legislative priorities in his final two years in office. One commonly used measure of legislative productivity is Mayhew's class of "sweep one" significant enactments. In raw numerical terms, the emergence of sustained, significant congressional challenges to the war in

18. See Brody and Shapiro 1989, Brody 1991, Lian and Oneal 1993, Berinsky 2007.

Iraq did not dampen legislative productivity. The 110th Congress enacted thirteen pieces of landmark legislation, versus fourteen in the 109th Congress, although this total was boosted significantly by three bills responding to the financial crisis. However, a simple comparison of numbers obscures precisely whose agenda items comprised these lists of significant enactments. Landmark initiatives passed in the 109th Congress included a major reform of bankruptcy laws that favored lenders over consumers; the Class Action Fairness Act, which made it more difficult for individuals to bring such suits against businesses; billions of dollars of tax breaks to increase energy production; the Central American Free Trade Agreement; and the opening of more than eight million acres of the Gulf of Mexico to offshore drilling. These and most other items on the list clearly reflected Bush's legislative priorities. By contrast, many of the landmark initiatives enacted by the 110th Congress clearly reflected the priorities of the Democratic majority: an increase in the minimum wage; ethics and lobbying reform; an overhaul of the student loan program that cut subsidies to private lenders and increased federal aid to low-income families; an energy bill raising automobile gas mileage standards and encouraging conservation; and a bill requiring insurance companies to provide equal coverage for mental and physical illnesses.[19]

All second-term presidents at some point grapple with the reality of becoming a lame duck, and all presidents in periods of divided government must grapple with legislatures possessing their own programmatic agendas. By almost any standard, however, Bush succeeded in achieving even fewer of his legislative priorities in the final two years of his presidency than his immediate predecessors. The reasons for this are undoubtedly multifaceted. However, an important piece of the puzzle may well be that Bush, who in 2001 had been the most popular president in the history of the Gallup poll, was forced to expend every remaining bit of political energy in waging a rearguard action against Congress to preserve his policies in Iraq. The animus that his intransigence in Iraq had generated among the American people and many in Congress, even among some in his own party, left him stripped of the political capital needed to advance the remainder of his policy agenda.

19. One major enactment in the 110th Congress that was firmly on Bush's agenda was the significant expansion of the federal government's surveillance powers in the war on terror.

The Limits of Congressional Influence

If, as the preceding sketches suggest, congressional opposition to the Iraq War did raise the political costs of staying the course in the Middle East, why did it not precipitate a change in policy? Despite the considerable political costs it entailed, the Bush administration persevered in Iraq and refused to give any ground to its critics in Congress or in the public at large. In an interview on the fifth anniversary of the invasion, ABC News reporter Martha Raddatz asked Vice President Dick Cheney how he could square the administration's claims of major progress in Iraq with the judgment of more than 60 percent of Americans that the war had not been worth the cost. Succinctly capturing the administration's attitude toward all doubters throughout the war, Cheney's reply lasted but one word: "So?"[20] Why did the president prove so recalcitrant?

One explanation emphasizes the Bush administration's almost unique position in recent history on the eve of the 2008 election: neither the president nor the vice president stood at the top of the Republican ticket in November. The only other second-term president in the post-1945 era to not have his vice president running to succeed him, Harry Truman, himself was eligible to stand for re-election in 1952. As a result, every post–World War II president except Bush has faced the prospect of electoral punishment for his military policies if they proved politically costly. First-term presidents faced these costs themselves, while second-term presidents faced them in the persons of their vice presidents. Writing in *Federalist* no. 72 more than two centuries ago, Alexander Hamilton warned that removing the prospect of re-election would only lead to the "diminution of the inducements to good behavior." In the context of the Iraq War, because Bush could not stand for re-election, the electoral check on presidential policies, which the political costs generated by Congress usually can greatly strengthen, was absent from the equation.

Moreover, Bush had no close ties to any of his potential successors. Ironically, the only Republican front-runner to support the administration's Iraq policies consistently, Arizona Senator John McCain, was perhaps the candidate with whom Bush historically held the most poisoned political relationship dating back to the 2000 South Carolina primary campaign. As a result, Congress found itself in a considerably weaker

20. "Dick Cheney Calls Iraq War a 'Major Success.'" ABC News, March 19, 2008, http://abcnews.go.com/GMA/Vote2008/story?id=4479462. Accessed March 26, 2008.

position to influence Bush's conduct of the war in Iraq after 2004, pre-cisely because the political costs their opposition could generate had meager potential electoral ramifications for the president and his clos-est allies.

While this unique confluence of electoral factors may go a long way toward explaining the administration's indifference to political pressures in Iraq, more generally the Iraqi case reminds us of the limits on con-gressional influence over military affairs when exerting pressure on the White House exclusively through indirect means. Chapter 2 concluded with an important caveat: The theory does *not* predict that congres-sional opposition will *always* cause presidents to curtail their military plans. In some cases, the president may judge that the benefits of staying the course or the costs of withdrawing are so great that they exceed the heightened political and/or military costs of doing so. If the president is willing to pay these costs to pursue his military policy goals no matter how high they may grow, then there is little Congress can do to change his course short of a legislative remedy.

*   *   *

American history offers few examples of Congress using its legislative power to bring to heel a wayward commander in chief. Only in the rarest of cases will Congress be able to marshal the supermajorities required to pass legislation compelling the president to abandon his preferred policy preferences. However, to focus only on the lack of concrete legislation terminating an ongoing war or blocking the use of force altogether is to miss the more indirect, yet still powerful means of influence through which members of Congress have routinely shaped the course of Ameri-can military affairs. Even when Congress fails to write its military pref-erences into law, its members rarely stand on the sidelines of the policy process. Rather, members of Congress have historically engaged in a va-riety of actions from formal initiatives, such as introducing legislation or holding hearings that challenge the president's conduct of military ac-tion, to informal efforts to shape the nature of the policy debate in the public sphere. These actions can raise significantly the political and stra-tegic costs to the president of waging large-scale, long-duration military actions to pursue their policy goals. In some cases, presidents may judge that the benefits of responding militarily to a foreign crisis or continu-ing an ongoing military engagement may outweigh even the heightened costs that congressional opposition generates. In these instances, enacting legislation to compel the president to change course may be the only remedy available to congressional opponents.

In many other cases, however, congressional opposition has had tangible effects on policy outcomes. Again and again, the statistical and qualitative analyses have showed presidents modifying their policies, moderating the scale and duration of their military ventures, and sometimes foregoing a military response altogether, when faced with real or anticipated opposition on Capitol Hill. When exerted indirectly, congressional influence is less immediately visible and dramatic than it is in the rare occasions when Congress has enacted legislation to mandate a change in military policy. Yet through indirect mechanisms, Congress has often encouraged presidents to pursue significantly different military policies than they would have adopted in the absence of congressional opposition.

References

Aberbach, Joel. 1990. *Keeping a Watchful Eye: The Politics of Congressional Oversight*. Washington: Brookings Institution Press.

———. 2002. "What's Happened to the Watchful Eye?" *Congress and the Presidency* 29:3–23.

Achen, Christopher. 1975. "Mass Political Attitudes and the Survey Response." *American Political Science Review* 69:1218–31.

———. 1986. *The Statistical Analysis of Quasi-Experiments*. Berkeley: University of California Press.

Ackerman, Bruce. 2005. *The Failure of the Founding Fathers: Jefferson, Marshall, and the Rise of Presidential Democracy*. Cambridge, MA: Belknap Press.

Adler, David, and Larry George, eds. 1996. *The Constitution and the Conduct of American Foreign Policy*. Lawrence: University of Kansas Press.

Adler, E. Scott. 2003. "Congressional District Data File," University of Colorado, Boulder.

Aldrich, John. 1995. *Why Parties? The Origin and Transformation of Political Parties in America*. Chicago: University of Chicago Press.

Aldrich, John, and David Rohde. 1998. "Theories of Party in the Legislature and the Transition to Republican Rules in the House." *Political Science Quarterly* 112:112–35.

———. 2001. "The Logic of Conditional Party Government: Revisiting the Electoral Connection." In *Congress Reconsidered*, ed. Lawrence Dodd and Bruce Oppenheimer. Washington: Congressional Quarterly Press.

Aldrich, John, John Sullivan, and Eugene Borgida. 1989. "Foreign Affairs and Issue Voting: Do Presidential Candidates 'Waltz' Before a Blind Audience." *American Political Science Review* 83:123–41.

Alexseev, M., and W. Lance Bennett. 1995. "For Whom the Gates Open: Journalistic Norms and Political Source Patterns in the United States, Great Britain, and Russia." *Political Communication* 12:395–412.

Allison, Graham. 1977. "Making War: The President and Congress." In *The Presidency Reappraised*, ed. Thomas Cronin and Rexford Tugwell. New York: Praeger.

Allison, Paul. 1982. "Discrete-time Methods for the Analysis of Event-Histories." In *Sociological Methodology*, ed. S. Leinhardt. Beverly Hills: Sage.

Almond, Gabriel. 1960. *The American People and Foreign Policy*. New York: Praeger.

Altfeld, Michael, and Bruce Bueno de Mesquita. 1979. "Choosing Sides in War." *International Studies Quarterly* 23:87–112.

Althaus, Scott. 2003. "When Norms Collide, Follow the Lead: New Evidence for Press Independence." *Political Communication* 20:381–414.

Althaus, Scott, Jill Edy, Robert Entman, and Patricia Phalen. 1996. "Revising the Indexing Hypothesis: Officials, Media, and the Libya Crisis." *Political Communication* 13:407–21.

Alvarez, R. Michael, and John Brehm. 1995. "American Ambivalence towards Abortion Policy: Development of a Heteroscedastic Probit Model of Competing Values." *American Journal of Political Science* 39:1055–82.

Alvarez, R. Michael, and John Brehm. 2002. *Hard Choices, Easy Answers: Values, Information, and American Public Opinion*. Princeton, NJ: Princeton University Press.

Arnold, R. Douglas. 1990. *The Logic of Congressional Action*. New Haven: Yale University Press.

Asch, Solomon. 1987 (1952). *Social Psychology*. Oxford: Oxford University Press.

Auerswald, David. 2000. *Disarmed Democracies: Domestic Institutions and the Use of Force*. Ann Arbor: University of Michigan Press.

Auerswald, David, and Peter Cowhey. 1997. "Ballotbox Diplomacy: The War Powers Resolution and the Use of Force." *International Studies Quarterly* 41:505–28.

Bachrach, Peter, and Morton Baratz. 1962. "The Two Faces of Power." *American Political Science Review* 56:947–52.

Barrett, Andrew. 2004. "Gone Public: The Impact of Going Public on Presidential Legislative Success." *American Politics Research* 32:338–70.

Bartels, Larry. 1991. "Constituency Opinion and Congressional Policy Making: The Reagan Defense Buildup." *American Political Science Review* 85:457–74.

Baum, Matthew. 2002. "The Constituent Foundations of the Rally-Round-the-Flag Phenomenon." *International Studies Quarterly* 46:263–98.

———. 2004. "How Public Opinion Constrains the Use of Force: The Case of Operation Restore Hope." *Presidential Studies Quarterly* 34: 187–226.

Baum, Matthew and Timothy Groeling. 2005. "What Gets Covered? How Media Coverage of Elite Debate Drives the Rally-'Round-the-Flag Phenomenon, 1979–1998." In *In the Public Domain: Presidents and the Challenges of Public Leadership*, ed. Lori Cox Han and Diane Heith. Albany, NY: State University of New York Press.

———. 2009. "Shot by the Messenger: Partisan Cues and Public Opinion Regarding National Security and War." *Political Behavior* 31:157–86.

Bean, Louis. 1948. *How to Predict Elections*. New York: Knopf.

Bennett, D. Scott. 1999. "Parametric Models, Duration Dependence, and Time-Varying Data Revisited." *American Journal of Political Science* 43:356–270.

Bennett, D. Scott, and Matthew Rupert. 2003. "Comparing Measures of Political Similarity: An Empirical Comparison of S versus Tau(b) in the Study of International Conflict." *Journal of Conflict Resolution* 47:367–93.

Bennett, D. Scott, and Allan Stam. 1996. "The Duration of Interstate Wars, 1816–1985." *American Political Science Review* 90:239–57.

———. 2000. "*EUGene*: A Conceptual Manual." *International Interactions* 26:179–204.

Bennett, W. Lance. 1990. "Toward a Theory of Press-State Relations in the United States." *Journal of Communication* 40:103–25.

———. 1996. "An Introduction to Journalism Norms and Representation of Politics." *Political Communication* 13:373–84.

Berinsky, Adam. 2007. "Assuming the Costs of War: Events, Elites, and American Public Support for Military Conflict." *Journal of Politics* 69:975–97.

———. 2009. *In Time of War: Understanding American Public Opinion from World War II to Iraq*. Chicago: University of Chicago Press.

Bernstein, Robert, and William Anthony. 1974. "The ABM Issue in the Senate, 1968–1970: The Importance of Ideology." *American Political Science Review* 68:1198–1206.

Bianco, William. 1994. *Trust: Representatives and Constituents*. Ann Arbor: University of Michigan Press.

———. 2005. "Last Post for 'The Greatest Generation': The Policy Implications of the Decline of Military Experience in Congress." *Legislative Studies Quarterly* 30:85–102.

Binder, Sarah. 1997. *Minority Rights, Majority Rule: Partisanship and the Development of Congress*. New York: Cambridge University Press.

Blechman, Barry. 1990. *The Politics of National Security*. New York: Oxford University Press.

Blechman, Barry, and Stephen Kaplan. 1978. *Force without War: U.S. Armed Forces as a Political Instrument*. Washington: Brookings Institution Press.

Boehmke, Frederick, Daniel Morey, and Megan Shannon. 2006. "Selection Bias and Continuous-Time Duration Models: Consequences and a Proposed Solution." *American Journal of Political Science* 50:192–207.

Boettcher, William A. III, and Michael D. Cobb. 2006. "Echoes of Vietnam? Casualty Framing and Public Perceptions of Success and Failure in Iraq." *Journal of Conflict Resolution* 50:831–54.

Box-Steffensmeier, Janet, and Bradford Jones. 1997. "Time is of the Essence: Event History Models in Political Science." *American Journal of Political Science* 41:1414–61.

Brace, Paul, and Barbara Hinckley. 1992. *Follow the Leader.* New York: Basic Books.

Brady, David, and Phillip Althoff. 1974. "Party Voting in the U.S. House of Representatives, 1890–1910: Elements of a Responsible Party System." *Journal of Politics* 36:753–75.

Brady, David, and Craig Volden. 1998. *Revolving Gridlock: Politics and Policy from Carter to Clinton.* Boulder, CO: Westview Press.

Brands, H. W. 1987. "Decisions on American Armed Intervention: Lebanon, Dominican Republic, and Grenada." *Political Science Quarterly* 102:607–24.

Bremer, Stuart. 1992. "Conditions Affecting the Likelihood of Inter-state War, 1816–1965." *Journal of Conflict Resolution* 36:309–41.

Brody, Richard. 1991. *Assessing the President: The Media, Elite Opinion, and Public Support.* Stanford, CA: Stanford University Press.

———. 1994. "Crisis, War and Public Opinion." In *Taken By Storm: Media, Public Opinion, and U.S. Foreign Policy in the Gulf War*, ed. W. Lance Bennett and David L. Paletz. Chicago: University of Chicago Press.

Brody, Richard, and Catherine Shapiro. 1989. "A Reconstruction of the Rally Phenomenon in Public Opinion." In *Political Behavior Annual*, ed. Samuel Long. Boulder, CO: Westview Press.

Brown, Alan. 2003. "U.S. Armed Forces Abroad: Selected Congressional Roll Calls Since 1982." Congressional Research Service. Code RL 31693.

Bueno de Mesquita, Bruce. 1975. "Measuring Systemic Polarity." *Journal of Conflict Resolution* 19:187–215.

———. 1978. "Systemic Polarization and the Occurrence and Duration of War." *Journal of Conflict Resolution* 22:241–67.

———. 1981. "Risk, Power Distributions and the Likelihood of War." *International Studies Quarterly* 25:541–68.

Bueno de Mesquita, Bruce, and David Lalman. 1992. *War and Reason: Domestic and International Imperatives.* New Haven: Yale University Press.

Bueno de Mesquita, Bruce, and Randolph Siverson. 1995. "War and the Survival of Political Leaders: A Comparative Study of Regime Types and Political Accountability." *American Political Science Review* 89:841–55.

Bueno de Mesquita, James Morrow, Randolph Siverson and Alastair Smith. 1999. "An Institutional Explanation of the Democratic Peace." 93: 791–807.

Bueno de Mesquita, James Morrow, Randolph Siverson and Alastair Smith. 2003. *The Logic of Political Survival.* Cambridge: Cambridge University Press.

Bueno de Mesquita, James Morrow, and Ethan Zorick. 1997. "Capabilities, Perception, and Escalation." *American Political Science Review*: 91:15–27.

Burk, James. 1999. "Public Support for Peacekeeping in Lebanon and Somalia: Assessing the Casualties Hypothesis." *Political Science Quarterly* 114: 53–78.

Burnham, Walter Dean. 1970. *Critical Elections and the Mainsprings of American Politics*. New York: Norton.

Buzzanco, Robert. 1999. *Vietnam and the Transformation of American Life*. Malden, MA: Blackwell Publishers.

Caldwell, Dan. 1991. *The Dynamics of Domestic Politics and Arms Control*. Columbia: University of South Carolina Press.

Cameron, Charles. 2000. *Veto Bargaining: Presidents and the Politics of Negative Power*. Cambridge: Cambridge University Press.

Campbell, Andrea, Gary Cox, and Mathew McCubbins. 2002. "Agenda Power in the U.S. Senate, 1877–1986." In *Party, Process and Political Change in Congress*, ed. David W. Brady and Mathew D. McCubbins. Stanford, CA: Stanford University Press.

Campbell, James. 1986. "Presidential Coattails and Midterm Losses in State Legislative Elections." *American Political Science Review* 80:45–63.

———. 1991. "The Presidential Surge and its Midterm Decline in Congressional Elections, 1868–1988." *Journal of Politics* 53:477–87.

———. 2000. *The American Campaign: U.S. Presidential Campaigns and the National Vote*. College Station: Texas A&M University Press.

Campbell, James, and Joe Sumners. 1990. "Presidential Coattails in Senate Elections." *American Political Science Review* 84:513–24.

Canes-Wrone, Brandice. 2001. "The President's Legislative Influence from Public Appeals." *American Journal of Political Science* 45:313–19.

———. 2005. *Who Leads Whom? Presidents, Policy, and the Public*. Chicago: University of Chicago Press.

Canes-Wrone, Brandice, Michael Herron, and Kenneth Shotts. 2001. "Leadership and Pandering: A Theory of Executive Policymaking." *American Journal of Political Science* 45:532–50.

Cannon, Lou. 2000. *President Reagan: The Role of a Lifetime*. New York: Public Affairs.

Carmines, Edward, and James Stimson. 1989. *Issue Evolution: Race and the Transformation of American Politics*. Princeton, NJ: Princeton University Press.

Carpenter, Daniel. 2005. *The Forging of Bureaucratic Autonomy: Reputations, Networks and Policy Innovation in Executive Agencies, 1862–1928*. Princeton, NJ: Princeton University Press.

Carson, Jamie, Jeffrey Jenkins, David Rohde, and Mark Souva. 2001. "The Impact of National Tides on District-Level Effects on Electoral Outcomes: The

U.S. Congressional Elections of 1862–1863." *American Political Science Review* 45:887–98.

Carter, Ralph, and James Scott. 2009. *Choosing to Lead: Understanding Congressional Foreign Policy Entrepreneurs.* Durham, NC: Duke University Press.

Center for Naval Analyses. 1991. "The Use of Naval Forces in the Postwar Era: U.S. Navy and U.S. Marine Corps Crisis Response Activity, 1946–1990." Alexandria, VA: Center for Naval Analyses.

Clark, David. 2000. "Agreeing to Disagree: Domestic Institutional Congruence and U.S. Dispute Behavior." *Political Research Quarterly* 53:375–401.

Clinton, Bill. 2004. *My Life.* New York: Alfred A. Knopf.

Cooper, Phillip. 2002. *By Order of the President: The Use and Abuse of Executive Direct Action.* Lawrence: University of Kansas Press.

Corwin, Edward. 1940. *The President: Office and Power.* New York: New York University Press.

Corwin, Edward. 1970 (1917). *The President's Control of Foreign Relations.* Princeton, NJ: Princeton University Press.

Cotton, Timothy. 1986. "War and American Democracy: Electoral Costs of the Last Five Wars." *Journal of Conflict Resolution* 30:616–35.

Cowhey, Peter. 1993. "Domestic Institutions and the Credibility of International Commitments: Japan and the United States." *International Organization* 47:299–326.

Cox, Gary, and Jonathan Katz. 2002. *Elbridge Gerry's Salamander: The Electoral Consequences of the Reapportionment Revolution.* Cambridge: Cambridge University Press.

Cox, Gary, and Matthew McCubbins. 1993. *Legislative Leviathan: Party Government in the House.* Berkeley: University of California Press.

Cox, Gary, and Matthew McCubbins. 2005. *Setting the Agenda: Responsible Party Government in the U.S. House of Representatives.* New York: Cambridge University Press.

Crabb, Cecil. 1957. *Bipartisan Foreign Policy: Myth or Reality?* Evanston, IL: Row, Peterson.

Crabb, Cecil, and Pat Holt. 1988. *Invitation to Struggle: Congress, the President, and Foreign Policy.* Washington: Congressional Quarterly Press.

Den Hartog, Chris, and Nathan Monroe. 2008. "The Value of Majority Status: The Effect of Jeffords's Switch on Asset Prices of Republican and Democratic Firms." *Legislative Studies Quarterly* 33:63–84.

DeRouen, Karl. 1995. "The Indirect Link: Politics, the Economy, and the Use of Force." *Journal of Conflict Resolution* 39:671–95.

DeRouen, Karl, and Uk Heo. 2004. "Reward, Punishment or Inducement? US Economic and Military Aid, 1946–1996." *Defence and Peace Economics* 15:453–70.

Destler, I. M., Leslie Gelb, and Anthony Lake. 1984. *Our Own Worst Enemy.* New York: Simon and Shuster.

Druckman, James. 2001. "On the Limits of Framing Effects: Who Can Frame?" *Journal of Politics* 63:1041–66.

Dutton, Donald. 1973. "The Maverick Effect: Increased Communicator Credibility as a Result of Abandoning a Career." *Canadian Journal of Behavioral Science* 5:145–51.

Eagly, Alice, Wendy Wood, and Shelly Chaiken. 1978. "Causal Inferences about Communicators and their Effects on Opinion Change." *Journal of Personality and Social Psychology* 36:424–35.

Edwards, George. *On Deaf Ears: The Limits of the Bully Pulpit.* New Haven: Yale University Press.

Edwards, George, and Dan Wood. 1999. "Who Influences Whom? The President, Congress, and the Media." *American Political Science Review* 93: 327–44.

Eichenberg, Richard. 2005. "Victory Has Many Friends: U.S. Public Opinion and the Use of Military Force, 1981–2005." *International Security* 30: 140–77.

Eichenberg, Richard, Richard Stoll, and Matthew Lebo. 2006. "War President: The Approval Ratings of George W. Bush." *Journal of Conflict Resolution* 50:783–808.

Ely, John, ed. 1993. *War and Responsibility: Constitutional Lessons of Vietnam and Its Aftermath.* Princeton, NJ: Princeton University Press.

Entman, Robert. 2004. *Projections of Power: Framing News, Public Opinion, and U.S. Foreign Policy.* Chicago: University of Chicago Press.

Entman, Robert, and Benjamin Page. 1994. "The Iraq War Debate and the Limits to Media Independence." In *Taken By Storm: Media, Public Opinion, and U.S. Foreign Policy in the Gulf War,* ed. W. Lance Bennett and David L. Paletz. Chicago: University of Chicago Press, 82–101.

Epstein, David, and Sharyn O'Halloran. 1999. *Delegating Powers: A Transaction Cost Politics Approach to Policy Making under Separate Powers.* New York: Cambridge University Press.

Erikson, Robert. 1978. "Constituency Opinion and Congressional Behavior: A Reexamination of the Miller-Stokes Representation Data." *American Journal of Political Science* 22:511–35.

Farrand, Max, ed. 1966. *The Records of the Federal Convention of 1787.* 4 volumes. New Haven: Yale University Press.

Fearon, James. 1994. "Domestic Political Audiences and the Escalation of International Disputes." *American Political Science Review* 88:577–92.

———. 2004. "Why Do Some Civil Wars Last So Much Longer than Others?" *Journal of Peace Research* 41: 275–301.

———. 1997. "Signaling Foreign Policy Interests: Tying Hands Versus Sinking Costs." *Journal of Conflict Resolution* 41:68–90.

Feaver, Peter, and Christopher Gelpi. 2004. *Choosing Your Battles: American Civil-Military Relations and the Use of Force.* Princeton, NJ: Princeton University Press.

Fenno, Richard. 1973. *Congressmen in Committees.* Boston: Little, Brown.

———. 1975. "If, as Ralph Nader Says, Congress is 'The Broken Branch,' How Come We Love Our Congressmen So Much?" In *Congress in Change: Evolution and Reform*, ed. Norman Ornstein. New York: Praeger.

Ferejohn, John. 1986. "Logrolling in an Institutional Context: A Case Study of Food Stamp Legislation." In *Congress and Policy Change*, ed. Gerald Wright, Leroy Rieselbach, and Lawrence Dodd. New York: Agathon Press.

Fisher, Louis. 1995. *Presidential War Power.* Lawrence: University of Kansas Press.

———. 2000. *Congressional Abdication on War and Spending.* College Station: Texas A&M University Press.

Fleisher, Richard. 1985. "Economic Benefit, Ideology, and Senate Voting on the B-1 Bomber." *American Politics Quarterly* 13:200–211.

Flemming, Gregory. 1995. "Presidential Coattails in Open-Seat Elections." *Legislative Studies Quarterly* 20:197–211.

Foglesong, David. 1995. *America's Secret War against Bolshevism: U.S. Intervention in the Russian Civil War, 1917–1920.* Chapel Hill: University of North Carolina Press.

Fordham, Benjamin. 1998a. "The Politics of Threat Perception and the Use of Force: A Political Economy Model of U.S. Uses of Force, 1949–1994." *International Studies Quarterly* 42:567–90.

———. 1998b. "Partisanship, Macroeconomic Policy, and U.S. Uses of Force 1949–1994." *Journal of Conflict Resolution* 42:418–39.

———. 2002. "Another Look at 'Parties, Voters and the Use of Force Abroad.'" *Journal of Conflict Resolution* 46:572–96.

———. 2005. "Strategic Conflict Avoidance and the Diversionary Use of Force." *Journal of Conflict Resolution* 67:132–53.

Fordham, Benjamin, and Christopher Sarver. 2001. "Militarized Interstate Disputes and United States Uses of Force." *International Studies Quarterly* 45:455–66.

Fowler, Linda, and Seth Hill. 2006. "Guarding the Guardians: U.S. Senate Oversight of Foreign and Defense Policy 1947–2004." Paper presented at the annual meeting of the American Political Science Association, Philadelphia.

Foyle, Douglas. 1999. *Counting the Public In: Presidents, Public Opinion, and Foreign Policy.* New York: Columbia University Press.

Franck, Thomas, ed. 1981. *The Tethered Presidency: Congressional Restraints on Executive Power.* New York: New York University Press.

Friedberg, Aaron. 1988. *The Weary Titan: Britain and the Experience of Relative Decline 1895–1905.* Princeton, NJ: Princeton University Press.

Gailmard, Sean, and Jeffery Jenkins. 2007. "Negative Agenda Control in the Senate and House of Representatives: Fingerprints of Majority Power." *Journal of Politics* 69:689–700.

Garnham, David. 1976. "Dyadic International War, 1816–1965: The Role of Power Parity and Geographical Proximity." *Western Political Quarterly* 29:231–42.

Gartner, Scott, and Gary Segura. 1998. "War, Casualties, and Public Opinion." *Journal of Conflict Resolution* 42:278–320.

——. 2008. "All Politics are Still Local: The Iraq War and the 2006 Midterm Elections." *PS: Political Science and Politics* 41: 95–100.

Gartner, Scott, Gary Segura, and Bethany Barratt. 2004. "War Casualties, Policy Positions, and the Fate of Legislators." *Political Research Quarterly* 53:467–77.

Gartner, Scott Sigmund, Gary M. Segura, and Michael Wilkening. 1997. "All Politics Are Local: Local Losses and Individual Attitudes toward the Vietnam War." *The Journal of Conflict Resolution* 41:669–94.

Gartzke, Eric. 1998. "Kant We All Just Get Along? Opportunity, Willingness, and the Origins of the Democratic Peace." *American Journal of Political Science* 42:1–27.

Gartzke, Erik, and Dong-Joon Jo. 2002. *United Nations General Assembly Voting, 1946–1996.* Version 3.0. http://www.columbia.edu/~eg589/datasets.

Gaubatz, Kurt. 1991. "Election Cycles and War." *Journal of Conflict Resolution* 35:212–44.

Gelb, Leslie. 1972. "The Essential Domino: American Politics and Vietnam." *Foreign Affairs* 50:459–75.

Gelpi, Christopher, and Peter Feaver. 2002. "Speak Softly and Carry a Big Stick? Veterans in the Political Elite and the American Use of Force." *American Political Science Review* 96:779–93.

Gelpi, Christopher, Peter Feaver, and Jason Reifler. 2005/06. "Casualty Sensitivity and the War in Iraq." *International Security* 30:7–46.

——. 2007. "Iraq the Vote: Retrospective and Prospective Foreign Policy Judgments on Candidate Choice and Casualty Tolerance." *Political Behavior* 29:151–74.

——. 2009. *Paying the Human Costs of War: American Public Opinion and Casualties in Military Conflicts.* Princeton, NJ: Princeton University Press.

Gerring, John. 1998. *Party Ideologies in America, 1828–1996.* New York: Cambridge University Press.

Ghosn, Faten, Glenn Palmer, and Stuart Bremer. 2004. "The MID3 Data Set, 1993–2001: Procedures, Coding Rules, and Description." *Conflict Management and Peace Science* 21:133–54.

Gibbons, William. 1986. *The U.S. Government and the Vietnam War: Executive and Legislative Roles and Relationships.* Princeton, NJ: Princeton University Press.

Ginsberg, Benjamin, and Martin Shefter. 1995. "Ethics Probes as Political Weapons." *Journal of Law and Politics* 11:497–511.

Ginsberg, Benjamin, and Martin Shefter. 2003. *Politics by Other Means: Politics, Prosecutors, and the Press from Watergate to Whitewater.* New York: W. W. Norton.

Gleditsch, Nils Petter, and J. David Singer. 1975. "Distance and International War, 1816–1965." In *Proceedings of the International Peace Research Association's Fifth General Congress*, ed. M. R. Khan. Oslo: International Peace Research Association.

Glennon, Michael. 1990. *Constitutional Diplomacy.* Princeton, NJ: Princeton University Press.

Gowa, Joanne. 1998. "Politics at the Water's Edge: Parties, Voters and the Use of Force Abroad." *International Organization* 52: 307–24.

———. 1999. *Ballots and Bullets.* Princeton, NJ: Princeton University Press.

Gowa, Joanne, and Edward Mansfield. 2004. "Alliances, Imperfect Markets and Major-Power Trade." *International Organization* 58:775–805.

Graber, Doris. 1989. *Mass Media and American Politics.* Washington: Congressional Quarterly Press.

Green, Donald, Alan Gerber, and Suzanna De Boef. 1999. "Tracking Opinion over Time: A Method for Reducing Sample Error." *Public Opinion Quarterly* 63:178–92.

Greene, William. 2003. *Econometric Analysis.* Upper Saddle River, NJ: Prentice Hall.

Grieco, Joseph, Christopher Gelpi, Jason Reifler, and Peter Feaver. n.d. "Let's Get a Second Opinion: International Institutions and American Public Support for War." Typescript, Duke University and Georgia State University.

Grimmett, Richard. 2001. "Congressional Uses of Funding Cutoffs since 1970 Involving U.S. Military Forces and Overseas Deployments." Congressional Research Service. Code RS20775.

———. 2004. "The War Powers Resolution: Thirty Years Later." Congressional Research Service. Code RL32267.

———. 2007. "Congressional Use of Funding Cutoffs since 1970 Involving U.S. Military Forces and Overseas Deployments." Congressional Research Service. Code RS20775.

Groeling, Timothy, and Matthew Baum. 2008. "Crossing the Water's Edge: Elite Rhetoric, Media Coverage, and the Rally-Round-the-Flag Phenomenon." *Journal of Politics* 70:1065–1985.

Grofman, Bernard, and Thomas Brunell. 2005. "The Art of the Dummymander: The Impact of Recent Redistrictings on the Partisan Makeup of Southern House Seats." In *Redistricting in the New Millennium*, ed. Peter Galderisi. Lanham, MD: Lexington Books.

Gronke, Paul, and John Brehm. 2002. "History, Heterogeneity, and Presidential Approval: A Modified ARCH Approach." *Electoral Studies* 21:425–52.

Grose, Christian, and Bruce Oppenheimer. 2007. "The Iraq War, Partisanship, and Candidate Attributes: Variation in Partisan Swing in the 2006 Election." *Legislative Studies Quarterly* 32:531–57.

Hallin, Daniel. 1986. *The 'Uncensored War': The Media and Vietnam.* New York: Oxford University Press.

Hamilton, James. 1994. *Time Series Analysis.* Princeton, NJ: Princeton University Press.

Hartley, Thomas, and Bruce Russett. 1992. "Public Opinion and the Common Defense: Who Governs Military Spending in the United States?" *American Political Science Review* 86:361–87.

Heckman, James. 1978. "Dummy Endogenous Variables in a Simultaneous Equation System." *Econometrica* 46:931–59.

———. 1979. "Sample Selection Bias as a Specification Error." *Econometrica* 47:153–61.

Herring, George. 1987. "The Executive, Congress, and the Vietnam War, 1965–1975." In *Congress and United States Foreign Policy*, ed. Michael Barnhart. Albany: State University of New York Press.

Hersman, Rebecca. 2000. *Friends and Foes: How Congress and the President Really Make Foreign Policy.* Washington: Brookings Institution Press.

Hess, Stephen, and Michael Nelson. 1985. "Foreign Policy: Dominance and Decisiveness in Presidential Elections." In *The Elections of 1984*, ed. Michael Nelson. Washington: Congressional Quarterly Press.

Hetherington, Marc. 2001. "Resurgent Mass Partisanship: the Role of Elite Polarization." *American Political Science Review* 95:619–31.

Hibbs, Douglas. 2000. "Bread and Peace Voting in U.S. Presidential Elections." *Public Choice* 104:149–80.

Hickey, Donald. 2004. "The War of 1812." In *The American Congress: The Building of Democracy*, ed. Julian Zelizer. Boston: Houghton Mifflin.

Hinckley, Barbara. 1994. *Less Than Meets the Eye: Foreign Policy Making and the Myth of the Assertive Congress.* Chicago: University of Chicago Press.

Hirsch, Sam. 2003. "The United States House of Unrepresentatives: What Went Wrong in the Latest Round of Congressional Redistricting." *Election Law Journal* 2:179–216.

Hofstadter, Richard. 1955. *The Age of Reform: From Bryan to F.D.R.* New York: Vintage Books.

Holsti, Ole. 1992. "Public Opinion and Foreign Policy: Challenges to the Almond-Lippman Consensus." *International Studies Quarterly* 36:439–66.

———. 1998. "A Widening Gap between the U.S. Military and Civilian Society? Some Evidence, 1979–1996." *International Security* 23:5–42.

———. 2001. "Of Chasms and Convergence." In *Soldiers and Civilians*, ed. Peter Feaver and Richard Kohn. Cambridge, MA: MIT Press.

———. 2004. *Public Opinion and American Foreign Policy*. Ann Arbor: University of Michigan Press.

Holsti, Ole, and James Rosenau. 1984. *American Leadership in World Affairs: Vietnam and the Breakdown of Consensus*. London: Allen and Unwin.

———. 1988. "The Domestic and Foreign Policy Beliefs of American Leaders." *Journal of Conflict Resolution* 32:249–94.

———. 1990. "The Structure of Foreign Policy Attitudes among American Leaders." *Journal of Politics* 52:94–125.

———. 1996. "Liberals, Populists, Libertarians, and Conservatives: The Link between Domestic and International Affairs." *International Political Science Review* 17:29–54.

Hoogenboom, Ari. 1961. *Outlawing the Spoils System: A History of the Civil Service Reform Movement, 1865–1883*. Urbana: University of Illinois Press.

Howell, William. 2003. *Power without Persuasion: The Politics of Direct Presidential Action*. Princeton, NJ: Princeton University Press.

Howell, William, and Douglas Kriner. 2006. "Power without Persuasion: Identifying Executive Influence." In *Presidential Leadership: The Vortex of Power*, ed. Bert Rockman and Richard Waterman. New York: Oxford University Press.

———. 2007. "Bending so as Not to Break: What the Bush Presidency Reveals about Unilateral Action." In *The Polarized Presidency of George W. Bush*, ed. George Edwards and Desmond King. Oxford: Oxford University Press.

———. 2009. "Congress, the President, and the Iraq War's Domestic Political Front." In *Congress Reconsidered*, 9th edition, ed. Lawrence Dodd and Bruce Oppenheimer. Washington: Congressional Quarterly Press.

Howell, William and Jon Pevehouse. 2005. "Presidents, Congress, and the Use of Force." *International Organization* 59:209–32.

———. 2007. *While Dangers Gather: Congressional Checks on Presidential War Powers*. Princeton, NJ: Princeton University Press.

Huntington, Samuel. 1957. *The Soldier and the State: The Theory and Politics of Civil Military Relations*. Cambridge, MA: Belknap Press of Harvard University Press.

———. 1961. *The Common Defense: Strategic Programs in National Politics*. New York: Columbia University Press.

Hurwitz, John, and Mark Peffley. 1987. "The Means and Ends of Foreign Policy as Determinants of Presidential Support." *American Journal of Political Science* 2:236–58.

Huth, Paul, D. Scott Bennett, and Christopher Gelpi. 1993. "System Uncertainty, Risk Propensity, and International Conflict Among the Great Powers." *Journal of Conflict Resolution* 36:478–517.

Iyengar, Shanto, and Donald Kinder. 1987. *News that Matters: Television and American Opinion*. Chicago: University of Chicago Press.

Jackson, John, and John Kingdon. 1992. "Ideology, Interest Group Scores, and Legislative Votes." *American Journal of Political Science* 36:805–23.

Jacobs, Lawrence. 2003. "The Presidency and the Press: The Paradox of the White House Communications War." In *The Presidency and the Political System*, ed. Michael Nelson. Washington: Congressional Quarterly Press.

———. 2007. "The Promotional Presidency and the New Institutional Toryism: Public Mobilization, Legislative Dominance, and Squandered Opportunities." In *The Polarized Presidency of George W. Bush*, ed. George Edwards and Desmond King. Oxford: Oxford University Press.

Jacobs, Lawrence, Eric Lawrence, Robert Shapiro, and Steven Smith. 1998. "Congressional Leadership of Public Opinion." *Political Science Quarterly* 113:21–41.

Jacobs, Lawrence, and Benjamin Page. 2005. "Who Influences U.S. Foreign Policy?" *American Political Science Review* 99:107–23.

Jacobs, Lawrence, and Robert Shapiro. 2000. *Politicians Don't Pander: Political Manipulation and the Loss of Democratic Responsiveness*. Chicago: University of Chicago Press.

Jacobson, Gary. 2004. *The Politics of Congressional Elections*. New York: Pearson Longman.

James, Patrick, and John Oneal. 1991. "The Influence of Domestic and International Politics on the President's Use of Force." *Journal of Conflict Resolution* 35:307–32.

Jentleson, Bruce. 1992. "The Pretty-Prudent Public: Post-Post Vietnam American Opinion on the Use of Military Force." *International Studies Quarterly* 36:49–73.

Johnson, Robert David. 1995. *The Peace Progressives and American Foreign Relations*. Cambridge, MA: Harvard University Press.

———. 2006. *Congress and the Cold War*. New York: Cambridge University Press.

Johnston, Harry, and Ted Dagne. 1997. "Congress and the Somalia Crisis." In *Learning from Somalia: The Lessons of Armed Humanitarian Intervention*, ed. Walter Clarke and Jeffrey Herbst. Boulder, CO: Westview Press.

Jones, Daniel, Stuart Bremer, and J. David Singer. 1996. "Militarized Interstate Disputes, 1816–1992: Rationale, Coding Rules, and Empirical Patterns." *Conflict Management and Peace Science* 15:163–213.

Jones, David. 2001. "Party Polarization and Legislative Gridlock." *Political Research Quarterly* 54:125–41.

Jordan, David, and Benjamin Page. 1992. "Shaping Foreign Policy Opinions: The Role of TV News." *Journal of Conflict Resolution* 36:227–41.

Kagay, Michael, and Greg Caldeira. 1975. "I Like the Look of His Face." Presented at the Annual Meeting of the American Political Science Association, San Francisco.

Kant, Immanuel. 1983 (1795). *Perpetual Peace and Other Essays.* tr. Ted Humphrey. Indianapolis: Hackett.

Karol, David, and Edward Miguel. 2007. "The Electoral Cost of War: Iraq Casualties and the 2004 U.S. Presidential Election." *Journal of Politics* 69: 633–48.

Katzmann, Robert. 1990. "War Powers: Toward a New Accomodation." In *A Question of Balance: The President, Congress, and Foreign Policy*, ed. Thomas Mann. Washington: Brookings Institution Press, 35–69.

Katznelson, Ira. 2002. "Flexible Capacity: The Military and Early American Statebuilding." In *Shaped by War and Trade: International Influences on American Political Development*, ed. Ira Katznelson and Martin Shefter. Princeton, NJ: Princeton University Press.

Kennedy, Robert. 1999 (1971). *Thirteen Days: A Memoir of the Cuban Missile Crisis.* New York: W.W. Norton.

Keohane, Robert. 2002. "International Commitments and American Political Institutions in the Nineteenth Century." In *Shaped by War and Trade: International Influences on American Political Development*, ed. Ira Katznelson and Martin Shefter. Princeton, NJ: Princeton University Press.

Kernell, Samuel. 1978. "Explaining Presidential Popularity." *American Political Science Review* 72: 506–22.

———. 1997. *Going Public: New Strategies of Presidential Leadership.* Washington: Congressional Quarterly Press.

Kessell, John. 1988. *Presidential Campaign Politics: Coalition Strategies and Citizen Response.* 3rd edition. Homewood, IL: Dorsey.

Kiewiet, D. Roderick. 1983. *Macroeconomics and Micropolitics.* Chicago: University of Chicago Press.

Kiewiet, D. Roderick, and Matthew McCubbins. 1991. *The Logic of Delegation: Congressional Parties and the Appropriations Process.* Chicago: University of Chicago Press.

Kimball, Jeffrey. 2004. *Nixon's Vietnam War.* Lawrence: University of Kansas Press.

Kinder, Donald, and Lynne Sanders. 1996. *Divided by Color: Racial Politics and Democratic Ideals.* Chicago: University of Chicago Press.

King, Gary, and Langche Zeng. 2001. "Explaining Rare Events in International Relations." *International Organization* 55:693–715.

Kissinger, Henry. 1979. *White House Years.* Boston: Little, Brown.

Klarevas, Louis. 2002. "The 'Essential Domino' of Military Operations: American Public Opinion and the Use of Force." *International Studies Perspectives* 3: 417–37.

Koetzle, William. 1998. "The Impact of Constituency Diversity upon the Competitiveness of U.S. House Elections, 1962–96." *Legislative Studies Quarterly* 23:561–73.

Koeske, Gary, and William Crano. 1968. "The Effect of Congruous and Incongruous Source Statement Combinations upon the Judged Credibility of a Communication." *Journal of Experimental Psychology* 4:384–99.

Koh, Harold. 1990. *The National Security Constitution: Sharing Power after the Iran-Contra Affair.* New Haven: Yale University Press.

Krehbiel, Keith. 1990. "Are Congressional Committees Composed of Preference Outliers?" *American Political Science Review* 32:1151–74.

———. 1991. *Information and Legislative Organization.* Ann Arbor: University of Michigan Press.

———. 1993. "Where's the Party?" *British Journal of Political Science* 23: 235–66.

———. 1996. "Institutional and Partisan Sources of Gridlock: A Theory of Divided and Unified Government." *Journal of Theoretical Politics* 8:7–40.

———. 1998. *Pivotal Politics: A Theory of U.S. Lawmaking.* Chicago: University of Chicago Press.

Kriner, Douglas. 2006. "Examining Variance in Presidential Approval: The Case of FDR in World War II." *Public Opinion Quarterly* 70:23–47.

———. 2009. "Can Enhanced Oversight Repair the 'Broken Branch?'" *Boston University Law Review* 89: 765–93.

Kriner, Douglas, and William Howell. n.d. "Congressional Leadership of War Opinion: Conditional Influence and the Risk of 'Backlash.'" Typescript. Boston University.

Kriner, Douglas, and Liam Schwartz. 2008. "Divided Government and Congressional Investigations." *Legislative Studies Quarterly* 33:295–321.

———. 2009. "The Variance of Presidential Approval." *British Journal of Political Science* 39:609–31.

Kriner, Douglas, and Francis Shen. 2007. "Iraq Casualties and the 2006 Senate Elections." *Legislative Studies Quarterly* 32:4.

———. 2010. *The Casualty Gap: The Causes and Consequences of American Wartime Inequalities.* New York: Oxford University Press.

———. n.d. "All Politics (Even Wars) Are Local: Local Casualties, Congressional Rhetoric and Popular Support for the War in Iraq." Typescript: Boston University.

Krosnick, Jon, and Donald Kinder. 1990. "Altering the Foundations of Support for the President through Priming." *American Political Science Review* 84:497–512.

Kronsnick, Jon, and Laura Brannon. 1993. "The Impact of the Gulf War on the Ingredients of Presidential Evaluations: Multidimensional Effects of Political Involvement." *American Political Science Review* 87: 963–975.

Kryder, Daniel. 2000. *Divided Arsenal: Race and the American State During World War II*. New York: Cambridge University Press.

Kull, Steven, and I. M. Destler. 1999. *Misreading the Public: The Myth of a New Isolationism*. Washington: Brookings Institution Press.

Lake, David. 1992. "Powerful Pacificsts: Democratic States and War." *American Political Science Review*, 86:24–37.

Lalman, David, and David Newman. 1991. "Alliance Formation and National Security." *International Interactions* 16:239–53.

Larson, Eric, and Bogdan Savych. 2005. *American Public Support for U.S. Military Interventions from Mogadishu to Baghdad*. Santa Monica: RAND.

Lee, Jong. 1977. "Rally Around the Flag: Foreign Policy Events and Presidential Popularity." *Presidential Studies Quarterly* 7:252–56.

Lee, Frances. 2008. "Agreeing to Disagree: Agenda Content and Senate Partisanship, 1981–2004." *Legislative Studies Quarterly* 33:199–222.

Leeds, Brett. 2003. "Do Alliances Deter Aggression? The Influence of Military Alliances on the Initiation of Militarized Interstate Disputes." *American Journal of Political Science* 47:427–39.

Levy, Jack. 1989. "The Diversionary War Theory: A Critique." In *Handbook of War Studies*, ed. Manus Midlasky. Boston: Unwin Hyman.

Levy, Jack, and Lily Vakili. 1992. "Diversionary Action of Authoritarian Regimes: Argentina in the Falklands/Malvinas Case." In *The Internationalizaton of Communal Strife*, ed. M. Midlarsky. London: Routledge.

Lewis, David E. 2003. *Presidents and the Politics of Agency Design*. Stanford, CA: Stanford University Press.

Lewis-Beck, Michael, and Tim Rice. 1992. *Forecasting Elections*. Washington: Congressional Quarterly Press.

Lian, Bradley, and John Oneal. 1993. "Presidents, the Use of Military Force, and Public Opinion." *Journal of Conflict Resolution* 37:277–300.

Light, Paul, and Celinda Lake. 1985. "The Election: Candidates, Strategies and Decision." In *The Elections of 1984*, ed. Michael Nelson. Washington: Congressional Quarterly Press.

Lincoln, Abraham. 1953 (1809–65). *The Collected Works of Abraham Lincoln*. ed. R. P. Basler. New Brunswick, NJ: Rutgers University Press.

Lindsay, James. 1990. "Parochialism, Policy and Constituency Constraints: Congressional Voting on Strategic Weapons Systems." *American Journal of Political Science* 34:936–60.

———. 1991. "Testing the Parochial Hypothesis: Congress and the Strategic Defense Initiative." *Journal of Politics* 53:860–76.

———. 1992. "Congress and Foreign Policy: Why the Hill Matters." *Political Science Quarterly* 107:607–28.

———. 1994. *Congress and the Politics of U.S. Foreign Policy*. Baltimore: Johns Hopkins University Press.

Lindsay, James, Lois Sayrs, and Wayne Steger. 1992. "The Determinants of Presidential Foreign Policy Choice." *American Political Quarterly* 20:3–25.

Livingston, Steven, and Todd Eachus. 1995. "Humanitarian Crises and U.S. Foreign Policy." *Political Communication* 12:413–29.

Lippmann, Walter. 1922. *Public Opinion*. New York: MacMillan.

Lodge, Milton, Marco Steenbergen, and Shawn Brau. 1995. "The Responsive Voter: Campaign Information and the Dynamics of Candidate Evaluation." *American Political Science Review* 89:309–26.

Lofgren, Charles. 1972. "War-Making under the Constitution: The Original Understanding." *Yale Law Journal* 81:672–702.

———. 1986. *"Government from Reflection and Choice": Constitutional Essays on War, Foreign Relations, and Federalism*. New York: Oxford University Press.

Lupia, Arthur, and Matthew McCubbins. 1998. *The Democratic Dilemma: Can Citizens Learn What They Need to Know?* Cambridge: Cambridge University Press.

MacKuen, Michael, Robert Erikson, and James Stimson. 1992. "Peasants or Bankers? The American Electorate and the U.S. Economy." *American Political Science Review* 86:597–611.

Mandelbaum, Michael, and William Schneider. 1978. "The New Institutionalisms." *International Security* 2:81–98.

Mann, Thomas. 1990. "Making Foreign Policy: President and Congress." In *A Question of Balance*, ed. Thomas Mann. Washington: Brookings Institution Press.

Manning. William, ed. 1932–39. *Diplomatic Correspondence of the United States: Inter-American Affairs, 1831–1860*. Washington: Carnegie Endowment for International Peace.

Mansfield, Edward, and Jack Snyder. 2002. "Incomplete Democratization and the Outbreak of Military Disputes." *International Studies Quarterly* 46:529–49.

Maoz, Zeev, and Bruce Russett. 1993. "Normative and Structural Causes of Democratic Peace, 1946–1986." *American Political Science Review* 87:624–38.

Margolis, Michael, and Gary Mauser. 1989. *Manipulating Public Opinion: Essays on Public Opinion as a Dependent Variable*. Pacific Grove, CA: Brooks/Cole.

Marra, Robin, Charles Ostrom, and Dennis Simon. 1990. "Foreign Policy and Presidential Popularity: Creating Windows of Opportunity in the Perpetual Election." *Journal of Conflict Resolution* 34:588–623.

Marshall, Monty G., and Keith Jaggers. 2007. *Polity IV Project: Political Regime Characteristics and Transitions, 1800–2007*. Center for International Development and Conflict Management, University of Maryland.

Martin, Lisa. 1993. "Credibility, Costs, and Institutions: Cooperation on Economic Sanctions." *World Politics* 45:406–32.

———. 2000. *Democratic Commitments*. Princeton, NJ: Princeton University Press.

Mayer, Kenneth. 1999. "Executive Orders and Presidential Power." *Journal of Politics* 61:445–66.

———. 2001. *With the Stroke of a Pen: Executive Orders and Presidential Power*. Princeton, NJ: Princeton University Press.

Mayhew, David. 1974. *Congress: The Electoral Connection*. New Haven: Yale University Press.

———. 1991. *Divided We Govern: Party Control, Lawmaking, and Investigations 1946–1990*. New Haven: Yale University Press.

———. 2000. *America's Congress: Actions in the Public Sphere, James Madison through Newt Gingrich*. New Haven: Yale University Press.

———. 2005. "Wars and American Politics." *Perspectives on Politics* 3:473–93.

McCarty, Nolan, Keith Poole, and Howard Rosenthal. 2006. *Polarized America: The Dance of Ideology and Unequal Riches*. Cambridge, MA: MIT Press.

McCormick, James. 1985. "Congressional Voting on the Nuclear Freeze Resolutions." *American Politics Quarterly* 13:122–36.

McCormick, James, and Michael Black. 1983. "Ideology and Voting on the Panama Canal Treaties." *Legislative Studies Quarterly* 8:45–63.

McCormick, James, and Eugene Wittkopf. 1990. "Bipartisanship, Partisanship, and Ideology in Congressional-Executive Foreign Policy Relations, 1947–1988." *Journal of Politics* 52:1077–1100.

———. 1992. "At the Water's Edge: The Effects of Party, Ideology, and Issues on Congressional Foreign Policy Voting, 1947 to 1988." *American Politics Research* 20:26–53.

McFarlane, Robert. 1994. *Special Trust*. New York: Caldwell & Davies.

McNulty, Timothy. 1993. "Television's Impact on Executive Decision-Making and Diplomacy." *Fletcher Forum of World Affairs* 17:67–83.

Meacham, Jon. 2003. *Franklin and Winston: An Intimate Portrait of an Epic Friendship*. New York: Random House.

Meernik, James. 1993. "Presidential Support in Congress: Conflict and Consensus on Foreign and Defense Policy." *Journal of Politics* 55:569–87.

———. 1994. "Presidential Decision-Making and the Political Use of Force." *International Studies Quarterly* 38:121–38.

———. 1995. "Congress, the President and the Commitment of the U.S. Military." *Legislative Studies Quarterly* 20:377–92.

Meernik, James, and Peter Waterman. 1996. "The Myth of the Diversionary Use of Force by American Presidents." *Political Research Quarterly* 49:573–90.

Mermin, Jonathan. 1999. *Debating War and Peace: Media Coverage of U.S. Intervention in the Post-Vietnam Era*. Princeton, NJ: Princeton University Press.

Miller, Arthur, and Warren Miller. 1976. "Ideology in the 1972 Election: Myth or Reality?" *American Political Science Review* 70:832–49.

Miller, Arthur, Martin Wattenberg, and Oksana Malenchuk. 1986. "Schematic Assessments of Presidential Candidates." *American Political Science Review* 80:521–40.

Miller, Warren, and Donald Stokes. 1963. "Constituency Influence in Congress." *American Political Science Review* 57:45–56.

Millner, Helen. 1997. *Interests, Institutions and Information: Domestic Politics and International Relations*. Princeton, NJ: Princeton University Press.

Mitchell, Sara, and Brandon Prins. 1999. "Beyond Territorial Contiguity: Issues at Stake in Democratic Militarized Interstate Disputes." *International Studies Quarterly* 43:169–83.

Moe, Terry, and William Howell. 1999a. "The Presidential Power of Unilateral Action." *Journal of Law, Economics, and Organization* 15:132–79.

———. 1999b. "Unilateral Action and Presidential Power: A Theory." *Presidential Studies Quarterly* 29:850–72.

Moe, Terry, and Scott Wilson. 1994. "Presidents and the Politics of Structure." *Law and Contemporary Problems* 57:1–44.

Mondak, Jeffrey, and Carl McCurley. 1994. "Cognitive Efficiency and the Congressional Vote: The Psychological Coattail of Voting." *Political Research Quarterly* 47:151–75.

Monroe, Alan. 1998. "Public Opinion and Public Policy, 1980–1993." *Public Opinion Quarterly* 62:6–28.

Moore, Will, and David Lanoue. 2003. "Domestic Politics and U.S. Foreign Policy: A Study of Cold War Conflict Behavior." *Journal of Politics* 65:376–96.

Morgan, Clifton, and Kenneth Bickers. 1992. "Domestic Discontent and the External Use of Force." *Journal of Conflict Resolution* 36:25–52.

Morgan, Clifton, and Sally Campbell. 1991. "Domestic Structures, Decisional Constraints, and War." *Journal of Conflict Resolution* 35:187–211.

Morrow, James. 1986. "A Spatial Model of International Conflict." *American Political Science Review* 80:1131–50.

Mouw, Calvin, and Michael MacKuen. 1992. "The Strategic Configuration, Personal Influence, and Presidential Power in Congress." *Western Political Quarterly* 45:579–608.

Mueller, John. 1970. "Presidential Popularity from Truman to Johnson." *American Political Science Review* 64:18–34.

———. 1973. *War, Presidents, and Public Opinion*. New York: John Wiley and Sons, Inc.

———. 1994. *Policy and Opinion in the Gulf War*. Chicago: University of Chicago Press.

———. 2005. "The Iraq Syndrome." *Foreign Affairs*. November/December 2005.

Murtha, John. 2003. *From Vietnam to 9/11: On the Front Lines of National Security*. University Park: Pennsylvania State University Press.

Nagel, Jack. 1975. *The Descriptive Analysis of Power*. New Haven: Yale University Press.

Nathan, James. 1993. "Salvaging the War Powers Resolution." *Presidential Studies Quarterly* 23:235–68.

Neuman, W. Russell, Marion Just, and Ann Crigler. 1992. *Common Knowledge: News and the Construction of Political Meaning*. Chicago: University of Chicago Press.

Neustadt, Richard. 1990. *Presidential Power and the Modern Presidents*. New York: Free Press.

Nicholson, Stephen, and Robert Howard. 2003. "Framing Support for the Supreme Court in the Aftermath of *Bush v. Gore*." *Journal of Politics* 65:676–95.

Nincic, Miroslav. 1990. "U.S. Soviet Policy and the Electoral Connection." *World Politics* 42:370–96.

Nincic, Miroslav, and Barbara Hinckley. 1991. "Foreign Policy and the Evaluation of Presidential Candidates." *Journal of Conflict Resolution* 35:333–55.

Olson, Mancur. 1965. *The Logic of Collective Action*. Cambridge, MA: Harvard University Press.

O'Neill, Thomas. 1987. *Man of the House: The Life and Political Memoirs of Speaker Tip O'Neill*. New York: Random House.

Ostrom, Charles, and Bryan Job. 1986. "The President and the Political Use of Force." *American Political Science Review* 80:541–66.

Page, Benjamin, and Robert Shapiro. 1983. "Effects of Public Opinion on Policy." *American Political Science Review* 77:175–90.

———. 1992. *The Rational Public: Fifty Years of Trends in Americans' Policy Preferences*. Chicago: University of Chicago Press.

Page, Benjamin, Robert Shapiro, and Glenn Dempsey. 1987. "What Moves Public Opinion?" *American Political Science Review* 81:23–44.

Parker, David, and Matthew Dull. 2009. "Divided We Quarrel: The Politics of Congressional Investigations." *Legislative Studies Quarterly* 34:319–45.

Paterson, Thomas. 1979. "Presidential Foreign Policy, Public Opinion, and Congress: The Truman Years." *Diplomatic History* 3:1–18.

Peffley, John, and Mark Hurwitz. 1992. "International Events and Foreign Policy Beliefs: Public Responses to Changing Soviet-American Relations." *American Journal of Political Science* 36:431–61.

Peppers, Donald. 1975. "The Two Presidencies: Eight Years Later." In *Perspectives on the Presidency*, ed. Aaron Wildavsky. Boston: Little, Brown.

Peterson, Mark. 1990. *Legislating Together: The White House and Capitol Hill from Eisenhower to Reagan*. Cambridge, MA: Harvard University Press.

Peterson, Paul, ed. 1994. *The President, Congress, and the Making of U.S. Foreign Policy.* Norman: University of Oklahoma Press.

Phillips, Cabell. 1949. "The Mirror Called Congress." In *Public Opinion and Foreign Policy*, ed. Lester Markel. New York: Harper.

Popkin, Samuel. 1991. *The Reasoning Voter: Communication and Persuasion in Presidential Campaigns.* Chicago: University of Chicago Press.

Powlick, Philip, and Andrew Katz. 1998. "Defining the American Public Opinion/Foreign Policy Nexus." *Mershon International Studies Review* 42:29–61.

Prins, Brandon, and Christopher Sprecher. 1999. "Institutional Constraints, Political Opposition, and Interstate Dispute Escalation: Evidence from Parliamentary Systems, 1946–1989." *Journal of Peace Research* 36:271–87.

Ray, James Lee. 1995. *Democracy and International Conflict: An Evaluation of the Democratic Peace Proposition.* Columbia: University of South Carolina Press.

Reagan, Ronald. 1990. *An American Life.* New York: Simon and Schuster.

Reeves, Richard. 1993. *President Kennedy: Profile of Power.* New York: Simon and Schuster.

———. 2005. *President Reagan: The Triumph of Imagination.* New York: Simon and Schuster.

Regan, Patrick. 2002. "Third-Party Interventions and the Duration of Interstate Conflicts." *Journal of Conflict Resolution* 46:55–73.

Regan, Patrick, and Allan Stam. 2000. "In the Nick of Time: Conflict Management, Mediation Timing, and the Duration of Interstate Disputes." *International Studies Quarterly* 44:239–60.

Reichley, James. 2000. *The Life of the Parties: A History of American Political Parties.* Lanham, MD: Rowan & Littlefield.

Reiter, Dan, and Erik Tillman. 2002. "Public, Legislative and Executive Constraints on the Democratic Initiation of Conflict." *Journal of Politics* 64:810–26.

Reveley, W. Taylor. 1981. *War Powers of the President and Congress.* Charlottesville: University of Virginia Press.

Richards, Carl. 1995. *The Founders and the Classics: Greece, Rome, and the Enlightenment.* Cambridge, MA: Harvard University Press.

Richards, Diana, Rick Wilson, Valerie Schwebach, and Gary Young. 1993. "Good Times, Bad Times, and the Diversionary Use of Force." *Journal of Conflict Resolution* 37:504–35.

Richardson, James, ed. 1917. *A Compilation of the Messages and Papers of the Presidents.* New York: Bureau of National Literature.

Ripley, Randall. 1969. *Majority Party Leadership in Congress.* Boston: Little, Brown.

Ripley, Randall, and James Lindsay, eds. 1993. *Congress Resurgent: Foreign and Defense Policy on Capitol Hill.* Ann Arbor: University of Michigan Press.

Roberts, Jason, and Steven Smith. 2003. "Procedural Contexts, Party Strategy, and Conditional Party Voting in the U.S. House of Representatives, 1971–2000." *American Journal of Political Science* 47:305–17.

Robinson, Piers. 1999. "The CNN Effect: Can the News Media Drive Foreign Policy?" *Review of International Studies* 25:301–9.

Rohde, David. 1991. *Parties and Leaders in the Postreform House.* Chicago: University of Chicago Press.

———. 1994. "Partisanship, Leadership, and Congressional Assertiveness in Foreign and Defense Policy." In *The New Politics of American Foreign Policy,* ed. David Deese. New York: St. Martin's Press.

Rourke, John. 1983. *Congress and the Presidency in U.S. Foreign Policymaking: A Study of Interaction and Influence, 1945–1982.* Boulder, CO: Westview Press.

Rubner, Michael. 1985/86. "The Reagan Administration, the 1973 War Powers Resolution, and the Invasion of Grenada." *Political Science Quarterly* 100:627–47.

Rudalevige, Andrew. 2002. *Managing the President's Program: Presidential Leadership and Legislative Policy Formulation.* Princeton, NJ: Princeton University Press.

———. 2005. *The New Imperial Presidency: Renewing Presidential Power after Watergate.* Ann Arbor: University of Michigan Press.

Russett, Bruce. 1970. *What Price Vigilance?* New Haven: Yale University Press.

———. 1990. *Controlling the Sword: The Democratic Governance of National Security.* Cambridge, MA: Harvard University Press.

Russett, Bruce, and John Oneal. 2001. *Triangulating Peace: Democracy, Interdependence, and International Organizations.* New York: W. W. Norton.

Russett, Bruce, John Oneal, and David Davis. 1998. "The Third Leg of the Kantian Tripod for Peace: International Organizations and Militarized Disputes, 1950–1985." *International Organization* 52:441–67.

Sarkesian, Sam, John Williams, and Fred Bryant. 1995. *Soldiers, Society, and National Security.* Boulder, CO: Lynn Rienner.

Sartori, Anne. 2003. "An Estimator for Some Binary-Outcome Selection Models without Exclusion Restrictions." *Political Analysis* 11:111–38.

Schickler, Eric. 2001. *Disjointed Pluralism: Institutional Innovation and the Development of the U.S. Congress.* Princeton, NJ: Princeton University Press.

Schlesinger Jr., Arthur. 1973. *The Imperial Presidency.* Boston: Houghton Mifflin.

———. 1974. "Congress and the Making of Foreign Policy." In *The Presidency Reappraised,* ed. Rexford Tugwell and Thomas Cronin. New York: Praeger.

Schultz, Kenneth. 1998. "Domestic Opposition and Signaling in International Crises." *American Political Science Review* 92:829–44.

———. 1999. "Do Democratic Institutions Constrain or Inform? Contrasting Two Institutional Perspectives on Democracy and War." *International Organization* 53:233–66.

———. 2001. *Democracy and Coercive Diplomacy.* New York: Cambridge University Press.

Schultz, Kenneth, and Barry Weingast. 2003. "The Democratic Advantage: International Foundations of Financial Power in International Competition." *International Organization* 57:3–42.

Shaw, Martin. 1993. *Civil Society and Media in Global Crises.* London: St. Martin's Press.

Shefter, Martin. 1994. *Political Parties and the State: The American Historical Experience.* Princeton, NJ: Princeton University Press.

———. 2002. "War, Trade, and U.S. Party Politics." In *Shaped by War and Trade: International Influences on American Political Development,* ed. Ira Katznelson and Martin Shefter. Princeton, NJ: Princeton University Press.

Shepsle, Kenneth, and Barry Weingast. 1987. "The Institutional Foundations of Committee Power." *American Political Science Review* 81:85–104.

Shultz, George. 1993. *Turmoil and Triumph: My Years as Secretary of State.* New York: Scribner's.

Shultz, George. "Sustaining Our Resolve." *Policy Review* 138 (August 2006), Hoover Institution Press.

Sigal, Leon. 1973. *Reporters and Officials: The Organization and Politics of Newsmaking.* Lexington, MA: D. C. Heath.

Sigelman, Lee, and Pamela Johnston-Conover. 1981. "The Dynamics of Presidential Support During International Conflict Situations." *Political Behavior* 3:303–18.

Signorino, Curtis, and Jeffrey Ritter. 1999. "Tau-b or Not Tau-b: Measuring the Similarity of Foreign Policy Positions." *International Studies Quarterly* 43:115–44.

Silverstein, Gordon. 1994. "Judicial Enhancement of Executive Power." In *The President, Congress, and the Making of U.S. Foreign Policy,* ed. Paul Peterson. Norman: University of Oklahoma Press.

Silverstein, Gordon. 1997. *Imbalance of Powers: Constitutional Interpretation and the Making of American Foreign Policy.* New York: Oxford University Press.

Sinclair, Barbara. 1983. *Majority Leadership in the U.S. House.* Baltimore: Johns Hopkins University Press.

———. 1989. *The Transformation of the U.S. Senate.* Baltimore: Johns Hopkins University Press.

———. 1995. *Legislators, Leaders and Lawmakers: The U.S. House of Representatives in the Postreform Era.* Baltimore: Johns Hopkins University Press.

———. 2000. *Unorthodox Lawmaking: New Legislative Processes in the United States Congress*. 2nd edition. Washington: Congressional Quarterly Press.

Singer, Judith, and John Willett. 1993. "It's About Time: Using Discrete-Time Survival Analysis to Study Duration and the Timing of Events." *Journal of Educational Statistics* 18:155–95.

Siverson, Randolph. 1995. "Democracies and War Participation: In Defense of the Institutional Constraints Argument." *European Journal of International Relations* 4:481–89.

Skocpol, Theda. 1992. *Protecting Soldiers and Mothers: The Political Origins of Social Policy in the United States*. Cambridge, MA: Belknap Press of Harvard University Press.

Skowronek, Stephen. 1982. *Building a New American State: The Expansion of National Administrative Capacities, 1877–1920*. New York: Cambridge University Press.

Slantchev, Branislav. 2004. "How Initiators End Their Wars: The Duration of Warfare and the Terms of Peace." *American Journal of Political Science* 48:813–29.

Small, Melvin, and J. David Singer. 1990. National Material Capabilities Database. Inter-University Consortium for Political and Social Research Study No. 9903. ICPSR, University of Michigan, Ann Arbor.

Smith, Alastair. 1998. "International Crises and Domestic Politics." *American Political Science Review* 92:623–38.

Smith, Steven. 2007. *Party Influence in Congress*. New York: Cambridge University Press.

Smith, Steven, and Christopher Deering. 1990. *Committees in Congress*. Washington: Congressional Quarterly Press.

Smith, Steven, Jason Roberts, and Ryan Vander Wielen. 2006. *The American Congress*. New York: Cambridge University Press.

Smyrl, Marc. 1988. *Conflict or Codetermination*. Cambridge, MA: Ballinger.

Sniderman, Paul, Richard Brody, and Philip Tetlock. 1991. *Reasoning and Choice: Explorations in Political Psychology*. Cambridge: Cambridge University Press.

Sobel, Richard. 1993. *Public Opinion in U.S. Foreign Policy: The Controversy over Contra Aid*. Lanham, MD: Rowan Littlefield.

———. 2001. *The Impact of Public Opinion on U.S. Foreign Policy since Vietnam*. New York: Oxford University Press.

Sobel, Richard, and Eric Shiraev, ed. 2003. *International Public Opinion and the Bosnia Crisis*. Lanham, MD: Lexington Books.

Sparrow, Bartholomew. 1996. *From the Outside In: World War II and the American State*. Princeton, NJ: Princeton University Press.

Stam, Allan. 1996. *Win, Lose or Draw*. Ann Arbor: University of Michigan Press.

Stokes, Donald. 1966. "Some Dynamic Elements of Contests for the Presidency." *American Political Science Review* 60:19–28.

Stoll, Richard. 1984. "The Guns of November: Presidential Reelections and the Use of Force, 1947–1982." *Journal of Conflict Resolution* 28:231–46.

Stonecash, Jeffrey, Mark Brewer, and Mark Mariani. 2003. *Diverging Parties: Social Change, Realignment, and Party Polarization.* Boulder, CO: Westview Press.

Sundquist, James. 1973. *Dynamics of the Party System: Alignment and Realignment of Political Parties in the United States.* Washington: Brookings Institution Press.

———. 1981. *The Decline and Resurgence of Congress.* Washington: Brookings Institution Press.

Tananbaum, Duane. 1987. "Not for the First Time: Antecedents and Origins of the War Powers Resolution, 1945–1970." In *Congress and United States Foreign Policy,* ed. Michael Barnhart. Albany: State University of New York Press.

Tomz, Michael. 2007. "Domestic Audience Costs in International Relations: An Experimental Approach." *International Organization* 61:821–40.

Tomz, Michael, Gary King, and Langche Zeng. 2003. "Relogit: Rare Events Logistic Regression." *Journal of Statistical Software* 8:137–63.

Tomz, Michael, and Paul Sniderman. 2004. "Constraint in Mass Beliefs Systems: Political Brand Names as Signals." Paper presented at the annual meeting of the American Political Science Association, Chicago, September 2004.

Trubowitz, Peter. 1992. "Sectionalism and American Foreign Policy: The Political Geography of Consensus and Conflict." *International Studies Quarterly* 36:173–90.

———. 1998. *Defining the National Interest: Conflict and Change in American Foreign Policy.* Chicago: University of Chicago Press.

Tuchman, Gaye. 1978. *Making News: A Study in the Construction of Reality.* New York: Free Press.

Tulis, Jeffrey. 1987. *The Rhetorical Presidency.* Princeton, NJ: Princeton University Press.

Turner, Julius. 1970. *Party and Constituency: Pressures on Congress.* Baltimore: Johns Hopkins University Press.

Voeten, Erik. 2000. "Clashes in the Assembly." *International Organization* 54:185–215.

Voeten, Erik, and Paul R. Brewer. 2006. "Public Opinion, the War in Iraq, and Presidential Accountability," *Journal of Conflict Resolution* 50:809–30.

Walker, Jack. 1977. "Setting the Agenda in the U.S. Senate: A Theory of Problem Selection." *British Journal of Political Science* 7:433–45.

Wang, Kevin. 1996. "Presidential Responses to Foreign Policy Crises: Rational Choice and Domestic Politics." *Journal of Conflict Resolution* 40:68–97.

Waterman, Richard, Bruce Oppenheimer, and James Stimson. 1991. "Sequence and Equilibrium in Congressional Elections: An Integrated Approach." *Journal of Politics* 53:372–93.

Wayman, Frank. 1985. "Arms Control and Strategic Arms Voting in the U.S. Senate." *Journal of Conflict Resolution* 29:225–51.

Wawro, Gregory. 2000. *Legislative Entrepreneurship in the U.S. House of Representatives.* Ann Arbor: University of Michigan Press.

Weinberger, Caspar. 1990. *Fighting for Peace: Seven Critical Years in the Pentagon.* New York: Warner Books.

Weingast, Barry, and William Marshall. 1988. "The Industrial Organization of Congress; Or, Why Legislatures, Like Firms, are not Organized as Markets." *Journal of Political Economy* 96:132–63.

Weissman, Stephen. 1995. *A Culture of Deference: Congress' Failure in Leadership on Foreign Policy.* New York: Basic Books.

Wildavsky, Aaron. 1966. "The Two Presidencies." *Trans-Action* 4:7–14.

Wildavsky, Aaron, and Duane Oldfield. 1991. "The Two Presidencies Thesis Revisited at a Time of Political Dissensus." In *The Beleaguered Presidency,* ed. Aaron Wildavsky. New Brunswick, NJ: Transaction Publishers.

Wilentz. Sean. 2005. *The Rise of American Democracy: Jefferson to Lincoln.* New York: Norton.

Wittkopf, Eugene. 1987. "Elites and Masses: Another Look at Attitudes toward America's World Role." *International Studies Quarterly* 31:31–159.

———. 1990. *Faces of Internationalism: Public Opinion and American Foreign Policy.* Durham, NC: Duke University Press.

Wittkopf, Eugene, and James McCormick. 1998. "Congress, the President, and the End of the Cold War: Has Anything Changed?" *Journal of Conflict Resolution* 42:440–66.

Wlezien, Christopher, and Robert Erikson. 1996. "Temporal Horizons and Presidential Election Forecasts." *American Politics Quarterly* 24:492–505.

Yamaguchi, Kazuo. 1990. "Logit and Multinomial Logit Models for Discrete-Time Event History Analysis: A Causal Analysis of Interdependent Discrete-State Processes." *Quality and Quantity* 24:323–41.

Yoo, John. 2005. *The Powers of War and Peace: The Constitution and Foreign Affairs after 9/11.* Chicago: University of Chicago Press.

Zaller, John. 1992. *The Nature and Origins of Mass Opinion.* New York: Cambridge University Press.

———. 1994. "Elite Leadership of Mass Opinion: New Evidence from the Gulf War." In *Taken By Storm: Media, Public Opinion, and U.S. Foreign Policy in the Gulf War,* ed. W. Lance Bennett and David L. Paletz. Chicago: University of Chicago Press, 186–209.

Zaller, John, and Dennis Chiu. 1996. "Government's Little Helper: U.S. Press

Coverage of Foreign Policy Crises, 1945–1991." *Political Communication* 13:385–405.

Zaller, John, and Stanley Feldman. 1992. "A Simple Theory of the Survey Response: Answering Questions versus Revealing Preferences." *American Journal of Political Science* 36:579–616.

Zelikow, Phillip. 1987. "The United States and the Use of Force: A Historical Summary." In *Democracy, Strategy, and Vietnam*, ed. George Osborn. Lexington, MA: Lexington Books.

Zelizer, Julian. 2004. *On Capitol Hill: The Struggle to Reform Congress and its Consequences, 1948–2000*. New York: Cambridge University Press.

Index

The letters *f* or *t* following page numbers indicate figures or tables, respectively.